"Weaving together stories of youth ministry pioneers and their organizations, Senter provides an intriguing historical perspective on the church's concern for its young people. Drawing on the lessons from history, Senter provides insight into this frustrating area of ministry and the challenges the church must address in order to spiritually engage young people. *When God Shows Up* is required reading for anyone remotely concerned with the future of the church's ministry to young people."

—**Darwin Glassford**, associate professor of church education, Calvin Theological Seminary; book reviews editor, *The Journal of Youth Ministry*

"Like a wise docent, Senter generously guides us through the archives of the history of youth ministry. Embracing a cyclical description of the evolution of youth ministry in America, Senter insightfully presents a well-researched, creative engagement with youth ministry in the Protestant church. Faithfully reporting the stories of our past, the text concludes with current observations and questions regarding our future direction. Comprehensive, accessible, and vital—a one-of-a-kind book that needs to be savored by every youth ministry professional!"

—**Cheryl A. Crawford**, assistant professor of practical theology, Azusa Pacific University

"Every family, every organization, and every movement has a history that informs, explains, and inspires. Mark Senter has done a wonderful job of providing historical context for American Protestant youth ministry, which is a family, an organization, and a movement all in one. A thorough understanding of the contents of this book will help those who care about youth ministry to appreciate its roots and to be awed and inspired by youth ministry leaders from the past."

—**Dan Lambert**, professor of youth ministries, John Brown University

"This is not merely a history book; it is a compelling story of young lives— thousands of lives—transformed by the surprising grace of God. As a keen historian and reflective theologian, Senter provides a fresh perspective on the past that illuminates the future. *When God Shows Up* encourages those who care about young people to understand their past and challenges them to maintain the historic core conviction of helping young people encounter God."

—**Mark W. Cannister**, professor of Christian ministries, Gordon College

"This book establishes Mark Senter as today's foremost youth ministry historian. *When God Shows Up* is a seminal work providing a historical analysis of Protestant youth ministry in America. Yet Senter goes beyond a historical survey to provide a sociological and theological exegesis of youth ministry from 1824 to 2010. *When God Shows Up* is a significant contribution to both the field of youth ministry education and modern American church history."

—**Fernando Arzola Jr.**, associate dean, College of Arts and Sciences, Nyack College; author, *Toward a Prophetic Youth Ministry: Theory and Praxis in Urban Context*

Youth, Family, and Culture Series

Chap Clark, series editor

The Youth, Family, and Culture series examines the broad categories involved in studying and caring for the needs of the young and is dedicated to the preparation and vocational strengthening of those who are committed to the spiritual development of adolescents.

WHEN GOD
SHOWS UP

A History of Protestant
Youth Ministry in America

Mark H. Senter III

Chap Clark, Series Editor

Baker Academic
a division of Baker Publishing Group
Grand Rapids, Michigan

© 2010 by Mark H. Senter III

Published by Baker Academic
a division of Baker Publishing Group
P.O. Box 6287, Grand Rapids, MI 49516-6287
www.bakeracademic.com

Printed in the United States of America

Library of Congress Cataloging-in-Publication Data
Senter, Mark.
    When God shows up : a history of Protestant youth ministry in America / Mark H. Senter III.
        p.   cm. — (Youth, family, and culture)
    Includes bibliographical references and index.
    ISBN 978-0-8010-3590-6 (pbk.)
    1. Church work with youth—Protestant churches—History. 2. Church work with youth—United States—History. I. Title.
    BV447.S46 2010
    259′.23—dc22   2009047802

Scripture quotations are from the HOLY BIBLE, NEW INTERNATIONAL VERSION®. NIV®. Copyright © 1973, 1978, 1984 by International Bible Society. Used by permission of Zondervan. All rights reserved.

10 11 12 13 14 15 16   7 6 5 4 3 2 1

green
press
INITIATIVE

To
my grandchildren,

Elijah Houston Senter,

Emmy Ruth YeYe Susanka,

and

Aubrey Olivia Senter,

with the prayer that God shows up in their lives.

Contents

Series Preface

In many ways, youth ministry has come of age. No longer seen as "a stepping-stone to real ministry in the church," especially in North America, youth ministry is now seen as a viable career option. Over the last few decades a wide range of professional resources, conferences, periodicals, and books have been developed on this topic. Most Christian colleges and seminaries now offer a variety of courses—if not degree programs—in youth ministry. Youth ministry has all it needs to continue to push the church to care about and serve the needs of the young in God's name, except for one thing: we have a long way to go to develop a rich, broad, and diverse conversation that frames, defines, and grounds our missional call.

There is good news, of course. There is a professional organization, Association of Youth Ministry Educators, that sponsors an annual conference and publishes a solid emerging journal. Several thoughtful books have helped to shape the discipline's future. There are also now two major publishers who have academic lines dedicated to furthering the field of youth ministry. We have made great progress, but we must all work together to continue deepening our understanding of what youth ministry should be.

The purpose of Baker Academic's Youth, Family, and Culture series is to raise the level of dialogue concerning how we think about, teach, and live out youth ministry. As a branch of practical theology, academic youth ministry must move beyond a primarily skills-based focus to a theologically driven expression of a contextualized commitment of the local church to a targeted population. James Fowler defines practical theology as "theological reflection and construction arising out of and giving guidance to a community of faith in the *praxis* of its mission. Practical theology is critical and constructive reflection leading to ongoing modification and development of the ways the church shapes its life to be in partnership with God's work in the world.[1] And as Scott Cormode reminds us, we must not shirk our calling, but "must strive to nurture leaders that are faithful. . . . Schools must prepare leaders to translate this faithfulness into effective action."[2] This is precisely what those of us who are called to engage the church in theological reflection of contemporary youth and family issues must do—develop a practical theology that takes seriously the reality of the context we are in, regardless of how and where it takes us. This is the future of youth and family ministry in the church.

Mark Senter's *When God Shows Up* is the third book in the Youth, Family, and Culture series. A long-time leader of youth ministry thinking and writing, Dr. Senter brings a fresh perspective on where we have been and how we need to think about youth ministry as we move forward. The book offers a historical, cultural, and ecclesiological angle for those who serve the young and their families in the name of Christ, and therefore brings a helpful addition to the Youth, Family, and Culture academic series on youth ministry issues. As is the mark of this series, this volume once again is framed in a practical theology of youth and family ministry.

Chap Clark
Fuller Theological Seminary
August 2009

Preface

God Shows Up

Protestant youth ministry in America expected God to show up. Prayer meetings, camps, revivals, youth rallies, mission trips, service projects, and even the weekly meeting served as contexts where God demonstrated his presence in the lives of Protestant young people. Youth programming served as prologue. Activities retained the attention and loyalty of youth until such time as Jesus Christ became reincarnated in their lives either individually or in a group experience.

This history of Protestant youth ministry in America is the story of a search for Christian spirituality in young people. While not defined in terms of the classical writings of the desert fathers or medieval mystics, the desire was much the same. Prayer served as a central discipline, and faith communities provided support and accountability. The Bible provided a portal for youth to establish and maintain a personal relationship with God.

Approaches varied at different times and in different contexts. Some used their minds to engage the God of Scripture. Others experienced God emotionally through their hearts. Still other young people found God as they served others. Yet Protestant youth groups had one conviction in common: young people, especially the most faithful participants in youth groups, expected to experience God's presence during the years of their youth.

A majority of clergy at one time supposed the normal worship services to be sufficient for ushering the youth of their church into the presence of God, but those assumptions proved flawed. From the earliest days of the American experience, isolated clergy experimented with gatherings outside the Sunday morning worship service to engage the rising generation in a quest to know God and live lives in conformity with God's will.

The Industrial Revolution complicated the ability of churches and families to shape the lives of their youth. Many moved to the cities in order to make their fortune, an expectation that rarely succeeded. The move away from family and church caused great concern on the part of churchgoers, who responded by forming agencies that addressed this youth problem.

Periodic revivals swept the nation, and in most of them, young people were very responsive. Yet these revivals were neither uniformly spread across the nation nor frequent in their recurrence. In fact, most of the contributions made by youth ministry in America took place either between revivals or far removed from the places where such revivals happened. Further complicating our understanding of youthful spirituality in American history is the realization that eventually many youth grew up in Christian homes never thinking of themselves as anything but followers of Jesus Christ.

Youth ministry was an attempt to sustain God's presence and activity in the lives of young people. Responding to the changing challenges of the societies in which they lived, church leaders created or re-created youth groups in order to design environments that were conducive to youth experiencing God's presence.

For many Protestants in America, spirituality was measured by lifestyle. This was especially true of young people. While some historians viewed the apparent emphasis on youthful morality as a desire for social control, the leaders of these youth groups had what they considered a higher agenda. They wanted young people to experience God in a biblical manner, as understood by various faith communities.

As the American experience changed so did the manner in which youth groups functioned. New forms for highly focused youth groups developed and, at times, the organized activities or philosophy of ministry became more important to participants and leaders than the spiritual aspects. Despite ongoing changes in the functions of youth groups, the consistent desire in the early years of youth ministry was to create social settings in which young people could experience God.

In the first cycle of youth ministry (1824–75), young people sought to encounter God through the organization of societies dedicated to the task. The creation of these societies paralleled the organization of groups, such as firefighters and militia, that addressed other social needs. Major youth ministry agencies—Sunday school associations, the YMCA, and Protestant juvenile temperance societies—focused on young people's outward lifestyle, a sanctified way of living that previously had been the product of spiritual awakenings or revival meetings. In time, the expectation of God showing up was lost, except on rare occasions. Consequently, a new approach to youth groups developed.

The second cycle (1881–1925) emphasized education as a means of experiencing God. Especially by the end of this cycle, youth societies took on educational functions and were compared with the approaches of progressive education. Christian Endeavor and various denominational youth societies became nonformal educational agencies that helped young people to learn biblical content and denominational distinctives with the goal of bringing about a lifestyle in harmony with the values of the sponsoring society. At first, prayer meetings and union (i.e., regional) gatherings created anticipation of God's presence, and in various ways these anticipations were realized. However, as activities became routine in this second cycle of youth ministry, God's presence seemed more and more contrived or nonexistent.

In the third cycle (1933–89), youth fellowships became relational at their cores. This was especially apparent as parachurch agencies attempted to win the right to be heard by unchurched youth. In church-based youth groups, fellowship became the focus, and Christ's relationship with his disciples served as the model for youth ministry. The leadership encouraged adolescents to live out the Great Commandment (to love God with their whole body, soul, and spirit and to love their neighbor as themselves) and the Great Commission (to disciple all nations including their own). In time, however, entertainment superseded a search for God's presence, and youth groups once again began to change.

A transition to a fourth cycle of Protestant youth ministry began in the 1990s. As with previous transitions between cycles, it has taken time for the nature of youth ministry in the twenty-first century to define itself. A pluralistic culture that values religious tolerance has made clarity elusive. Clear descriptors of a fourth cycle have yet to emerge. Yet a desire among young people to experience God's presence persists, perhaps even intensifies, as young people continue to gather in youth ministry settings.

How God Showed Up in Youth Ministry

When God Shows Up: A History of Protestant Youth Ministry in America is divided into five parts. The first part clarifies three terms—*youth* (chapter 1), *adolescent* (chapter 2), and *spirituality* (chapter 3)—then explains the cyclical nature of Protestant youth ministry in America (chapter 4). While readers have some understanding of the three terms, the meaning of each has changed since the inception of youth ministry in America. People tend to think of youth groups either as uniform throughout America or as primitive expressions of current forms of youth ministry. While there is continuity in how these terms have been used in youth ministry, putting them into context and tracing them through the short history of youth ministry will enable us to better understand where youth ministry stands at the beginning of the twenty-first century.

Parts 2 through 5 are built upon the assumption that youth ministry in America has followed a cyclical pattern. Each cycle began with a ministry innovation responding to changes in American society and within fifty years found that the social milieu of youth had changed so significantly that the earlier innovations had become somewhat irrelevant to the current generation of young people. While the agencies of youth ministry continued to exist, their emphasis had changed. No longer were they as relevant to the expectations of young people that God would show up in their individual and collective experiences.

Part 2 focuses on the beginnings of youth groups in America. Local improvisation begun in England but adapted to the American experience shaped the beginnings of Protestant youth ministry in America. This period of associations (1824–75) was dominated by three agencies from England—the Sunday school, the juvenile temperance movement, and the YMCA. In typical American fashion, each movement formed associations to promote their attempts to reach young people.

The Sunday school and YMCA (chapter 5) share clear concerns for the spirituality of youth, while the juvenile temperance movement (chapter 6) dealt specifically with the lifestyle issue of alcohol consumption, and thus was more concerned with an evidence of sanctification over which Protestants differed in opinion. Nonetheless the temperance movement set the structure for the formal emergence of Protestant youth groups in the second cycle of youth ministry.

While these three movements shaped much of what we know about the early years of Protestant youth groups in America, local churches took many initiatives to enable their youth to experience God's presence in their lives. Responding to the spiritual needs of the youth of the city, Rev. Theodore Cuyler, pastor of Lafayette Avenue Presbyterian Church, drew upon his experience in the prayer revival of 1857–59 to foster Christian spirituality among his young people. Cuyler's innovations in one local church became the basis for the next cycle of youth ministry (chapter 7).

Part 3 describes the formal emergence of Protestant youth groups in America. It was a period of organization as national youth ministry programs shaped local youth groups. The period of youth societies (1881–1925) unfolded as America struggled to recover from the Civil War. There was an air of optimism in the nation. An experiment with the young people at Williston Church in Portland, Maine, conceived by

Rev. Francis E. Clark, produced such immediate results that regional churches quickly sought help from the young pastor (chapter 8). Other church leaders hoped to achieve the dramatic birth and growth of the Society of Christian Endeavor in which youth found an attractive way to focus on their endeavor to know God. Nearly as quickly as the Society of Christian Endeavor sprang up, denominational youth societies followed (chapter 9). The Baptists, Lutherans, Methodists, and Presbyterians developed programs that encouraged youthful spirituality as well as denominational loyalty.

Part 4 captures the rise of the American *teenager*, the transition to a relational approach to youth groups, and the evangelical attempt to reach youth for Christ. Fellowship with Christian peers and friendships with unchurched friends shaped Christian formation during this phase. Proclaiming the gospel became the emphasis that reshaped the Protestant youth group in the period of the relational outreach (1933–89). Mainline Protestant denominations became dissatisfied with aging youth societies and reoriented themselves toward peers, while emphasizing the role youth should have in addressing the pains of the world (chapter 10). Dissatisfied with the lack of Christian influence on the peer culture in the public high school, parachurch agencies came into being that would evangelize students who had little if any knowledge of or experience with the Christian gospel. This Christian youth movement included the Miracle Book Club, Young Life, Youth for Christ, Fellowship of Christian Athletes as well as many smaller agencies (chapter 11). Newer evangelical movements stirred in the same relational direction while continuing to stress personal salvation, holiness, and other emphases characteristic of their movements (chapter 12). For a relatively brief period of time in the middle of the twentieth century, youth rallies came to characterize youth ministry in America (chapter 13).

The final section of the book (part 5) looks at the period that combines old and new (1990–2010). Chapter 14 critiques how parachurch ministries have tried to reinvent themselves while struggling with how to address a youth culture influenced by the erosion of certainty. The last chapter looks at the legacy youth ministers in the first decade of the twenty-first century are leaving behind in formal and nonformal training of the next generation of youth ministers. While modernity still exists, and, with it, established approaches to youth ministry remain effective in certain settings, the pluralism of the twenty-first century requires a far different response by youth ministry leaders. Whereas in the third cycle of youth ministry, a handful of strategies dominated youth ministry with an emphasis on evangelization, the fourth cycle, if it develops, appears to be returning to a more clearly defined effort to experience the presence of God.

In the epilogue I acknowledge the gaping holes in the book—areas in the history of Protestant youth ministry in America that still need to be studied and considered. Hopefully other researchers will pick up on some of the themes of the history of youth ministry and weave them into this jam session.

As a historian, I have attempted to make sense out of the heritage in which youth workers have participated. My conclusion is that Protestants in America have been very concerned with ensuring that their children, especially during their teenage years, have an opportunity to be present when God "shows up." As imperfectly as youth workers have done the job, as unevenly as they have employed educational or sociological theory, as simple and even naïve as has been their faith, and as easily as they have slipped from theological visions to programmatic formulas, Protestants nonetheless have a rich heritage of utilizing youth ministry to encounter the God of the Bible. And God has shown up.

Acknowledgments

As I reflect on the number of people who assisted in the research and writing of this book, I feel a significant level of emotion. A wide range of people assisted my process of gathering information. Several organizations funded aspects of my research. Some asked critical questions that improved the final product. To all of these I am indebted and grateful.

My greatest appreciation goes to my wife, Ruth, who stood with me throughout the writing process and in the final stages accompanied me to the mountains of North Carolina, isolated from friends and family as well as the interruptions of daily life in Illinois, to allow me to complete the final stages of research and writing.

In the early stages of this project, Rev. Michael Perko, SJ, PhD, coached and encouraged my doctoral research at Loyola University of Chicago. Robert Schuster and his staff at the Billy Graham Archives made available rare documents while the Billy Graham Center Library provided a study room in which I wrote much of my dissertation and *The Coming Revolution in Youth Ministries*. These served as a basis for this current work.

Funding for research included grants from the Youth Ministry and Theological Schools Project, Union Seminary in connection with the Lilly Endowment Center, and from the Association of Youth Ministry Educators. The generous sabbaticals provided by Trinity Evangelical Divinity School, a part of Trinity International University, provided the blocks of time necessary for the completion of the book.

I appreciate the professionalism of the staff and availability of materials in the libraries and special collections of the Billy Graham Center Library and Archives, Garrett Evangelical Theological Seminary, Moody Bible Institute, Louisville Presbyterian Theological Seminary, Princeton

Theological Seminary, Seabury-Western Theological Seminary, Southern Baptist Theological Seminary, Trinity International University, Union Theological Seminary and Presbyterian School of Christian Education, and Wheaton College.

Access to materials and information from both former and current leaders of parachurch organizations proved invaluable. My special thanks goes to Jay Kesler, Dick Wynn, and Roger Cross of Youth for Christ, USA, along with June Thompson, as well as Bill Muir and Dave Rahn; to Doug Burleigh and Denny Rydberg of Young Life, and associates Suzie Coddington and Greg Kinberg; to Hal Merwald of Young Life Canada; to Richard F. Abel and Dal Shealy of Fellowship of Christian Athletes, along with Rod Handley, Kevin Harlan, Ralph Stewart, Carey Casey, Milt Cooper, and Julie Brown; and to Evelyn M. McClusky, founder of the Miracle Book Club.

Research about church-based youth ministry was aided by conversation, research materials, and/or articles written by Wes Black, Bo Boshiers, Richard Castleberry, Jim Forstrom, Roger McKenzie, Dan Webster, and Bob Yoder and his students. Especially helpful was the critical eye of fellow youth ministry historian Tom Bergler.

Interaction with Mark Cannister, Dann Spader, Wayne Rice, Mike Yaconelli, Thom Schultz and Rick Lawrence, Dean Borgman, and Pete Ward as well as the members of the Association of Youth Ministry Educators, have informed the writing of this book. I am especially grateful for the encouragement and patience of Bob Hosack, along with the critical editorial help of Brian Bolger at Baker Academic. To all of you as well as the students I have had over the nearly three decades of teaching, I say thank you.

Mark H. Senter III
Lake Forest, Illinois
October 6, 2009

part 1

Birth of Youth Ministry Jazz

The Context

Jazz is America's classical music," commented my friend Bob Ligon as we rode to high school one day. The idea stopped me short. Jazz? Classical? How could the two genres be mentioned in the same sentence?

We were sophomores and sophomores know everything, so I had to argue. But Bob stopped me short. "Think about it," Bob challenged, "what makes a piece of music qualify as being classical? It is primarily because of its ability to endure, its distinctive structure, its reflection of the context in which it was created, and the quality of the musicians to whom it appeals." He went on to explain how jazz music satisfied all four criteria.

I don't know where Bob got his definition of classical music, but it made sense to me. The conversation was short but it left me with an entirely new perspective on that distinctive American contribution called jazz. It seems fascinating to me that fifty years later I am using jazz as a metaphor for understanding the development of Protestant youth ministry in America. Like jazz, Protestant youth ministry has proven to endure, has distinctive structures, has fit into the culture of the day, and has attracted an outstanding cast of leaders.

Basic to this classical theme in Protestant youth ministry is the theology that ties a biblical understanding of God as present but not yet in evidence in the lives of humankind. The book primarily deals with how Protestant churches lived out the conviction that God would become a part of the lives of young people in a meaningful, and in a majority of cases, permanent way.

In this first section of the book, I will place the history of Protestant youth ministry in America into four contexts. The first chapter has to do with the widely-varied manner in which young people experienced their lives prior to adulthood. The various sections of the country as well as the changing dynamic of the American experience imprinted youth in very different ways.

The second chapter explores the meaning of *adolescence*. While the reader may assume that *adolescence* has always applied to teenagers or perhaps persons between the ages of twelve and twenty-five, for much of youth ministry in America the word hardly appeared. Some now question if *adolescence* can accurately describe the differences between later stages of childhood and an ever-extending period of young adulthood.

The third chapter looks at the history of *spirituality* as it has been applied to the lives of Protestant young people in America. Grounded in various traditions of pietism and connected to a broad cross section of Protestant churches, the common denominator appears to be the conviction that God would be active in the lives of young people and Christian people had the obligation to provide opportunities for this to happen.

The fourth chapter describes the distinctive characteristics of three *cycles* of youth ministry that stretched across the nineteenth and twentieth centuries. This description provides the structure upon which the history of Protestant youth ministry is built.

1

Newsies

A Survey of the Diverse Experiences of Youth in America

The 1899 strike of the newspaper boys in New York City shocked the city. Boys could fight with each other, but they were not expected to challenge authority figures, no matter how corrupt. These news boys were quite different from the classic ideal of family life formed by the middle of the twentieth century. Few enjoyed the safety of families, schools, churches, and communities that prepared them to participate in the American dream.

The 1992 movie *Newsies* captured some of the dynamics of the era. Jack "Cowboy" Kelly, an orphan, and David Jacobs, who needed to support his family due to a job-related injury experienced by his father, typified many youth at the turn of the twentieth century. "Cowboy" was a hustler who did not worry about ethics when selling newspapers, while Jacobs was an educated Christian boy with organizational skills. The two found themselves pitted against the political and newspaper business establishment of New York City. Publishers William Randolph Hurst and Joseph Pulitzer vie for profits at the expense of the newsies until the lead characters rally the news boys to strike and, with the help of Governor Theodore Roosevelt, gain some degree of justice for their peers.

The strike was noteworthy since it was one of the few times prior to the twentieth century when young people came out on top. For the most part young people of their day had no rights, no protection, no access to political leaders, and no resources other than what they could muster through their own efforts.

Protestant young people in early America also experienced a surprisingly diverse set of life circumstances. The dynamics of the teenage years varied widely based on region of the country (not everything was like New England), ethnic background (not everything was English), religious conviction (not every Protestant was shaped by Puritanism), and economic position (not everything was economic middle class).

While youth ministry gained its earliest notoriety in New England with the birth in Portland, Maine, of the Society of Christian Endeavor in 1881, Brooklyn had provided a focal point for youth ministry experimentation thirty years earlier. Yet the nation was populated with a wide variety of young people for whom Protestants shaped by regional differences shared concerns.

Growing Up in America

The experience of people in their teenage years varied greatly as the American expansion shaped a wilderness into a nation. The contrasting opinions and experiences between Anglicans in South Carolina (where the passion for wealth trumped all other concerns), Puritan families in the Massachusetts Bay Colony (where Christian convictions commanded the attention of civic leaders), and the Dutch Reformed Church (supported by the Dutch West India Company–financed schools in New Amsterdam [New York]) created enormous disparities in attitudes toward education and religion in the lives of young people. French Huguenots in the Southern colonies, German Lutherans in the Midwest, English Quakers in the mid-Atlantic colonies, and English Wesleyans up and down the East Coast all brought their concepts of Christian formation of children and youth to the new world.

The role of youth in American society varied not only regionally but also according to the period of history being considered. Joseph Kett indicates three distinct periods for youth: (1) in the early republic, 1790–1840; (2) toward the age of adolescence, 1840–1900; and (3) in the era of adolescence, 1900–1977.[1]

The three-volume *Children and Youth in America: A Documentary History* divides its study of public policy toward children and youth into three somewhat similar periods: (1) from the earliest English settlements to the close of the Civil War (roughly 1600–1865), (2) Reconstruction to the New Deal (1865–1932), and (3) the New Deal of Franklin Roosevelt to 1973.[2] While the foci of the two works differ (the former on understanding adolescence; the latter on public policy), the dynamics of the youthful experience discussed in them are very similar. Since Kett's purpose is closer to the purpose of this work, I will follow his periodization, with the exception that I give more attention to colonial life before the early republic.

Colonial Period and Early Republic (1600–1840)

From the time British people first settled in Jamestown or the Mayflower landed at Plymouth Rock, American society has abounded with young people. Many of the settlers in Virginia were the younger brothers of British noblemen. Of the 102 passengers aboard the Mayflower, thirty-one were children. The average age at the birth of the republic was under thirty-five years. Yet in 1800 the median age was only sixteen.[3] This meant that if all people living in the newly formed United States of America were lined up according to age, a sixteen-year-old would have been exactly in the middle of the lineup.

To put this into perspective, the median age in the United States as of the 2000 census, was 35.3 years. With such a high proportion of the population being young in the early years of the American experience, life for young people differed greatly from the youth culture of the twenty-first century.

Life for youth in the thirteen colonies spread along the Atlantic seaboard, though differing according to the colony in which a young person lived, had one common theme: work. When a child was big enough to contribute to the family or community, he or she began to work. With the exception of children from the few wealthy families, young people were needed to enable the family to survive, and so without regrets they worked. The problem that faced young people was not self-esteem but survival.

For many, maintaining a lively spiritual life proved to be difficult in America; the survival of the soul of the rising generation became a pressing matter. Protestant dissenters from the authorized churches of Europe (Church of England, Lutheran, Roman Catholic, and Reformed Church) came to the New World in search of religious freedom. Quickly they found that their newly-found freedom put their children at risk. The persecution experienced in Europe forced a spiritual solidarity on families; but the enemy in America became freedom and the spiritual apathy that it engendered.

Leaders of the various colonies, and especially church leaders, took responsibility for training young people to contribute to the common life. Maintaining spiritual convictions was a key aspect of local communities. The ability to read provided a minimal spiritual and intellectual training for youth, enabling them to know the Scriptures, while skills for providing food, shelter, and safety sustained life. Exactly how the leaders prepared youth varied according to the section of the nation in which the young person grew to maturity.

New England

By far the greatest influence on young people outside their families came from the American educational system, which was birthed in New England where Puritans stressed education as a means of cultivating values of righteousness in children beset by their sinful nature. Reading and understanding the Bible formed the cornerstone of education for Christian families. Massachusetts Bay Colony enacted legislation demonstrating governmental concern for schools and providing taxation for supporting public schools. As early as 1642 and 1647, laws required the teaching of reading, writing, arithmetic, and religion in vernacular schools.

From these beginnings grew the common school movement championed by James Carter, Horace Mann, and Thaddeus Stevens that resulted in legislation in 1827 supporting common schools by means of compulsory taxation. Governmental institutions needed literate voters to make decisions in order for the American democratic experiment to be effective. All citizens needed to be educated.

This shift from education in the home to the public schooling necessary for the building of a democracy began a process of removing the Christian Scriptures from a central place in education. In some communities Protestant parents and clergy sensed the need to train young people in Bible knowledge and application. In others, clergy felt a lack of parental support for their concerns for encounters with God and lives of personal holiness among youthful attendees, so ministers sought to create methods for attracting and holding the youth of their day.

The family-church-school symbiosis may have seemed simple, but young people in New England differed from one another in a multitude of ways. Unlike the ideals of economic middle-class America in the twenty-first century, families seldom functioned as depicted in a Norman Rockwell painting with father going off to work, mother taking care of the house, and children splitting their time between play and school. Life in early America was hard. Virtually every person above seven years of age worked to contribute to the welfare of the family. It was commonly understood that children owed their parents the labor they could render.[4] This was not a violation of child labor laws since such laws were nonexistent. Child labor was a necessity of life.

In poor Massachusetts families life was especially harsh on children. In 1672, Boston Commissioners ordered that poor families "bind out" their children as servants in order to satisfy family indebtedness.[5] Orphans in England endured even harsher treatment. At a merchant's bequest, three hundred pounds were "employed in the taking out of the street or out of the Bridewell (London's house of correction) twelve fatherless and motherless boys and eight girls from seven years old and upwards and for furnishing them with necessities and paying for their passage to New England and for being bound apprentices to some such as will be careful to bring them up in the fear of God and to maintain themselves another day." Though more common in other colonies, these youth and others, including the unruly sons of English gentlemen, were sent to Boston primarily because of New England's reputation for piety.[6]

In fact, life was so hard that the health or physical condition of many parents suffered due to working conditions to the extent that many times children provided a bulk of family income. Frequently children essentially skipped adolescence and functioned as adults before entering their teenage years. Churches seldom had special meetings for young people because there simply was no time or energy for extra activities when life hung by a thread.

The more mouths there were to feed, the greater the difficulty parents had in making ends meet. Yet every additional mouth meant additional labor to help the family survive when the children were old enough to work. With a high level of infant and child mortality, less than half of the children survived until adulthood. Families had to be large merely to guarantee that the family would perpetuate itself.

If children survived into their teenage years, two customs of the day removed many from their homes. For girls, marriage was not uncommon soon after menarche, which occurred at age fourteen or fifteen. For boys, the common feeling was that in their early teenage years, sons should be placed as apprentices in the homes of other families. The reason most frequently given was that another father would have a better chance of properly disciplining and training the lad than would his biological parents.

As an example, Benjamin Franklin was the tenth son of a Boston soap maker. His father, who eventually had seventeen children, could only afford one year of schooling for Ben, and so at age twelve Ben was allowed to be an apprentice in his brother James's print shop. He never lived at home again. Unlike some apprentices whose master craftsmen were church-oriented, Ben's teenage contacts with the church were negative. He and his brother engaged in a feud with Puritan ministers Cotton and Increase Mathers over the use of smallpox vaccine in Boston (not a typical youth group discussion topic). At age seventeen, after a falling-out with his brother, Ben struck out for Philadelphia, where he became an entrepreneur, writer, publisher, statesman, and diplomat.[7]

Other factors shaped the manner in which children grew to adulthood in New England. The death of a father, mother, or both required children, if fortunate, to live with a relative. Francis Clark, the founder of Christian Endeavor, was born Francis Symmes, but lost his father, Charles, to cholera when the boy was only three years old. His seventeen-year-old brother, Charles Henry, died apparently of pneumonia four years later, and shortly thereafter his mother, Lydia, also passed away. Frank (as they called him) was an orphan at age seven in 1859. As was common, his mother made provision before her death that Frank would be raised by her younger brother, Edward Clark, a minister in Massachusetts. His uncle, who was childless, adopted him.[8] The saga of the Symmes family was common, not only in New England, but throughout America.

Often boys left home to seek their fortune while still in their teens. Dwight L. Moody, born on a small New England farm on February 5, 1837, was only four when his father, an alcoholic, died at age forty-one. Twins were born one month later to the family. His mother, Betsy, a thirty-six-year-old widow, had nine children at home and hardly any income. After years of struggle, D. L. left home on his seventeenth birthday to sell shoes for his uncle in Boston on the condition that he would attend church once a week. He found church boring but succeeded in selling shoes. Moody was on his own.[9]

While church attendance was a factor in the lives of New England youth in the colonial and early republic of the American experience, few if any churches treated young people as anything but either children or adults. Like D. L. Moody, most young people found their church experience rather boring. After all, it was assumed that they were adults because in many other aspects of life they functioned as adults.

Middle Atlantic Region

Life in the Middle Atlantic colonies (the current states of New York, New Jersey, Maryland, Pennsylvania, and Delaware) was equally challenging for children and youth. Whereas the settlers of New England early on required public schooling, private or parochial schooling was the norm in the Middle Atlantic colonies. Unlike the religiously homogeneous New England colonies, the Middle Atlantic colonies were havens for religious diversity—Dutch Calvinists, Anglicans, Lutherans, German Pietists, Quakers, Presbyterians, Roman Catholics, and Jews.

In New Amsterdam, private teachers provided instruction until 1664 when the Dutch Reformed Church persuaded the Dutch West India Company to finance schools. Like the Puritans in New England, the Dutch Reformed Church valued an educated laity and wanted everyone to be able to read the Scriptures in the vernacular. After the English took over and called the settlement *New York*, the Dutch continued schooling in their own language as a means of maintaining their cultural distinctives.[10]

The Church of England, however, used the English language and continued the same emphasis on reading, writing, arithmetic, catechism, and religion, extending educational opportunities in the form of charity schools to the poor. At the same time, "private venture schools" operated on a for-profit basis to teach practical skills and knowledge. These prepared young people for certain commercial trades.

Pennsylvania, initially settled by Quakers, later became the home of followers of the German Pietist Menno Simons, who became known as the Mennonites. Both groups provided schooling that protected their religious convictions and cultural heritage. In 1749, the civic leader Benjamin Franklin published *Proposals Relating to the Education of Youth in Pennsylvania*. The ideas he espoused lay the groundwork for a school system that moved from a heavy dependence on the classical languages to a more diversified curriculum that included vocational subjects.[11]

For a variety of reasons it was more common for settlers to come from Europe to the Middle Atlantic region individually rather than as families. Whereas it was normal for children of New England families to provide much of the labor supply, the absence of families in the Middle Atlantic colonies meant labor shortages. To address the shortage the directors of the West India Company in 1645 urged the importation of poor and orphaned children from the Netherlands. The first of these arrived in New Amsterdam in 1658.[12] These children would serve as indentured servants for six years and then be on their own, free to seek their fortunes.

Factory work occupied children in the Middle Atlantic colonies and later states. George Washington favorably reported in his diaries in 1789 of a visit to a mill where duck (cotton or linen cloth like canvas) was made. For ten hours a day, fourteen girls worked twenty-eight looms while other girls turned the wheels for them. The practice was both profitable and quite common. Sunday was the only day off. James Davenport received the first patent issued in the United States (1794) and set up the Global Mills in Philadelphia, where labor was performed primarily by boys. Dickson's Cotton Factory in Hell-Gate near New York employed mostly women and children who were bound as apprentices until age twenty-one.[13]

Most of the Middle Atlantic region depended on agriculture. Families expected their children to contribute to the family's survival through seasonal work on the farm. By the time a child was able to do the physical labor of the farm (somewhere between ages six and twelve depending on the child's size and the number of older siblings), school attendance, if at all, occurred only in the winter months.

Church was an important factor of solidarity in rural Middle Atlantic communities. Though it was a place of worship, the social aspect of the faith community was very significant. Until the introduction of the Sunday school, young people expected no special programming for their age group, and nothing was provided. Socializing with friends before and after church was a fringe benefit of church attendance.

The South

Young people in the Southern colonies experienced life quite differently than their peers to the north. The plantation system that dominated much of the South, especially along the coastal areas, separated families by many miles and made community schools impractical. In addition, wealthy landowners viewed themselves as a British-style aristocracy who felt no obligation to provide education to people with whom they had little or no relationship. Tutors for the children of plantation owners sometimes taught the children of others associated with the plantation and even slaves, but formal education was scarcely available to back-country youth.[14]

Private schools served the children of those who could afford the cost. Many of the Southern aristocracy chose instead to send their sons for education in England. Girls seldom had the benefit of formal education, but many knew how to read. Though the first free school in the colonies was founded by Benjamin Syms in Virginia in 1634, most schooling in Virginia and the rest of the South was private, scanty, and haphazard.[15] When public-supported education was provided, the intent was to educate poor white children, though some attention was paid by the Church of England and Quaker missionary societies to the education of slave children and Indians, with the intent of bringing them into the Christian faith.[16]

The labor shortage that caused indentured children to be brought to New England and New Amsterdam was even more acute in the South. Before the arrival of African slaves, children ten years and older were brought in significant numbers to Southern colonies. Before the Mayflower landed in Massachusetts, "idle and needy" children from England were transported to the Caribbean and Virginia as servants or apprentices. The action was seen as a boon to both the colony and the children who, at age twenty-one, would be "placed as tenants upon public land with best conditions where they shall have houses with stock of corn and cattle to begin with, and afterward the moiety [*sic*] of all increase and profit whatsoever."[17]

Not all transportation of children to Virginia was so protected. A report to the Lord Mayor of London (ca. 1638) expressed concern about "certain persons called spirits, do inveigle and by lewd subtleties entice away youth, against the consent of their parents, friends, or masters; whereby oftimes great tumults and uproars are raised in the city, to the breach of the peace, and the hazard of men's lives."[18] What began as a type of youth work that aimed to provide new beginnings in the colonies for indigent children turned into an industry built around opportunistic kidnapping of children from the streets of London.

Even more ugly was the traffic in African slaves. Since slaves were property, African children were legally sold and separated from parents.[19] The same was true for slave children captured from Indian tribes. In both cases Protestant churches gave complicit consent, with the justification that both were heathen and could become Christians under the care of Christian masters.

Whereas in New England and the Middle Atlantic colonies dissenting Protestant groups provided a moral core to the cultural ethos, the religious force dominating the South was the enfranchised Church of England. Supported by governmental prescription, the church was aligned with the business and governmental interests that drove the Southern colonies. In South Carolina, for example, understaffed priests found themselves burdened with civic duties when the Election Act of 1712 made parishes the local governmental unit rather than counties.[20] Even though dissenting groups settled in the South, their influence and concern for their communities' children and youth was minor compared with colonies farther north.

Toward the Age of Adolescence, 1840–1900

From the middle of the nineteenth century people began viewing young people in a somewhat different light. The word *adolescence* began to work its way into the American vocabulary. The culture started to view the time between the end of childhood and the assumption of adult responsibilities as a distinct stage in life. The change was gradual, but by the time G. Stanley Hall wrote his classic work, *Adolescence*, in 1904, American society had begun accepting the concept.

The Industrial Revolution and the challenge of the western frontier changed life for youth in America during the nineteenth century. While most of the nation remained rural, two migrations reshaped the manner in which young people lived. Wages for factory work attracted young people to the cities; and adventure and the endless potential of the American frontier lured young men, some with families, to seek their fortunes westward as the nation spread beyond the Allegheny Mountains and on toward the Pacific Ocean. Opportunities abounded, especially for the young.

Not only did young people migrate to the cities in search of economic gain, five million immigrants, primarily from northern Europe, flooded into America between the War of 1812 and the Civil War. Two million Irish Catholics came primarily after the potato blight brought about famine and death in the 1840s. German Lutherans flooded northern East Coast ports of entry in Boston, New York, and Philadelphia, as did Protestants from Scandinavian and other northern European countries. Thousands of Chinese laborers (primarily male) arrived on the West Coast to work on the railroad. In the South, only New Orleans saw a significant influx of people seeking to become a part of the American experience. By the time of the Civil War, many of these immigrants migrated up the Mississippi to St. Louis or Louisville, while Chicago and Milwaukee became home to Germans and Irish from the East Coast.[21] Virtually all the new Americans of this period came because of economic or political reasons.

Sacrifice characterized life for nineteenth-century immigrants. Giving up the country and culture of their parents and their grandparents, many left the friendly villages of their motherland to settle in growing cities where they were not wanted. Because of language barriers the jobs available to these immigrants often ignored their skills and clustered them at the bottom of the economic scale.

The children of immigrants suffered as well. The English-speaking, white American children, in part because of their parent's attitudes, looked down upon and bullied the newly-arrived children. Most immigrant kids had to work just to help their families make ends meet, while others were cut loose to live by their wits on the streets. The American dream for many was a nightmare. In addition to the financial struggles and the language and cultural barriers they faced, religious differences also made life for immigrants very challenging. Established youth, for the most part, came from families of eighteenth-century Protestant dissenters who shared both a Protestant work ethic and a culture of morality prescribed by biblical passages. Because immigrant children seldom shared the Protestant perspective on work, they were often viewed as lazy.

Immigrants faced religious challenges in their new land as well. Many had never read Scripture in their own language and certainly did not understand the English Bible. None had a memory of the Great Awakenings that, in part, shaped Protestant lifestyles. A legacy of conflicts between Protestants and the Roman Catholics in Europe spilled over into the

New World. Cities became more of a tossed salad of nationalities and religious expressions than the traditional concept of a melting pot.

Schools became an oasis of hope. During the period from 1840 until the end of the century, the public school came to the fore and began its expansion in shaping the lives of children and youth in America. With economic prosperity came the formation of the economic middle class. One of the characteristics of this class of Americans was that adults began looking at their children as something other than adults in little bodies. Values initially promoted by wealthy Protestants and Protestant ministers came to be normative expectations for the youth of the era.

Public high schools were rare in 1840. More than a thousand private academies dotted the land, educating the sons and daughters of those wealthy enough to pay the fees. Names varied widely—academies, seminaries for boys or girls, institutes, collegiate institutes, even colleges. Benjamin Franklin's Academy in Philadelphia, initially proposed in 1749, is perhaps the best known of this genre of schools for youth. Some academies continued the tradition of education in the classical languages as had been the curriculum in Latin schools. But most were conducted in English and included in their curriculum reading, writing, arithmetic, grammar, composition, rhetoric, and geography. In the nineteenth century, graduation from an academy constituted the highest level of education for those who attended. The few young people who went to college seldom attended academies and certainly did not see an academy education as preparatory for college since college studies primarily focused on the literature written in classical languages.[22]

By the end of the nineteenth century, however, high schools surpassed academies both in number and attendance. While still sparsely scattered across the United States, the commissioner of education reported 2,526 public high schools, enrolling 202,063 students, during the 1889–90 school year, while 1,632 private secondary schools and academies educated 94,391 young people. High school students represented less than 1 percent of the population in the United States. It was a rare thing to go to high school.[23]

So, where were all the rest of the young people of the nation? Working. Whether on the farm, in city mills and factories, in sales positions, or as apprentices training to be artisans (though the number of apprentices had begun to decline), young people in their teenage years accepted adult responsibilities and moved ahead with life as their parents had done. Few of these working youth were from the fledgling economic middle class. Even younger adolescents often worked. Robert H. Bremner comments:

> The nation-wide extent of child labor became visible in 1870 when the Census Bureau established a separate category of the gainfully employed

who were from ten to fifteen years of age. According to the 1870 census about one of every eight children were employed. By 1900 approximately 1,750,000 children, or one out of six, were gainfully employed. Sixty percent were agricultural workers; of the 40 per cent in industry over half were children of immigrant families.[24]

While most young people were working, not all had left home. The decline in apprenticeships, extension of public schooling to the second-ary years, willingness of fathers to deed tracks of land to their sons at an earlier age, declining family size, and stronger appeal of home life led many young people to remain at home until they married and established their own homes.[25]

Families changed as well. After touring America, French social analyst Alexis de Tocqueville concluded that the autocratic rule of fathers com-mon in Europe had been abandoned in favor of a more relaxed approach to raising children. Except for the earliest years of a child's life, children were encouraged to become increasingly independent.[26] The democratic ideal had begun making its way into family life. Mathew Carey, an Irish publisher in Philadelphia who migrated to the United States in 1824, commented similarly, "The endearing relationship between parents and children partakes largely of the same mild character. The austerity, the harshness, and the severity which characterize this relationship in some parts of Europe, are here unknown, except among a few foreigners, who have brought hither the manners of their own countries."[27]

Yet even middle-class values failed to penetrate all regions of the country. President Martin Van Buren led a nation in 1840 that included all states east of the Mississippi River except Florida, plus Louisiana, Arkansas, and Missouri. By the end of the century, President William McKinley's America consisted of the rest of the forty-eight continental states with the exception of Oklahoma, Arizona, and New Mexico. As the nation expanded westward, Protestant church ministers and lay leaders expressed concerns for the problems young people faced both in their communities and across the nation.

New England

By 1840 free universal elementary schools, known as common schools, had been legally established in the industrial northeast. Motivation be-hind the common school movement has been widely discussed. Idealists claimed that common schools were a means of forming or reforming culture through its children. Critics suggest the schools primarily rein-forced the status quo as defined by a Protestant consensus.[28] Following the lead of English educational reformer Thomas Arnold of Rugby, com-mon school advocates decided that "no longer were the public schools to be dumping grounds for the dissolute sons of gentlemen. . . . [T]hey were to become nurseries of character."[29]

High schools developed in New England about as rapidly as in any other section of the nation. In 1885 the Massachusetts Board of Education reported 224 high schools in the state. These, however, were not evenly distributed across the state. High schools were not found in rural areas and small villages, and even in towns like Worcester and Fall River, the attendance of students of high school age was only 38.4 percent and 12.3 percent respectively.[30]

Much of what historians know about youth before the twentieth century comes from records of various sorts written in New England. In his well-documented analysis of the period, Joseph Kett primarily cites authors from New England. The highly literate society and stable community allowed documents to be written and then maintained for historians to review. In critiquing the movement of the period that laid the groundwork for teenagers to be treated as being in a distinct place in life called *adolescence*, Kett accurately described the New England experience for young people.

> The concept of adolescence, from the beginning of its modern form, was intertwined with a romantic view of childhood, with articulate fears of modern life, cities, overpressure, and overcivilization. In the form it assumed by mid-century, the concept of adolescence was the creation of a distinctive mind-set, an expression of a mélange of nostalgia and anxiety, and in its crudest mold of Victorian prejudices about females and sexuality.[31]

Middle Atlantic States

President George W. Atherton of Pennsylvania State College reported in 1882 that 8,608 students were enrolled in the state's fifty-seven high schools. Yet only 236 of these students entered college.[32] Both numbers reflected the ambivalence over the role that high schools should play in the lives of young people.

Until 1880, child labor was viewed as a part of the normal way in which society worked. While reformers in New England addressed issues regarding child employment in factories, their counterparts in the Middle Atlantic states addressed their child labor issues. The news boys in New York City (newsies) provide a not uncommon picture of young people in Middle Atlantic urban settings. Describing the children in American street trades, Myron E. Adams comments:

> The newsboy has become a part of our city environment. A familiar figure, rather undersized as we know him best, flipping the street cars, or standing on street corners holding his stock under his arm. A veritable merchant

of the street, who scans each passer-by as a possible customer. Quick of wit and intent upon his trade he reads their peculiarities at a glance, and makes the most of their weaknesses. The public sees him at his best and neglects him at his worst. He is not considered a problem of child labor, because he works in the open and is seemingly apart from the associations which are so hostile to the health and happiness of the factory child.[33]

The South

While the common school had become a fixture to the north, Southern states did not share the same passion for a literate population. In South Carolina, tax dollars were controlled by the aristocrats from Charleston while the bulk of the population lived in the "backcountry." Schools in Charleston, both public and private, were comparable to other sections of the nation. Yet away from the coastal city of Charleston public education was stigmatized as schools for the poor, that is, charity schools. So as late as 1860 only about half of the state's white population was in school. When it came to educating African children, South Carolina had some of the most stringent laws in the nation outlawing the education of slave or free in the years leading up to the Civil War.[34]

In 1885, A. D. Mayo reported that in the sixteen Southern states, there were four million white students and nearly two million "colored" children, with no more than a third enrolled in any effective form of schooling. Charles Forster Smith of Vanderbilt University bemoaned the fact that his state of Tennessee had but four public high schools, though hosting twenty-one male colleges and universities and sixteen female colleges and seminaries.[35] Much of the blame for this inattention to schooling may be attributed to the lingering effects of the reconstruction period following the Civil War.

As textile mills relocated to the South from New England, child labor increased. Bremner reports that "by 1900 one-third of the workers in southern mills were children. More than half of them were between ten and thirteen years of age; and many were under ten. In the absence of legislative restrictions the South repeated the experience of New England in its early period of industrialization."[36]

The West

Benefiting by the experiences of cities in the east, cities throughout the Ohio River Valley and along the Great Lakes developed school systems. As much as being good for children, schools were good for business. They gave rapidly growing cities like Buffalo, Cincinnati, and Chicago a feeling of sophistication. Police departments, fire departments, water systems, and publicly funded schools retained the type of people necessary to turn a frontier village into a viable city.

Chicago illustrates the manner in which schools developed in western cities. The first school in Chicago to receive public funds was that of Miss Eliza Chapell in 1833. The school started as a charity school in a storeroom but moved to a Presbyterian church and was as much an evangelistic ministry as a school.

The first high school in Chicago opened in 1856 with 169 pupils. Four years later, the same year Abraham Lincoln was elected president, public school records showed 312 students enrolled in high school. By that time, the population of the city on the southern tip of Lake Michigan had grown to over one hundred thousand. Even after the population of the city passed the one million mark in 1890, high school students numbered only 2,825. Only after the 1893 Columbian Exposition—called by some the greatest nineteenth century world's fair—did high school enrollment increase to 10,201 at the turn of the century when the Chicago population topped a million and a half. Total public school enrollments that year were over a quarter of a million.[37]

But where were the high school–aged young people in Chicago at the end of the nineteenth century? The answer is complex since the diversified economy of Chicago was booming. The poorest section of the city was the Nineteenth Ward, home to immigrants from twenty-six nations.[38] It was there that Jane Addams established the Hull House Settlement to help women and children survive the rough-and-tumble city. A study by Hull House staff members found children working as boot blacks, newsboys, and cash-children (they carried money to and from departments in stores to a central teller as sales were made), but the majority worked in factories, the largest of which was a caramel works where children wrapped and packed candies.[39]

The booming economy of Chicago, as with the rapidly growing cities of the Midwest and West, was a haven for entrepreneurial young people. School and church failed to be a priority in this frontier environment. Even though G. Stanley Hall would soon describe adolescents as people in a turbulent transition from childhood to adult status, most young people in the region functioned as what Daniel Levinson would later call "novice adults," a term Levinson used to describe people in their early twenties.[40]

The Era of Adolescence, 1900–1977

As far as young people were concerned, the twentieth century started with a formal statement of the nature of adolescence with the publication of G. Stanley Hall's *Adolescence* in 1904; morphed into the age of the "teenager" following World War II; and was proclaimed a "youth culture" as the century came to an end. In each phase of this progression, adults determined how the culture should understand people in the years between twelve and twenty and how these young people should view themselves. Though the idea of adolescence was celebrated by most, toward the end of the century some questioned the validity of the concept. Thomas Hine provocatively asked, "Are teenagers necessary?" in his description of the "rise and fall of the American teenager."[41]

One of the great difficulties in tracing the history of youth ministry in America is the manner in which the concept of youth is understood (see chapter 2). While much of the world still thought of "youth" as starting sometime after infancy and concluding in a person's late twenties, youth ministry people came to use the term first to refer to boys and girls in their teenage years and then focused primarily on high school students—grades nine through twelve. Social commentators, especially in the first part of the twentieth century, focused on students residing at colleges and universities. Paula Fass commented, "I have narrowed the focus of investigation to one major segment of the youth population— native, white, middle-class, and almost exclusively college-going—and I have given particular attention to the role of the family and of school peer groups in determining the experience of [these] youth."[42] Churches, however, shifted their attention to the young people who remained under the roofs of their parents.

For college and university students and young professionals, the Roaring Twenties marked a change from the world of their parents. World War I broke the provincialism of American youth when more than two million of them joined forces with the Allies of France to defeat the nations aligned with Germany. Upon their return home, a booming economy and a pervasive sense of optimism set the stage for building a new world. After all, they had fought and won the war to end all wars.

Economic changes produced a growing middle class. Fewer young people needed to work in order for families to survive, so more young people remained in school, attending high school and college. At the same time, family size decreased. With the decreased number of children per family came an increased sense of warmth and affection among family members and especially between parents and children. The American experiment had brought democracy to the family. Austere and authoritarian forms of fatherhood gave way to a more affectionate and relational approach.

In the years between 1890 and 1920, secondary school enrollment mushroomed from three hundred sixty thousand to two and a half million, which included almost a third of the fourteen- to seventeen-year-old population as the twenties began. While most of the students enrolled in large urban schools, the majority of high schools were small and rural.

Yet the story of the founding of Crossnore School in western North Carolina by medical doctors Mary T. Martin Sloop and her husband Eustace was typical of many rural communities. Uneducated parents saw little need for "book larnin'." Children assumed adult responsibilities shortly after puberty. Commenting on the needs for the school, the founder said:

> Frequently girls married at thirteen; they considered themselves old maids if they were not married at fifteen or sixteen. And if a boy hadn't married at sixteen or seventeen, his fellows would begin to poke fun at him and charge him with being "a poor hand with the wimmenfolks." A boy who reached voting age without being married was a rarity indeed; he was headed toward permanent bachelorhood, everyone agreed.[43]

By 1929–30, enrollment in secondary schools grew to 4,804,000 which was 51.3 percent of fourteen- to seventeen-year-olds. The percentage increased to 83.2 percent by 1959–60.[44] For teenagers, life shifted from the workplace to the high school and provided a common experience for the adolescent population.[45] Compulsory school attendance laws extended into middle adolescence in many states and prohibitions against child labor that were enacted during the Great Depression forced young people into high schools. Nationally high schools took on such a unified character that Ralph Keyes would describe high school as the last tribal experience in America and ask, "Is there life after high school?"[46]

What high schools attempted to accomplish solidified early in the twentieth century. While some had seen the high school as "the people's college," an alternative to a college or university education in the late nineteenth century, the secondary school curriculum shifted to preparation for college based on the blueprint laid out by President Charles W. Elliot of Harvard and the Committee of Ten appointed in 1892 by the National Education Association. While "life preparation" curricular tracks followed, the dominant emphasis of high school throughout the twentieth century was academic.

The greatest social impact of the rise of high schools was the influence of the peer society.[47] The currency of this newly-formed society was *status*. While adults controlled the academic aspects of high school and closely supervised extracurricular activities, students themselves designated who was "in" and who was "out," who was "cool" and who was a "dork." In smaller and rural high schools the social pyramid was rather well defined. The larger the school, the greater likelihood of multiple status pyramids. By the 1970s, social pyramids proliferated in part due to entitlement legislation that made it possible for specialized extra-curricular groups to receive the same funding as the traditional status activities such as football and cheerleading.

Several dynamics made the peer group significant as the twentieth century progressed. Though the school day was highly structured, after-noons and evenings gave adolescents unstructured time to be together. The automobile provided mobility and, though few owned cars until midcentury, many had access to family vehicles. Commercial establish-ments such as drugstores with soda fountains, drive-in restaurants, and movie theaters became places to gather apart from adult supervision. By midcentury radio and soon television began catering to a new market of high school students, and teenagers gained their own style of music that allowed them to differentiate from their parents and form a peer society. The peer group became central to understanding what adoles-cence was all about.

Two factors, however, isolated some high school students outside the dominant social pyramids: race and poverty. Race kept African Americans from accessing the better funded high school of the dominant culture, but the social dynamics of black students were similar. Only after the *Brown v. Board of Education of Topeka* desegregation ruling by the United States Supreme Court in 1954 did African students slowly begin to gain access to the better-funded high schools of white Americans.

Poverty broke across race, ethnic, and religious barriers and made life difficult for high school students caught in its clutches. Dropping out of school and episodic unemployment were closely associated with poverty throughout the century. Still the peer factor shaped how adolescents used their time and creativity. In urban settings, gangs of peers served as families for many teens who saw little hope in escaping the poverty cycle. For teens from low-income families who proved resistant to gang influence, inadequate food and clothing and poor housing conditions left them outside the mainstream of the high school society and eventually on the fringes of American life.

While the high school experience standardized the lives of American teenagers in the twentieth century, and the media created what some called a "youth culture" in the later half, regional differences remained, urban and rural gaps widened, and ethnic diversity increased.

Regional Differences

The number of children ages ten to fifteen working in 1930 varied according to where a child lived. While the national average was 8.5 percent, the South East Central region (Kentucky, Tennessee, Alabama, and Mississippi) more than doubled that figure (17.5 percent) while the South Atlantic region (Delaware, Maryland, Washington, DC, Virginia, West Virginia, North Carolina, South Carolina, Georgia, and Florida) saw 14.3 percent of their ten- to fifteen-year-olds working. In contrast, the Pacific region (Washington, Oregon, and California) saw only 3.1 percent of the age group working and West North Central (Minnesota, Iowa, Missouri, North Dakota, South Dakota, Nebraska and Kansas) saw only 3.9 percent of its kids in the group working.

When 5.2 percent of ten- to fifteen-year-olds in the United Sates worked on farms, the percentage in South East Central (15.5 percent) and South Atlantic (11.2 percent) were again the highest while New England (Maine, New Hampshire, Vermont, Massachusetts, Connecticut, and Rhode Island) had the fewest ten- to fifteen-year-old farm workers (.4 percent), followed by the Pacific region (.7 percent).[48] These regional differences in youthful employment merely demonstrate the regional variation at one point in the century. Differences in other aspects of adolescent lives suggest a wide variation in the experiences of early adolescents in different parts of the country.

Urban and Rural Gaps

As machinery replaced manual labor on the farms of America, entire families moved to nearby cities. Wartime shortages of workers during World War I brought a flood of workers from farms to factories in the cities. To put the migration to the cities into perspective, at the beginning of the Civil War in 1860, 80.2 percent of the population of the nation was rural. At the turn of the century, that percentage had dropped to 60.4 percent. By the end of World War I, 48.8 percent of the population remained rural, and this would drop to 36 percent at the beginning of the Korean conflict at midcentury and reach 30.1 percent a hundred years after the beginning of the Civil War.[49]

Especially notable was the influx of African Americans from the South to northern cities beginning just before World War I. William J. Collins comments:

> More than 50 years after the Emancipation Proclamation freed their parents and grandparents, African Americans initiated the Great Migration. Whereas only about 535,000 blacks emigrated from the South on net between 1870 and 1910, the following 40 years witnessed the net emigration of 3.5 million, primarily to the urban North.[50]

There was another American migration: out of the cities into suburbs surrounding the cities. During the early part of the century, economic middle-class families clustered in sprawling cities throughout the

United States. The idea of moving to the suburbs was not new, having begun when some of the upwardly mobile citizens of New York City left Manhattan, crossed the East River, and settled in Brooklyn in the mid-nineteenth century. Following the Great Depression of the 1930s and World War II (1941–45), a migration of middle-class families settled in suburbs around major cities. Immigrants who came to the cities saw their children gain an education in public schools and universities, and settled with their families in newly formed communities adjacent to the cities. By the 1970s, the suburbs were understood to be the domain of the economic middle class.

Ethnic Diversity

The desegregation of American schools, changes in immigration laws, and civil rights legislation changed the American high school, especially in the second half of the twentieth century. Combined, these factors changed the complexion of the high schools of America.

When the United States Supreme Court concluded that the separate-but-equal concept of public schools was in fact separate and unequal, they issued the *Brown v. Board of Education of Topeka* decision, which integrated America's public schools. Life for American teenagers changed dramatically as a result. Along with children, they became the focal point of the Court's attempt to extend the Constitution of the United States to people of all colors. Public schools were the starting point for providing equal education opportunities to all Americans. Though the process was slow and antagonistic at times, the rising generation of white students began to see black, Hispanic, and Asian students as classmates and friends.

The first permanent immigration law in the United States passed in 1924. One of its limitations related to national origins. Quotas were set on ethnic groups from nations deemed undesirable. In 1952, the Immigration and Nationality Act (the McCarran-Walter Act) abolished race as an overall barrier to immigration, but kept particular forms of national bias. The act was amended in 1965, abolishing the national origins quota. Because of these changes a strong influx of educated people from Asian countries relocated to the United States, and many settled in American suburbs. At the same time, Hispanic immigrants became the largest ethnic group in America.

Civil rights legislation of the sixties and seventies, combined with entitlement legislation in the 1970s, further changed the high school landscape. For high school students, the laws required parity in the manner in which educational dollars were spent. The great beneficiaries were students of color, females, and arts programs. No longer would black female actresses have to take a back seat to white male football players. Or, at least, that was the intent.

For teenagers, life in the latter part of the twentieth century was very different from that experienced by their counterparts either earlier in the century or in the other two periods Joseph Kett identified. Rites of passage had changed.

Conclusion

The newsies of New York symbolized one segment within the diversity of life for American young people. Youth was a broad category in the nineteenth century, stretching from the time a child could assume work responsibilities until sometime in their late twenties or early thirties. For Protestant youth, the home and church gradually gave way to the marketplace and, later, the public school as the places where they moved from childhood to adulthood.

Following Kett's outline of the history of adolescence in America and expanding the focus initially into regional differences and, finally, into changing social factors in the high school culture, this chapter described the unity and diversity of the American experience for young people. It will be in this context that the book will examine the response of Protestant churches to the changing needs of both their youth and the youth in the broader society.

Yet, before tracing the history of youth ministry in America, one basic question needs to be asked: "What is adolescence?" If youth is a distinct period in the process of human development, what describes and characterizes that period of life? The next chapter attempts both to address the question and to examine how the Protestant church responded with the creation of special ministries distinctly for adolescents.

Rebel Without a Cause

The Rise and Fall of Adolescence in America

The 1955 movie *Rebel Without a Cause* marked a watershed in the way in which teenagers in America viewed themselves. James Dean, the leading actor, came to symbolize the angst of the post–World War II generation. Even at the beginning of the twenty-first century, his picture on movie posters can be found in stores selling CDs and DVDs to teenagers in the emerging world.

Jim Stark (played by James Dean) came to town to escape his troubled past. He hoped to find the love he didn't get from his middle-class family. Though he found some in his relationship with Judy (Natalie Wood), and a form of it in both Plato's (Sal Mineo) adulation and juvenile officer Ray's (Edward C. Platt) real concern for him, Jim still felt the need to prove himself to his peers in switchblade knife fights and "chickie" games, in which cars raced toward a seaside cliff.

The story ends tragically, in a Romeo and Juliet–type scene, as Jim proved he was not a chicken but crashed over the cliff to his death as his peers watched. Ironically, James Dean crashed his own sports car and died a month before the movie was released, perhaps reinforcing the theme of the story.

The most poignant tragedy of the story, however, was found in the alienation between adults and teenagers. Framed in an era when parents of the "greatest generation," formed by the Depression and World War II, had difficulty coming to terms with the peer influence and personal freedom of their children, generational tension ran throughout the movie.

One scene captured the estrangement Judy felt from her father. Judy told a very patient, sympathetic juvenile offenders officer, Ray, that she was experiencing problems with her father who had withdrawn his physical affections and love now that she was older and wore lipstick. Unlike many teenager-oriented films that followed, the police officer was the only truly responsible adult figure (father figure) in the film. Judy sobbed that her father resisted and reproached her newly found grown-up maturity. He caused her pain when he labeled her a "dirty tramp" after she applied red lipstick and dressed up for him. Rejecting her, he showed his disapproval by smearing the lipstick off her lips. Judy reacted by running out of the house.

At one o'clock that night, well after curfew, Judy was picked up wandering about alone. Mistaken for a streetwalker "looking for company," Ray concluded her behavior was one way to get back at her father, to get him to pay attention.[1]

Rebel Without a Cause captured the fears of parents and educators in the mid-twentieth century. More importantly, the movie gave teenagers a voice and an excuse to turn to their peers for advice and friendship. Yet, this transition from parental control to peer influence had been growing since the 1920s, starting with university campuses and working its way down to public high schools.[2]

It was in the *Rebel Without a Cause* context that much of contemporary youth ministry was formed. Youth ministries became oases where teenagers could find themselves within Christian peer groups. Youth pastors and lay youth directors were hired by churches. Parachurch youth ministries flourished. Yet to assume that characters played by James Dean, Natalie Wood, and Sal Mineo were representative of youth before or after the second half of the twentieth century would be highly misleading. In fact, the generational alienation of the middle-class family captured in the film probably describes the youth culture ethos for only about twenty years, 1955–75.

Various types of youth ministry preceded and followed this period when youth ministry was professionalized and grew into a visible influence in shaping the ministries of Protestant churches. So, before we proceed in exploring the history of Protestant youth ministries, it is essential that we understand the evolution of two ideas—the term *youth* and the concept of *middle class*.

Defining *Youth*

Even at the beginning of the twenty-first century, the word *youth* has a wide variety of usages. In the majority of the world, *youth* means everyone under the midthirties. If a person is not an adult, she or he is a youth. Adults are people who have acquired an age and social status in the community to be looked to for leadership. Frequently, the indicators of adulthood are that people are in their midthirties, are married, and have children. Though sometimes *children* is used to differentiate *youth* prior to age six or seven, for much of the world *youth* means everything not adult.

Three words, *adolescence*, *youth*, and *teenage*, have described this period prior to adulthood. The term *adolescence* comes from the Latin word *adolescere*, meaning to grow up. Used by churchmen and other scholars from classical times to the Middle Ages, the term referred to young people who had reached puberty but had not achieved full adult social rights. Frequently this did not occur until a man was in his late thirties.[3] For women whose social rights were seldom considered, achievement of adulthood related more to marriage and childbearing.

Youth before the Twentieth Century

Though first use of the term *adolescence* occurred in the fifteenth century, Plato and Aristotle proposed three periods of development in the fifth century BC. Each period before adulthood lasted seven years—infancy, boyhood, and young manhood.[4] Toward the end of the Middle Ages, the word *youth* largely replaced *adolescence* in the English-speaking world. The beginning of the years of youth came when a child could be gainfully employed. This usually was at about the age when children enter the first or second grades in the American school system today. The word applied until such a time as a young person was married or self-employed. Though the end of youth might be as late as thirty years of age, it generally referred to people between the ages of ten and twenty-five.[5]

The idea that employment separated young people from children and that self-employment or marriage distinguished youth from adults may seem odd to the reader. Yet family survival depended on the work of every able-bodied family member. Schooling was available to very few. Even for those for whom schooling was available, attendance patterns adjusted to work schedules, especially in dominantly agrarian societies. It was not infrequent for youth to leave home in order to obtain suitable employment. In fact it was the necessity of youth working that gave rise to youth ministries of the nineteenth century.

The word *adolescence* was seldom used in America until the twentieth century. *Youth* described everyone who was not an infant and not yet self-supporting with a family. At about age seven, boys moved from the care of mothers to the supervision of their fathers. Girls remained under the care of their mothers, for it was assumed they would become wives and mothers. Mothers, it was commonly felt, were too indulgent with their male children, and so the responsibility for preparing boys for adulthood passed to fathers. Because not all fathers performed their task well, apprenticeships, tutors, schools, guilds, and clubs were utilized to supplement their training.[6]

The size of a young person was far more important than chronological age during this period. Size was assumed to indicate usefulness in the work that supported the family. If a fourteen-year-old boy or girl could "work like a man" then they were considered grown-up. If a sixteen-year-old was small in stature or sickly in health, he or she was seen as childlike.[7]

For youth ministry prior to the twentieth century, chronological age was not a determining factor. There was no youth culture. Marriage and the beginning of a family determined the conclusion of the period of life known as youth. Marriage was generally postponed until the young man was able to support a wife and family, so this meant that the period of life described as *youth* concluded for most men in their late twenties. For women the age of marriage was much younger and with marriage came the passing from youth to adulthood.

Few of the rites associated with youth in the twenty-first century even occurred to nineteenth century youth. Since few high schools existed and only scattered academies or seminaries dotted the landscape, formal education for boys in their teenage years was reserved for the sons of the wealthy who attended colleges founded, for the most part, by Protestant denominations. The formal education of girls was generally considered a waste of time since they would become wives and mothers.

Leisure time activities were limited to a few hours on Sunday afternoon and were spontaneous gatherings, generally associated with church attendance. Nor were coeducational activities commonly available. Families regulated courtship, and as a result, spontaneous gatherings of people of the opposite sex were viewed as a threat to family authority and custom. Dating, especially as a casual means of getting to know people of the opposite sex, did not exist. Courtship was a prelude to marriage.

Even for the wealthy, the social protocols for men and women in their late teens and early twenties were carefully prescribed. For the few wealthy enough to escape the heat of the summer and retreat to mountain resorts, the gathering of people of the opposite sex was ritualized. For example, at an immense hotel in White Sulphur Springs, West Virginia, just after the Civil War, families of the wealthy from North and South gathered.

In the evenings . . . there was a custom known as "the treadmill." This was a great promenade. The guests walked up and down the long uncarpeted parlor in lines of three or four, stopping to chat and to make introductions. This was followed by a dance in the dining room, which nightly converted to a ballroom by the removal of many of its tables.[8]

In time, the social customs at White Sulphur Springs were further ritualized as "the nightly Treadmill and ball were no longer enough; there were square dances, concerts, and even dances known as 'morning germans' which began at eleven and went on until one in the afternoon. The lawns were filled with people playing a new game called croquet."[9]

Such luxuries were not available to most youth in the nineteenth century. Vacations were unknown. For most young people, life came closer to that described by Laura Ingalls Wilder in her *Little House on the Prairie* series, set in the heartland of America where all family members worked year-round simply to survive. In the cities, life for the working poor was equally demanding.

Only late in the nineteenth century did organized games begin providing social releases for young people. Basketball and volleyball, inventions of the YMCA, along with baseball encouraged young men to play on weekends and in their few leisure moments. Young women, for the most part, were expected to be spectators.

Youth from 1900 to 1975

With the Progressive Era and the rise of publicly-funded high schools, the word *adolescence* came back into usage, primarily because of the publication of *Adolescence* by G. Stanley Hall in 1904.[10] The book attempted to provide a scientific basis for the public high school by demonstrating that adolescence was a distinct period between childhood and the adult years that was filled with such turbulence and stress that special attention should be paid to the period. Soon thereafter the term *adolescence* began appearing in the artistic world, and using Hall's description of this season of life, the word became a metaphor for life between puberty and the time in the midtwenties when life stabilized with the acceptance of the adult responsibilities of family, home, and job. "Part 2 of Stravinsky's Rites of Spring, titled 'Dance of the Adolescents' with its thumping sexual rhythms written in 1912, and Edvard Munch's painting 'Adolescence' of the same period, portraying a frail vulnerable girl in her mid-teens, reflected two contrasting artistic expressions of the same subject."[11]

In G. Stanley Hall's attempt to ground his concept of adolescence in scientific evidence, he extended the research of Ernst Haeckel in the field of embryology into a life stage theory of human development. Haeckel proposed the idea of recapitulation, in which the history of ancestors within a species was compressed into the prenatal period of development. Using the same idea and wedding it with the writings of Jean-Jacques Rousseau, Hall presented adolescence as parallel to the evolutionary period when human ancestors went from being beastlike to living civilized lives.[12] With a theoretical framework that viewed adolescence as a period of turmoil, Hall then utilized evidence from various fields of scientific study to explain adolescent angst.

For the next seventy years, adolescence was understood much as Hall defined it. Researchers focused on gaining a greater understanding of this developmental stage while practitioners (educators, social workers, and youth workers) paid more attention to the context in which the adolescent lived. Unfortunately, the researchers and practitioners failed to collaborate in their studies and as a result the uniqueness of the adolescent experience was seldom challenged. *Youth* and *adolescence* was that period of internal disorder and chaos and yet idealism that humorist Garrison Keillor described as being from age fourteen on up to whenever you recover.[13]

Three sets of legislative acts further defined adolescence as a distinct and vulnerable period of life. These dealt with child labor, compulsory school attendance, and the establishment of a juvenile court system. While all three had their roots in the nineteenth century, each peaked in the early years of the twentieth century and shaped the culture's understanding of the teenage years.

Child labor laws went through three phases. In the first (1830–60), states primarily in New England and to a lesser extent in the Middle Atlantic region, required employers of children to provide education of various types. This was followed by a period (1860–1929) when various states limited the employment of children, primarily in factories, starting with age ten and gradually raising the minimum age to sixteen. Federal legislation just before World War I, while not taking away the authority of states to regulate labor practices within their borders, prevented the interstate shipment of products produced or manufactured by children. Though the act was later declared unconstitutional by the United States Supreme Court, the process of removing adolescents from the workplace had begun.[14]

With the stock market crash in 1929 and the Great Depression of the 1930s, the third phase of child labor laws began. Unemployment was so great that adults began competing with children for the few available jobs. In 1938, President Franklin Delano Roosevelt signed the Fair Labor Standards Act into law and in so doing prohibited most employment of minors. Though there were exceptions, adolescents were no longer part of the American workforce. Their place in society was distinct from the labor-intensive lives of nineteenth-century young people.

Compulsory school attendance was closely connected with child labor laws. Compulsory school attendance legislation was first enacted in New England with a Massachusetts law in 1852. Mississippi was the last state to pass similar legislation in 1918. Motivation for these laws varied from humanitarian impulses, to keeping children and youth out of mines and factories, to providing the advantages of education in a democracy, to maintaining social control over children and youth who otherwise may be a problem to society.[15] Though compulsory attendance laws were relatively ineffective through the end of World War I, the correlation between such legislation and high school completion increased significantly between 1920 and 1934.[16]

The combination of child labor laws and compulsory school attendance further defined adolescence. Public high schools became the gathering place for youth. It was expected that most people ages fourteen through seventeen would no longer have the option to live independently or set out to seek their fortunes. Nor would they contribute to the economic viability of their family. Adolescence became a period of dependence and postponed dreams. The real world would have to wait.

A third factor that helped define adolescence was the juvenile court system. For youthful offenders who performed antisocial acts beyond those tolerated by parents and communities, an alternative justice system had to be created. Because adolescence was understood to be a time of turbulence and stress, authorities concluded that young people should not be permanently scarred by having a criminal record or being incarcerated with hardened adult criminals. So a juvenile justice system was established.

At the end of the nineteenth century, children under age seven were legally considered incapable of committing a crime. For children between seven and fourteen, criminal intent had to be proved by prosecutors. But for youth from puberty on (fourteen and older), the law treated their crimes like adults' crimes. A coalition of lawyers and philanthropic leaders in Chicago objected to this procedure, and in 1899, Judge Harvey B. Hurd and Mrs. Lucy L. Flower spearheaded an effort that established the first juvenile court in America. Other states followed.[17] The assumption was that the *character* of children was still forming so instead of punishment or reformation, youth offenders stood in need of the formation of good habits and character. So the aim of the juvenile court became correction and training rather than punishment. Once again, adolescents were placed into a suspended stage of life, but troubled youth were viewed as salvageable when properly managed.[18]

By the end of the Great Depression, *youth* had taken on a meaning significantly different than was employed in the nineteenth century or before. Youth and adolescence were used interchangeably. No longer did they include prepubescent children. While educators would continue to describe college-age people as adolescents, legal definitions of child workers, truancy, and juvenile delinquency concentrated on high school–age students. The stage was set for the emergence of America's love-hate relationship with "teenagers." The rise of an economic middle class following the Great Depression provided the resources to make young people a new factor in virtually every aspect of American life.[19]

The word *teenager* was a product of the World War II era. Apparently first used in the magazine *Popular Science* in 1941, the moniker was quickly adopted by the world of advertising to label the demographic group between thirteen and nineteen years of age.[20] The war prematurely transformed older youth into adults, claiming their efforts either in the armed services or as support in the war effort through employment for vital industries. This left high school students and their junior high school counterparts as a unique group. They became that distinct group called *teenagers*.

While Protestant churchmen made new efforts to reach youth for Christ, initially the "youth" evangelical leaders had in mind included military personnel who soon after the war entered colleges and universities courtesy of the G.I. Bill, which funded higher education for returning soldiers and sailors and kept the job market from being flooded. During the war, evangelical periodicals, such as *Moody Monthly*, the evangelical voice of Moody Bible Institute, changed their youth focus to military personnel. "Youth Page" changed to "Soldiers, Sailors, Marines" in July of 1942, and in the process retained an older perception of *youth* while ignoring teenagers.[21]

After World War II, the focus of youth ministry became teenagers. University and college ministries accommodated the twin factors of higher levels of critical thinking capacity evidenced in late adolescence and, more importantly, the fact that college and university students had moved away from the homes of their parents and were free to experiment with ideas and lifestyles not necessarily permitted while living under their parents' roofs. Teenagers, by contrast, were still at home. Youth ministry adjusted, focusing on the same demographics as did Madison Avenue. Denominational and independent publishing houses addressed problems of teenagers. Camps and conferences specialized in ministries to high school students. Clubs sponsored by Protestant groups met in or near high schools. Teens became the focus of youth ministry.

Still using the G. Stanley Hall framework of understanding adolescents, youth workers, educators, and legislatures assumed teenagers to be pretty much the same anywhere in the nation or the world. Based on the common assumptions, church programs were designed to address the "problems" of teens. Ministry strategies, built upon the assumption that teenagers were attempting to discover their identity, provided opportunities for young people to associate with student body leaders in order to enhance their status among their peers.[22] Youth workers appealed to student body leaders in the persons of high school athletes and cheerleaders in the hope that others would follow their lead and attend meetings and camps. Everyone was assumed to be college-bound. Little thought was given to the actual social diversity found in high schools and junior high schools.

Youth from 1975 to 2000

Social turbulence in the late 1960s and early 1970s along with the arrival of a new generation of researchers forced a new look at adolescence. The idea that adolescence was a developmental life span came into question among researchers. Though Hall's framework for understanding adolescence remained in place, theories of adolescence expanded throughout the second half of the twentieth century.

If human development in this adolescent period were a function of biology, why did young people react so differently to various life circumstances such as the Depression (primarily viewed negatively), world wars (generally viewed positively), or the Vietnam conflict (viewed both positively and negatively)? The Vietnam conflict brought the differing reactions of young people into public scrutiny. Why did some youth in a given generation respond differently to the same set of circumstances (Vietnam: "America, Love it or leave it" vs. "Hell no, we won't go [to Vietnam]")? Or why did so many African American youth see the war effort as irrelevant to their lives as Americans?

Cognitive theorist Jean Piaget emphasized that children changed as they adapted their thinking to include new ideas. Lev Vygotsky went a step further, asserting that culture played a formative role in human development. Lawrence Kohlberg and Carol Gilligan examined moral reasoning, including that of adolescents. James W. Fowler, John Westerhoff, Mary Wilcox, Bruce Powers, and others explored the nature and structure of faith. B. F. Skinner and Albert Bandura looked at the impact of the learner's environment on learning, including that of adolescents. Urie Bronenbrenner and Glen H. Elder Jr. examined the ecology and life course of adolescent development, suggesting a strong social and historical interaction with their various life systems.[23]

Each theory viewed adolescence as part of a larger environment. As Bronenbrenner put it, there are microsystems (in which the person lives—family, peers, school), mesosystems (relations between contexts—family vs. peers), exosystems (settings with which a teen does not have direct contact but influence him or her anyway—parents' workplaces), macrosystems (culture in which one lives), and chronosystems (one's life course and sociohistorical circumstances). To minister to adolescents, youth workers had to take all of these into account. Unsurprisingly, many had done so nearly instinctively, hardly knowing that theories existed validating their field-based experience.

While the study of adolescence progressed, the legal position of young people in American society changed as well. Prerogatives previously reserved for adults were granted to young people. In *Tinker v. Des Moines Independent School System* (1969), the United States Supreme Court granted high school students the right to wear black armbands in protest of the Vietnam conflict, stating that high school students were persons who "did not shed their constitutional rights to freedom of speech or expression at the schoolhouse door." Middle adolescents received similar constitutional rights. Two years earlier the Supreme Court ordered (*In re: Gault, 1967*) that fifteen-year-old Gerald Gault had the same right to council and other elements of due process as any other citizen. The juvenile court system was changing. Then in 1971, the Twenty-sixth Amendment to the United States Constitution granted voting rights to eighteen-year-olds.[24] One more adult privilege had been granted to young people. The uniqueness of the adolescent period of life began eroding.

Using interesting parallels with the nineteenth century, Walter Kirn raised some intriguing scenarios in his 2000 *Time* magazine essay entitled "Will Teenagers Disappear?" Citing changes in economic issues ("The right to be economically unproductive until the day after college graduation—amendment one of the teenage constitution"); social issues ("One thing that used to make teenagers teenagers was the postponement of family responsibilities, but these days even 30- and 40-year-olds are postponing family responsibilities, often permanently"); and legal issues ("The teenage years, as formerly defined, were a time for people to get away with things, to make mistakes and not really have to pay for them. The legal system has changed all that by trying kids as adults for serious crimes"), Walter Kirn concludes, "The age of James Dean, the Ford Mustang and making out will seem, in retrospect, like what it was: a summer vacation from larger human history."[25]

Despite the changing nature of adolescence, Protestant teenagers continued to embrace the Christian faith much as they had in the past. Even with a dramatic rise in lay and ordained youth ministers in Protestant churches, parents, particularly mothers, continued to have the greatest impact upon their teenagers' Christian faith.[26] Consequently, God continued to show up in meaningful ways.

With adults acting like teenagers and teenagers granted full access to the adult world, whether they exercised their option or not, the whole notion of *adolescence*, and maybe even *youth*, began to seem quaint and perhaps obsolete. The dilemma, as David Elkind suggested, was that teenagers were all grown up but had no place to go.[27] The adolescent angst G. Stanley Hall saw at the beginning of the twentieth century had changed to a social angst. The issues were no longer internal to the individual adolescent, they were now issues of connectedness to society. For youth workers the issue was at its heart a spiritual question.

Youth in the Twenty-first Century

With the advent of the twenty-first century, a precise understanding of what *youth* is seems firmly planted in midair. Prozac has removed much of the turbulence and angst formerly associated with the teenage years. Birth control devices and the availability of abortion to terminate unwanted pregnancies have made sexual experimentation a game engaged in at ever-younger ages. Fears of HIV/AIDS, rather than creating greater chastity, have produced a tidal wave of personal and nonvaginal sexual activity.

Cultural diversity in the high schools of the nation brought a clash of expectations for adolescents in the early twenty-first century. Elementary and high school students in 2003 were more diverse than the baby-boom generation of students. In 1970, the student population was 79 percent non-Hispanic white, 14 percent black, 6 percent Hispanic, and 1 percent Asian and Pacific islander and other races. In 2003, 60 percent were non-Hispanic white, 16 percent black, 18 percent Hispanic, and 4 percent Asian.[28] In many states and major cities nonwhite students outnumbered those of European descent.

While the high school remains the town square where adolescents gather daily, the assembled multitude is far from a homogeneous unit. Perhaps it never was. Not only are young people fragmented by ethnic origin, they are further divided into social subgroupings on campus. In a recent nonscientific survey conducted in the affluent northern suburbs of Chicago, high school students identified forty-three distinct groupings of students, and many of the groupings had a significant number of subgroupings. While all of the students were enrolled in high school, their experiences of being a young person in America were significantly different.[29]

Popular culture, focused on the youth market and championed by cable and satellite channels, niche magazines, the Internet, and iPhones, further confuses the nature of adolescence. When adult channels and Web sites provide the passive sexual activity previously reserved for curious junior high boys, and MTV's *Jackass* features adults performing "double-dog-dare" stunts previously the domain of unsupervised preteen backyard challenges, the question of who is an adult and who is an adolescent seems absurd.

Researcher George Barna sent shockwaves through the evangelical portion of Protestant youth workers by demonstrating that as few as 5 percent of American youth affirmed an evangelical perspective.[30] At the same time Princeton Theological Seminary Associate Professor of Youth, Family, and Culture, Kenda Creasy Dean, called mainline Protestant denominations to task for their failure to connect the passion of their youth with the passion of Christ.[31]

Despite the hand-wringing, the massive National Study of Youth and Religion, spearheaded by Christian Smith at the University of North Carolina, identified far more continuity of religious beliefs between parents and their high school teenagers than discontinuity. Conservative Protestants and Mormons consistently showed the greatest religiosity with Black Protestants close behind. Mainline Protestants lagged significantly, as did youth in the Catholic tradition of Christianity.[32] While their concept of God was at best imprecise, one expectation seemed consistent: when needed, God would show up.

As the twenty-first century began, the use of the word *youth* continued to morph. While MTV targeted the eighteen- to twenty-eight-year-old male for marketing purposes, the impact in culture was far younger. So it was with youth ministry. The primary focus of most Protestants involved in youth ministry remained high school students but a growing amount of attention shifted to middle school/junior high students and even younger. Post–high school youth were increasingly treated as novice adults while high school dropouts, which constituted 3 to 4 percent of the adolescent population, dropped off the screen altogether. The children of undocumented residents, while present, were seldom the recipients of Christian youth ministry.

Even though the understanding of what constituted "youth" changed over the past two centuries, at the core of the church's concern was the desire of parents to pass their values to the next generation. For most conservative Protestants this meant passing along the expectation that God would be an active part of their lives. Pastors and parishioners continued to focus attention on the time young people remained under the roof of their parents. While the great wealth of materials on youth ministry tends to trace the work of organizations, this study will attempt to cull out the concerns and ministry responses of Protestant pastors and parents during the years prior to graduation from high school (or its equivalent before the existence of public high schools).

What Is the Middle Class?

One issue should be addressed before moving on. Much of the discussion of Protestant youth ministry assumes it to be a product of the economic middle class. If the idea is understood in economic terms, it appears to accurately describe most of what happened from the second decade of the twentieth century onward. Yet the genesis of youth ministry in the economic middle class needs some explanation.

Joseph Kett in his classic analysis of adolescence in America admits, "historians overuse and under-specify the term 'middle class.'"[33] Unfortunately, Kett falls prey to his own criticism. At this stage of our examination of Protestant youth ministry, we pause to ask, "Who exactly are these middle class people and how do they relate to the youth of America?" The next few pages address the first question, and the latter we will engage throughout the rest of the book.

Since Kett remains the premier historian of adolescence in America, an analysis of his use of *middle class* would provide an appropriate context for understanding for whom the description was designated and how the middle class shaped youth ministry in America. This is not to diminish the fine work of Elliott West and Paula Petrik in their edited work, *Small Worlds: Children and Adolescents in America, 1850–1950;*[34] of Paula Fass's *The Damned and the Beautiful: American Youth in the 1920's;*[35] of Thomas Hine's *The Rise and Fall of the American Teenager;*[36] or of Jon Pahl's *Youth Ministry in Modern America: 1930 to the Present,*[37] each of which contributes to the role of the middle class in the study of youth or youth ministry in America. Kett simply provides the most comprehensive survey of the middle class and youth ministry.[38]

Forms of youth ministry existed prior to the middle of the nineteenth century. Pastors Cotton Mather and Jonathan Edwards as well as many other ministers held weekday meetings for the youth of their churches.[39] The Sunday school served as a strategy for lay Christians to touch the young lives of both the urban poor and settlers on the American frontier. Yet neither of these does Kett attribute to the middle class.

When addressing the various youth movements that arose in the nineteenth century, most of which were identified in Frank Otis Erb's groundbreaking research, Kett groups them together as self-improvement societies initiated voluntarily by young people.[40] No doubt some were initiated by youth but more often these self-improvement societies were shaped by Protestant pastors wishing to retain a Protestant expectation of God's presence in the lives of their young people that would result in a Christian value system despite a changing world.

Only after the middle of the nineteenth century does Kett begin associating youth ministry with the middle class. As young people moved to the cities in search of employment, urban life forced social roles and economic functions on teenagers with which they were unfamiliar in their rural settings. The city magnified everything young people touched. The scale of just about everything was greater. Kett comments:

> By mid-century these differences in scale were creating qualitative differences in the life-style of urban youth of rival social classes. The novel element lay not in the class differences as such but in the self-conscious efforts of moralists of the propertied classes to demarcate the life-style of middle-class youth from the children of the laboring poor.[41]

It is the young people moving to the city from rural communities and farms whom Kett describes as *middle class*. They were boys and girls in their late teens and early twenties, impacted by the Industrial Revolution, who moved to the cities to find jobs. In New England and to a lesser extent the Middle Atlantic states, their values were primarily shaped by rural Protestantism. *Middle class*, as Kett used it, was primarily associated with a traditional Protestant world and life view.[42]

Kett designates a group of adults as *middle class* as well. The phrase "self-conscious efforts of moralists of the propertied classes" provides an additional hint as to whom Kett's *middle class* designation belonged: they were wealthy people in the city who had convictions about how young people should live as they migrated from rural areas surrounding industrial cities. These urban property owners, for the most part, acted in response to concerns of the Protestant faith communities led by ministers. Kett cites ministers from across the theological spectrum including Methodist L. M. Pease in New York, Congregationalist Henry Ward Beecher in Litchfield, Connecticut (close to Hartford), Universalist E. H. Chapin in Boston, and Union Theological Seminary–trained Charles Loring Brace.

Who these "moralists of the propertied class" were is illustrated by James McCabe in describing the support received by L. M. Pease in establishing the Five Points Mission in one of the toughest sections of New York City. "A number of Christian women of position and means, who knew the locality only by reputation, determined, with a courage peculiar to their sex, to break up this den, and make it a stronghold of religion and virtue."[43] As was the case of many philanthropists in the years before there was a federal income tax, these women chose to use their wealth to help people less fortunate than themselves. To call these women *middle class*, however, stretches the definition.

Kett described neither these "women of means" nor the Methodist pastor they supported at the Five Points as *middle class*. Yet somehow the values they espoused were so designated. Perhaps better stated, the values reflected the same broad Protestant world and life view as did the youthful immigrants to the city from rural New England. Even in their day, Beecher, Brace, and Chapin espoused fairly liberal views of Christianity and so the twentieth-century concept of a conservative suburban "middle class" hardly would apply.

A second clue to Kett's understanding of *middle class* can be found in his distinguishing them from the "new middle class" in 1912. With the Industrial Revolution well under way in America, this new middle class featured "white-collar professionals and clerical employees" while the older version of "middle class" included "small traders, shopkeepers, self-employed professionals, and independent artisans." Both of these groups Kett distinguished from the *working class* who were from the skilled trades and manual labor sectors.[44] In so doing, Kett both complicates and simplifies the reader's understanding of the *middle class*.

The complication comes in the fact that most of the youthful immigrants from rural New England took jobs as manual laborers in factories. This might place them outside the middle class if defined merely by profession. Yet, for many, their factory jobs were transitional, designed to earn them enough money to settle into a different profession or station in life as adults. Thus, Kett simplifies the identification of the middle class by associating them with the values of people who took personal and/or entrepreneurial initiatives as they established families and patterns of work.

Stretching the historical understanding of *middle class* a bit, Kett offers a third perspective on the term linking middle-class families with Horace Bushnell's concept of Christian nurture. For Bushnell, nurture of children was the responsibility of parents and happened in the home especially before children acquired language skills. Kett suggests this was scarcely possible for poor families in the nineteenth century, in which all family members needed to work. "It was most likely to occur in middle-class families where mothers had the undisputed custody of children after their fathers left for work in the commercial district."[45] But this scenario included a relatively small percentage of mid-nineteenth century family life. More frequently than not, shopkeepers, self-employed professionals (including ministers), and even independent artisans either worked out of their homes with their wives assisting in their work or relied on the wife to help to manage the family business.

A fourth clarification of *middle class* employed by Kett is the distinction between those who sent their sons to high school and college and those who needed their children to provide income for the family in the late nineteenth century.[46] Between 1875 and 1925 both high school and college attendance grew dramatically. With the increase of laws requiring school attendance into middle adolescence and labor laws restricting the age at which young people could begin working, high school and college attendance grew rapidly. Education provided a ladder for upward mobility. This postponement of adulthood by prolonged education provided a hope of a better adult life. For many, "middle class" youth meant those willing to engage in "higher" education with a dream of financial security later in life.

While Joseph Kett sprinkled the *middle class* descriptor across the pages of his classic work, the term morphed over time. Prior to the second decade of the twentieth century, it referred to people who shared a Protestant world and life view, most typical of New England village life. After the First World War, *middle class* took on the meaning of people who were upwardly mobile, especially those using formal schooling as a means to better their station in life.

Youth ministry was defined by both usages of *middle class*. Prior to World War I, youth ministry protected young people from competing world and life views most easily typified by the cacophony of voices in the growing cities. Following the war, however, this city jazz became part of the greater culture as "middle class" youth became consciously upwardly mobile, seeking to improve their station in life. In this new environment, youth ministry sought to train leaders of the church in a manner similar to how universities prepared leaders for diverse fields of endeavor.

Paula Fass makes a similar distinction. During the 1920s, America came to view young people in one of two ways. Though vulnerable to Kett's comment that *middle class* was overused and underdefined, Fass aligns the middle class with people she called "traditionalists" who looked back at the nineteenth century values and wrung their hands at the new freedoms late adolescents were experiencing. People embracing the new freedoms she called *progressives*. In her study, Fass viewed middle class youth as those who used higher education as a means of liberation from the older values.[47]

Conclusion

As a generation of youth researchers look back at James Dean's portrayal of a teenage rebel, Jim Stark, quite a different picture emerges. As it turns out, young people may not have changed as much as has the world around them. When parents find their children growing up in a world that is different from the one they experienced at the same stage of life, parents become alarmed and struggle to find help in passing their values along to the next generation.

In *Rebel Without a Cause*, the only sympathetic adult was a juvenile officer who tried to console Judy when she became frustrated by her father's lack of empathy. Without a doubt situations like Judy's happened throughout the second half of the twentieth century, but seldom were young people as isolated from their parents' generation as was Judy or as alienated as was Jim Stark.

Parents have always been concerned about the survival and health of their children. Before the twentieth century youth remained in close proximity to their families until well into their twenties or even thirties. Youth merely meant that boys had not worked long enough to be able to provide for a wife and family or that girls, similarly, had not married and started a family. When this tradition began to change in the nineteenth century and young people left home to seek work, parents felt a loss of control and turned to their pastors for help. *Youth* came to be defined as that period, frequently in their middle teens, when young people began leaving home until they were established as parents supporting a family. Youth ministries became the local face of the support provided by Protestant churches during this period of life.

By the beginning of the twentieth century, the help parents sought from their Protestant faith community came to be described by many as the values of the middle class. Though Catholic and non-Christian faiths responded in a similar manner, youth ministries became synonymous with the Protestant church's response to its youth. Thus, when it was said that youth ministries cultivated middle-class values, what was being described was a Protestant world and life view with the God of the Bible in the center of the picture.

With the rise of the high school, the definition of youth changed to focus on adolescence. Initially *adolescence* indicated young people ages twelve to twenty-four, but during the Great Depression and the Second World War it came to signify those in their teenage years, that is, those still living at home and not employed. The word *teenager* took center stage and youth ministries invested their energies in helping young people survive high school as Christians.

As the twentieth century came to a close, questions began to be asked about the end of the term *adolescence* and with it the distinctiveness of the teenage years. The answers are yet to be found, but with this framework in mind, we turn the reader's attention to youth ministry as the vehicle of the Protestant church that provided support to families and churches over the past two centuries as they worked together to pass Christian values from generation to generation.

3

Bruce Almighty

A History of Spirituality in Youth Ministry

ruce Almighty (2003) tells the story of Bruce Noland (Jim Carey), a television reporter in Buffalo, New York, who angrily criticizes God on what he considers the worst day of his life. To his amazement, God shows up as a man (Morgan Freeman) and endows Noland with divine power. As a selfish human, the television reporter uses his powers for selfish ends until he becomes overwhelmed with the constant flood of prayer requests. In frustration, he answers *yes* to everyone and in the process satisfies no one, even himself.

The movie is part of the Hollywood attempt to raise the question, "What would it be like if God showed up in today's world?" More than the other movies of this genre (*Oh, God* [including sequels] and *Evan Almighty*), *Bruce Almighty* provides clever insights into the complexities of the nature of God. However, Hollywood is late in coming to the question. For two centuries Protestant youth ministries have addressed the question with various expectations of how it would be answered.

As they frequently do, a group of ministers gathered some years ago to compare notes on trends in their congregations. Sometimes such meetings degenerate into sanctified "can you top this one?" conversations about congregational life. But on this occasion, the conversation focused on youth. A quick consensus revealed their churches had a youth problem. Public worship attendance at best appeared stagnant, except among young people, whose attendance was definitively declining. Parents seemed apathetic. Many children came to physical, social, and mental maturity without a spiritual or moral compass to guide their lives. Few had experienced God's presence in their world. The year was 1881.[1]

Though this youth problem in Protestant churches persists into the twenty-first century, it can be traced all the way back to the earliest settlements in North America. Much of the discussion focused on what constituted evidence of a Christian life appropriate for church membership. While many of the efforts ministers made on behalf of youth focused on their conversion, most church leaders felt dismay at the absence of sustained change in lifestyle.[2]

Through the years church leaders co-opted the Sunday school and made it the "nursery" of the church or adapted public educational structures as the most efficient way in which to manage this youth problem, yet the dominant theme of youth ministry experiments related more closely to changing understandings of youthful spirituality. What would make more likely the possibility of God showing up and changing their lives? What constituted appropriate expressions of sanctification in the lives of young people? Pastors and parishioners from diverse denominational backgrounds and geographical regions all expressed the common desire for their young people to grow up in harmony with their various perspectives of Christian spirituality and godly living.

Throughout the history of Protestant youth ministry in America, there has been a consistent connection between religious socialization and spiritual experiences. Activities associated with various youth group traditions have served as means of maintaining relationships with and between young people in anticipation that God will show up and shape their lives. The structured social experience and the spontaneous spiritual experience have been expected to go hand in hand.[3]

G. Stanley Hall, author of the 1904 classic description of youth, *Adolescence,* was the first student of adolescence to collect information about its spiritual aspects. He concluded that the adolescent years produced the most concentrated period of religious conversions in life. A normal expression of adolescent spirituality in the eighteenth and nineteenth centuries focused on nearly annual periods of spiritual awakenings that visited college campuses and on occasion, far beyond.[4] Even G. Stanley Hall briefly had just such an awakening of his spirit while at Williams College. In a letter to his parents, Hall described his experience:

Yesterday (Sunday) morn I had not the slightest serious impression. I spent the morning, I am sorry to say, in the secular pursuit of study, attending church in the P.M. and involuntarily fell into a train of reflection which led to my conversion. My impressions were deepened by the sermon on the general subject "The Ark of Safety." I then and there resolved that God assisting me I would give myself no rest until I had found rest and safety therein. Then followed a season of fear, then doubt, and darkness, perplexity and painful anxiety. I sought advice and counsel of Christians and their prayers, but no light. My conviction of sin and of the terrible doom which hung over me I fear were not strong enough and I thought that I could have no hope till they were more vivid. But the feeling paramount was all the time a desire, deep, strong, and ardent to become a Christian. In accordance with the counsel of others I tried to give myself fully into the hands of Jesus, relying on his promises but got no light until this morning when I began to feel that a burden was very gradually lifted from my mind, as though the night of wrestling was far spent and the day was dawning. Gradually this feeling has increased during the day and I began to feel such a delightful but indescribable change coming over me and now I can say without distrust, though it does once in a while creep in, that I think and hope I have found acceptance through the blood of the Lamb.[5]

Later Hall would describe adolescence as a period of young people's lives in which such conversion experiences were common, if not expected. The fact that his resulting spiritual tranquility did not last beyond his freshman year, however, did not suggest that the adolescent spiritual experiences of others were always so temporary.

Not all expressions of adolescent spiritual fervor followed Hall's description, which was common specifically in New England. Youth in Middle Atlantic colonies and states were far more parochial, secular, and diverse. Religious diversity in the Middle Atlantic colonies and states gave rise to parochial schools, each with its own perception of the spirituality of youth. By and large the emphasis was on conformity to the norms of the sponsoring church. Like New England youth, most young people in the Middle Atlantic colonies worked to supplement family incomes. For most families, income was more important than schooling, except for the more wealthy classes. In their urgency to survive in the new land, Christian nurture issues were ignored. Yet in Pennsylvania, a nearly legal German pietism shaped the manner in which rural churches conceived of the spiritual development of their youth.

Youth in the Southern colonies and states experienced the fewest advantages of spiritual formation outside the family. The Carolinas (including Georgia and north Florida) were established as proprietary colonies and were expected to return a profit to the seven proprietors who had gotten the Carolina Grant from the King. Because they were run as a business venture (poorly handled), the colonies paid little attention to providing educational opportunities or Christian nurture. Tensions created by slavery further complicated the spiritual development of youth in the South, black or white.

Uncle Tom's Cabin tells the fictitious story of the black experience in the antebellum South. While Uncle Tom became the antitype of human dignity in the African American experience, the slave lived a life highly compatible with biblical instructions in the first-century Roman world. Tom grew up in the spiritually rich experience of many Christian black people on Southern plantations. Heaven was real. Submission to slave masters followed the example of Christ and his crucifixion. Freedom was a distant hope. Music and preaching shaped the spiritual experiences of young and old alike.

In stark contrast to Tom's story is the story of Lottie Moon. Charlotte Diggs Moon grew up on her family's Georgia plantation, which was staffed by fifty-two slaves. She was born in 1840, and tutors provided her education—though little religious instruction—until age thirteen. When her father died prematurely, fourteen-year-old "Lottie" Moon enrolled in Hollins Institute. Compulsory chapel and Sunday church attendance at Enon Baptist Church exposed the teenager to Christian teaching, but these influences demonstrated little evidence of spiritual fruit in her life. At age sixteen, the able student enrolled in Albemarle Female Institute. In her second year, following a revival meeting conducted by Dr. John W. Broadus in 1858, Lottie's examination of Christianity led to her conversion. In time Lottie Moon became a missionary to China.[6]

The contrasting experiences of the fictitious Uncle Tom and missionary pioneer Lottie Moon characterized the development of adolescent spirituality in the South before the Civil War. Whether influenced by slave preachers or revival meetings, young people in their spiritual journeys were part of the adult faith community at church or in camp meetings.

Youth in the frontier states functioned like adults. There were a disproportionate number of youth on the frontier since many had left their families along the East Coast to seek their fortunes. What schools there were tended to be denominational colleges whose purpose was to train pastors. Little formal education preceded college. The Great Valley Campaign sponsored by the American Sunday School Union planted Sunday schools throughout the Midwest and laid the groundwork for public schools and libraries. Spiritual development tended to be tied to camp meetings and revivals.

Hall Explores Adolescent Spirituality

G. Stanley Hall shaped the understanding of adolescence by writing his classic work, *Adolescence*, published in 1904. Built on the best research of the day, Hall attempted to isolate the distinctive characteristics of the period of life stretching from ages thirteen to twenty-four. This period, characterized by Hall as a period of turbulence, had special spiritual implications, which he then explored. Current researchers take a less dramatic view of adolescence as a unique period of turbulence, stressing that only a low percentage of adolescents experience turbulence out of line with other age groups.

Hall linked together genetic psychology and education. The theory for which Hall is known is adapted from the theory of recapitulation to adolescent development. This theory poses that each person goes through changes in both the psychic and somatic senses that follow the evolution scale of the mind and body. Hall believed that the preadolescent child develops to its best when it is not forced to follow constraints, but rather is allowed to go through the stages of evolution freely. Before a child turned six or seven, the child should be able to experience how one lived in the simian stage, in which the child could express his animal spirits. The child grows rapidly at this stage and the energy levels are high. The child is unable to use reasoning, or to show either sensitivity toward religion or social discernment.

By age eight, the child should be at stage two. This, Hall believed, is the stage where formal learning should begin. This is when the brain is at full size and weight. In this stage, people considered it normal for children to be cruel and rude to others, for the reasoning skills are still not developed. The child should not have to deal with moralizing conflicts or ideas, because his brain is not yet ready at this stage. The child's physical health is most important now.

In the stage of the adolescent, the child has a rebirth into a sexed life. Hall argued that at this point, there should no longer be coeducation. Both sexes can't optimally learn and get everything out of the lessons in the presence of the opposite sex. And, this is when true education can begin. The child is ready to deal with moral issues, kindness, love, and service for others. Reasoning powers are beginning to develop, but are still not strong. Hall argued that the high school should be a place similar to a "people's college" so that it could be more of an ending for those who would not be continuing their education to the next level.

Hall associates the idea of spiritual rebirth, as advocated by Puritans in the First Great Awakening and Methodists in the Second Great Awakening, with his concept of recapitulation. Jonathan Edwards, according to Hall, grasped the need for new birth with a precision and clarity that defied the theological trends of the day. Hall stated,

> There is, I think, abundant evidence that he [Edwards] deliberately decided to attempt a new use of the great Protestant principle of justification by faith alone, to insist on God's absolute sovereignty and "just liberty of election"

and to teach, in place of the current conception of human initiative, the notion that all persons not specifically converted are sinners that "have merited and now deserve instant damnation," that this is wholly just, and there is nothing to do but to call upon God for mercy through Christ.[7]

Adolescence, according to Hall, was the period of life when people were most responsive to this call for rebirth. Citing impressive anecdotal evidence from Protestant evangelists and pastors of the day, he built a case that a vast majority of Christian conversions took place during the adolescent years.[8] The types of conversion experiences cited complied with Hall's conception of adolescence as a time of turbulence. Emotional expressions invariably accompanied new birth experiences.

Conveniently, there was no reference in the chapter on the adolescent psychology of conversion to the idea of Christian nurture proffered by Horace Bushnell, in which children raised in Christian families grew up never knowing themselves as unbelievers and consequently in need of dramatic conversion experiences. Hall neglected attention to Christian nurture despite the fact that the idea of Christian nurture was over fifty years old and was deeply embedded in the literature of youth ministry at the turn of the twentieth century.

Historians View Spirituality of Youth in America

Historians of youth in America (Kett, Fass, Bremner, Hine) paid little attention to tracing the spiritual formation of youth, choosing rather to inaccurately suggest that conservative Protestants mobilized the middle class (seldom defined) to impose a value system upon America, utilizing youth ministry agencies to do so.

Joseph Kett, in *Rites of Passage*, described the influence the revivals and religious enthusiasm had upon the boys and young men who entered urban areas from villages, but he limits their influence to moral issues. Omitting any consideration of spiritual formation or the possibility that God might be present in any special way, Kett critiqued those Protestants who worked with the gangs of youth in the cities in the mid-nineteenth century as "the self-conscious efforts of moralists of the propertied classes to demarcate the life-style of middle-class youth from that of children of the laboring poor."[9]

Kett described the conflicting emphases of conversion and nurture on the part of Protestant adults but attributed both to forms of social control of the moral lives of young people.[10] Kett saw the pledges utilized most prominently by Christian Endeavor and the temperance movement to be rather meaningless. He commented, "The Christian Endeavor pledge . . . was not the product of any kind of self-analysis. It was devoid of theological content and nearly devoid of moral content."[11] If adolescent spirituality was no more than providing theological rationale for moral behavior, Kett may have been right. But at the core of adolescent Christian spirituality was communion with the triune God, and of this Kett appears to have been blissfully ignorant.

Paula Fass, in *The Damned and the Beautiful*, similarly viewed religion in the 1920s as focusing on maintaining the moral standards of the traditionalists. Accurately critiquing churches in the 1920s as having left firm dogma and doctrines for liberal idealism, she commented that morals without religious absolutes could not keep youth in control. Citing an article in *Atlantic* magazine, where "wild young people" were seen as the progressives of the era, Fass quotes, "The 'wild young people' don't believe that faith can be confined to a dogma or reduced to a creed. We think of religion as the spiritual stream in which we are floating or swimming, or struggling or sinking, and how can we deny the existence of the very element in which we live?"[12]

But even with such a progressive definition of spirituality, Fass concluded, "By the twenties the [college and university] young people had transferred their allegiance from the churches, broad or narrow, to a different sort of God, as they invested a kind of religious devotion to their leisure pursuits, to sports, dating, and song."[13] At Duke [originally called Trinity College] the university newspaper editorialized, "While revivals were greeted enthusiastically before the twenties as a proud tradition, the revival exercises were on the wane during the early twenties." In typical cynical editorial fashion the writer commented, "The very idea of a revival 'is repugnant to us' because it was no more than 'emotional debauch, an opportunity to put feelings above reason.'"[14] It would be in the *reason above emotions* context that spirituality would be defined for young people for the remainder of the twentieth century.

Thomas Hine in *The Rise and Fall of the American Teenager* identified teenage spirituality with the Protestant faith community in New England and focused on lifestyle issues. Hine suggests that the Second Great Awakening taught young people that they could now trust their emotions. This was expressed both in dramatic conversion experiences and in a willingness to violate traditional family norms and call parents and other family members to repentance. What had broken down in New England was the Puritan practice of strong family ties with the father as primary teacher and priest. Whether this was the result of the rise of the common school or the common school was an initial attempt to correct the problem is a matter of debate that Hine does not address.

One implication of the Great Awakening and the emphasis on direct personal contact with God was the opportunity it gave women to participate in Christian spirituality.[15] This would make it possible for girls to later partake as full participants in youth ministries, missionary efforts, and churches. A second implication that Hine identified growing out of the Second Great Awakening was the emergence of churches that embraced young people and took their emotions seriously.[16] Writing at the end of the twentieth century, Hine identified personal contact with God as being at the core of adolescent spirituality.

Sociologists View Adolescent Spirituality

In 1929, Robert and Helen Lynd published their study of American culture and called the place they studied "Middletown." The portion of their study that focused on youth noted a lot of extracurricular activities centered around the high school, with a smattering of activities connected with churches, the YMCA, and YWCA. The town had a fifteen-to-one ratio of Protestants (twenty-eight different denominations) to Catholics with virtually no other religions represented.

The belief system of youth in Middletown assumed the all-sufficiency of Christianity for all mankind, the sacredness of the Bible, various shades of emphasis on God as completely revealed in Jesus Christ, and the generally held belief that there is a life after death in either heaven or hell.[17] Churches saw their responsibility toward young people in schooling terms. The schools were places where youth were trained in their Christian faith. Observing that little had changed since the 1890s, the Lynds commented:

> The Sunday School is the chief instrument of the church for training the young in religion; of secondary importance is the "young people's society" meeting in each Protestant church Sunday evening for an hour before the evening service. Like the prayer meetings, these discussion hours attracted few people, attendance ranging from fifteen to fifty, almost invariably with girls in the heavy majority.[18]

From a sociologist's perspective, education served as training for young people to assume leadership roles in their church, replacing the nineteenth-century emphasis on repentance and conversion. Revival and camp meetings were no longer the norm for the religious experience of youth. Yet, in a follow-up study eight years later, the Lynds detected a shift in the religious experience of Middletown with an increased "fundamentalism" among "the more primitive South Side sects," while the older denominations became doctrinally less demanding.[19] The researchers had detected the rise of smaller evangelical churches, rooted in nineteenth-century expressions of evangelization and holiness, that would shape evangelical youth ministry through the middle of the twentieth century.

The Elmtown study of youth followed. From May 1941 to December 1942, August B. Hollingshead, a sociologist on the faculty of Indiana University, studied the adolescents in a Middle West Corn Belt town, which he called Elmtown. One chapter in the study focused on religion and religious behavior, looking primarily at the participation of youth in church activities. The study concluded that much of the approach of ministers focused on sin avoidance, an approach that elicited little enthusiasm from the youth of Elmtown.

While Sunday schools and youth societies provided instruction and activities for the youth who attended, Hollingshead's findings concluded that only about 50 percent of students listed on church rolls attended church activities with any degree of regularity. Girls far outnumbered boys. Students' strongest criticism had to do with the social pecking order within church activities for youth. The social elite made others feel unwanted. The result was that attendance decreased as young people progressed through high school.

Despite the efforts of church leaders, Hollingshead concluded, "Young Elmtowners acquire religious beliefs from their parents in the same way as they learn that the parental home is their home."[20] It was more of a process of enculturation than of spiritual engagement. To these young people, commented the researcher,

> Church is a place where one goes to Sunday School, to a young people's meeting, to a church party, and, to a small segment, it is a place to worship or to hear a sermon. It is not something special or supernatural as the ministers and some elders would have them believe.[21]

Without questioning Hollingshead's methodology, one would wonder how well his conclusions applied to the rest of the country. If youth ministry was not in some sense special or supernatural, then what was it? Was there any sense in which the God of the Bible showed up in the youth ministries of the nineteenth century and following?

Developmentalists View Adolescent Spirituality

Protestant writers concerned with the spiritual formation of adolescents tended to frame their understanding in developmental terms related to young people's capacity to believe (have faith). James Fowler connected the faith of young people with their ability to reason, discovered to begin at about the time of puberty. He called this "stage" of faith "Synthetic-Conventional," meaning that beginning in early teenage years, people attempt to synthesize what they believe with what others in their world value (synthetic), and yet they are not highly critical of the faith community in which they find themselves (conventional). The focal point for Fowler was how faith happens rather than the content of faith.[22]

The synthetic-conventional stage of faith development results in various levels of doubt as young people struggle to conform to the view of a widening circle of others, including peers, while seeking to retain the beliefs of their family and faith community. The struggle results in a creation of a *hierarchy* of social authority in the teenagers' lives whereby the values and convictions of one group gain a dominant influence on their beliefs and actions. For some Protestant youth this *faithing* process results in forms of rebellion either into or away from Jesus Christ, while others retain a stable spiritual growth trajectory.

John Westerhoff suggested "that faith (understood as a way of behaving) can, if provided with the proper interactive experiences, expand through four distinct *styles* of faith." The *style* most common for adolescents is what he called the *affiliative faith*, which includes participation in the activities of the faith community, religious affections (religion of the heart, not just the head), and a sense of authority drawn from the story of the faith community.[23] In Protestant youth ministry this story was grounded in the Bible and doctrines of their denominational community.

James Bryan Smith, perhaps influenced by Eric Erikson's concept of identity development, suggested that Christian spiritual formation for adolescents involved coming to the right answer to the question "Who am I?" and then living their lives on the basis of that proper identity. He cited Dallas Willard's definition of spiritual formation as "the process through which those who love and trust Jesus Christ effectively take on His character."[24] Adolescence, according to Smith, shaped a person's spirituality for the rest of life.

The history of Protestant youth ministry incorporated at various times and in diverse ways these aspects of adolescent spirituality and formation. Because of young people's newfound capacity for abstract reasoning, their growing need for social interaction, their newly discovered sense of and capacity for affection, all wrapped up in a discovery of personal identity within the various communities vying for their loyalty, adolescents were thought to explore their spiritual lives in a jumbled fashion. Adults in and from the church supported parents as they assisted young people on their spiritual journeys.

Reflecting on Fowler's understanding of adolescent experiences of faith, Duffy Robbins comments:

> One of the interesting implications of Fowler's work is that faith is affirmed empirically as a universal facet of human experience. In other words, we are never working with a faithless teenager. They may not be conscious of their beliefs, or the implications of their beliefs, or even how those beliefs

came to be. But we are not trying to start a fire from coals that do not exist. The students who walk into the youth group on Friday night have a faith shaped significantly by childhood and community experiences—for good or for ill—and we must meet them at their point of development, and help them progress to the next stage.[25]

The Gospel and Spirituality in the Youth Group

A careful study of the development of youth ministry in America and its predecessors in Great Britain suggests a central theme (if not *the* central theme): that the Christian gospel produces evidences that influence and even change the lifestyle of believing youth. The questions being asked within various denominational settings remained rather consistent though answers varied.

1. What is the gospel? (Soteriology) The answers remain fairly consistent until the early part of the twentieth century when liberal theology began filtering down to the church's ministry to youth.
2. What evidence can we expect when the gospel has been applied to the life of a young person? (Sanctification) The responses to this question varied from denomination to denomination and were the primary reason various denominations left Christian Endeavor and began their own youth societies.
3. What contributions do faith communities make in helping youth answer these questions? (Ecclesiology) Lay initiatives shaped church ministry to youth, first outside the church and then progressively within local churches. Denominational initiatives followed and eventually people were added to the church staff with responsibilities for youth ministry.

Over the years the emphasis in youth ministry shifted between stressing the gospel in a narrow sense and exploring the gospel in a more holistic manner. Not much attention was paid to classic expressions of spiritual formation. But always, the driving force was the corporate initiatives of the local church. In its narrow sense the Christian gospel stressed the good news of redemption through Jesus Christ; in its broader sense the Christian gospel emphasized the entire story of redemptive history that embraced the kingdom of God. In its narrow sense the Christian gospel in youth ministry transformed young people; in its broader sense the Christian gospel transformed youth culture. In its narrow sense the Christian gospel in youth ministry stressed salvation; in its broader sense the Christian gospel focused on the changes in the lives of young people in whom salvation was applied.

Adolescent Spirituality before the Sunday School in America

Concern for adolescent spirituality in Protestant churches in America, while more evident in the second half of the twentieth century, has roots that have run throughout the history of youth ministry. Views of adolescent spirituality are hard to identify in eighteenth- and nineteenth-century America because "adolescence" had not been identified as a special time span in the life cycle, and "spirituality" was not a central concern of Protestants in America.

The greatest concern of the church, especially in New England, was a Christian lifestyle—the outward evidences of spiritual maturity necessary for young people to join the church. Church membership seldom came before the mid to late twenties and generally came after a period of "sowing their wild oats," so adolescent spirituality as they understood it was quite different from what concerns youth ministers today.

Outside of New England and especially where the Church of England (Anglican) was the established church (i.e., the South), the subject of spirituality appears to be seldom discussed. While there were pockets of concern over the spiritual condition of youth in places like Savannah, Georgia (John Wesley ca. 1737); Ephrata, Pennsylvania (German Baptist Brethren, 1732); Bethlehem, Connecticut; and Philadelphia, these were exceptions to the concerns of the day.[26]

One of the earliest advocates for addressing the spiritual condition of youth in America was Cotton Mather (1663–1728). Richard Lovelace traced the history of spiritual accountability in Western Christianity, citing Gerard Groote (Brethren of the Common Life), Catholic Quietists, Jesuit retreats, Luther's suggestions that were adopted by itinerant radical Caspar Schwenckfeld, and reformers like Zwingli as well as various groups of Pietists.[27]

The Pietists, including Cotton Mather, focused on the nurture of spirituality through objective study of Scripture and devotional works, for the purpose of the edification and renewal of small group members.[28] Wesley added an evangelistic intent to these gatherings.[29] Mather was involved in a religious society when he was eighteen and repeatedly attempted to engage others in such societies. He provided advice for a Society of Negroes, women, ministers, and families.[30] The primary emphasis of these groups was personal piety and worship of God.

The most apparent evidence of spiritual vitality, according to Jonathan Edwards, was the working of the Holy Spirit that "opened the eyes of their hearts and illuminated the theological concepts. . . . [T]he opaque orthodoxy of the laity suddenly became a transparent medium for vision through which they saw the glory of God."[31] Edwards wrote of this in

Faithful Narrative of the Surprising Work of God, describing the beginning of the Great Awakening in Northampton, Massachusetts, in 1734.

About the same time, a similar awakening took place in at least one location in the Middle colonies as graduates of William Tennent's Log College (later Princeton College) went door to door taking the Puritan message.[32] Most of the churches in the Middle and Southern colonies showed little concern for such awakening. The agricultural economy widely separated young people while the Church of England as the established church in the Southern colonies had little vision for ministering to the youth of their parishes. The Second Great Awakening (1790–1840) had similar manifestations associated with Timothy Dwight, president of Yale, and the grandson of Jonathan Edwards.

The spiritual experience was measured by Edwards, not as a "special season of religious excitement . . . rather it (was) an outpouring of the Holy Spirit which restores the people of God to normal spiritual life after a period of corporate declension."[33] The essential elements of revivalism included:

1. The proclamation, primarily within the church, at its regular meetings of God's provision of justification through faith in Jesus Christ and on man's response (faith, repentance, conversion, and sanctification).
2. A conception of the church's task of leavening society by witness and action.
3. The presence of a strong and widespread sense of the need for the Holy Spirit's empowering.[34]

The public meetings of George Whitefield and Charles Finney and later itinerant evangelists caused great growth among Baptists and Methodists and shifted the emphasis from sanctification to conversion. Young people were among the primary concerns of the two Great Awakenings but the category described as youth stretched far beyond adolescence.

Adolescent Spirituality in the Sunday School Era (1780–1880)

The earliest expression of Sunday school in Great Britain emphasized reading and social skills. Though the Bible was used for a textbook and Christian people provided the leadership for bringing a better life to children, spiritual formation was not emphasized.[35] Initially the Sunday school taught a social ethic drawn from a Christian worldview without overt emphasis on personal salvation. It does not appear that the intent of Robert Raikes and his followers was to ignore personal salvation; they merely felt that proper training, and especially education, would bring about a desire for becoming a Christian. Then God would show up.

Sunday school pupils learned hygiene and manners as well as how to read the Bible, and they memorized hymns and catechisms. It would appear that the early Sunday school leaders (Robert Raikes, Thomas Stork, William Fox) viewed children holistically and felt that children would become Christians as they became enlightened. Childhood or adolescent spirituality was expected to be a by-product of the early Sunday school.

Earliest efforts in America to establish Sunday schools followed a similar pattern, especially in dealing with slaves and American Indians. Schools similar to that popularized by Robert Raikes were scattered throughout the American colonies even before Raikes established his Sunday school in 1780. In the Southern colonies where little education was available, William Elliot, Francis Asbury, and others introduced Sunday schools after the model of Raikes as early as 1785. The founding of the First Day (Sunday) School Society in Philadelphia in 1790 was heavily influenced by the Wesleyan revival, and the school became a powerful evangelistic tool.[36]

For the first thirty-five years or so, the Sunday school was, for the most part, led by lay people outside and without the blessing of the church. Its emphasis was on salvation, reading of the Scriptures, and a rote memorization of the Bible. Historian Anne Boylan, commenting on the spiritual receptiveness of children in the 1820s, says, "Most important, Sunday school organizers argued that it was possible for children to experience conversion. Using examples from local school reports, they noted that children as young as seven or eight had given evidence of experiencing the change of heart associated with conversion, and some had applied for full communion in churches."[37]

The "evidence of experiencing the change of heart associated with conversion" meant living a life in harmony with a Protestant worldview. It would appear that the explicit trust in the work of the Holy Spirit made any human attempts at spiritual formation inappropriate or at least of a lower priority than evangelization.

In 1830, the American Sunday School Union took on the staggering task of placing a Sunday school in "every desolate place" throughout the Mississippi Valley, a track of land stretching from Harrisburg, Pennsylvania, to the Rocky Mountains and from Canada to the Gulf of Mexico.[38] The overriding goal was to "bring every child and youth . . . under the influence of the gospel."

It should be noted that strict instruction was given to the missionaries to avoid the controversial issue of slavery.[39] A de facto division was made between conversion and the moral implications of the slavery issue; however, readers today should recognize that the moral issues are far clearer now than they were in the dominant society in the pre–Civil War era. A similar effort at establishing Sunday schools in the South met with much less success.

As churches embraced the Sunday school, a transition took place that shifted the emphasis from evangelization to biblical instruction. Child and adolescent spirituality was measured by public conversion and conformity to the standards and norms of the churches with whom the youthful converts were associated.

Adolescent Spirituality in Juvenile Temperance Societies (1830–80)

The juvenile temperance movement was perhaps the first attempt to shape a specific aspect of the child's moral life. Though this may not be considered *spirituality* by today's understandings, it was about as close a parallel as could be found among Protestants in the nineteenth century. The juvenile temperance movement grew out of the broader temperance movement that began in the early nineteenth century. The juvenile temperance movement developed like most movements, with local responses to alcohol abuse arising from the grass roots and eventually developing into nationwide organizations with networks across national boundaries—especially in the United States and Europe.

Two phases of the temperance movement gave rise to different emphases. The earlier phase emphasized moderation and focused much of its effort on rescuing men who had fallen prey to "demon rum." Primary attention was paid to "ardent spirits" (hard liquors), while wine and beer were assumed to be normal parts of church and social life. The second phase shifted to abstinence and included preventive measures for those who had not begun to partake of alcoholic beverages. This second phase began about 1830, though there was conflict over the validity of the two perspectives for many years to come. The second phase gave rise to juvenile temperance societies.[40]

Probably the earliest temperance training took place in the homes where parents had adopted a life of temperance. Early local temperance societies included both adults and children and were said to be most effective where mother, father, and children practiced the total abstinence principle. Like adults, children were allowed to join abstinence societies by signing a pledge to abstain. Pledging sobriety allowed them to obtain cards of membership as well as to buy and wear medals of the society. Yet early on certain temperance movement leaders decided that children would benefit from societies of their own.[41]

The idea of a pledge shaped youth ministry for the next one hundred years. Christian Endeavor and denominational youth societies utilized pledges to enable young people to know what the church expected from them in living the Christian life. A survey of the various pledges provides an overview of adolescent spirituality as understood by the agencies of youth ministry.

As early as 1832, the youth's temperance societies formalized a pledge of abstinence from ardent spirits, with the promise to discontinue intemperance. This practice quickly became a key element of juvenile temperance societies. One version of the pledge stated:

> I do voluntarily promise that I will abstain from Ale, Porter, Wine, Ardent Spirits, and all intoxicating Liquors and will not give nor offer them to others, except as medicines, or as a religious ordinance, and I will endeavor to discontinuance [sic] the cause and practice of intemperance.[42]

If there was a barometer of spirituality in this early juvenile temperance pledge, it had to do with the desire to avoid a practice that would have a negative effect upon one's relationship with God, family, and the broader community. Later temperance pledges broadened their prohibitions to include other activities deemed vices (smoking, other uses of tobacco, and gambling, in particular). These vices violated Protestant societal lifestyle expectations primarily because they were seen as detrimental to holiness and godliness.

Adolescent Spirituality in the Christian Endeavor and Denominational Youth Society Era (1881–1925)

By the 1880s ministers in New England were speaking of the "youth problem" in their congregations.[43] Many were concerned that young people were growing up unconverted. Christopher Lee Coble, following the analysis of Edmund Morgan, describes four stages in Christian conversion:

1. Conviction of sin and recognition in vivid detail of his or her state of depravity;
2. Experiencing a deep sense of crisis and despair leading to repentance for sin;
3. Feelings of joy and peace resulting from accepting God's unconditional grace;
4. Experiencing a transformed life marked by good deeds and a cheerful disposition.[44]

Pastors were concerned that true conversion had not taken place in the lives of young people because they seemed to disregard reverence for the Sabbath and the restraints and inspirations of the principles of Christian religion. Even when young people responded to the moving of the Spirit at annual revivals, the impact appeared to fade quickly. Fueling the discussion was the growing influence of Horace Bushnell's *Christian Nurture*, which called into question the idea of a dramatic conversion experience for children raised in Christian homes.

Christian Endeavor, founded on February 2, 1881, redefined (or perhaps defined) *spirituality* for Protestant youth. At the core of the Christian Endeavor system was a pledge that all members were required to take. The founder, Francis E. Clark, initially stated the pledge simply:

> Trusting in the Lord Jesus Christ for strength, I promise Him that I will try to do whatever He would have me do; that I will pray to Him and read my Bible every day, and that, just so far as I know how, through my whole life I will try to lead a Christian life.[45]

The pledge provided a formula for youthful spirituality shared across Protestant denominations in America. Elastic enough to assume either a conversion experience or Bushnell's understanding that children raised in the faith community could grow up never thinking of themselves as anything but Christian, the point of the pledge was to continuously foster the work of Christ in the life of youthful believers. It had to do with Christian spirituality.

As Christian Endeavor expanded, the pledge became more general. Perhaps avoiding the criticism that Christian Endeavor took young people away from the services of their home churches, Clark included specific commitments for these youth to be involved in the services of their church. Writing in 1890 at which time the Society had grown to associate with churches of many denominations, Clark recommended a revised pledge:

> Trusting in the Lord Jesus Christ for strength, I promise Him that I will strive to do whatever He would have me do; that I will make it the rule of my life to pray and read my Bible every day; that I will support my own church in every way, especially by attending all regular Sunday and mid-week services, unless prevented by some reason which I can conscientiously give to my Saviour, and that, just so far as I know how, I will endeavor to lead a Christian life.[46]

Writing in *The Golden Rule* (October 31, 1889), Clark identified two essential ideas the Christian Endeavor pledge stood for: "private devotion, and loyalty to our own church; private devotion as exemplified by prayer and Bible reading, loyalty to the church as expressed by regular and constant attendance upon her public services."[47]

The Christian Endeavor pledge was described as "a standard of character and action which we promise to try to reach."[48] Anyone joining Christian Endeavor was expected to make the pledge believing it would help him or her in the Christian life. The word *spirituality* was never associated with the pledge. The focus was on behaviors that aided people in living the Christian life. Yet the expectation was that the pledged actions were essentially spiritual disciplines that produced a stronger relationship with God and could be seen by the faith community. It should be noted that as the Christian Endeavor pledge was being introduced, the temperance movement was moving away from its pledge, judging it ineffective.

Denominations soon followed the lead of Christian Endeavor in forming youth societies and included pledges of their own. Concepts of holiness stated both as prohibitions and affirmations, saturated the Methodist pledge. Spirituality for the youthful followers of Wesley took on the concepts of sanctification but also embraced a mandate for evangelization. Methodist youth pledged:

> I enjoy or will seek the blessing of heart purity as taught in the Scriptures. I promise to abstain from the use of tobacco and of all intoxicants as beverages, to refrain from card-playing and dancing, and from attending the theatre, the opera, the circus, and all other questionable places of amusement. I agree to have stated seasons of private prayer, to pray for my pastor and for the members of the Young People's Methodist Alliance, to study the Bible each day, and to give thought to winning souls, by personal conversation, letter writing, tract distribution, prayer, and other means.[49]

Baptists formed the Baptist Young People's Union in 1891. Organization for local churches varied but in time common statements of purpose came into common usage. A handbook issued by the Department of Religious Education of the Iowa Baptist Convention, which was frequently copied, placed "increased spirituality" as the foremost purpose of BYPU. It states:

> The object of this organization shall be to secure the increased spirituality of our Baptist young people; their stimulation in Christian stewardship and service; their edification in scriptural knowledge; their instruction in Baptist doctrine and history; their enlistment in all missionary and social service activities through existing denominational organizations; and their definite commitment to Christian Life Service.[50]

The "life service" emphasis, though a subset of the objects of BYPU, had a consecration pledge which helped define spirituality as understood by Baptist youth workers. To join the Baptist Life Service League, the young person was to pledge:

> I will live my life under God for others rather than for myself; for the advancement of the kingdom of God rather than for personal success.
> I will not drift into my life work, but will do my utmost, by prayer, investigation, meditation, and service to discover that form and place of life work in which I can become of the largest use to the kingdom of God.
> As I find it I will follow it, under the leadership of Jesus Christ, wheresoever it takes me, cost what may.[51]

The pledge combined Christian piety (prayer, meditation, submission to the leadership of Jesus Christ) with a commitment to Christian service (advancement of the kingdom of God, form and place of life work, wherever it takes me, cost what may). While suggesting this type of service would result in pastoral or missionary careers, the wording is broad enough to include other forms of advancing the kingdom of God.

Lutherans had their manner of including spirituality in their denominational youth ministries. The pledges for Lutheran youth shared similar concerns with Methodists for separation from worldly practices. In commenting on the Augustana Luther League, Clarence Peters observed,

> Most of these early societies had a common underlying purpose. Primarily they were spiritual in nature. They were to assist youth in Christian growth. Many of the early societies' constitutions emphasized especially the Word of God and the confessions of the Lutheran Church. In a number of instances societies were organized to counteract the influence of the dance, the saloon, the theatre, and whatever bad companions young people might pick up in the community.[52]

Unlike most other denominational groups, Lutheran churches in America were organized in various synods that functioned autonomously. Though Peters spoke of the underlying spiritual purposes of their youth organizations, few pledges for spirituality or Christian living are on record. More than other denominations, the stated purposes of their youth organizations had to do with maintaining doctrinal purity, retaining youth within Lutheran churches, and promoting relationships within Lutheran youth societies.[53]

Many denominational youth societies merely used the Christian Endeavor pledge. Influenced by the Progressive Era (especially following 1917), the attention of Christian Endeavor and her denominational sisters shifted from spiritual endeavors to training young people for church leadership. Joseph Kett was appropriately critical of these professed training efforts, claiming that the desired church leadership skills were never clearly defined. In reality, Christian Endeavor had strayed from its original concern for fostering spirituality to an effort to be efficient in retaining and delivering experienced young adults for membership in their local churches.

In the 1920s and following, both Christian Endeavor and denominational youth societies attempted to redeem their floundering movements from the obscurity of the direction in which they were moving by appealing to the idealism of youth and focusing on changing society, bringing social systems into compliance with the Christian gospel. The movement moved youth ministry further from its roots, in which it had emphasized personal salvation, personal holiness, and full incorporation into the faith community. Any emphasis on *spirituality* was lost.

Adolescent Spirituality in Mainline Denominational Youth Fellowships (1936–65)

One of the major reasons why denominational youth societies emerged in the late nineteenth century was the discomfort felt by denominational leaders with either the obligatory nature of the Christian Endeavor pledge, the concept of religious living implied in the organization's program and pledge, or the lack of balance in Christian Endeavor, which centered primarily on a prayer meeting and personal piety.[54] Though other reasons relating to organizational conflicts between Christian Endeavor and Protestant denominations may have been more influential, varying understandings of adolescent spirituality were major factors.

Influenced by the Progressive Era and the liberal theology of such people as George Albert Coe, mainline denominational youth ministries looked to educational methods to replace the *spiritual* passion associated with evangelical conversions and expected a more reasoned approach to generate a "mature mind."[55] Kenda Creasy Dean comments:

> Yet early in the twentieth century, mainline Protestants broke ranks with American evangelicals over liberal theology, eschewing evangelical purity movements in favor of a social gospel that emphasized "doing good" over "being good"—and divested themselves of the soteriological urgency of youth ministry's revivalist beginnings.[56]

One manifestation of the mainline denominational movement toward "doing good" was the United Christian Youth Movement, a cooperative venture begun in 1934. Its bold objective, expressed in its overarching theme, was "Christian youth building a new world." Gone was the emphasis on conversion and holy living. In its place came an emphasis on social action, which climbed and then declined in a relatively brief period of time. Reactions from denominational churches forced leaders to retreat from the social action emphasis. Critiquing the youth ministry trends of the previous decade in 1943, Nevin Harner commented, "The changing emphasis . . . namely, from social action to Biblical and doctrinal content—will bear watching. If it can be allowed to go just far enough to redress the balance, and then stop short, we shall be all right."[57] The desired balance, however, looked to a more effective schooling approach (better biblical and doctrinal content) rather than a growth in personal salvation and piety.

Following two world wars and the Great Depression, liberal assumptions failed to apply to youth ministry. Even an infusion of neosupernaturalism stemming from neo-orthodox theology failed to infuse a new surge of Christian spirituality into mainline denominational churches. Some, instead, aligned their methods with a relational face on the redemption story pioneered by Jim Rayburn and Young Life. The result was a cheerful version of reformed theology.[58]

Incarnational ministry, as Young Life's approach came to be known, however, tended to deemphasize biblical content and stress the role of the faith community (but not churches) in shaping the lives of new believers. Spiritual disciplines were for the most part ignored. The work of spiritual formation was left to the Holy Spirit with a minimum of systematic efforts on the part of church or parachurch agencies.

Adolescent Spirituality in the Youth for Christ Movement and Youth Fellowship Era (1933–89)

In the 1930s and 1940s three movements began to reshape youth ministry. This began refocusing youth ministry on *koinonia* (fellowship) and *evangelium* (outreach evangelization). Mainline denominational youth societies reshaped themselves into youth fellowships that made room for adolescent ownership and leadership. At the instigation of the International Council of Religious Education, denominational youth leaders began asking how youth ministries could be done better. With fifty years of experience with young people's societies, they began to ask how the two aspects of religious education (Sunday school and youth society) could be made more effective. Schooling had become the model for religious education and efficiency the standard by which it was judged. Youth societies with their committees and pledges simply did not match up to the educational standards of the mid-1930s.[59]

Into this gap stepped youth fellowships. The concept tied together the Sunday school and a new kind of Sunday evening meeting designed to foster fellowship with both God and peers. Luke 2:52 provided the cornerstone, for young people were to grow as Christ had, "in wisdom and stature, and in favor with God and [people]." Some would call this the "balanced life." By the mid-1940s fourteen mainline denominations had adopted the approach.[60]

Materials published by denominational publishers became the primary programming resource for youth fellowships. *Spirituality* had very little appeal on the printed page and so the themes appealing to youthful idealism continued to provide the content for youth fellowship gatherings led by peer group leaders.

Parachurch youth ministry agencies arose from Protestant fundamentalism with the express purpose of evangelizing adolescents. Called by some the "youth for Christ" movement because of its explicit desire to reach young people for Christ, the movement included leaders from evangelical churches who felt their churches had lost the vision and/or capacity to evangelize the new generation for Christ. The movement followed a pattern of starting with public evangelization (rallies, radio programs, clubs, camps) and moved into a form of discipleship that primarily focused on increased Bible knowledge and spiritual disciplines similar to those embraced by Christian Endeavor in her early years.

Small evangelical denominations and independent churches began creating youth ministries tied to the distinctives of these new movements. In some of these denominations, churches were so small that few youth ministries existed and young people were expected to be a part of "their church." Churches from the Wesleyan traditions emphasized sanctification; churches from northern Europe stressed international missionary efforts; independent and fundamentalist church movements taught their youth to live lives separated from worldly influences. *Spirituality* for small evangelical denominations was measured by conformity to the norms and values of their churches. When God showed up, usually at camps or special meetings, commitments were made consistent with these evangelical priorities.

One of the earliest evangelical denominations was the Church of the Nazarene. Following the Wesleyan tradition their youth ministry included a strong emphasis on holiness. While the Nazarene Young People's Societies began two decades after the youth societies of mainline denominations, the need to redefine youth ministry came during the 1930s. Society was changing. The Church of the Nazarene recognized this change and in 1932 formed the "Intermediate Society" or "High School Nazarene Young People's Society." Four years later it was renamed Hi-NY. Yet the emphasis on holiness remained the same.

A pledge expected from society members read: "Realizing my duty to God and His church I promise by His grace to seek the New Testament standard of heart purity; to strive always to live consistently for my Master; to make it the rule of my life to read the Bible and pray daily; to attend faithfully all services of N.Y.P.S.; and to take an active part in the services as opportunity affords me."[61]

Personal holiness and piety remained a consistent emphasis of the youth ministry of the Church of the Nazarene through the middle of the twentieth century. For Nazarene youth, living their Christianity was closely tied to Bible reading and prayer. Purity of heart evidenced its existence in holiness of life and separation from worldly activities.

Adolescent Spirituality in the Youth Pastor Era (1979 to Present)

The formation of the National Network of Youth Ministries at a mountain retreat in Colorado in 1979 was symbolic of the transition from the youth fellowship era to a new stage of youth ministry. Though youth ministers (called by various names) existed as early as the beginning of the youth fellowship era and had mushroomed in the 1960s and 1970s, the focus of professionalized youth ministry activity began to tip back toward the local church as the 1980s began.

Joseph Bayly, at that time the editor of David C. Cook Publications, asked the author why youth ministers insisted on creating their own Sunday school curriculum when publishing houses such as the one he represented put so much research into product development. The author responded that the Sunday school material, as well researched as it was, was not relevant to the needs of the kids in the church in which he served. The same was true of youth ministries. Youth fellowship–era material no longer reflected the lives of either the young people or the youth ministers who had taken responsibility for their pastoral care. Youth ministers, like their senior pastors, began shaping local ministry to youth around the needs of the young people and their own personal skill sets. Three other organizations came into being about the same time, all focused on assisting local church youth ministers in their ministries: Youth Specialties (1968), Group Publishing (1974), and Sonlife Ministries (1979).

Youth Specialties led the way in suggesting a shift in youth ministry toward an emphasis on *spirituality*. A survey of the first dozen *Ideas* books (which to many youth ministers of the day ranked alongside the Bible), finds that the "Creative Communication" section included at least fifteen descriptions of worship experiences that shifted youth group meetings from novel approaches to meeting the needs of teenagers to contemporary means of fostering worship and reflection on the God of the Scriptures.

By the mid-1980s YS began introducing the Protestant youth ministry fraternity to speakers who offered a more classical approach to spirituality than had been available elsewhere at their National Youth Workers Convention. These included Brennan Manning, Walter Wangerin Jr., and Tom Howard among others.

Mike Yaconelli, one of the founders of YS, credited Henri Nouwen and the L'Arche community in Toronto, Canada, with starting him on "this wild and terrifying journey with Jesus" that he describes in *Dangerous Wonder*.[62] Yaconelli's son, Mark, picked up on his father's growing interest in spirituality and initiated the Youth Ministry and Spirituality Project (1997–2004) described in *Contemplative Youth Ministry* (2006) and *Growing Souls* (2007).[63] These books reflected the classical spirituality writings dating back to Ignatius of Loyola.

In the Youth Ministry and Spirituality Project, Mark Yaconelli concluded that youth workers don't know how to be with their kids, themselves, or God. His conclusion was that "if we want our young people to live lives of faith, we need to live into the presence of Jesus." Using principles of classical contemplative spirituality, Yaconelli provided a process for adults who are concerned about youth to grow as a faith community. The core idea was that a love for God on the part of adolescents would result from experiencing the model of spiritually-sensitive adults in community.

The emergent church movement was a product of youth ministry during the last two decades of the twentieth century. Reacting to the exclusion of classical practices of spirituality (primarily Catholic and Anglican) from Christian worship and formation, the movement began attempting to discover "another kind of Christian."

Conclusion

Unlike the movie *Bruce Almighty*, where God shows up unexpectedly in the life of a self-centered television reporter, Protestant youth ministries in America have been concerned with setting the stage for God to become a real presence in the lives of young people. In some traditions, God's presence was very private. In others, public expressions of God's working were the norm. Youth ministries became the focal point for the faith community to encourage youthful Christian *spirituality*. To gain a sense of God's work in young people's lives, Christian behaviors were the primary concern of pastors and Christian leaders throughout most of the history of youth ministry.

Different faith traditions paid attention to various behaviors but at the core was a type of Christian piety that included profession of personal salvation, Bible study, prayer, church attendance, and Christian service. Those denominations or cooperative movements that drifted from these emphases appeared to lose their compasses and floundered for direction. Throughout all of the disciplines taught and the strategies employed was a constant desire for young people to experience God's presence in their lives.

As the twenty-first century began, portions of youth ministry began to stress being rather than doing. Some felt as if the heart of youth ministry had at last been discovered. Yet pastors from Cotton Mather and Jonathan Edwards onward had sought to foster the inward life only to settle for types of programs, many of which did bring about vital Christian living for brief periods of time.

The type of *being* reflected in twenty-first-century youth ministry requires a pursuit of God in a communal setting. While this appears to be something new when compared to the silliness of the fun-and-games approach evident in the late twentieth century, it is very much in harmony with the early years of each new effort to shape the Christian spirituality of youth. Once again or perhaps for the first time, Christian spirituality may be moving to the heart of Christian youth ministries.

4

Whatever Goes Around
Comes Around

The Concept of Cycles in History

Writing a history of Protestant youth ministry is much like viewing a mosaic. Individual Protestant youth ministries are like the
colorful tile fragments that compose the work of art. Up close
they appear to be a collection of pieces embedded in a layer of plaster,
but when the viewer steps back a bit, the fragments blend into a picture.
The farther back the viewer stands, the more the picture communicates
the artist's vision and the less the viewer notices the individual tile
fragments.

Yet the mosaic analogy is static and the history of Protestant youth
ministries has been anything but static. In fact, efforts to standardize
youth ministries produced a paint-by-numbers effect in the churches of
North America. From a distance, they look barely passable as an imitation work of art but up close they look awful.

Jazz may be a more useful metaphor for viewing history. In live musical improvisation there are themes and variations. The lead moves from
musician to musician but retains a certain integrity to the very end. Every
jam session is a creative act. Performances utilize the best of the jam
sessions, either consciously or by raw instinct. Eventually the music is
recorded or written as a musical score, and at this point creativity ends

and imitation begins. Others, sometimes less talented musicians, attempt to duplicate the jazz sounds with varying results. In time a given jazz piece or style will become rather common and uninteresting. It is then that new forms of jazz emerge.

History is much like jazz. It too goes in cycles, but not in the sense of repeating itself. History is more like a spiral that revolves upward or downward depending on the viewer's perspective.

Economic Cycles

The cyclical nature of history finds roots in various disciplines. Peter Drucker, author and consultant to Fortune 500 companies, wrote of economic cycles in *Innovation and Entrepreneurship*. He proposed an idea that growth in the entrepreneurial sector of the United States economy was based on a model created by a Russian economist named Nikoli Kondratieff, who was executed in the mid-1930s on Stalin's orders because his model predicted the failure of the collectivized Russian agricultural policies. Drucker called it the "fifty-year Kondratieff cycle."

Simply stated the theory was this: Every fifty years a long technological wave crests. For the last twenty years of each cycle the growth industries of the previous technological advance appear to be doing exceptionally well but what they really are doing is using up the capital that was no longer needed to grow. The situation never lasts more than twenty years. Then there is a sudden crisis followed by twenty years of stagnation before which new and emerging technologies can overcome the sluggishness of the economy.[1]

This pattern can be found in youth ministry as well. Researchers call them youth movements. Similar fifty-year cycles, even broken down into innovation, stagnation, and transition periods, characterize Protestant youth ministries in America. Three cycles of youth movements have passed into history. For approximately the first twenty to thirty years of each youth movement, an excitement and continual innovation drove it forward in attempts to reach young people for Christ and help them experience God's presence in their lives. Then around year thirty something happened. Stagnation began to characterize each movement. This continued for the next twenty years while the movement's earlier momentum and good reputation carried it along. Finally, a crisis happened and there was no longer a way to disguise the fact that the movements were bankrupt. For an additional twenty years youth work would struggle before entrepreneurial innovations in working with young people could set in motion a new cycle of youth ministry.

Historical Cycles

The mere existence of economic cycles does not mean this phenomenon will show up in youth ministry. Arthur M. Schlesinger Jr., in *The Cycles of History*, traced just such thinking down through American history. Starting with Henry Adams's analysis of the presidential administrations of Thomas Jefferson and James Madison, and following the idea of historical cycles through the writings of his father, historian Arthur M. Schlesinger (*Paths to the Present*), economist Albert O. Hirschman (*Shifting Involvements*), and political scientists Herbert McClosky and John Zaller (*The American Ethos*), Schlesinger Jr. developed his argument for historical cycles.[2]

"Among democratic nations," Schlesinger Jr. quotes Alexis de Tocqueville, "each generation is a new people."[3] The historian then goes on to suggest that a political generation lasts thirty years, made up of fifteen years coming of age and fifteen years resisting the advancing of ideas of the next generation. The political ebb and flow seemed analogous to the cycles in youth ministry, though youth ministry cycles lasted longer. Other writers cited by Schlesinger suggest longer cycles of forty years (Phillips) and forty-eight years (Klingberg).[4]

While Schlesinger confined his comments primarily to the political arena, the concept appears applicable to broader areas as well. Weather, population growth, and as Drucker pointed out, economic cycles appear to have validity as well. While this historian will not force the cyclical idea in the history of Protestant youth ministries too far, he finds it very convenient to use some fairly apparent trends in youth ministry to provide structure for this historical journey.

Cycles of history are associated by various researchers with economic fluctuations, political effectiveness, life-cycle revitalization movements, and scientific revolutions. Seeing these cycles as periods of social disequilibration, society looks for fresh answers to their problems. Church leaders do the same. The remainder of this book is organized around the new challenges associated with the emergence of new expressions of the "youth problem" as viewed by Protestants in America and the responses utilized by churches. At stake is the spiritual vitality of the rising generation.

Revivals and spiritual awakenings, similarly, have been cast in cyclical terms, though some doubt the criteria for identifying such revivals or awakenings, suggesting them to be local or at best regional affairs and hardly marker events for a generation of Christians.[5] Yet there seems to be a pattern loosely associated with periods of awakenings in Protestant churches. New forms of youth group ministry take shape some years after the awakenings have passed as if church leaders wish to structure for the rising generation a working of the Spirit that will perpetuate a sense of awakening.

Sociological Cycles

Religious sociology suggests a similar cyclical pattern in churches. German theorists Ernst Troeltsch and H. Richard Niebuhr as well as the American student of religious sociology David O. Moberg suggest a predictable cycle as churches develop.[6]

Sociologists describe the first stage of a religious movement using the word *cult*. The phase was characterized by a visionary and authoritarian leader, tight and somewhat arbitrary rules, and an antagonism to anyone who did not understand God in the exact way in which they did. After the original leader passed from the scene, the movement took on the characteristics of a *sect* with a plurality of leaders, a more systematic set of rules, and an increasing tolerance for other groups who shared essential convictions.

In the third stage of a religious movement, a group reached its peak of efficiency while increasing its willingness to engage with culture. Religious sociologists described this as an *organized church*. In this phase the church was characterized by a broadened leadership base that included a cross-section of the church, democratically chosen, rules that had been softened to be understood as principles, and cooperation with other churches of like mind. Stage four some characterize as being a *denomination* with a wide range of tolerance for everything from leadership styles to doctrinal issues. Though the church had gained more credibility and power, by this time the church was beginning to decline. This stage was inevitably followed by *disintegration* during which time people tended to leave the church either for a church earlier in the cycle or for nothing at all.

Though the time it took to move through the cycle was longer than for youth ministries, the pattern was quite similar. These cycles may not have been as rigid as Troeltsch and Niebuhr had theorized but they did, in fact, exist. Yet people were not locked into the cycle in which they found themselves. Individually or in groups they had the freedom to escape at any time and in effect start new cycles. However, history suggests that few escaped. Most stayed with their church even when it was apparent that the final notes were being played.

Biblical Cycles

Some Protestant leaders react negatively to the possibility that the God of Scripture could be trapped into mechanistic patterns of economic, historical, or sociological paradigms. In all likelihood God would not work in fifty-year cycles or any other type of predictable paradigm. He operates strictly in accord with His own sovereign wisdom.

Yet the concept of recurring cycles also appeared in the Scriptures. It was hard to detect in the New Testament, which was stretched over little more than one fifty-year period. The Ephesian church was an interesting case study. Founded by the Apostle Paul along with Aquila and Priscilla in the middle of the first century (Acts 18–20) and pastored by a young Timothy (1–2 Timothy), the Ephesian church appeared very healthy as Paul wrote a letter to them around AD 62. Yet thirty years later the angel to the church in Ephesus in the book of Revelation critiques them as having left its first love (Rev. 2:4). Symptoms of a cycle characterize the church in Ephesus.

The Old Testament, which covers more than a thousand years, presented a clearer picture of the cyclical nature of God's work in history. Though not in clear fifty-year sequences, the general pattern can be seen both in the book of Judges and among the Kings of Judah in the divided kingdom. In both cases God worked through a person to bring about a spiritual awakening followed by a gradual period of stagnation ending in divine wrath before God raised up another person and a spiritual awakening followed.[7]

The book of Judges, for example, organizes itself in a cyclical fashion. The second chapter explains the pattern. Jehovah raised up a leader who followed the commandments given to Moses. When the leader and the people of his generation died, the people of Israel went native and began conforming to the norms of the people around them who did not share a loyalty to Jehovah. As a result, oppressors took control and made life miserable for the Israelites. Then in approximately fifty-year cycles, Jehovah raised up a new leader and people returned to following the Lord (Judg. 2:6–22).

Though the Bible does not clearly specify a recurring pattern of revival which could be considered normative for the church today, the idea is by no means in violation of either God's character or God's Word.

Youth Movements

If youth ministries run in a cyclical fashion (as described throughout the rest of the book), then some recurring patterns could be expected. S. N. Eisenstadt, in his work entitled *From Generation to Generation*, described youth movements as social constructs that pass values from generation to generation.[8] Tracing Protestant ministry to youth in America, three distinct patterns emerge, each of which impact Protestant youth ministries.

As a youth pastor I often wondered why youth did such a poor job of reaching their peers for Christ. Though most of the youth workers I knew encouraged and even trained high school students to carry the Christian gospel to their friends at school, the actual results of evangelistic efforts by students were minimal. Understanding youth movements provides an answer to this dilemma. The primary function of youth movements is that of *passing the values of one generation to the next.* That was probably the reason why youth ministries were not particularly evangelistic—the parents of youth group members, despite what they claimed, did not particularly value evangelism. What parents appeared to hold in highest esteem was having their adolescents survive the teenage years, not become the "black sheep" of their families, and encounter God in a manner somewhat similar to what they had known as they grew up.

The process of value passing, however, finds three different expressions in youth movements. The first can be described as *spontaneous youth ministries* or *student movements.* These arise at the instigation of young people themselves and find leadership and direction from within the peer group. They perform two functions for youth. Either they become a means for alienated youth to reenter the mainstream of society or they allow idealistic youth a socially acceptable outlet for their militancy.

The Jesus Movement of the sixties, though short in duration, was a classic illustration of a spontaneous student movement. During the Vietnam conflict, a period of extreme social unrest in the United States, young people felt alienated from adult values. The media described it as a "generation gap." Clothing, hair styles, music, and the flaunting of societal taboos symbolized the disaffection felt first by adolescents and later by even grade school children. The movement was led primarily by young adults who were uncomfortable with the status quo, especially in the church, or who had experimented with countercultural lifestyles and had found them empty.

The movement died when well-meaning Christian adults began organizing the movement in behalf of youth. Mike Yaconelli correctly wrote the obituary for the Jesus Movement after the Campus Crusade for Christ–sponsored Explo '72.[9] The media-oriented Jesus Festival drew eighty thousand students and laypersons to Dallas, Texas, for what was suggested to be "the most significant Christian student gathering in history." But after the buses and vans filled with young people left the Cotton Bowl and headed home, the Jesus Movement was dead. Though symbols of the movement lingered on, the heart of the movement had died. It was no longer led by youth.[10]

Rarely is this type of youth movement found on the high school or junior high school level. Early and middle adolescents do not seem to have the social maturity, cognitive development, or leadership skills necessary to sustain such a movement for more than a few weeks. Thus student movements led by students below the college level are virtually absent from the annals of youth ministry.

The second type of youth movement is that which *utilizes adult leadership* sponsored by church or parachurch agencies to work with young people *in nonformal settings. Nonformal settings* means places outside the formal classroom where attendance is required. These adults may be paid for their work with youth but for the most part they are volunteers who donate five to twenty hours each week to help young people reaffirm and strengthen their Christian faith.

Most of the parachurch youth ministries fall into this category. Fellowship of Christian Athletes, Young Life, Youth for Christ USA, and Student Venture were the best known efforts to minister to high school students outside the context of the church in the second half of the twentieth century. Another set of organizations exist outside the local church but are designed to service club programs within the context of the church. These include interdenominational agencies such as Awana, Pioneer Clubs, Christian Service Brigade, Adventure Clubs, and Word of Life clubs. Denominational youth organizations also fall into this category.

The highly structured nature of the materials published by these groups makes their various systems most attractive to churches that have no paid youth ministry personnel. Area, regional, and sometimes national rallies, social activities, camps, and conferences provide additional opportunities for adults and young people from local churches to spend valuable time together. Lay leaders enjoy the freedom of spending their volunteer hours in face-to-face contact with students rather than toiling behind the scenes to create programs that they only hoped would be productive.

Youth ministers employed by local churches have adapted many of the ministry strategies developed by parachurch workers and used them within local church youth ministries. For the most part these are people highly skilled in interpersonal relationships who can use those abilities to convey Christian truth from one generation to the next.

The third type of youth movement is that of the *graded educational system*. Most youth workers may not consider a system of parochial schools as a method of doing youth ministry, and yet for many years Catholic, Lutheran, and Christian Reformed Church leaders placed a majority of their time, energy, and financial support of youth work into their school systems. More recently independent Protestant churches followed the same approach to passing their values and view of the world to a new generation.

Parochial schools found their genesis in reaction to the secularization of public schools and the teaching of a worldview in conflict with those of their church or family. At the beginning of the twenty-first century some publicly-financed charter schools have satisfied this need as well.

Though this type of youth movement may lack the spontaneity and voluntary attendance many people associate with youth ministry, the method precedes most of today's approaches. New England's "common school," which was the forerunner of the public school system in America, came into being to achieve the same ends as youth ministries do today. Leaders of the colonies wanted to teach young people to live moral and Christian lives and thus required school attendance.

Another reaction to both the secularization and the ineffectiveness of public schools has been the home schooling movement. A significant portion of those participating in the movement, now approaching two million children, have as part of their motivation the conveying of a Christian worldview. A portion of this later group, calling themselves the family integrated church movement, go so far as to advocate the elimination of church youth ministries because of the deeply held conviction that fathers should provide Christian training for their children.[11] While not a graded educational system, both the home schooling and family integrated church movement fit in this category because of the structure provided by parents.

Why Youth Movements Began: Secularization

Youth ministry as it is known today is a late addition to the work of the church. No youth ministries can be found in the pages of Scripture, try as we might to find them. The stories of Martin Luther, John Calvin, Menno Simons, and John Wesley are nearly exclusively the stories of adults.

Not until the late eighteenth century is there a concerted effort to minister to young people within the context of the church. The Sunday school was first. Then came the juvenile temperance movement and the Young Men's and Young Women's Christian Associations. Throughout the nineteenth century individual churches in a wide variety of denominations provided activities for their youth, but it was a visionary pastor named Francis E. Clark who put together the ideas for a youth society in his own church and then successfully promoted the idea to a nation that was waiting. It was an idea whose time had come.

But why did youth societies begin in the nineteenth century and not before? Why did they flourish in England and the United States long before the idea of a youth movement took root in other nations? Several suggestions might describe the context.

During the 1800s a process of secularization began to decrease the influence which church and home had previously exerted over young people. The 1859 publication of Darwin's *On the Origin of Species* symbolized the change. A Christian understanding of the world was no longer the principal view in the environment in which young people were being raised.

Many people think of secular ideas as being those that have no religious content, and this is partially true. More accurately, however, secular thinking divides all of life into categories which can be verified through scientific reasoning. Math, biology, chemistry, physics, sociology, economics, and anthropology are but a few of these categories. To the extent that religion could be "proven" it could then be considered a category. The problem was not with the categories but with the lack of Christian theology both within the categories and tying all of the categories together.

As the Christian worldview lost its authoritative place, parents felt like they were losing control. The formal educational process that shaped the lives of their children had begun to reflect the growing diversity of America. Gradually religious and moral influences, including the teaching of the Bible, were excluded from the public schools. The mores of the farm or small community were not the convictions of city dwellers, and young people were migrating to urban areas in search of jobs.

Reactions to secularization intensified from time to time, frequently related to changes in public schooling with Supreme Court decisions and other court cases. Decisions seen as logical extensions of the disestablishment of religion in America and the equal rights premise of the Constitution increased the distrust of Protestant parents and church leaders in America and provided an openness to innovations in youth ministry.

When Youth Movements Began: Times of Social Unrest

Youth for Christ leaders always had a sense of the dramatic, so kneeling in prayer on an airport runway was no big deal. After all, if youth evangelists Billy Graham, Torrey Johnson, Charles Templeton, and Strat Shufelt were to carry the good news of Jesus Christ to a war-hardened Europe, the whole effort had to be bathed in prayer. So as cameras snapped their picture, the team bowed in prayer before boarding a plane at Chicago's Midway Field.

It was March of 1946. Saturday night Youth for Christ rallies had drawn thousands of young people to hear fiery speakers with a flair for the dramatic. So now the first of many Youth for Christ teams was headed for England, Ireland, Scotland, Sweden, and Norway with the express purpose of sharing their youth evangelism know-how with the religious leaders in Europe. The sad irony of the trip was that it was a journey to the birthplace of youth ministry, an expedition made necessary by the absence of European Christian youth movements during the forties.

Youth ministry began in England during the Industrial Revolution in the late eighteenth and early nineteenth centuries. This dramatic period of economic and technical change began on the continent and in England well before it happened in the United States. Factories had replaced family-owned shops, and mass production became the normal process for making everything from clothing to buggies. With this change in the manner of production came the need for a new labor force. Factories began to employ children, and young people moved to the cities to obtain jobs that were no longer available in rural areas.

Concerned over the ragamuffins who worked twelve- to fourteen-hour days, six days a week, Robert Raikes popularized a ministry to children in Gloucester that came to be known as Sunday school. Its purpose was to teach children to read and behave properly using the Bible as a textbook. Within five years the idea had spread to Virginia and by 1790 Boston, New York, Philadelphia, and a host of other cities were imitating Raikes's ideas.[12]

As the Industrial Revolution continued, many expressed concern for young adults who had left their families for jobs amid the worldly influences of the cities. Few places in the growing urban centers were friendly to young people who wished to retain their Christian values. Housing was awful, sexual temptation was everywhere, and crime and violence were nearly unavoidable. Something needed to be done to redeem the youth of England.

George Williams was a prime mover in responding to this need. As a youthful dry goods merchant he began a Bible study for apprentices, clerks, and young male assistants in the dry goods industry. From this modest beginning in 1841 came the founding of the Young Men's Christian Association on June 6, 1844, in London. Like the Sunday school before it, the YMCA quickly found its way to North America and by 1851 the ministry had established roots in Montreal and Boston.[13]

Though the YMCA of the twenty-first century is thought of primarily as an athletic facility that also provides camps and educational services, its original objectives were distinctly Christian. Bible studies and prayer meetings, training classes for Sunday school teachers, and athletic competition were all seen as ways to reinforce Christian beliefs and values.

Before the Industrial Revolution such activities were not necessary. The extended family and the church combined to do all the teaching most people felt was necessary. Though a strong case can be made demonstrating the ineffectiveness of the traditional delivery systems for instruction in Christian truth and values, Christian people of the eighteenth century felt little need for help. The boundaries of their worlds were the fields surrounding their villages. Traditional taboos were held in place by the unchanging fabric of the local social system.

By the nineteenth century those feelings of self-sufficiency had begun to evaporate. Even adults responded as college students paved the way for the modern missionary enterprise.[14] Influenced by the organizational structures of the Methodists as well as the success of the Sunday school and YMCA/YWCA movements, new systems were created for working with young people. A new day had dawned in the concern to bring the light of the gospel to youth.

The Roaring Twenties, two world wars, the Great Depression, the counterculture of the 1960s, and the collapse of Communism in the late 1980s created similar disruptions in the twentieth century. The wars in Iraq, collapse of the housing market in America, and the resulting worldwide recession during the first decade of the twenty-first century provided times of unrest suited to new youth movements.

In addition to secularization and the impetus of social unrest, however, there was a third element that influenced the development of youth ministry. It was not enough to sense a need for ministry to youth; people had to mobilize to deal with the concerns. A rapidly growing segment of the population, the products of the Industrial Revolution, came to fill this void. They were members of an economic middle class.

With Whom Youth Movements Began: The Economic Middle Class

I saw plainly how youth work is determined by economic conditions when I spent a week teaching youth ministry at Mexico's National Christian Education Conference as a part of a team sponsored by the National Association of Directors of Christian Education. It was held in the nation's capital, Mexico City, which was at the time the world's largest city. Each day, hundreds of middle-class Mexican lay people made their way via the Metra (subway system) to the church where the conference was being held. Even though the conferees were not poor, few would have been able to afford the conference if it had been held in a hotel as many youth conferences are in the United States.

There were no youth pastors present, and the only parachurch ministry people in attendance drew at least part of their support from people outside of Mexico. Consequently the style of youth ministry promoted at the conference looked very much like youth societies from the United States during the early part of the twentieth century. Elected officers presided over weekly meetings that sounded like youth-led imitations of their church's worship service. Social events were an integral part of their monthly cycle of activities.

One Sunday evening I traveled with my interpreter to the outskirts of that great city. The farther we traveled away from the grandeur of the central business district, the smaller the houses and shops became. Just before we turned down a tiny street where stood the half-remodeled boxing gymnasium that served as his father's church, Ricardo stopped his truck and pointed to a sea of huts located on the other side of an arroyo. "That's where the poor people live" was his wistful comment.

I knew, as did Ricardo, there was no youth ministry happening on the other side of the arroyo. It barely existed on our side where an articulate young man in his early twenties could work a normal job during the day and then help his father start a church during the evening hours. The needs were so great in both neighborhoods that any specialized ministry was impractical. This experience taught me, more graphically than ever before, that youth work was a by-product of the economic middle-class people of a nation. Its style and strategy was, in part, dictated by the economic conditions of its environment.

Youth ministry in the United States has been able to flourish because of the presence of a growing economic middle class of people who were both the leaders and benefactors of the movement. Economic middle-class adults and occasional upper-class benefactors have provided leadership for keeping adolescents off the streets and on the straight and narrow. But seldom have people emerged after ten or twelve hours of filthy, sweaty, exhausting labor in coal mines or textile mills and hustled off to church for a busy night of working with youth. For most lower-class parents, such a scenario was not possible.

It has consistently been people who are relatively secure financially and have been appropriately educated who have had the time, creativity, and energy to work with young people. Though people like Jim Rayburn, founder of Young Life, and Torrey Johnson, first president of Youth for Christ, were not wealthy people, they benefited from both education and the financial resources of loyal supporters. Jack Wyrtzen, founder of Word of Life Fellowship, and Percy Crawford, originator of the Young

People's Church of the Air, attracted emerging middle-class support by means of their radio programs. Francis E. Clark, father of the Society of Christian Endeavor, and Evelyn M. McClusky, mother of the Miracle Book Club, captured the interest of middle-class Christians through articles and books.

Though many youth workers, especially during the early days of a movement, live at or below the poverty line, their status is not measured by personal income. Ability is a far better criteria of their social standing. In fact, when some of these poverty-stricken youth workers leave youth ministry behind, they do exceedingly well in their next chosen field of endeavor, whether in Christian ministry or in the world of business or education, because they have developed entrepreneurial instincts.

More important than the personal status of the leadership of a youth movement is the existence of a significant pool of economic middle-class young people from whom to draw support. If young people have no time for a youth movement due to more pressing needs for food, shelter, or safety, a youth movement will not exist. Charles Dickens's story *Oliver Twist* described the slums of London where youth ministry should have been happening. There was an enormous pool of needy children, but the economic necessities of life had left them victims to the likes of Fagin, a master thief, who provided room and board in exchange for stolen goods.

The economic climate of the United States during the past two centuries, by contrast, has provided a virtual reservoir of middle-class youth, and it has been on these people that a majority of church and parachurch activity has been focused. The Society of Christian Endeavor found a stream of middle-class young people in the closing years of the nineteenth century as is evidenced by the fact that 56,425 delegates registered at an 1895 convention in Boston. Resort-like camps sponsored by Young People's Church of the Air (Pinebrook), Word of Life Fellowship (Island), and Young Life at various sites around the nation are another evidence of the appeal of youth movements to the economic middle class. Someone had to pay the bills for transportation to and from those camps as well as the higher-than-normal fees, which covered professional staff and programming costs. The young people who attended were either children of economic middle-class parents or received scholarship assistance from middle- or upper-class adults.

It should be noted that youth ministry does exist in countries where the economic middle class has been systematically repressed. Christian youth movements in Eastern Europe during the Communist era challenged the faith of the people with whom they had contact. But the forms were far different from the models seen in the United States.

They more closely parallel the dynamics of the Jesus Movement and depend on college-age leadership rather than upon adult sponsors or paid youth ministry specialists. These dissimilarities continue in emerging economies until a functional middle class develops within these countries.

The Spread of a Christian Youth Movement

Even when all the conditions appear to be right, there is no guarantee a Christian youth movement will happen. While teaching at Torch Trinity Graduate School of Theology in Seoul, Korea, in 1997, the economies of several Asian countries considered "economic tigers" collapsed, sending world markets into a tailspin. The exchange value of the Korean currency, the Wan, suddenly was worth only half of what it was just days before. In the months ahead, I asked my students to watch for signs of a new Christian youth movement in their land. But to our surprise, even when Koreans showed signs of repentance for their materialism and arrogance, no such youth movement emerged. This seemed incongruous until we recognized that certain characteristics of Christian youth movements were missing.

In the 1990s I wrote of "the coming revolution in youth ministry."[15] One question that I was asked repeatedly was, "Is what I am doing revolutionary?" Repeatedly, my answer was that I did not know, because only time will tell whether a youth ministry will thrive and become a movement. Once under way, Christian youth movements explode rapidly, though frequently not in the places people are looking to find them. Nonetheless, there are some observable characteristics common to the Christian youth movements that shaped the Protestant youth ministries of America.

A Visionary

The story of youth ministry is filled with people who had great ideas and used them in a local context but did not see them spread any farther. Others are visionaries whose ideas spread far beyond their communities. Theodore Cuyler was one of the former while Francis E. Clark demonstrated the latter.

Pastor Cuyler's concern was for the young people of his Presbyterian church in Brooklyn. He started a youth society by adapting the methodologies of the YMCA and the juvenile temperance movement for use within his church. Cuyler freely shared what his group did as they structured themselves for evangelizing and discipling young men and women. One of his many articles about his young people's association caught the attention of a Congregational pastor from Portland, Maine, occasioning a trip to Brooklyn for him to see what was happening.

The young Congregational pastor was Francis E. Clark. After trying a number of unsuccessful approaches to working with the youth of his church, Clark came across Cuyler's ideas and blended them with some his wife had been using with girls of Williston Church. Adding the Methodist idea of a class-meeting, which he called the consecration meeting, he formed the Society of Christian Endeavor. Like Cuyler, Clark was an innovator, but the latter was also a visionary. Within a year the young pastor began sending information about the society to other pastors in New England.

From the early years Francis Clark's vision was ambitious. Though most of his objectives had to do with the godly vitality and piety of individuals, he had dreams about the impact the society might have on the church and the world. His desire for interdenominational fellowship, manifested in conventions and conferences, illustrates Clark's ambition for a larger impact. Less than eighteen months after the Young People's Society of Christian Endeavor was founded Clark hosted a conference at his Williston Church. The gathering became an annual event.

As the idea spread, Clark was instrumental in promoting the organization around the world. Traveling and writing while still a pastor became too much for him, so on September 4, 1887, only six years after the first meeting of the society in Portland, Maine, the young husband and father resigned his pastorate, stepped out in faith, and became the first full-time employee of Christian Endeavor. By the turn of the century there were close to a million young people associated with the movement.

Each youth movement has a visionary who sees beyond what his or her peers think possible and then attracts capable people to put legs on the vision. In most cases the vision is progressive and grows in response to opportunities, usually against the advice of more experienced voices.

Jack Wyrtzen, founder of Word of Life Fellowship, is a classic example of a visionary. While still in his twenties, Wyrtzen experimented with radio broadcasting and mass evangelism of youth. Against the advice of most seasoned churchmen in the New York area, Jack felt led of God to begin Saturday night rallies in the heart of Times Square and broadcast the meetings over WHN, which became a fifty thousand watt station at about the time of the first transmission. Only two hundred fifty people showed up for the first rally but within a few weeks crowds had swelled to over a thousand.

From those bold steps of faith in 1941 came Word of Life rallies and broadcasts around the world. Gil Dodds, an early participant in Wyrtzen's meetings and later a chronicler of the Youth for Christ movement, states, "It was not until Jack Wyrtzen stepped out to [follow] God's call that the reality of Youth for Christ caught fire in the hearts of other . . . Youth for Christ leaders. Had he failed, it is safe to say that there would be no Youth for Christ as we know it."[16]

Another visionary was Young Life's Jim Rayburn. Like Wyrtzen, Rayburn had an instinct for ministry that others saw as folly. The purchase of Star Ranch near Colorado Springs in late 1945 seemed absurd to the Young Life board members since the organization had been unable to pay staff salaries and had ended the fiscal year in the black only as a result of a last-minute gift of twenty-five hundred dollars from the board chairman, Herbert J. Taylor. The idea of investing fifty thousand dollars they did not have into a camp they did not need and then attempting to attract high school students from as far away as Texas, New York, and Bellingham, Washington, to that camp in Colorado seemed like a fantasy.[17]

Yet industrialist Herbert J. Taylor was captured by Rayburn's idea. Selling his preferred stock in Club Aluminum, Taylor bought the camp site himself and then leased it back to Young Life at a minimal cost. From that vision for ministry came an entirely new concept of resort camping to reach high school students for Christ. Camp began playing a key role in the evangelization of nonchurched young people. High school students came by the busload first to the Star Ranch and other Young Life camps in Colorado and then to other facilities located in picturesque locations across the continent. The vision shaped the ministry.

Evelyn M. McClusky was a visionary of a different kind. Her idea of teaching the Bible to high school young people caused her to found the Miracle Book Club in 1933. In the process she formed the first parachurch high school youth ministry in the United States. The timing was right. People from Wapato, Washington, to De Land, Florida, shared McClusky's vision. Women spearheaded the movement from which the clubs of Young Life, Youth for Christ, and High School Crusaders (Hi-C) would eventually grow. Numbers vary regarding chapters associated with the club in the thirties. The *Sunday School Times*, which was sometimes known to publish numbers associated with ministries without careful scrutiny, generalized that there may have been a thousand clubs.[18] Yet no matter what the exact numbers were, one conclusion could be drawn safely: a revolutionary type of youth ministry that was specifically focused on high school students, located on or near public school campuses, and not under the direct control of churches or denominations was changing the face of youth ministry across America.

History is filled with visionaries whose brilliance died with them and extended no farther than their individual capacities could carry them.

To create a Christian youth movement, systems were needed for spreading these dreams. To complicate matters, the systems had to be simple enough to tolerate the leadership of people who were not as insightful as the originator.

Simple System

Most of the people who have done youth ministry over the years have been lay people. Even those who have been paid a stipend for their efforts, such as the early Sunday school teachers, were not professionals in any sense. Their time for working with youth was limited. What they needed was a method compatible with their abilities, training, passion, and time constraints for presenting the Christian message to young people.

The Sunday school is the earliest example of a simple system that was used to reach and hold young people. Though there were a number of variations on how to organize a Sunday school the basic components remained the same: an adult used free time, usually on Sunday, to teach biblical truths to a small group of children. Even without curricular materials or training as a teacher, a dedicated person could use this formula and be effective in assisting children to discover the God of the Bible.

D. L. Moody was not an educated man or a trained theologian. Yet the nineteenth-century evangelist started his ministry by gathering children from the streets of Chicago and teaching the Bible to them. Children were delighted to be a part of Mr. Moody's class because they felt loved by the bearded shoe salesman who was their teacher. The more Moody taught the Bible, the more children and adults responded. In time this group grew to become the Moody Church, which now stands at Clark Street and North Avenue in Chicago.

Another example of simple organization was Francis E. Clark's Young People's Society of Christian Endeavor. The activities of the organization were built around a simple pledge. It required each individual in the society to endeavor to know God, participate in the society's committee work, pray, and read the Bible daily as well as support the church and its services unless a person had an excuse that Christ would accept.

Accountability within the Society of Christian Endeavor was important. Once a month, at a consecration meeting, a roll call was held to allow every member to report on his Christian endeavor. Daily prayer and Bible study were assumed to be part of that process, which reminded a person of his consecration to God made once and for all. Participating in committee work was another visible way to demonstrate one's growth process and at the same time to learn skills of church leadership.

The pledge concept was simple. If young people were willing to live up to the pledge they remained members in good standing. If they did not, they were "weeded out." Though the idea seemed rather legalistic to many people, it remained the central core of the society and distinguished Christian Endeavor from what was described as "the old type young people's meetings that made so manifest a failure."[19]

Evelyn M. McClusky's Miracle Book Club, founded a half century later, provided a simple formula of a different sort. Instead of being located in churches under ecclesiastical sponsorship and held on Sunday afternoons, the chapters met as neighborhood study groups during the week for the express purpose of knowing what God has to say in the Bible (i.e., the Miracle Book). Adults were the leaders but young people were the ones who were responsible to get their friends, both churched and unchurched, to attend.[20]

The parachurch club was entrepreneurial in character. Leaders did not have to wade through layers of bureaucratic red tape in order to begin their ministries. Most merely read about Mrs. McClusky's idea and quickly organized chapters in their own communities. Enacting the concept was further simplified when Mrs. McClusky began publishing Bible study materials for these teachers. Though the lessons were criticized as being "prepared by a woman who has a penchant for 'lilies and lace' that make her writing not only feminine but absurd,"[21] they captured the imagination of such figures as Francis and Edith Schaeffer who became the Pennsylvania State Chairpeople for the movement in 1939.

Percy B. Crawford pioneered a fourth simple delivery system for youth ministry. This was the *radio rally*. Actually it was an old idea with a new twist. For years evangelists had held revival services as they traveled from town to town. But with the advent of commercial radio in the late twenties, a new generation of preachers had the opportunity to address entire regions of the country and eventually the whole country through the new medium. The radio audience demanded a different set of communication skills from the evangelists. Sermons that droned on and on were not tolerated by youthful listeners. Crawford became known as the master of the seven-minute sermon. Jack Wyrtzen, who began the longest running series of radio rallies ten years after Crawford originated his broadcasts in Philadelphia, was said to have forbidden anyone on his broadcasts to speak any longer than forty-five seconds. This of course excluded his messages, which carried much of the staccato rhythm learned from Percy Crawford.

The radio rally before a live audience became the focal point for the Youth for Christ movement in the forties. Torrey Johnson and Robert Cook used the idea to give birth to Chicagoland YFC Rallies and then described how such efforts could be made successful in communities across the nation in the book *Reaching Youth for Christ*.[22]

In the 1990s two simple systems sprang out of Southern Baptist churches. True Love Waits mobilized hundreds of thousands of teenagers to make public declarations of their intent to remain sexually pure until marriage before friends and families. See You at the Pole brought millions of students to the flagpole on their high school campuses in mid-September of each year to pray for their campuses and declare their faith before their watching peers.

These simple systems may seem like mere programs today. But in the day in which they were introduced, and for the students who embraced the challenge of serving Christ by utilizing them, each of these systems was enthusiastically received by a loyal band of followers who had been looking for a workable way to touch the lives of young people.

As good as these ideas were, Christian youth movements would not have been created without some promotion and a rapid distribution of their ideas, so the media became the third link in the development of a cycle of youth ministry.

Media Coverage

When we think of media today our minds focus on television, music, movies, Internet, and portable media players. The media of the first three cycles of youth ministry were far less dynamic but still powerful and persuasive. Newspapers and magazines were the agents that stimulated movements and communicated trends in the early days of youth ministry.

Robert Raikes was not the first person to teach or sponsor what came to be known as a Sunday school. Such efforts had been happening in scattered pockets all over England and America. Raikes was a journalist, however, and when he began describing the work of Sunday schools in the *Gloucester Journal*, the response was swift and gratifying. People who thought of themselves as being alone in their efforts discovered they were part of a grassroots movement to minister to children. Others who had never attempted to reach young people were challenged by published reports and became involved in the Sunday school movement.

The formula repeated itself with the coming of the Christian Endeavor movement. After Francis E. Clark had been successful in reaching the youth of his community and other churches in the region had experienced similar achievements, he wrote an article for *The Congregationalist* entitled "How One Church Looks After Its Young People." The response was dramatic. Letters came from all over the nation and as far away as Foochow, China, inquiring about the society.

In order to keep up with the flood of questions, Clark wrote a book that placed in manual form the procedures for molding a Christian Endeavor Society. The book standardized the development of the society while keeping the spotlight on the essential elements of the movement.[23] By 1887 it was essential to provide a regular publication to tie the rapidly growing movement together and so *The Golden Rule*, later called *The Christian Endeavor World*, was begun. It was both a constant source of new programming ideas and a means of cross-pollinating ideas.

Fifty years later the *Sunday School Times* popularized the Miracle Book Club. After the first six chapters were formed in Portland, Oregon, Charles G. Trumbell, editor of the *Sunday School Times*, heard about the club and asked Mrs. McClusky to write several articles for his nationally circulated paper. They appeared during the summer of 1935 and the mail came pouring in. McClusky, who, like the founder of Christian Endeavor, was an excellent writer, determined to set the criterion for Miracle Book Club chapters and so wrote a book entitled *Torch and Sword* in 1937. At about the same time she began publishing *The Conqueror*, a monthly report of ideas and news from chapters as far away as Adelaide, Australia.

Unlike the leaders of Christian Endeavor, who had outstanding organizational skills and an ability to use the media effectively, Mrs. McClusky's abilities were primarily in writing and public speaking. As radio began to supersede the printed page as the primary means of stimulating a Christian youth movement and men with stronger organizational skills absorbed the fragmented Miracle Book Club chapters into new club systems, Mrs. McClusky's publications faded from sight. Yet her imprint had been left primarily through a very effective use of media.

It was the Youth for Christ movement that made the switch from the passive medium of the printed page to a more active channel of communication, radio. No longer were leaders dependent upon adults to read youth ministry ideas and then translate them into ministry structures for young people. Young people of the thirties and forties became the consumers. Percy Crawford, Jack Wyrtzen, and Billy Graham spoke directly to the youth of the nation. It was like having a national youth group.

The peak of the radio rally era was in the late forties. If the influence of Youth for Christ was to be sustained, resources had to be provided for youth work on the local level. Adults were still the key for continuity and leadership, and magazines were important for exchanging ideas and feeding the grassroots movement. *Youth for Christ Magazine* and *Young Life Magazine* became a virtual bulletin board of ideas. Then *Moody Monthly* got into the act. Hazel Goddard, Wally Howard, and later Tom

Bade left Young Life to edit the young people's section of the magazine while Youth for Christ leaders like Jack Daniel, Gordon McLean, and Warren Wiersbe later contributed articles.

True Love Waits and See You at the Pole received similar media attention. Popular interest brought over four hundred national and international news outlets to inquire about True Love Waits including *Newsweek*, *Rolling Stone*, *Teen Magazine*, *Family Circle*, *Life* magazine, *The Phil Donohue Show*, and many newspapers and radio stations. Far less attention was paid to See You at the Pole, but it was still enough to spread the idea around the world.

Throughout the history of denominational Protestant youth ministries in America, articles in denominational publications led to the development of magazines and program materials dedicated to the development of youth ministries in their local churches. As denominational youth societies grew, attention shifted toward national and regional conferences that attracted denominational young people from across the nation.

Media coverage alone was not enough to sustain the new Christian youth movements. There had to be face-to-face contact in large group settings.

A Spokesperson

Enthusiasm for a movement is seldom maintained in isolation. In each cycle of youth ministry there have been people who have traveled extensively in order to spread the vision and reinvigorate the people already committed to the movement. "Mail-order" clubs do not last very long.

Jack Hamilton, the father of the Youth for Christ clubs, received hundreds of letters in response to his articles about high school clubs in *Youth for Christ Magazine* during the early fifties. Since there were relatively few materials available, all Jack could do was send out a few mimeographed sheets and keep their addresses on file. Then when he had a trip scheduled, instead of taking public transportation, the master club man would obtain a car from an agency that wanted a car moved from Chicago to the East or West Coast and set up a route that would allow him to meet groups of these young people face-to-face without risking automobile breakdowns in his aging car. Sometimes Hamilton's stopover would be no longer than an hour or two before he was off to meet the next group of students a hundred miles down the road.

Hamilton was the spokesman for YFC clubs. His constant travel enabled him to both spread and strengthen the vision held by students of reaching their high school peers for Christ through their clubs. The pace was exhausting and yet personal contact was essential if the club strategy was going to work.

Incessant travel appears to be essential during the early days of a movement. The Wesleyan movement was weaned as John Wesley traveled by horseback preaching several times each day. The Sunday school movement was extended into the Mississippi Valley as missionaries sent by the American Sunday School Union traveled to "every desolate place" in the midwest planting Sunday schools to reach young people.

Before his death in 1927 it was estimated that Francis Clark traveled over a million miles doing the work of Christian Endeavor. Though he served as statesman for the movement his primary responsibility was addressing every level of the movement from the great conferences to individual societies.

Evelyn McClusky, the founder of Miracle Book Club, and Maurice Jacques, the national president, traveled constantly in the late thirties, addressing MBC rallies, conferences, and chapters. There appears to be a strong correlation between the strength of the movement and the travels of its leaders.

Billy Graham, the first employee of Youth for Christ International, reported that he traveled one hundred thirty five thousand miles during the 1945–46 school year and that he "got a little note from the United Air Lines saying that [he] had traveled on United Air Lines more than any other civilian in the United States last year." Graham was only one of many Youth for Christ speakers of that era but it was the slender North Carolinian who captured the attention of the media and inspired the Saturday night rally movement. In 1949 the Minneapolis Star asserted that Youth for Christ had covered 1,450 cities.

Richard Ross, who had his youth group sign True Love Waits commitment cards at Tulip Grove Baptist Church in Hermitage, Texas, became the spokesman for the movement and appeared on numerous television programs and provided a steady flow of interviews to journalists who fed information to outlets across the nation.

Face-to-face contact between youth leaders and their constituency in the field was essential for these Christian youth movements. This personal contact in turn stimulated the last vital organ that goes into the anatomy of a Christian youth movement: the sense that God is doing something special. Some people would call it revival.

Revival

Up to this point, the social scientist might point out, the description of a Christian youth movement could be explained entirely in sociological terms. It might even be depicted as mechanical or contrived. But the participants and those who have studied youth movements over the years have an entirely different perspective. They were convinced they were part of a special working of God and that God would show up, changing the lives of youthful believers.

"Revival is here!" wrote Harold J. Ockenga in *Youth for Christ Magazine*, describing the meetings held by Billy Graham in Boston as the second half of the twentieth century began.[24] In a city that was 76 percent Roman Catholic, was traditionally hostile to revivalism, and was a mecca for the hundred thousand students who came to Harvard, MIT, Boston University, and a host of other great institutions of higher learning, the pastor of historic Park Street Church could explain the overflow crowds in the city's largest arenas in no other way.

A sense of revival was the mood of the movement. Reports from college campuses to major cities, from rural communities to private high schools, were constantly published in evangelical periodicals. As early as 1944 the *Sunday School Times* linked Jack Wyrtzen and Percy Crawford to "The Revival in Our Midst."[25] Conservative Christians were convinced that God was doing something special, and the Youth for Christ movement was near the heart of it.

Leaders were so convinced of the revival that one person documented a prayer meeting on movie film before a Chicago Stadium rally that twenty-eight thousand people attended during October 1944. There was a sense of destiny. These young visionaries wanted to document for history not only the large events but the smaller events that led up to them.

This same sense of revival was associated with the earlier cycles of youth ministry. R. P. Anderson, in reflecting back over the first fifty years of Christian Endeavor commented, "The church was ripe for such a Movement. Christian Endeavor . . . brought to young people of the world a new and easily comprehended ideal: 'What would Jesus do if He were in my place?' It opened up new fields of service. It stimulated the spiritual life of the multitudes, and above all it enthroned Christ."[26]

Robert W. Lynn describes the role of revival in the American Sunday school movement in the nineteenth century. "At the very heart of the educational ecology of the evangelical Protestants was revival. Around this center clustered an array of enterprises, propelled into existence and maintained by a determination to convert the whole population. The Sunday school, as embodied by the American Sunday School Union, was one of the first offshoots of the Revival."[27]

A report from a section of New Jersey during the 1820s speaks of just such a revival atmosphere:

No sooner were [Sunday] schools commenced in destitute places than a change was visible in the morals of the children and the inhabitants of the neighborhood. Profane swearing, intemperance, and Sabbath break-ing, which formerly prevailed to an alarming extent, in a great measure ceased. . . . This was not all; from a number of reports of [Sunday] schools belonging to this [Sunday school] Union, it appears that many teachers and scholars have been made recipients of divine and saving grace.[28]

Speaking at the Yale Divinity School in 1888, H. Clay Trumbull tied the Sunday school movement with the great religious reforms of the church since the days of John the Baptist and the Apostle Peter. Though such revivals have been brought about by preaching, "religious training of any people has been attained, and the results of any great reformation have been made permanent, only through . . . teaching such as forms the distinguishing characteristics of the . . . Sunday-school."[29]

There were pockets of spiritual awakening in the 1990s and early part of the twenty-first century. Christian colleges experienced extended periods of repentance and renewed commitment to Jesus Christ in the mid-1990s. The shootings on April 20, 1999, at Columbine High School in Littleton, Colorado, along with various other shooting episodes that targeted Christian students generated a temporary awakening among the circles of Christian young people affected by the violence. In Brownsville, Florida, a sustained period of spiritual awakening had an effect upon the young people of the church. Looking back on the decade, it would be inaccurate to describe it as a time of youthful revival. Yet the growing hunger for prayer, worship, singing, and contemplation among Chris-tian teenagers and their friends may suggest the coming of a revival of a different type.

In each youth ministry cycle the participants and observers sensed that God was doing something exciting and they felt privileged to be a part of that moving of the Spirit. Extended times of prayer were common in the early stages of each movement along with the sense that there was a fresh wind of the Spirit blowing.

But Fifty Year Cycles?

Once I was convinced that the idea of youth ministry going in year cycles was valid, one question lingered. Would Kondratieff's idea of a fifty-year economic cycle transfer to a sequence of similar length in youth ministry? The history of youth ministry seemed to suggest such a pattern but I wondered if anyone else had identified the half-century configuration.

John Perkins, the founder of Voice of Calvary Ministries, envisioned a fifty-year span of effectiveness for his Mississippi-based organization. Regarding the people who had been trained through his ministry Perkins commented, "I feel good about the black leaders that have emerged in Mendenhall and Jackson. Things will go on in Mendenhall for fifty years. Things will go on in Jackson for fifty years. After fifty years, anything can go wrong."[30]

Though the black leader was not a youth worker, his idea of a span of effective ministry corresponded with the Kondratieff cycle in duration. It suggested a length of time in which the founder and those most closely associated with him could keep a ministry on track. While the organization might continue beyond that period, effectiveness of efforts would not be as certain.

The most startling confirmation came from the archives of Young Life. As the movement prepared for its fiftieth anniversary in 1990 (celebrated nearly eighteen months shy of the fiftieth anniversary of its incorporation), word circulated that the founder had anticipated that Young Life would only last fifty years. I wrote to Doug Burleigh, then president of Young Life, and he graciously confirmed the rumor by providing a copy of the original articles of incorporation dated October 16, 1941.

Article IV stated simply, "The term for which it [Young Life] is to exist is fifty years." Whether it was a legal formality of the day or a purposeful statement by Jim Rayburn and the board of directors is not clear. The thought, however, does seem to be consistent with the founder and his concepts of ministry.[31] The idea of a fifty-year cycle in the field of youth ministry appears to be a valid concept for understanding Protestant youth ministries in America.

Conclusion

Three factors tended to converge when a new cycle of youth ministry began. *Secularization* and a loss of Christian moorings, compounded by times of *social unrest* and change, in settings where there was a critical mass of Christians from the *economic middle class*, gave rise to innovation in helping young people experience God's presence. Five characteristics shaped these movements—a visionary, a simple system, media coverage, a spokesperson, and a sense of revival, that is, the sense that God was actually involved in what was happening both individually and on a larger scale. In the remainder of the book this pattern will be traced through three cycles of youth ministry, and the potential for a fourth cycle will be examined.

part 2

Youth Ministry Jazz

The Period of Associations (1824–75)

Jazz is created out of dissatisfaction. It is a fusion of old and new. A reaction to accepted harmonic structure and rhythms set the stage for this distinctively American sound. New forms of syncopation dominate, clashing with the ears of traditionalists and appealing to the tastes of a new audience. For many the New Orleans "noise" of black musicians was just that. Jazz, to traditionalists, sounded like a gigantic clash characterized by an "every man for himself" struggle among musicians who wanted to grab the limelight. The call for musical revolution was a rejection of classical music.

To many Protestant church leaders, the youth group resembled jazz. Their sounds did not fit the accepted norms of Christian spirituality. Traditionalists believed that young people should be satisfied, even proud, of Christian worship and church traditions. The means of coming to God, refined over the years, provided the clarity of an oratorio. The pastor was the conductor, and the instrumentalists and vocalists were to respond on cue.

In my book *The Coming Revolution in Youth Ministry* I argued that youth ministry followed a cyclical pattern, starting with appropriate responses to the issues facing youth at a given time and stagnating within fifty years. The study focused primarily on parachurch ministries like the Sunday school, YMCA, Christian Endeavor, and the Youth for Christ movement (in which I included Young Life and Fellowship of Christian Athletes).

After *The Coming Revolution in Youth Ministry* was published, readers and reviewers asked, "What about the church? Weren't any revolutionary initiatives taken in local churches?" This question has stimulated further research. In one sense, all improvisation in youth ministry emanated from local churches. After all, it was Christian parents and church leaders who had the most vested interests in the spiritual journey of their children. In fact, church people were the ones who created the new sounds for youth ministry, though many found their only audience outside the walls of the church. Yet at key times and in key places the sounds of youth ministry jazz were found within the church as well.

The frustrating part about such a study was that people who did work with adolescents seldom took the time to record or carefully document what they were doing. Most just did the work of helping form the spiritual lives of the rising generation. Then, without fanfare, these dedicated people went on with their Christian lives never dreaming that someone would be interested in what they had done to disciple youth.

Hundreds of pastors in churches across the United States and Canada experimented with forms of youth groups. Each of these youth ministry improvisations addressed local concerns for the "youth problem." One pastor who left a record behind was Rev. Theodore Cuyler of Lafayette Avenue Presbyterian Church in Brooklyn, New York, often considered the first American suburb. Cuyler's efforts form the basis for describing how an early church-based youth group functioned.

The second section of this book focuses on the beginnings of youth groups in America. Local improvisation begun in England but adapted to the American experience shaped the beginnings of Protestant youth ministry in the United States. This first of three cycles of Protestant youth ministry in America was the period of associations (1824–75).

Chapter 5 uses Mark Twain's classic, *The Adventures of Tom Sawyer*, to describe life in the early 1840s at St. Petersburg, Missouri. Tom and his friends live right in the middle of the first cycle of youth ministry in the United States. This period was dominated by three agencies from England: the Sunday school, which Tom hated, the juvenile temperance movement, which initially appealed to Tom, and the YMCA, which came after the period covered in Twain's book. The Sunday school and

YMCA share clear concerns for the spirituality of youth and are the focus of the chapter.

The juvenile temperance movement is the focus of chapter 6. While the temperance emphasis dealt with the lifestyle issue of alcohol consumption and thus was more concerned with an evidence of sanctification (over which Protestants differed in opinion) than with Christian spirituality, the movement nonetheless set the structure for the formal emergence of Protestant youth groups in the second cycle of youth ministry.

Chapter 7 draws upon Martin Scorsese's graphic depiction of *The Gangs of New York*, set in the years leading up to the Civil War, to capture the turbulent life of young people in America's first world class city. Responding to the spiritual needs of the youth of the city, one pastor, Rev. Theodore Cuyler, in one church, Lafayette Avenue Presbyterian Church, drew upon his experience in the Prayer Revival of 1857–59 to foster Christian spirituality among his young people. Cuyler's innovations in one local church became the basis for the next cycle of youth ministry.

This period of associations (1824–75) was perhaps the most improvisational period of youth ministry. Like Dixieland Jazz, the theme of helping youth to know and experience God in life-changing ways jumped from player to player. Sometimes pastors and at other times parishioners led the way. The lead switched between men and women. Occasionally young people stepped in to improvise and assume the lead. Yet amid all the variations, the constant theme was preparing young people to be available when God showed up in their lives. The major associations formed during this period shaped the sounds of youth ministry for years to come.

From this period came the highly structured church youth groups that would sweep across the nation and the world at the end of the nineteenth century. Seldom led by educational theory, Protestant adults merely responded to the needs they observed in the young people around them and attempted to make a difference.

Tom Sawyer and the British Invasion

The Period of Associations (1824–75)

In Mark Twain's *The Adventures of Tom Sawyer*, Tom hated Sunday school passionately. It was downright unnatural to him. Aunt Polly made the boy wash himself with soap and water. Then he had to put on the "other clothes," ones used only on Sundays. The Sunday attire included his neat roundabout buttoned up to his chin, shirt collar turned down over his shoulders, and shoes thoroughly coated with tallow adorning his feet.

Sabbath-school hours were from nine to half past ten and it was followed by the church service. It was a long time for a fellow to sit and do recitations, which is why "showing off" occupied so much of the time for Tom and his buddies.

Mr. Walters, the superintendent, was a very earnest man with a sincere and honest heart. He had set up a system by which a student could earn different colored tickets for reciting Bible verses. When the tickets collected indicated that a person had memorized two thousand verses he would be honored by the superintendent and be awarded with a Bible. It was not the Bible Tom wanted, but the honor of being acknowledged in front of the entire Sunday school. To that end Tom traded his treasures, such as fish hooks and licorice, for enough tickets to obtain the award.

Then, to the amazement and dismay of the adults present, Tom proudly paraded to the front and claimed his prize.

Usually it was the older children, the teenagers, who had learned enough verses to be acknowledged by Mr. Walters. Tom, by contrast, was not old enough to have lost his first tooth. But in St. Petersburg, Missouri, during the 1840s there was little distinction between grade schoolers and adolescents. They were all considered to be children until they started working or got married. Yet even at his young age Tom Sawyer had learned to play the Sunday school game.

The Sunday school Tom Sawyer attended was a vital part of the first cycle of youth ministry in the United States. This cycle received its initial boost in 1824 when the American Sunday School Union was formed in Philadelphia and became the first national parachurch agency dedicated to establishing Sunday schools throughout the West. Of course, "West" at that time meant anything beyond New York's Hudson River. For the American Sunday School Union, the West stretched from Harrisburg, Pennsylvania, through the Ohio Valley and down the Mississippi River to New Orleans.

Of course there had been local attempts to help young people mature in their Christian faith, some of which looked very much like the British initiative called Sunday school, which quickly became a national movement. Within the following decade, the juvenile temperance movement, a second movement from the British Isles, gave Christian adults another means of shaping the lives of young people. Though focused on abstinence from alcoholic beverages, the movement provided a means of preserving youth for a life of Christian living.

Both movements were stimulated during the middle of the century by the introduction of the Young Men's Christian Association and Young Women's Christian Association, two parachurch agencies that, like the Sunday school and juvenile temperance movements, had their roots in England. The first youth ministry cycle began to wane following the Civil War and came to a conclusion in 1875 with a Supreme Court decision that was instrumental in establishing the modern-day public high school.

Westward Expansion of the Nation

Tom and his buddies, Huck Finn and Joe Harper, peered at the ferryboat from the bushes on Jackson's Island. Playing out a fantasy of childhood, the three boys had run away from home to become "pirates" and had set up camp on the island three miles below their home town of St. Petersburg. While the steam-driven ferryboat was being used to look for the "lost" boys, it and many like it were key factors in the settlement of little towns all along the Mississippi River and beyond. The boys were viewing not only a search for themselves but also for a national destiny.

As long as the nation was nestled along the eastern sea coast of North America in relatively isolated pockets, the Christian education of each succeeding generation of young people was not of great concern to the broader Christian community. The responsibility was fulfilled fairly adequately by the family and such school systems as were available.

But as the west began opening to settlement and people moved beyond the Allegheny Mountains of western Pennsylvania, concerns were expressed about the undisciplined frontier environment and the damage it might inflict upon young people. Enormous changes took place within society that set the context for the first cycle in American youth ministry.

Tom Sawyer was a product of the westward expansion of the nation. His hometown on the banks of the Mississippi River was settled in 1818, just about the time a financial panic was felt across the young nation. Steamboats, which carried goods and raw products along the muddy waters of the Mississippi River, occasionally stopped at their little town and served as the community's link with the rapid changes in the country.

The technology of the steam engine and the beginnings of the Industrial Revolution in America altered the patterns of people's lives, especially the manner in which they earned their livelihood. Factories replaced family-run shops for the production of goods. Informal patterns of support and education found in the established communities of the east shattered as families migrated west and young people moved to cities in search of jobs and to the frontier in search of adventure.

A network of canal systems connected the heartland of America with the rivers and lakes of the nation, allowing raw goods to move to the markets of the nation and the world. Best known is the Erie Canal, opened in 1825, which linked the Hudson River with Lake Erie and the rest of the Great Lakes. The Illinois and Michigan Canal opened in 1848 connecting Lake Michigan with the Mississippi River. Before the railroad, canals provided transportation for people as well as goods, employed vast numbers of immigrants, and fed the Industrial Revolution that changed the lives of rural youth.

The slavery issue, as Huck Finn would later find out, alienated brother from brother and divided the nation. Tension was increased in 1928 when Andrew Jackson, an unrefined frontiersman and military hero, was elected president of the United States. Though popular with the common people, Jackson was feared by the eastern business interests. These fears were further agitated in 1832 when he vetoed a bill and effectively killed the national bank giving the impression that he was not in favor of sound economic policies.

Change surged like a wave across the nation, breaking briefly along the banks of the Mississippi and then cresting again as the tide of events continued to carry a new generation westward. Left in the backwater of the nation's expansion, however, were the children of the frontiersmen whose values were shaped more by a desire for adventure and wealth than by a desire to know God or embrace historic Christian convictions.

Grassroots Movements

Social societies brought youth together. In the rapidly growing cities of the nineteenth century, few governmental services protected citizens. Voluntary fire companies and militias, boarding houses for people from similar industries or places of origin in rural America, and ethnic and native gangs provided opportunities for young people to find places to belong. Many of these agencies informally included younger adolescents and even children. While many social reformers of the day focused on the fighting, excess drinking, and other negative aspects of these societies, the informal structures gave young people an identity and a place to belong in otherwise impersonal cities.[1]

Efforts to protect the youth of America from the evils of society and to build Christian character sprang up all over the nation. The old music of the church no longer appealed to young people. The Tom Sawyers of the world needed new sounds. One attempt to provide fresh sounds was the Cadets of Temperance, which Tom joined, being attracted primarily by their flashy regalia rather than their requirement that members promise to abstain from smoking, chewing, and profanity.

The Cadets of Temperance originated in 1843 for the purpose of maintaining the good moral character of young persons of either sex between the ages of twelve and twenty-one. In order to ensure good character, members took a pledge not to drink, as a beverage, any intoxicating liquor, wine, or cider, so long as they remained a member. By 1891, membership had grown to ten thousand adolescents.[2] Mark Twain took the liberty of adding smoking, chewing, and profanity to the obligations for the purposes of his novel.

Immediately upon joining the Cadets a problem arose for Tom. He found himself suddenly tormented with a desire to drink and swear, which only the hope of wearing the Cadet's red sash on the fourth of July could temporarily allay. Even with such motivation, Tom could only endure the agony for a few days. He resigned only to discover that once he was free to drink and swear, he had no desire to do so.

Throughout the 1830s and 1840s, young men's temperance societies came into being in the cities of the land. Many were sponsored by employers who were concerned both with the moral standards of their employees and the loss of productive labor that would result from a lack of sobriety. The activities of the societies would indicate, however, that the primary objective of these groups was not the redemption of lower-class workers so much as the preservation of literate, respectable, and evangelical youth.[3] (The contribution of the juvenile temperance movement will be covered more fully in chapter 6.)

Such were the dynamics of grassroots associations that sprang up all across the nation during the first half of the nineteenth century. Most of these societies featured a type of pomp and ceremony that attracted young people to participate, and then the associations attempted to stimulate an interest in accepting the Christian values they advocated. Frank Otis Erb documented a number of such endeavors formed during this period, of which the temperance societies were but one example.[4]

Singing-schools, though dating back to the previous century, became more popular during the early years of the nineteenth century. The schools, which some people feel were the forerunners of modern church choirs, provided a place where young people could meet together in a socially acceptable manner apart from most adults and participate in an activity which they found enjoyable.

Music books suitable for such classes began to multiply as early as 1770. The *Salem Gazette* of September 1808 invited the public to a performance of the *Hallelujah Chorus* by a choir under the direction of Samuel Holyoke, and by 1821 the *Enterpeiad* of Boston reported similar concerts from Portland, Maine, to Augusta, Georgia. The significance of singing-schools was that they were essentially parachurch functions in which young men and women could gather in a natural setting and join in a common enterprise. It should be noted that even after youth societies were established later in the nineteenth century, choirs remained in existence by becoming a part of the church's program.

Young people's missionary societies were another expression of the era. While college students were highly influential in beginning the modern missionary movement early in the century, by the time the first cycle of youth ministry was well under way, young people's missionary societies had followed the model of similar women's groups in the church and were attracting young people to donate money, study, and pray for the heathen of the world.

By midcentury Young Men's Christian Associations were common in larger cities. Catering to young businessmen, associations provided their membership with services appealing to needs to become established in business. Inspirational lectures, well-stocked libraries, and access to local business leaders provided incentives to join. Though limited to those between the ages of eighteen and thirty-five, the associations frequently included young boys seeking to find their way into the business community.[5]

Denominationally-sponsored "union" or citywide societies further enhanced the effectiveness of these efforts. The Missionary Assistance Society of London was composed

> chiefly of young persons of both sexes. Their officers are young men, whose ages according to their constitution must not exceed a certain limitation. They must be of the Baptist persuasion and in good standing in some church of that denomination. . . . They hold a monthly meeting for business, which is open and closed by prayer and singing appropriate hymns. They also have a monthly prayer meeting.[6]

It should be remembered that the definition of "young people" was far different in the nineteenth century than it is in the United States at the beginning of the twenty-first century. The phrase referred to people from puberty to their late twenties or beyond. Thus leadership for such parachurch union societies was drawn from what we would consider young adults today.

As early as the 1840s and 1850s local churches began experimenting with more generalized youth societies on a local basis. Some were designed only for young men, such as the Lutheran "Juenglingsverein" headed by Johann Buenger in St. Louis. But most were coeducational efforts in isolated churches scattered throughout Baptist, Presbyterian, Lutheran, and Brethren in Christ denominations. Instead of being as task-oriented as temperance societies, singing-schools, or missionary societies, these associations imitated the cultures of the sponsoring churches.

Scattered attempts to provide societies for Christian young people were identified with some of the leading pastors in New England. Cotton Mather, the fiery Baptist preacher from Rhode Island, introduced a "Devotional Society" in 1677 at which young people prayed, sang psalms, and then responded to a question proposed the week before. Despite his reputation for being stern, Mather permitted, even encouraged, anyone present to give whatever answer they pleased. Perhaps the most amazing aspect of Mather's proposal was that it was initially made when he was but sixteen years old.[7]

A half century later, Jonathan Edwards followed Mather's example in his Congregational church in Northampton, Massachusetts. Instead of discussion, however, Edwards emphasized prayer and the radical new idea of singing the hymns of Isaac Watts. Prayer manuals, such as Watts's *Guide to Prayer*, may have helped facilitate public prayer by young people. The music of public worship limited the congregation to singing the psalms using a limited number of worship tunes, so Watts's words and tunes provided a form of youthful innovation. Edwards used these times for instruction as well.[8]

The Sunday School

Late in the eighteenth century, Sunday schools modeled after the work of Robert Raikes in England began appearing in America. Yet it was "generally conceded by American students of the first-hand documents that such schools of a character founded by Raikes, with all their essential features, were found in America long before his day," commented historian Edwin Wilber Rice.[9] The sudden popularity of the English model gave rise to coordinated efforts to use the Bible or various catechisms to teach poor children to read.

In East Coast cities and the South, without a strong concept of the common school to provide education to all children as there was in New England, Sunday school became the de facto educational system. In Pawtucket, Rhode Island, Samuel Slater organized Sunday schools for the children who worked in his factories. On a plantation in Virginia, William Elliot set aside time each Sunday to instruct his own children. At a separate time, his slave children received similar instruction. Children from neighboring plantations were invited to join the efforts to learn to read the Bible. Under leadership by Francis Asbury, Methodists adopted the idea and made the teaching of slaves the primary purpose of the schools. Described in twenty-first-century terms, Sunday school began targeting at-risk children.

In urban settings the Sunday school was seen by Christian lay leaders as the hope for evangelizing the children of poor immigrants who had freshly arrived from Europe. Divie Bethune and Eleazer Lord founded the New York Sunday School Union to evangelize and transform the urban social structure of New York. Using the Bible as their textbook, Sunday school teachers attempted to correct the behavior of the "vilest classes" of children in New York. Patterns of Sabbath-breaking, improper dress, and disorderly behavior needed to be replaced by industrious behavior at work and punctuality at school and church. Though this approach generated criticisms of social control by writers such as Joseph Kett, the more basic desire was to introduce youth to the spiritual life characterized by personal salvation and the benefits resulting from sanctification. United efforts gave rise to missionary endeavors that resulted in thirteen schools for Native people and several for African Americans.[10]

In 1791, the First Day Society formed in Philadelphia, the nation's largest city. Concerned by the decline of the apprentice system, which served as a type of educational system, the society proposed providing "proper opportunities of instruction . . . (to) the offspring of indigent parents . . . pervious to their being apprenticed to trades."[11] Founded by an interdenominational group of primarily Protestant community leaders, the society hired instructors who taught reading skills for the purpose of enabling children to become contributors to the American experience. Occasionally teachers would take children to church with them, though the two institutions were quite separate.

Around 1800, enrollments in First Day Society schools began dropping. There was a growth of charity schools in Philadelphia run by Protestant congregations, and it was supposed that the decline was because of the redundancy of efforts. Throughout the country educational functions took the forms of free schools, pay schools, subscription schools, and common schools. The last First Day Society school closed in 1819.[12]

Alongside the decline of the Raikes type of school, a more evangelistic type of Sunday school emerged that continued to teach reading skills, but these were means to a greater end. The end for the schools was for children to adopt an evangelical worldview, including a personal experience of regeneration. The growth of this new form of Sunday school was remarkable. In the final full year of the First Day Society, four schools functioned, while forty-one of the evangelical Sundays schools spread across Philadelphia. In 1824, when the American Sunday School Union was founded, it included 723 affiliated schools, including sixty-eight in Philadelphia. By 1832, 301,358 children, nearly 8 percent of the children in the nation, were enrolled. In Philadelphia, the percentage was 27.9.[13]

One factor that contributed to the growth of the Sunday school was the inclusion of the children of church members in the schools. The strength of Bible instruction in Sunday schools aided Protestant parents in their role of Christian instruction. Anne M. Boylan reported:

> Members of New York's Brick Presbyterian Church, who had formed two Sunday schools for missionary purposes in 1816, noted in 1832 that their pupils "were no longer drawn exclusively from the poor and unchurched families, but included the children of Presbyterian parents." Likewise, members of Boston's Park Street (Congregational) Church, who in 1817 described the schools as "missionary instruction" for the poor, in 1829 organized a school for church member's children. In Richmond, Virginia, the Monumental (Episcopal) Church reported in 1829 that its Sunday school was "no longer confined to the poorer classes of society" but included church member's children.[14]

This simple but profound change established the Sunday school as essential to the fabric of Protestant churches in America.

Mississippi Valley Enterprise of the American Sunday School Union produced the first sounds of youth ministry, gaining a national hearing that resulted in the first cycle of youth ministry. Though grassroots youth ministries were growing more common, the vision of the Philadelphia-based union in 1830 defined the initial cycle of youth ministry. Simply stated, they wanted "in reliance upon divine aid, . . . within two years, [to] establish a Sunday-school in every destitute place where it is practicable throughout the Valley of the Mississippi."[15] The undertaking, which was first suggested and partially financed by New York businessman Arthur Tappan, targeted the nine states which stretched from Michigan to Louisiana, an estimated one million, three hundred thousand square miles with a population of four million, of which four hundred thousand were believed to be children and youth.

Stephen Paxson emerged as the best known Sunday school missionary of the campaign. Traveling on his horse, "Robert Raikes," he ventured from the Allegheny to the Rocky Mountains, organizing a reported 1,314 Sunday schools populated by 83,405 scholars and teachers.[16]

The campaign was an enormous success. It was computed that over half of the eight to ten thousand new communities in the Mississippi Valley were provided with Sunday schools in a two-year period. In addition, over a million volumes supplied by the American Sunday School Union were put into circulation through libraries in order that the young scholars would have something profitable to read. Professions of faith during the effort exceeded thirty thousand.

Encouraged by the response to the Mississippi Valley venture, the Sunday School Union accepted an invitation to attempt the same type of enterprise in the South. While hampered by financial problems, limited personnel, and less than adequate facilities, the effort still had an impact upon the youth of the region.

As the first cycle of youth ministry progressed, the Sunday school emerged as the most widespread agency for working with youth. Many of the key elements of the other grassroots movements were enfolded into the curriculum of the Sunday school. Singing, missions, and temperance all became part of the lay-led teaching program. Though many Sunday school missionaries took the initial steps to establish new ministries, the movement rapidly turned into a lay-driven enterprise with the strengths and weaknesses still encountered today.

Bethel Mission, a ministry of Brooklyn's Plymouth Church, pastored by Henry Ward Beecher, exemplified the breadth of the Sunday school strategy in the mid-nineteenth century. In addition to the educational programs the mission provided, Sunday evening services, weekly recreation and entertainment events, and reading rooms attracted and maintained the loyalty of mechanics and boys.[17]

By the time Tom Sawyer arrived on the scene in the mid-1840s, the Sunday school had fallen into some counterproductive ruts. The American Sunday School Union had found it impossible to provide leadership or supervision for the thousands of new Sunday schools they had established during the 1830s and before long the lay-led agencies had degenerated into oral recitations of memory verses and presentations of ill-prepared Bible lessons. The "Union" or community Sunday schools fragmented according to denominational lines in many locations and the influence of the Sunday school began to wane.

The American Civil War (1861–65) disrupted virtually every aspect of American life. The Sunday school was no exception. In the South the leadership of the lay movement volunteered or were conscripted for the war effort. Paper for Sunday school materials became scarce. Children once again assumed roles of adults to maintain life on the home front. In the North, though Sunday school efforts stalled, the effect of the war was not as great. In Illinois, Dwight L. Moody of Chicago and William Reynolds of Peoria strategized on how to reinvigorate the Sunday school after the war, claiming that "teaching the children of this country the way to Christ and then building them up in Christ was the greatest work in the world."[18] Their efforts served as but a rear guard action as the Sunday school would soon be captured by religious publishing houses with the creation of the International Uniform Lessons starting in 1872. Youth ministry would soon need a new champion.

Many youth workers may have a problem making Sunday school synonymous with youth ministry. For many youth pastors, the Sunday school, if the church maintains one on the high school level, is the least productive part of the ministry. But in the mid-nineteenth century the situation was far different. The Sunday school and church services may have been the only place in town where Christian young people could socialize in an acceptable manner. Few were in school. In most communities formal schooling ended before puberty began. As late as 1870 only 1.2 percent of all students enrolled in public education were in the ninth grade or above, including college. This compares with over 30 percent of the public school population enrolled at the ninth grade level or above as the nineteenth century came to a close.

Young people of the mid-nineteenth century experienced a vacuum. They were neither children nor adults, yet they were expected to work and live like adults. The problem was that society was changing so rapidly that no one knew exactly how adults should live. The discovery of gold in the Sierra Nevada mountains doubled the nation's wealth during the decade leading up to the Civil War. Foreign trade tripled during the

1850s, and when Commodore Perry opened Japan to trade the American merchant marine was the ruler of the seas. More than thirty thousand miles of rails connected every region of the country, replacing plank roads, canals, river boats, and short rail-lines except on the West Coast. Steam-driven factories continued to centralize job opportunities in cities and attract young people from the spiritual and social insularity of their home communities.

The YMCA

Midway through the nineteenth century, another youth movement arrived in North America. Though isolated associations for Christian young men functioned in various cities in America, the Young Men's Christian Association (1851) and later the Young Women's Christian Association (1858) became a movement and spread across the continent. Like the Sunday school and temperance societies before them, the movements began in England and then quickly spread to North America, where organizational mechanisms led to their rapid growth. The purpose of these parachurch agencies was to help Christian young people retain their Christian commitments after they had moved into the urban jungles where jobs were available.

Following twenty years of evangelistic efforts by a loosely connected Montreal group that called themselves "Young Men's Society," the YMCA took root in Montreal where church leaders approved it, and officers were elected on December 9, 1851. Just before the end of the year, a similar group meeting in Boston organized a second YMCA in America.

The constitution of the Boston YMCA describes the vision of the early ministry. It hoped to become

> a social organization of those in whom the love of Christ has produced love to men; who shall meet the young stranger as he enters our city, take him by the hand, direct him to a boarding house where he may find a quiet home pervaded with Christian influences, introduce him to the Church and Sabbath school, bring him to the rooms of the Association, and in every way throw around him good influences, so that he may feel that he is not a stranger, but that noble and Christian spirits care for his soul.[19]

Anxious for their vision for ministry to spread, the Boston YMCA, as would happen with the major agencies of the next two cycles of youth ministry as well, actively promoted their idea. Ten thousand copies of their constitution were distributed to clergymen and denominational leaders throughout New England and beyond. Soon membership in Boston reached sixteen hundred. By the end of 1853 the movement had spread to towns like Portland, Maine; San Francisco, California; and Peoria, Illinois. The following year the number had swelled to forty-nine and by the end of the decade there were said to be 205 YMCAs and twenty-five thousand members.

The idea was simple and easily reproducible. Young men were responsible for reaching their peers while a room was provided by the local organization where young men could gather with friends to read, relax, be trained as Sunday school teachers, and participate in Bible studies and weekly prayer meetings. Evangelical convictions that the Bible was the unique, supernatural repository of all truth, knowledge, and morality drove the movement not only to protect young men from the wiles of the city but also to seek the reformation of character and the improvement of human relationships.[20]

Despite the regional efforts of the Boston YMCA, most of the associations across North America were more localized efforts. They were born in isolation and ignorance of each other. One man, William Chauncy Langdon, cofounder of the Washington YMCA and founder of the Confederation of American YMCAs, was the prime mover in bringing about a national movement. Having overcome family difficulties that brought about his "nomadic boyhood," Langdon became a very successful organizer and leader. His travels enabled him to escape regional loyalties and bring the scattered associations together into a national movement despite the bitter regional allegiance of the 1850s.

The climax of the Confederation orchestrated by Langdon came at the 1859 gathering in Troy, New York, at which 237 delegates from sixty-eight YMCAs were present. At the request of the delegates the young minister wrote a document that would clarify the relationship between the YMCAs and the church. In the paper Langdon advocated that associations not pursue any course which violated the denominational principles of any of the supporting ecclesiastical organizations. This specifically included a ban on doing evangelistic work and instead stressed the formation of Christian character. The rejection of the proposal was nearly unanimous. The delegates wanted no limits placed on their future initiatives.

One need became apparent if young men would be attracted to join YMCAs: entertainment. Henry Ward Beecher of Brooklyn explained the need this way:

> There ought to be gymnastic grounds and good bowling alleys in connection with reading rooms, in every ward of the city, under judicious management, where, for a small fee, every young man might find various wholesome exercises, and withal good society, without the temptations

which surround all the alleys and rooms of the city, kept for bowling and billiards.[21]

In 1856, efforts to raise funds necessary to build facilities such as envisioned by Beecher began in Brooklyn and later in New York City. Two events intervened, delaying the adoption of the building of facilities suitable for such wholesome exercise. The first was the Prayer Revival of 1857–59, which resulted in prayer becoming the dominant characteristic of most YMCAs across America. The second was the Civil War, which increased the need to minister to young men but sapped the financial resources necessary to build recreational halls.

Revival of 1857–59

What happened next few could have anticipated and still fewer remember. Young men active in the YMCA became leaders for a revival that swept across the nation. Unlike other spiritual awakenings in the United States, the revival of 1857–59 found its momentum in prayer rather than in preaching. Churches and YMCAs became places where men would gather during their noon hours for prayer and the Spirit of God would drive them to repentance and public confession of sin.

While the nation was experiencing a period of unparalleled economic prosperity, the internal dissention over slavery caused an undercurrent of anxiety. The economic and social structures of the nation were not prepared for the stress brought about by the dynamics of the financial and political climate of the ensuing years. So when the Ohio Life Insurance and Trust Company failed during August 1857, panic swept the nation. Thousands of businesses were affected. Banks closed and railroads went into bankruptcy. The extreme optimism of the nation was shattered.

In this context a few members of the YMCA got the idea for a noon prayer meeting from the London Association. Jeremiah Lanphier, at the urging of Association member Richard C. McCormick, gave an open invitation for prayer in the Consistory building of New York's North Dutch Church at noon on September 23, 1857. Six showed up the first week, twenty the second, forty on the first Wednesday in October, and soon the prayer meeting was being held daily. Within six months ten thousand businessmen were gathering each day for prayer in New York and within two years a million converts had been added to the churches of America.[22]

Though the revival embraced men and women of all ages, members of the YMCA were the most active participants. A young man from Philadelphia attended the New York prayer meeting and upon his return home enlisted his friends from the YMCA to begin a similar noon prayer meeting in the United Methodist Episcopal Church. In Louisville the prayer gatherings were held in the YMCA room until crowds forced them to employ larger quarters. The role of the YMCA in Chicago in the prayer movement left such an impact on D. L. Moody that it became his favorite organization.

J. Edwin Orr, the premier authority on evangelical revivals, concluded:

> The Young Men's Christian Associations were already in existence when the Great Awakening began. Out of the Revival of 1858 came the introduction of the Y.M.C.A. to American cities, and the flowering of the movement in the United States. The influx of concerted men into Christian churches found an outlet in the evangelistic activities of the early Y.M.C.A.[23]

Then came the Civil War. The nation was shredded during four years of bloody struggle. Though at times the revival continued, especially in the Southern camp meetings, the losers in the conflict were the youth of the nation. Over six hundred thousand soldiers died and another half million were wounded during the carnage. The majority of the casualties were not much older than children.

The methodology employed by YMCA leaders after the war reflected the entrepreneurial spirit of the day. Though prayer meetings and Bible studies were thought to be central to the movement, the strategy was much more successfully employed in Canada and abroad than in the United States. By the early seventies only one out of seven or eight YMCAs reported having Bible studies.[24]

After the Civil War

The heart of the YMCA's ministry philosophy was symbolized by a triangle representing the unified whole of young men, integrating body, mind, and spirit. Initially activities and facilities designed to shape mind and spirit defined what the YMCA did. Reading rooms, Bible studies, prayer, and training for Sunday school teachers dominated their schedules. Later, in the third quarter of the nineteenth century, the idea of "muscular Christianity" came to be a major aspect of the program.[25] Using the concept that the discipline of the body could (should?) enable the young man to discipline his soul, Luther Halsey Gulick spearheaded the development of athletic programs for the YMCA.

The movement developed a student ministry in the 1870s when Luther Wishard began traveling to college campuses in the effort to extend the influence of the YMCA to the twenty-three thousand (primarily) young men enrolled in undergraduate programs in America.[26] While many of these students were as young as fifteen, they were a small minority of the youth of the day.

One of the most lasting aspects of the YMCA related to bringing young men into a relationship with the triune God was the Student Volunteer Movement. Though it came into being after the beginning of the next cycle of youth ministry, it was the culmination of years of effort by Luther Wishard when 235 students accepted invitations to have conversations with evangelist D. L. Moody at Mt. Hermon, in Northfield, Massachusetts. There, after twenty-six days of play, prayer, and Bible study, the Student Volunteer Movement was born with a commitment to "evangelize the world in this generation." A conservative estimate suggests that twenty thousand students spent a portion of their lives serving as Christian witnesses in nations outside North America.[27]

The YMCA in the United States was not an association built around one man or woman's vision, but within the movement different people arose to fulfill specific needs at appropriate times. They performed like a jazz ensemble with various people improvising based on a common progression or theme. William Langdon was only the first of many such national leaders.

Crisis: Birth of the Public High School

Though the Sunday school and YMCA continued to have an influence on the youth of America as the nation recovered from the Civil War, an event took place in 1875 that completely changed the nation's definition of youth. Until then they were understood to be either older children or younger adults. There was no clearly defined category in most people's thinking for *adolescence* until G. Stanley Hall popularized the concept with his book by that name published thirty years later in 1904.

The societal change that in effect brought to a close the first cycle of youth ministry was the decision by the United States Supreme Court that permitted tax money to be used to fund public high schools. Prior to the *Stuart et al. v. School District No. 1 of Kalamazoo* decision, the primary way in which to educate young people prior to college had been in private academies. Of course this limited such education to wealthier families.

Slowly the public high school began to take shape. By 1880 more students were enrolled in public high schools than in academies. Public high school enrollment had jumped from eighty thousand in 1870 to a half million at the turn of the century. These were people who, as G. Stanley Hall would point out, had adult bodies but were still undergoing a transition from childhood.

The discovery of adolescence both from a legal perspective and from an educational point of view meant that youth work would have to change. If the school system now had to provide educational services for people in their middle adolescence, the church would have to respond in a similar manner. It was time for improvisation.

Conclusion

Tom Sawyer and his friends lived in the middle of the first cycle of youth ministry and were part of the Sunday school movement after its effectiveness had peaked. Had Mark Twain written of Tom ten or fifteen years later he probably would have included references to the YMCA and its influence on the lives of young men.

The first cycle of youth ministry was an adaptation of British evangelical efforts to reach and hold the city youth of the day. Social dislocation caused by the westward expansion of the nation set the stage for a number of grassroots movements. These movements were then superseded by the Sunday school and YMCA movements before stagnating as effective evangelical tools and eventually giving way to new movements in the second cycle of youth ministry, when the public high school became a viable option in society.

It should be noted, however, that the various agencies and grassroots movements of the first cycle still exist in the twenty-first century. Singing-schools have become church choirs. Temperance societies have been succeeded by Students Against Drunk Driving. Young people's missionary societies now are student mission trips and agencies like Youth with a Mission and Teen Mission. While Sunday schools have become centers for students to socialize and learn in the church, the YMCA has settled for an educational and athletic focus in the young person's life.

6

Cadets of Temperance

Structuring Youth Societies

Although Tom Sawyer hated Sunday School, he was attracted to the Cadets of Temperance. Attracted, that was, until he realized the implications of the pledge. Tom had not thought much about the pledge before joining the Cadets because he was enamored by the showy character of their regalia—red sash and shackles. He envisioned himself sporting his newly-earned outfit on public occasions such as the Fourth of July or solemn processions mourning the death of leading citizens like old Judge Frazer, who was gravely ill at the time.

Now the pledge was the most important part of being a Cadet of Temperance, because a guy had to promise to abstain from drinking, smoking, chewing, and profanity as long as he remained a member. Tom quickly learned the difference between promising and doing. No sooner had he promised not to do these things than he was tormented by a desire to do them.

Tom's membership in the Cadets of Temperance lasted less than a week. He simply could not take the pressure. Besides, when Judge Frazer rallied and did not die, the next public occasion seemed too distant in the future to maintain his pledge. So Tom quit.

Juvenile temperance societies were as significant in the history of youth ministry as was the Sunday school. Unlike Mark Twain's parody, most juvenile temperance societies remained focused on training children to recognize the dangers of "demon rum." Led primarily by evangelical Christians who were concerned with alcohol's threat to family and spiritual life, the movement went beyond a focus on personal salvation and piety to an emphasis on one societal evil that would prevent the youth of the nation from living Christian lives. In the process, the juvenile temperance movement gave structure to what would become Christian youth ministries later in the century.

Voluntary Associations in the American Democratic Experiment

During the first half of the nineteenth century, Americans busied themselves with efforts to improve their lives. Sensing that the American democratic experiment provided a new opportunity for the human spirit, voluntary associations, utopian philanthropists, and religious communities addressed a wide variety of issues. Foremost among the concerns were education common to all children, abolition of slavery, curbing the abuses caused by alcohol consumption, and providing community services such as fire protection and police forces.

Most of the proposed solutions focused attention on the character of the people involved. Phrenology classified areas of the brain associated with human behavior and provided the basis for training children to behave appropriately. Communitarianism provided utopian settings for achieving democratic ideals. Labor reform started a process of humanizing the workplace. Abolitionists worked for the freedom of slaves. Temperance societies initially addressed drunkenness and later advocated total abstinence. Christian churches formed mission societies focusing on personal salvation and holiness in America and abroad, yet found their parishioners active in many of the other movements of the era.

Two unintended benefits resulted from these social movements. Women gained a voice in society, and youth societies developed for the intentional passing of values from generation to generation. Though affected in varying degrees by most of the voluntary associations, the temperance movement most profoundly influenced women and youth. In the twenty-first century, it is hard to envision the significance or impact of the temperance movement during the nineteenth century. Yet the movement overshadowed most of the other causes both in its general acceptance among the public and its organizational structures.

The factor that distinguished the juvenile temperance movement from the Sunday school and YMCA was that temperance only loosely connected with the desire by Protestants in America to enable young people to experience God. If anything, it was an attempt to prevent the negative influence of alcohol and only secondarily an effort to preserve young people, especially males, as children of God's covenant.

Volumes documenting the emergence of women in society appropriately link their current roles in society with the temperance movement. Curiously, little consideration has been given to the link between juvenile temperance societies and the myriad of youth societies, youth athletic leagues, and clubs that dominate the discretionary time of children and adolescents today. This chapter attempts to initiate discussion around the link between juvenile temperance societies and current youth ministry.

Of the three agencies that pioneered youth ministry in America, the temperance movement has been written about least as it touches on Protestant youth ministries in America. Each movement addressed issues related to the Christian character of young people. All were well established in America before the Civil War, which proved to be a watershed in the American experience.

The temperance movement in the first half of the nineteenth century, more than either the Sunday school or the YMCA, had its roots in the local community. The Sunday school, in its early days in America, attempted to educate the poor and children on the frontier. Only later did the children of church families become participants in Sunday schools. YMCAs located their ministries in urban centers. After the Civil War and the period of reconstruction, the movement found its impact among students. The temperance movement, by contrast, responding to local issues related to alcohol consumption, quickly transitioned from attempts to rescue drunkards to preventing Protestant children and adults from being captured by hard liquor. Juvenile temperance societies came into being, and meetings were held primarily in communities where Christian people lived. Methods appealed to children of the church. Volunteers, both men and women, provided leadership.

Whereas there is often discontinuity between one era and the next in youth ministry cycles, a formative influence exists between the juvenile temperance movement of the mid-nineteenth century and the Society of Christian Endeavor later in the century. This influence helped set the stage for youth ministry in the twentieth century.

The Development of the Juvenile Temperance Movement

The juvenile temperance movement grew out of the broader temperance movement in England that began in the early nineteenth century. As with most movements, local responses to alcohol abuse arose from the grass roots and developed into national organizations with networks across national boundaries—especially in the United States and Europe.

Two phases of the temperance movement gave rise to different emphases. The earlier phase emphasized moderation and focused much of its effort on rescuing men who had fallen prey to alcohol. Primary attention was paid to "ardent spirits" (hard liquors). Wine and beer were assumed to be normal parts of church and social life. The second phase shifted to abstinence and included preventive measures for those who had not begun to partake of alcoholic beverages. This second phase began around 1830, though there was conflict over the validity of the two perspectives for many years thereafter. The second phase gave rise to juvenile temperance societies.[1]

Probably the earliest temperance training took place in the homes where parents adopted a life of temperance. Early local temperance societies included both adults and children and were said to be most effective where mother, father, and children practiced the total abstinence principle. Like adults, children were allowed to join abstinence societies by signing a pledge to abstain. Pledging sobriety allowed them to obtain cards of membership as well as to buy and wear medals of the society. Yet early on, certain temperance movement leaders decided that children would benefit from societies of their own.[2]

The best known of the early juvenile temperance societies were in Great Britain. The name associated with the first juvenile society as early as 1829 was John Dunlop in Scotland. These groups generally consisted of boys from twelve or fourteen to twenty-one years of age. Girls were seldom included unless the society was situated in a school. Societies were said to be self-originated, self-governed, and self-sustained. Yet when the novelty of such societies began to wear off, committees from the senior societies prepared sets of rules and provided structure for officers (president, vice president, and committee). Membership in juvenile societies paved the way for membership in the senior societies.[3]

Most juvenile societies were small in number though at least one society in Airdrie, Scotland, boasted a membership of 210 children between ages six and fourteen in 1831. As early as 1832, the Youth's Temperance Society in Preston, Scotland, formalized a pledge of abstinence from ardent spirits, with the promise to discontinue intemperance. This practice quickly became a key element of juvenile temperance societies.

Frequently there were connections with Sunday schools and Sunday school societies. In 1834 the first Sunday School Temperance Conference was held in Bristol, England. By 1836 there was an attempt to establish a youth temperance magazine called *The Youthful Teetotaler*.[4]

The Birth and Influence of the Band of Hope (1847)

At the World Temperance Convention in London, August 4–8, 1846, a resolution on juvenile temperance was moved, supported, and carried unanimously, urging the formation of juvenile temperance societies. As best they could determine, there were already twenty-eight such societies with 19,512 members. Five societies accounted for nearly half of the total.[5]

One of the people responding to the call was Rev. Jabez Tunnicliff of Leeds. Supported by the Ladies Committee of the Leeds Temperance Committee, Tunnicliff held the first Band of Hope festival on November 9, 1847, attended by three hundred children who signed a temperance pledge. The membership card read simply,

> This is to certify that _____ is a member of the "Temperance Band of Hope" having signed the following declaration. "I do agree that I will not use intoxicating liquors as a beverage."[6]

At approximately the same time another Band of Hope emerged in Germany with no known connection to Tunnicliff's group. Other existing groups appropriated the name for their Sunday school groups or clubs. In the next two years, Band of Hope festivals following the Leeds model sprang up across England. Fueled by favorable publicity in newspapers, promoted in papers dedicated to temperance (*Band of Hope Review* being one), and supported by adult temperance societies, the festivals spread.

To attract greater numbers of children, novel methods were employed. Samuel Catton, a Quaker known as "the Children's Friend," made extensive use of the "magic lantern" to show images on a screen. Jonathan Revell used his musical gifts to attract and hold children. James Silk Buchingham, an ex-MP, arranged for a group of Band of Hope children to tour Surrey Zoological Gardens. The idea of using entertainment to attract children, an idea previously foreign to the church's ministry to children but more acceptable in Sunday schools, became a normal feature of their temperance rallies.

To enlist children, the Band of Hope utilized Sunday school teachers, divinity students, and teachers in day schools. To support these volunteers, funds were raised from tickets to the festivals, general solicitation, and underwriting from wealthy businessmen. Prayer meetings on Wednesday evenings and Saturday mornings encouraged adult leaders to pray for each other.

As the Band of Hope expanded, so did the methods used. Festivals became common. One gathering in London's Crystal Palace in 1862 attracted as many as thirty thousand children and adults. In these larger events children performed in choirs and orchestras. In local societies, committees of promising children worked to prevent absenteeism and especially gifted children were encouraged to make little addresses, tell temperance stories, or sing temperance songs. Readings or tracts dealing with everything from religious character to physiology were prepared to educate children. Temperance melodies multiplied through prize competitions. Temperance literature expanded to include printed sermons on temperance published in subscription-based papers (*The Juvenile Temperance Messenger* and *Juvenile Abstainers Magazine*). Teaching in day schools and apprentice evening schools further expanded the movement. Demonstrations, excursions, competitions (choruses, solos, glees, dialogues, recitations), and games in public parks all aided the cause of temperance.[7]

The Band of Hope Constitution formalized the organizational structure. The societies officially promoted as their purpose the "disuse of all intoxicating drinks as beverages among the young"; that is, they sought to prevent the "evil" rather than combating it after it has arisen. Funding came from fees paid by members. The business the societies conducted was handled by officers and committees. Parents were sought as partners in preventing intemperance.

Unlike the Sunday school and YMCA/YWCA, the juvenile temperance movement essentially focused on one moral issue—preventing the abuses commonly associated with the use of alcohol. The other youth movements, while including a moral component, were equally interested in fostering a personal relationship with God through a Protestant understanding of redemption. Though the narrow focus of the movement enabled some Catholics to align themselves with it, the bulk of its constituents were Protestants both in England and in America.

The Spread of Juvenile Temperance within the First Fifty Years

By 1897 the Bands of Hope in the United Kingdom claimed 21,645 groups with 2,952,580 members, or about 136 members per band. The juvenile temperance movement had bands in virtually all Christian denominations (Church of England, Baptist, Congregational, Methodist [of all varieties], Society of Friends, Presbyterian, Unitarian, Salvation Army, Catholic).[8]

Fellow workers in other temperance organizations gave birth to societies with similar purposes (as many as 4,710 more societies and 285,743 more members). These included Young Abstainers Union (sixty-one societies; five thousand members), Juvenile Rechabites (sixteen hundred "tents"; 81,924 members), Juvenile Temples (1,212 temples; 86,929 members), Cadets of Temperance, begun in Pennsylvania in 1887 (340 branches; eighteen thousand members), Juvenile Orders of the Total Abstinent Sons of the Phoenix (105 branches; forty-three hundred members), and Loyal Temperance Legion (twenty-three legions; 793 members).[9]

Juvenile temperance societies spread around the world. In Europe societies sprang up in Belgium, France, Holland, Germany, Sweden, Finland, Poland, Russia, Austria, Hungary, Italy, Malta, and Gibraltar. Asia saw similar societies emerge in India, Ceylon (Sri Lanka), Burma (Myanmar), China, and Japan. In Africa societies formed in South Africa and various areas influenced by Great Britain. In the Pacific, Australia, New Zealand, and Tasmania joined the nations with juvenile temperance societies. In the United States and Canada early societies formed in Massachusetts (1828), Pennsylvania (1846), New Jersey (1890), Chicago (1893), and Toronto.[10]

Impact of the Temperance Movement on Popular Culture

While juvenile temperance societies provided a structure within which the values of Christian people passed from generation to generation, the temperance movement had an impact on the popular culture of the nineteenth century. Temperance plays, dime novels, and public meetings proved very profitable as former drunkards (real and fictional) told stories describing their degradation in graphic detail before celebrating how their lives had been changed through a life of temperance. In turn, Christian people turned from resisting to embracing aspects of popular culture in much the same fashion that people in the medieval era responded to Catholic priests who employed morality plays to communicate the dangers of sin and the joys of a virtuous Christian life.

In "Selling Sobriety: How Temperance Reshaped Culture in Antebellum America," Graham Warder built a case for a change in the perception of popular culture by evangelical Protestants who thought of themselves as the moral middle of America.[11] He demonstrated that the temperance movement used popular culture to gain a hearing for the temperance message and in so doing allowed evangelical Protestants to embrace aspects of popular culture previously considered detrimental to the Christian life.

Warder's research focused on four uses of popular culture to communicate temperance messages. George B. Cheever's 1835 "Inquire at Amos Giles Distillery" used a temperance story to suggest limits to clerical authority resulting from the split between orthodoxy and Unitarianism in

Salem, Massachusetts, much in the same way that "Inherit the Wind" used the Scopes evolution trial in Dayton, Tennessee, to parody the activities of Senator Joseph McCarthy and the hearings of the House Un-American Activities Committee more than a century later. The story used temperance themes of greed by rum manufacturers, hypocrisy of drinking Christians, bodily disorders of drunkards, and the slippery slope of moderate drinkers into lives of drunkenness. Though many did not understand the intent of the story, the temperance theme appealed to their values.

The reformed drunkard, John Gough, gained notoriety telling his story of deliverance from alcoholism at meetings promoted by the American Temperance Union. Though his account was probably embellished for dramatic effect, the masterful storyteller moved paying audiences to delight in the glories of a teetotaler lifestyle. Though he later relapsed, his sensational testimonial was part of a shift of authority from biblical preaching to human experience.

William H. Smith's 1844 temperance melodrama, *The Drunkard*, helped defuse the antitheatricalism of many Americans, especially in Boston where it debuted. The impact was similar to the Billy Graham film *For Pete's Sake*, which showed in theaters in the late 1960s, softening evangelical resistance to theater attendance.

T. S. Arthur's popular novel, *Nights in a Bar-room* (1854), utilized "demon rum" as a metaphor for evil in a time of economic and theological optimism. Along with other books, like Sara Josepha Hale's *Godey's Lady's Book*, the temperance movement helped change evangelical perceptions of the popular publishing industry.

In effect, the impact on the evangelical culture in which youth ministry would emerge suggested that public entertainment could become a viable ally to the Christian message. This stood in contrast with the steady diet of mediocre preaching and unappealing Sunday school lessons offered weekly to the most faithful church attendees. Since the popular culture's temperance messages reinforced values in harmony with evangelical convictions, the idea of being entertained while learning Christian ideas began to change the manner in which evangelical convictions were taught. Though teaching by rote recitation continued well into the twentieth century, popular culture had begun to reshape youth ministry communication styles.

The Temperance Movement and the Society of Christian Endeavor

Defining himself as a teetotaler in his book *Recollections of a Long Life*, Brooklyn pastor Rev. Theodore Cuyler spoke of his early exposure to temperance, saying, "Though I became a teetotaler when I was a child, . . . the first public address I ever delivered was in behalf of temperance . . . in Glasgow [Scotland]." The experience guided him to "a sort of ordination to the ministry of preaching the Gospel of total abstinence."[12]

Cuyler returned to the United States and enrolled at Princeton Theological Seminary. He graduated in May 1846 and entered the pastoral ministry in New Jersey and soon New York. Part of his summer vacations were spent in Saratoga attending temperance conventions. In time he became one of the featured speakers at such conventions.

By the mid-1870s, Cuyler was a headline speaker with such notable persons as Rev. S. H. Tyng, D. L. Moody, John Wanamaker, and Francis E. Willard. Like his fellow temperance crusaders, Theodore Cuyler signed a number of temperance pledges. At least one version of the pledges he signed read as follows:

> We, the undersigned, do agree, that we will not use intoxicating Liquors as a beverage, nor traffic in them; that we will not provide them as an article of entertainment, or for persons in our employment; and that, in all suitable ways, we will discontinuance [sic] their use throughout the community.[13]

In 1865 Cuyler helped found the National Temperance Society and Publishing House and the American Juvenile Temperance Society, just two years before he formed the Young People's Association of the Lafayette Avenue Presbyterian Church in Brooklyn. Fifty-four persons signed the Young People's Association's constitution on November 6, 1867, and it went on to inspire the formation of the Society of Christian Endeavor a little over thirteen years later. Little is known about the American Juvenile Temperance Society to verify the apparent link between the temperance movement and Protestant youth societies, but Cuyler clearly shifted his focus from juvenile temperance to church-based youth ministry.

Francis E. Clark, the founder of the Society of Christian Endeavor, followed a different trajectory and eventually linked temperance to his society. While very careful to share the credit for the ideas that became part of the Christian Endeavor society, he never cited the juvenile temperance movement.

In the "Prefatory" of *The Children and the Church*, Clark acknowledged Horace Bushnell, Theodore Cuyler, and many of his brethren for their cordial sympathy and helpful counsel.[14] Yet, at the end of the first decade of Christian Endeavor, Clark carefully distinguished between the methods of the society he founded and Cuyler's Young People's Association in Brooklyn.[15] Clark went on to state, "The society of

Christian Endeavor sympathizes with temperance and all true moral reforms, with wise philanthropic measures, and especially with missions at home and abroad; yet it is not to be used as a convenience by any organization to further ends other than its own."[16] As Christian Endeavor grew, a temperance committee became one of the standing committees.[17] This, however, appears to be a late addition rather than an initial element.

Yet Francis Clark appears to have been influenced by people involved in the temperance movement. In his autobiography he spoke of his acquaintance with Neal Dow as he pastored Williston Church in Portland, Maine. Dow fathered the Maine law that voted the state dry in 1851. Arguably Dow was the most influential temperance advocate of the century.[18]

By 1881 the temperance movement was so ingrained in the northern culture of the United States that features of the movement may have seemed like natural aspects of any Protestant youth society being formed. Though relatively new to the state of Maine when he founded the Society of Christian Endeavor, Clark appeared to be aware of the methods employed by the temperance movement and the historic role the state of Maine played in the movement's development.

Striking Similarities between the Society of Christian Endeavor and the Juvenile Temperance Movement

The most striking similarity between juvenile temperance societies and Christian Endeavor was the use of the pledge to motivate members. While the temperance pledge was losing its central role in the fight against intemperance in 1881, Clark used a positive pledge to focus on what we today would call Christian formation. Writers like Mark Twain and Francis E. Willard argued that the temperance pledge was ineffective. As Twain pointed out, using Tom Sawyer as an illustration, "to promise not to do a thing is the surest way in the world to make a body want to go and do that very thing." Willard went on to formulate political and economic strategies for resisting alcohol consumption.

Even as Twain and Willard abandoned restrictive pledges, Francis Clark crafted a pledge that affirmed a desire for Christian piety. Like the temperance pledges, the Christian Endeavor pledge changed over time, but in its earliest form it committed the young person to endeavor to live a Christian life.

Both pledges proved to be lightning rods for criticism. For the temperance movement, questions revolved around the extent of abstinence. Teetotaling became the norm for juvenile societies, though some preferred abstinence from only hard liquors. Critics faulted the Christian Endeavor pledge for a variety of flaws from being too pietistic to a lack of attention to denominational distinctives. Yet without the pledges, the two movements would have lost their focal points.

In a second similarity, Christian Endeavor and the Band of Hope (as a sample juvenile temperance society) were structured with leadership offices and roles for young people to fill. Officers and committees took responsibility for public meetings. The leadership roles allowed adults to identify and work with young people who would in turn influence their peers.

In both societies, officers took initiatives in the learning process. No longer passive recipients of cognitive input provided by adults, officers assumed leadership roles and participated in communicating core convictions to their peers and people younger than themselves. While duties were defined by the two societies' constitutions, young people assumed a wide range of responsibilities that reinforced their commitment to the pledge they had made.

Public recitation and singing by young people, used as means of reinforcing the pledge, marked a third similarity between the two movements. Recitations warned of the dangers of intemperance and were recited both in union meetings and in individual society gatherings. Reciting of Scripture and reporting on a young person's endeavor to know God were central to Christian Endeavor meetings. Singing ranged from temperance hymns to oratorios to gospel-style songs. In both movements songbooks may have been the most common form of curricular materials, bringing about continuity from society to society.

For the temperance movement, *Hull's Temperance Glee Book*,[19] *Songs of the New Crusade*,[20] and *The Temperance Songster*[21] were used for participants to sing the praises of temperance as Christian Endeavor came into being.[22] The Society of Christian Endeavor in turn had its own set of songbooks that included *Junior Carols*[23] and *The Endeavor Hymnal for Young People's Societies, Sunday Schools and Church Meetings*,[24] published by the United Society of Christian Endeavor.

A fourth point of similarity was in the host of publications that reinforced commitments to their pledges. The Christian Endeavor had *The Golden Rule* while the Band of Hope had *The Juvenile Temperance Messenger* and *Juvenile Abstainers Magazine* as official organs of the organizations. Publishing houses sold program materials in great volumes to support the local societies.

A fifth similarity between the Society of Christian Endeavor and the juvenile temperance movement was the union rallies the groups held. Regional gatherings of societies for inspiration and motivation served to reinforce the activities of the individual societies. Sunday school societies similarly used such gatherings to rally volunteers and pupils alike. Ideas were passed along from society to society at the union meetings. Vision was cast, and methods modeled. The resulting publicity, primarily covered in local newspapers, spread the influence of the movements and helped them to gain new adherents.

Juvenile temperance societies and Christian Endeavor were both led and coached by lay people, a sixth similarity. In agreeing to leave his pastorate and accept the presidency of the Society of Christian Endeavor, one of Francis E. Clark's conditions stipulated that the society remain a volunteer-led organization with few paid personnel. Temperance societies appeared to have had even less professional structure than did Christian Endeavor. Sunday school associations modeled a similar pattern. This volunteer orientation reinforced the determination of the American people to improve their lives without dependence on government or church structures to make it happen. Some clergy resisted these lay initiatives, but they flourished where the local pastor supported them.

A seventh similarity evidences the highly ecumenical nature of two movements. Both groups ignored denominational barriers in search of the greater good. Perhaps most amazing was the manner in which Protestant and Catholic parishioners worked together for the cause of temperance. Even in the antipopish climate of the late nineteenth century, the temperance movement embraced the Catholic Total Abstinence League of the Cross, founded by Cardinal Manning in England. The Cardinal's work was well received by Americans as well.

Though the Society of Christian Endeavor failed to bridge the Protestant-Catholic divide, virtually every Protestant denomination embraced the movement. Even after denominational youth societies emerged, many local churches elected to retain their connections with the Society of Christian Endeavor and attend its union rallies.

In perhaps the most far reaching similarity between Christian Endeavor and juvenile temperance, the two movements embraced methods employed by popular culture to reinforce commitment to their pledges. These activities appealed to the imaginations of young people and allowed an element of entertainment to be part of their Christian experience. Though not all societies were highly religious in nature, by and large the juvenile temperance movement was an evangelical Protestant expression of morality.

Conclusion

There is a great deal of circumstantial evidence that the juvenile temperance movement influenced the youth ministry ideas of Theodore Cuyler and as a result helped shape the Society of Christian Endeavor, though to date there is no direct evidence that the juvenile temperance movement did anything more than help shape the context in which youth ministry would soon emerge.

As Erb pointed out in his 1917 publication, many approaches were used in the nineteenth century to shape the values of the young people of the nation. Ideas spread rapidly through the publications of the day. The dominance of the temperance movement throughout the nineteenth century and the energy focused on juveniles established a pattern of training youth that became a norm for Francis Clark and those who wished to focus the attention of Protestant youth on Christian piety.

A study of published juvenile temperance society program materials may prove a closer link than has yet been established. Yet more important than a point-by-point curricular comparison is the youth ministry ethos created by the juvenile temperance movement that empowered volunteers in America and around the world to utilize their own resources and methods current in the broader popular culture to address the issues that prevented young people from embracing the faith and values of their parents.

7

Gangs of New York

The Setting for Modern Youth Ministry

angs of New York captured the ferment of ethnic strife around the Manhattan intersection called Five Points in the middle of the nineteenth century. The Dead Rabbits, an Irish gang, battled a gang led by "the Butcher," Bill Cutting. At stake was control of the heart of the Sixth Ward near City Hall. The movie captured the struggle for power among hundreds of New York gangs of the era described in Herbert Asbury's book by the same name.

It was a dark time in American history. If the years of the Civil War (1861–65) were a national tragedy, this time was even more brutal for the impoverished masses that suffered at the plundering of the Tammany Hall politicians. Daily ships fueled the tensions of the city by discharging immigrants, Irish and German primarily, who hoped to find relief from the famine, conflict, and poverty of their native lands. Instead they discovered themselves struggling for survival in a hostile new environment.

Abolitionists, many of whom were evangelical Christians, championed the cause of Africans from the South. Freedmen settled in the Sixth Ward cauldron. Few were welcomed, either because of racial bias or for fear of further competition for already scarce jobs.

A draft law, the nation's first, created resentment among New York's poor at its inequity. Young men could avoid induction by paying three hundred dollars. Only the wealthy could afford the price. Tensions built.

Gangs of New York climaxes as draft riots broke out in July of 1863. For the better part of four days riots continued. Finally the militia brutally quelled the unrest. Injuries and property damage left New York looking somewhat like Gettysburg.

While *Gangs of New York* depicts a place of danger and exploitation for young people, New York also vibrated with spiritual hunger, economic progress, and cultural pride. Churches were abundant. Edgar Allan Poe, Herman Melville, Walt Whitman, and Horace Greeley wrote in and about the city, which was already a literary center for the nation. The port of New York serviced the nation and more importantly, the world. Samuel Morse's telegraph anchored the city as a center for communication. Industry boomed. The convergence of numerous factors created a viable economic middle class that would set the table for modern youth ministry.

Unmarried women from fifteen to twenty-five years of age, attracted by the rapidly expanding garment industry, opportunities to serve as domestics in wealthy homes, and other labor opportunities, left their rural backgrounds to settle in the excitement of the city. The ship and cart building industries, trades, and various labor opportunities attracted even greater numbers of young men.

To cater to this clientele, an entertainment industry emerged. A youth culture resulted in which

> tavern and small hotels provided free entertainment to draw in drinkers. These venues—known as "free and easies" or "varieties" or "vaudevilles" offered an ever changing if incoherent assortment of music, dance, magic, ventriloquism, comedy, skits, and tall tales, frequently provided by the audience itself.[1]

Young people from wealthier families clamored for new forms of entertainment as well. Exercise in gyms (there were seven by 1860), attendance at regattas, trotting meets, and pedestrian races attracted young men after work. A new game called Base Ball gathered clubs of young men and their friends to compete. By 1858 a formal set of rules guided the competition among the seventy-one clubs in Brooklyn, twenty-five in Manhattan, and others on Long Island and across the Hudson River in New Jersey.[2]

David Nasmith toured the United States and Canada during the winter of 1830–31 attempting to organize "American Young Men's Societies." One was briefly established in New York. Other societies designed for the betterment of youth appeared. The Young Men's Library Association and the Young Men's Society for Religious Improvement probably had expressions in New York as they did in other American cities. Not until

1852, however, would the Young Men's Christian Association take root and remain in the city.

Prayer Revival and Unrest Set the Stage

The events that influenced the emergence of modern youth ministry converged in the years just before the Civil War and culminated with the unrest exemplified by the draft riots in the summer of 1863. Unrest among the youth of New York led to a spiritual awakening that originated in the New York YMCA and swept across the nation. It came to be known as the Prayer Revival of 1857–59.

Revivals of religion had been closely linked to young people since the time of Jonathan Edwards and the First Great Awakening. Known for his piety and great intellect, Edwards demonstrated great distress for the youth of Northampton, Massachusetts, who concerned him by engaging in Sunday night "frolics" that lasted late into the night. In one sermon he commented, "Licentious and immoral practices seem to get a great head amongst young people, and how little appearance is there of a spirit of seriousness and religion among them? How little concern about their salvation and escaping eternal misery?"[3]

Edwards's preaching advocated piety and the rejection of sexual experimentation and other practices common within the youth culture of the day. Tragedy struck in 1734 when two young people from Northampton died in a short period of time. Shaken by their loss, a spiritual awakening began. Edwards convinced the young people to meet for times of "social religion" in smaller groups in homes scattered throughout the town. They met following the Thursday evening lecture, which had previously been a favorite time for frolicking. In a reversal of the previous pattern, young men brought their friends and led these times of social religion and prayer.[4]

The spiritual revival in Northampton brought many young people to faith and brought about lifestyle changes in others. The revival expanded across the colonies in what came to be known as the First Great Awakening. Another period of revival, the Second Great Awakening, happened at the beginning of the nineteenth century. These were followed by itinerant revivalists traveling from community to community holding revival meetings and calling children and adults to repentance and faith in Christ. When the Prayer Revival occurred in 1857–59 and adults repented of their sinfulness, young people were also a focus of intense prayer.

Starting in September of 1856, YMCA–sponsored noon hour prayer meetings met three times a week at the Dutch Reformed Church on the corner of Fulton and Williams Streets in New York. Prayers focused on young men living and doing business in the area.[5]

When a financial panic paralyzed the American money system in August 1857 and drove many businesses into bankruptcy, the prayer meetings swelled. Soon every available space in the church except the sanctuary was filled with people praying, each limited to five minutes to allow all to participate. Quickly the prayer revival spread across the nation and for two years the revival continued.

One of the people deeply involved with the revival was the pastor of Market Street (Dutch Reformed) Church, Theodore Ledyard Cuyler, who played an active role along with Jeremiah C. Lamphier, who had been a singer in the choir of the pastor's church.

The revival left an indelible imprint on Cuyler's life. He described it:

> It is not too much to say that often there were not less than 8,000 to 10,000 of God's people, who came together at the noon-tide hour with the spirit of supplication and prayer. The flame spread over the city, then leaped to Philadelphia. . . . And so it went on from town to town, and from city to city, over the length and breadth of the land.[6]

The idea of prayer meetings for young people became a vehicle for bringing about repentance from sin and sustaining the fruit of the conversions associated with the revival. Though young men's prayer meetings were not new, the timing and context was. Responding to the revival and expanding on the YMCA idea of prayer meetings, Theodore Cuyler anchored them firmly within the church's scope of ministry and made them coeducational. Thus it was in his Market Street Church that church-based young people's prayer meetings began, proving to be the seedbed from which modern youth ministry would sprout.

Gangs of New York and Youth Ministry

Gangs and revival gave youth ministry an entirely new face. Gangs threatened safety, while revival in the city provided hope, at least for evangelicals. Unlike the Sunday school that initially targeted children working in the sweatshops of America, a whole new understanding of youth ministry grew out of the needs of fifteen- to twenty-five-year-old men and women in New York City. The city exuded possibilities and excitement. At the same time, evangelical Christians saw a cloud of spiritual danger and vulnerability hanging over the very place from which the next generation of church leaders would come.

By age fifteen, most boys found their way into business as much to relieve their families of the economic drain imposed by their idleness as by any visions of wealth. The challenges for girls in the city were greater. Many girls found the workplace more alluring than marriage, and sometimes they had to enter it as a practical necessity. Public high schools rarely existed and those that did frequently graduated students by age fifteen.[7]

College enrollment was possible for only a handful of wealthy or gifted boys, and even fewer girls. Joseph Kett reports fewer than nine thousand undergraduates in the nation in 1850.[8] Churches offered some social structure to the urban cacophony, but their concerted efforts seldom brought harmony to daily life in their neighborhoods.

Formal education, however, was not the only safety net for urban young men. Volunteer fire and military companies provided purposeful activities and fellowship. Volunteer fire companies, for example, not only fought fires but also served as social fraternities where younger men could congregate while they served the good of the community. "Volunteer aides" provided a structure for those under eighteen in which they could socialize with the firefighters in the station house and assist in bringing equipment to the fires but not endanger themselves by actually fighting the fires.[9]

Literary societies, singing societies, Base Ball clubs, temperance societies, and missionary societies offered constructive alternatives to the temptations of the city. Sunday school unions and associations recruited young men and women to teach classes for urban children. Yet it appeared to be a losing battle. Cosmopolitan New York was no longer the New England of Jonathan Edwards and the Puritans of a century earlier.

Five years before the prayer revival began in New York, Theodore L. Cuyler, at age thirty-one, became the pastor of Market Street Church. The challenges of the city captured the young pastor. Reflecting back on those early days of ministry, Cuyler commented:

> The most hideous sink of iniquity and loathsome degradation was in the once famous "Five Points" in the heart of the Sixth Ward and within a pistol shot of Broadway. At the time of my coming to New York public attention had been drawn to that quarter with the opening of the "Old Brewery Mission" and by the first planting of a kindred enterprise which grew into the now well-known "Five Points House of Industry." . . . As my church was just off East Broadway, and within a short walk of the Five Points, I took a deep interest in [this] Christian undertaking.[10]

For years Cuyler has been linked to the beginnings of modern youth ministry. Francis E. Clark, the founder of the Society of Christian Endeavor, repeatedly acknowledged Cuyler's influence. Clark had been inspired by an article that Pastor Cuyler had written concerning the "Young People's Association" in Lafayette Presbyterian Church in Brooklyn.[11] Milford Sholund credits Cuyler with three ideas that endured—coeducational gatherings, weekly meetings, and participation through committees.[12] Roy Zuck mentions a pledge used in the Brooklyn church to assist young people in their spiritual growth.[13] Yet little more has been mentioned about the Brooklyn connection, much less the "Five Points" influence on Cuyler's creation of a local church-based youth ministry.

Theodore Ledyard Cuyler and the Young People's Association

On January 10, 1822, Louisa Frances Morrell Cuyler gave birth to Theodore Ledyard Cuyler in Aurora, New York. His father, Benjamin Ledyard Cuyler, practiced law, as had his father before him. At age four, the future pastor's twenty-eight-year-old father died, leaving him to be raised by his mother in what he described as "the beautiful farm of my grandfather, on the banks of the Cayuga Lake."[14] In this setting Theodore Cuyler grew to maturity and embraced the Christian faith under the "potent" influence of his mother.

During revival meetings led by Charles Finney in western New York state, Cuyler, at age nine, was deeply affected, but it was his mother who led him to Christ. "She was a remarkable woman in intellectual force, and in stalwart godliness of the old Puritan type," commented Cuyler writing after his retirement. "I revere her memory now as of a pastor, a Sunday-school teacher, and a parent, all combined in one."[15]

Cuyler's Education

At age sixteen, Cuyler entered Princeton University, where he took honors after three years of study. Upon graduation he visited Europe and amused himself by writing a series of sketches on travel and various men of eminence. His grandfather's thriving law practice apparently made possible his travels.[16] Yet it may have been the opportunity to address a group gathered at the Glasgow City Hall on the topic of temperance reform that established the direction of his life. He was age twenty at the time.

Still undecided on his career, Cuyler returned to the United States. His father's family urged him to study law and take his place in the family practice. A sense of being led to the Christian ministry came a few days later. On a business visit to a neighboring village an elder of the church asked Cuyler to speak at a meeting attended by nonbelievers. His impromptu message was so effective and to the point that eleven of the sixteen hearers yielded themselves to God. Young Cuyler's decision was made. In the fall of 1843, he enrolled at Princeton Theological Seminary to prepare for the Christian ministry and graduated in May 1846.[17]

Early Pastoral Ministry

After brief pastorates in Wilksbarre, Pennsylvania, and Burlington and Trenton, New Jersey, Cuyler married Annie Elisa Mathiot in Newark, Ohio, on March 17, 1853, and accepted a call to Market Street Dutch Reformed Church in New York City in May. Market Street Church placed him in the swirling vortex of the city, just blocks from the Five Points intersection.

With young people all around but not necessarily in the aging church, Cuyler tried to reach and hold fifteen- to forty-year-olds. Rejecting the trends of the day to provide literary clubs for educated youth, educational opportunities for the less privileged, and social entertainment for everyone, Cuyler focused on prayer. A coeducational prayer meeting for young people produced a positive response, especially when the Prayer Revival of 1857–59 swept the city.

Prayer and the preaching of the young pastor contributed to the growth of Market Street Church. Soon the limitations of their aging church building became apparent. The best idea appeared to be to move away from the Five Corners area to a place where more land was available, in the upper part of the city, but the church's Consistory voted not to move. Cuyler appeared to be trapped where church growth could not happen. Just weeks before, representatives from a newly established Presbyterian church in Brooklyn contacted Cuyler in their search for a pastor. The vote not to move freed him to leave New York for Brooklyn.[18]

Lafayette Avenue Church in Brooklyn

In 1860, Theodore L. Cuyler accepted that call to Park Church in Brooklyn, then two years later the church relocated and became Lafayette Avenue Presbyterian Church. Brooklyn was booming. Removed from the crowded conditions of New York and across the East River from the point of entry for foreign immigrants, Brooklyn was a place of opportunity. Residential developments like Cobble Hill and Brooklyn Heights attracted emerging economic middle class homeowners. The pastor found himself in a growing area where he served until retirement in 1890.

Cuyler ministered among the more affluent citizens of the city. "Brooklyn is not a city of slums," he commented, "nor does it abound with the sky-scraping tenement houses, like those in which myriads of New York live; but we have a large population of wage-earners of the humbler class. These mainly occupy streets by themselves. In order to do our part in giving the bread of life to these worthy people, Lafayette Avenue Church has always maintained two, and sometimes three, auxiliary chapels.[19]

Young people were a top priority for the new pastor. On the twenty-fourth of September 1860, forty young people joined him to establish a prayer meeting similar to the one held in New York. Meetings were held in private houses, and continued to increase in number until young people crowded into even the largest homes on every Monday evening.[20]

Revival and the Young People's Association

A period of revival once again shaped the pastor's ministry. "During the week of prayer in January, 1866, a work of grace commenced in this congregation, which, for extent and power, quite exceeded any that had gone before in the annals of Brooklyn. It occurred, too, not at a time of general revivals, like 1858, but as a sporadic case of extraordinary divine blessing. For several months our devotional meetings were thronged—sometimes as many as thirteen meetings in a week. God's spirit worked mightily."[21]

During this time, Cuyler found it necessary to open two houses for the accommodation of the crowds who flocked to these services. In an effort to conserve the fruit of this revival the weekly prayer meetings became the Young People's Association, which would later influence the establishment of the Society of Christian Endeavor.

The Young People's Association of the Lafayette Avenue Church was organized on the evening of November 6, 1867. Fifty-four persons signed its constitution. The purposes of the association were the conversion of souls, the development of Christian character, and the training of new converts in religious work.[22] Deeply influenced by revivals throughout his lifetime, Cuyler looked for both conversions of young people and Christian service for the total development of youthful followers of Jesus Christ.

The association convened every Monday evening in the private houses of church members. During the course of each year, forty or fifty families opened their doors for an evening visit from all who wished to come. An hour of devotion was spent in singing, prayer, and addresses, followed by a short time of giving introductions to strangers, conversation, and furthering the spiritual interests of the church in numerous ways. The rich and poor met together. Social caste was not a factor in Brooklyn, which may have been the nation's first suburb. In the freedom of a private house, the stuffiness of the church building was taken away. The system worked. Young people had a place of spiritual and social growth in the Brooklyn church.[23]

The affluence of Lafayette Avenue Church allowed the Monday night meeting to function. The fact that the church had forty to fifty homes that could accommodate sizable gatherings of young people suggests a distinct economically upper-middle-class group of people who had the financial capacity to undertake ministry to youth. The arrangements for each meeting further indicated a commitment by the church to their ministry to youth: "The sexton of the church [took] a load of camp stools to the house, for the accommodation of the guests. A box of 'Prayer- meeting Hymn-books' [were] taken also so that the family are [sic] asked to provide nothing but gaslight, house-room, and a hearty welcome."[24]

Though Theodore Cuyler was usually present at the meeting of the Young People's Association, he was not the center of attention. Young people led. Describing a meeting held in his own home, Cuyler said,

> The house was thronged, even on the stairways. Books were distributed, and the singing was social and inspiring. A word or two from God's Book was briefly expounded. Every one was welcome to speak or to pray, as the Spirit should give him utterance. And there was no "awful pause" in the whole happy, enlivening, and instructive hour.[25]

Mobilizing Young Men and Women

Cuyler understood the basic principles of discipleship for new believers. He made sure new believers quickly participated in the meetings. His conviction that a new convert's spiritual development depended on the first six months of his religious life required action. It was his idea that the new believer should be "put into the harness" at once—set to work, called on to pray in public—while he or she was still fresh in faith. The primary venue of service was the Monday night meeting.

A committee structure was established to mobilize the young men and women. While the committees appear to have expanded over the years, Cuyler commented,

> Several lines of labor are open to our Association, which embraces nearly 500 members. There is a "Devotional Committee" which oversees the weekly prayer-meetings. . . . There is a "Tract Committee" who circulated last year 50,000 tracts. An "Entertainment Committee" arrange [sic] for a monthly social gathering at which music, readings, and conversation are the chief attractions. A "Relief Committee" provides for the poor and the sick; and a "Temperance Committee" labors for the promotion of that especial work.[26]

Temperance was an issue close to Cuyler's heart. From the time of his temperance address at the City Hall in Glasgow, the problems related to alcohol consumption concerned him. One feature of the juvenile temperance society important to the Young People's Association was the abstinence pledge: "In reliance on the help of God, I hereby promise to abstain from all intoxicating liquors as a beverage, and to discontinuance [sic] their use in the community." In fact, so important in Cuyler's mind was the pledge, that he advocated its circulation at *every* public meeting held by the society.[27]

The social needs of young people were not overlooked. A half hour was spent at the close of each weekly meeting in friendly "intercourse." (It is interesting how *intercourse* has changed its meaning from wholesome conversation to a purely sexual connotation.) A committee on entertainments also provided for a large monthly gathering—sometimes reportedly attended by nearly a thousand people—in which choice music, readings, and popular lectures and artistic presentations as well as other attractive features were introduced.

Theodore L. Cuyler was the genius behind the Young People's Association. He was concerned for the young people of his church and found a way to reach and nurture them to spiritual maturity. In so doing his church became, by some accounts, the largest Presbyterian church and one of the largest churches in America by the last quarter of the nineteenth century.[28] Influenced by Cuyler's approach to young people, other churches in Brooklyn adapted his methodology with similar success.

Influence on Francis E. Clark

Buoyed by the impact of the Young People's Association, Cuyler wrote of his strategy in articles published for Christian readers. One such article captured the attention of a pastor in Portland, Maine, by the name of Francis E. Clark. Cuyler described what happened next:

> Several years ago an account of this vigorous association . . . fell under the eye of the Rev. Dr. F. E. Clark, who was then the pastor of a church in Maine. He came to our church—during a visit to Brooklyn—and learned more of the work carried on by our young people. . . . [That] was certainly an *inspiration to the first Christian Endeavor Society.*[29]

Horace Bushnell and the Christian Nurture Revolution

Not everyone was as enamored with the role of revival in bringing young people to faith in Christ as was Theodore L. Cuyler. In Hartford, Connecticut, Horace Bushnell served as pastor of North Congregational Church from 1833 to 1859. Though an 1831 revival at Yale College was instrumental in resolving his doubts about the Christian religion and led to his forsaking the pursuit of a law career in favor of pastoral ministry, Bushnell had difficulties with "the machinery system of revivals" in vogue in the mid-nineteenth century. He saw the spirit of pastors being broken when traveling evangelists brought things "to such a pitch in the churches, by the intensity of the revival system."[30]

Bushnell did not oppose revivals of the Christian religion, which he saw as periodic works of God to correct a Christian church grown cold, but he strongly reacted to the excesses of the revivalism of his day. His concern focused on the manner in which evangelical Christians after the Great Awakenings ignored the role of the family and loving care of the church family in favor of a nearly exclusive focus on generating emotion-laden conversions. Such experiences, Bushnell felt, excluded a normal process of incremental spiritual growth nurtured by the Christian family. The most crucial period in the nurturing process, Bushnell felt, occurred before the child learned to speak, the age he called the "age of impressions." To make plain his belief in the central role of Christian parents rather than revivals in shaping the character of their children, he stated, "Let every Christian father and mother understand, when their child is three years old, that they have done more than half of all they will ever do for his character."[31]

Bushnell's Childhood

Horace Bushnell was born on April 14, 1802, in the rural Connecticut community of Bantam. Ensign and Dotha Bishop Bushnell came from Methodist and Episcopalian backgrounds, respectively, and their granddaughter described them as "plain farming people, known to their neighbors . . . for their uprightness, industry, and kindness," all highly respected New England Protestant values.[32]

When Horace, their firstborn, was three years old, the family moved to a farmhouse near New Preston, Connecticut. There Horace joined the Congregational Church on profession of faith at age nineteen. Bushnell's youngest sister (he had two sisters and three brothers) reflected, "[Horace] was born in a household where religion was no occasional and nominal thing, no irksome restraint nor unwelcomed visitor, but a constant atmosphere, a commanding but genial presence."[33] It is quite understandable that Bushnell would have seen himself as having been nurtured in his home more than in his church.

Yet throughout his young adult years, Bushnell struggled with doubts about his Christian faith. Only through the aforementioned revival on the Yale campus, to which he returned as a tutor after graduation, did Bushnell set aside his doubts, concluding that the ultimate questions of religion are questions of the heart rather than of the mind.[34]

In the fall of 1831, Bushnell entered the Theological School in New Haven, and he was ordained as Pastor of North Congregational Church in Hartford on May 22, 1833. The following September, Bushnell married Mary Apthorp. He served North Church until ill health forced him to resign in 1859.

Discourses on Christian Nurture

Like Theodore Cuyler, Bushnell was a writer. His articles extended his ministry far beyond North Church. In 1844 he published an article in the popular *New Englander* magazine entitled "The Kingdom of Heaven as a Grain of Mustard Seed" that argued for Christian growth from within the church rather than through the current practice of revivals and conversions. The article led to a series of lectures for his Hartford ministerial association, which published them in April of 1847 as *Discourses on Christian Nurture*.[35]

Debate followed. Additional articles expanded and clarified his position, culminating in 1861 with the publication of *Christian Nurture*, in which the pastor argued that

> the child is to grow up a Christian, and never know himself as being otherwise. In other words, the aim, effort, and expectation should be, not, as is commonly assumed, that the child is to grow up in sin, to be converted after he comes to a mature age; but that he is to open on the world as one that is spiritually renewed, not remembering the time when he went through a technical experience, but seemed rather to have loved what is good from his earliest years.[36]

The book stimulated discussion among church leaders until his death in 1876 and continues to factor into discussions of youth ministry today.[37]

Revivalist preachers expected young people to sow their wild oats, to live lives of rebellion toward God before conversion. Convinced that this was wrong, Bushnell championed the view that this idea contradicted the teaching of Scripture as well as the history of the church. In so doing the Congregationalist pastor provided a theological basis for ministry by the church to youth and children. Reacting strongly against the individualism he associated with revivalism, he linked Christian nurture primarily with the family.

Influence on Cuyler and Clark

Both Theodore Cuyler and Francis E. Clark were influenced by Bushnell's concept of Christian nurture. In an article painting a "pen-picture" of Horace Bushnell as one of the eminent preachers of their day, Cuyler described him as "the most splendid genius who has stood in the New England pulpit during the present century."[38]

Yet little of what Theodore Cuyler did in establishing prayer meetings for young people or in creating the Young People's Association appeared to be connected with Bushnell's idea of Christian nurture. Obviously written for parents, *Christian Nurture* focused on the home. Cuyler hardly even used the language of nurture in reporting the structure and impact of the association. He desired to sustain the prayer revival of his New York days, and it had no connection with "the machinery system of revivals" against which Bushnell bristled. Nurture was for children, and Cuyler's concern focused on youth.

It would be left to Francis Clark, Pastor of the Williston Church in Portland, Maine, to connect Bushnell's concept of nurture to youth ministry. Yet not even Clark connected the dots between Christian nurture and Christian endeavor until after the structure of the society was successfully in place and had been replicated as far west as Ravenna, Ohio, and St. Louis, Missouri.

Clark Links Christian Nurture with the Young People's Association

Central to Francis Edward Clark's earliest attempts at youth ministry was revival. Serving in his first church after graduating from Andover Seminary, the young pastor crafted much of his preaching calendar in his first four years around a week of prayer just after the beginning of each new year. For four months he laid the ground work. In January a week of meetings focused on prayer. Conversions consistently resulted. Clark described these weeks of prayer more as revival meetings than as replications of the Prayer Revival experienced by Theodore Cuyler twenty years before.

> Special meetings were held every night, the claims of Christ for an immediate decision to serve Him were urged, an opportunity was given for all to declare themselves, and without exception, each year a religious awakening was the result, which usually brought from twenty to forty new members, most of them young people, into the church.[39]

As gratifying as were the initial results, the sustained impact upon the youth of his church appeared minimal. They failed to remain as "a company of devoted, earnest young people, outspoken among their companions in their acknowledgement [sic] of Christ's claim and ready to work for Him along all practical and systematic lines."[40] The problem was not new. In 1745 Jonathan Edwards grieved at the actions of the very young people who, only two years before, renounced sin and pledged themselves to holy and devout Christian living.[41] The fruit of revivals seemed to disappear in a relatively short period of time.

The circumstances of Francis E. Clark's life placed his understanding of Christian conversion somewhere between Cuyler's and Bushnell's.

> While I believe heartily in revivals, and in many revivalists, and in special periods of religious awakening, I also believe that there is a place for the Timothy type of conversion as well as for the Pauline, and that Mother Eunice and Grandmother Lois may be as much used of God in bringing their children to Christ, as the most fiery and eloquent evangelist.[42]

Clark's Childhood

Though born in Aylmer, Quebec (near Ottawa), to Lydia Fletcher Clark Symmes and Charles Carey Symmes, Francis Clark's parents were from prominent families in the Boston area.[43] Opportunities in the logging industry lured Clark's father northward, but on August 4, 1854, he died of cholera when Francis (they called him Frank) was three years old. Lydia remained in Canada with Frank and his older brother, Charles. In late 1858 Frank's brother died, and six months later, on March 26, 1859, his mother died. At age seven Frank Symmes was an orphan.

At his mother's request, Lydia's brother, Edward Warren Clark, and his wife, Harriet, adopted young Francis and gave him the Clark family name. With no children of their own, the Congregational clergyman and his wife raised Francis in a loving and nurturing environment first in Auberndale, Massachusetts, and later in Claremont, New Hampshire.

At age thirteen, in the prayer meeting at the Congregational Church in Claremont, Francis Clark stood up "trembling and abashed" and confessed his desire to be counted among the followers of Christ. No evangelist or season of religious excitement brought him to this decision. By his confession, it resulted from religious training and conviction.

Influence of Dartmouth College on Christian Endeavor

Since Clark lived before the era of the public high school, Kimball Union Academy, then one of the three largest and most important finishing schools in New England, prepared him for his college education at Dartmouth. In addition to academic development in college, Clark began formulating ideas that later would shape Christian Endeavor. Three impressions of Dartmouth stand out. First, in 1922 he wrote,

The class prayer meetings, though of course entirely voluntary, were usually attended by fully half of our class, most of whom took part briefly, according to the present Christian Endeavor custom. I am not sure that these class prayer meetings did not give me my first idea of what a church young people's society might be.[44]

A second impression was that of revival. Though the revivals didn't affect him personally, Clark described a genuine revival of religion that occurred in the midst of his college experience as happening at least once every four years. To his delight, some of the strongest men of his school, intellectually and socially (there were no women enrolled at that time), were thoroughly converted.

A third shaping influence in Clark's college days was the beginning of his literary efforts. His writings initially grew out of the two-week excursions in the White Mountains with half a dozen classmates at the close of his sophomore year. The yearly outing of the newly fledged juniors was a regular feature of those college days and rounded out his social and physical development. An article published in the *Old Curiosity Shop*, a Boston magazine, opened the way for Clark to become the editor of *The Dartmouth Magazine* during his senior year and eventually led to the publication of thirty-seven books and thousands of articles.

From Dartmouth College, Francis Clark matriculated at Andover Theological Seminary, graduating in 1876. In October he married Harriet Elizabeth Abbott and later that month was installed as pastor of the Williston Church, in Portland, Maine.

Similarities between Cuyler's and Clark's Churches

Like Theodore Cuyler's Lafayette Avenue Church, the youthful Williston congregation was an outgrowth of a mission begun only a few years before Francis Clark became pastor. Portland, Maine, like Brooklyn, was a city of churches and homemakers, insulated from the stresses of cities like New York or even Boston. Though initially neither Lafayette nor Williston were wealthy churches, both grew rapidly and attracted enough wealthy parishioners to relocate to larger and better located buildings within the first two years of their pastor's new ministry.

There was one other similarity between Cuyler's church in Brooklyn and Clark's ministry in Portland. Both stressed the role of prayer in the spiritual lives of the congregation. For both, prayer was associated with Christian conversion and revivals of religion. While these convictions ignored Horace Bushnell's idea of Christian nurture in the home, Clark would later incorporate a modified idea of nurture into his writings that promoted the Society of Christian Endeavor. From the beginning of his pastoral ministry, he saw the faith community, the local church, as an agency of Christian nurture.

The Evolution of Christian Endeavor

Thus it was that Francis E. Clark prepared for the fourth annual week of prayer in January of 1881 and, without realizing it, for what he would later describe as "the most important incident of my life in Portland," the founding of the Society of Christian Endeavor.[45] Like most innovations in youth ministry, the formation of the society was more like another jam session of ideas and experiments than the intentional launching of a new strategy of ministry. Only this time the youth ministry jazz fused revival and nurturing perspectives into a new form of youth ministry.

The pastor described his effort to solidify the church ministry to its young people as "an evolution, rather than a creation by the fiat of the minister."[46] For more than four years, Clark had experimented with his "Pastor's Class," a debating club, a musical society, social activities, and even a young people's missionary society founded by the pastor's wife, Harriet Abbott Clark, called the "Mizpah Circle." None of them worked to the satisfaction of the pastor, who concluded that two factors were missing. All other efforts added something else to the endeavor to know God, which then detracted from the Christian pursuit. None of the other efforts satisfactorily made young people accountable participants in reporting their spiritual journey.

Hardly alone in his quest for innovation, Clark joined literally thousands of pastors who felt they needed to find a better means of reaching and holding youth. Theodore Cuyler's efforts with his Young People's Association in Brooklyn captured Clark's attention. Stimulated and guided by an article written by Cuyler, followed by a visit to see the Brooklyn church's ministry to young people, Clark proposed the Society of Christian Endeavor to fifty-eight young people gathered in the parlor of the parsonage on February 2, 1881. Reinforced by his memory of prayer meetings at Dartmouth College, the organizational framework from Lafayette Avenue Church, and pledges from the temperance movement as well as others reaching back to the day of Jonathan Edwards, the pastor wrote out a proposal as the young people gathered downstairs for Mrs. Clark's cookies.

"Its object," wrote the pastor, "shall be to promote an earnest Christian life among its members to increase their mutual acquaintance, and to make them more useful in the service of God."[47] While the objective reflected more Baptist and revivalistic thinking than Horace Bushnell could have embraced, it proposed an alternative to the Christian individualism against which Bushnell railed. Staked out was the middle ground in which youth ministry would thrive into the twenty-first century, sometimes emphasizing nurture to the impoverishment of evangelism and at other times the other way around.

Conclusion

The gangs of New York were both a real threat and a metaphor against which youth ministry developed. Youth ministry played the sounds of the city. Urban experience replaced isolated village life, leaving the church struggling to adapt. While Horace Bushnell wrote of the nurturing impact of families, Theodore Cuyler, for a time, perpetuated the impact of the 1857–59 Prayer Revival, and Francis Clark merged and reconciled nurture and revival for Christians in the emerging economic middle class. The world had changed.

The jazz of youth ministry was continual improvisation, and all jam sessions were local. While union meetings (area rallies), denominational camps and conferences, and national and international youth conventions provided energy to support local ministry, the vitality of the music continued to depend on innovators like Bushnell, Cuyler, and Clark to create the new sounds and turn the sounds of the city into the music of the ages.

With or without Bushnell, Francis Clark probably would have developed Christian Endeavor in the same way. His efforts responded to a grassroots spiritual need among the young people of Portland, Maine. Only later, when correspondents asked about the relationship of Christian Endeavor to Christian nurture did Francis Clark bring educational theory to focus on his nonformal educational system. As this praxis emerged, Christian nurture became the expression of the faith community more than the nuclear family.

Without Theodore Cuyler's innovations in Brooklyn, it is unlikely that the supporting committee system would have been connected with either the prayer meeting or the Christian Endeavor pledge. Yet it was the committee system that gave the society social substance. Because of the committees, young people owned the society. Leadership roles provided niches for a wide variety of youth. The vigilance of the "Lookout Committee" cultivated new members and held existing members accountable for their Christian endeavor. The society provided a safe place where loving pastors or adult lay leaders could relate to the youth of the church and community. As a result, young people stayed within the church, experienced nurture in their Christian faith, and grew accustomed to experiences of God's presence privately and in group settings.

part **3**

Sheet Music Jazz

The Period of Youth Societies (1881–1925)

Jazz was created in the gut. Few of the musicians who expressed their pain in the music of New Orleans read music. Fewer still could reproduce what they had played on paper. Yet the sounds of the city spread. First traveling musicians played their musical expressions wherever people would gather for whatever coins they would toss into a hat.

As the sounds of jazz spread, publishers and conveyers of popular culture saw an opportunity for making money, and soon jazz started showing up as sheet music, and later, on 78 RPM records. The age of imitation had begun. Young musicians with nowhere near the musical skills of the original, primarily African American, musicians could mechanically copy the rifts of jazz artists, rendering a primitive but passable expression of jazz music.

The period of youth societies (1881–1925) unfolded in much the same way as the spread of jazz. Certain central themes remained the same as in previous days, but now rather than needing local leadership to create a score from which youth societies performed, national and international societies published the materials. National conferences annually brought the performers together to teach the music and inspire the novice musicians to return to their home churches and teach others this youth ministry jazz.

Of course these new sounds created resistance among advocates of the older forms of church music. Some felt that worship services and preaching should be sufficient to help young people experience God's presence. Sin avoidance lectures in Sunday school should be adequate to produce godly young people. Annual evangelistic meetings should be sufficient to bring about conversions in the community. Resistance to these new sounds, however, quickly fell away as Protestant youth societies increasingly facilitated youthful faithfulness in their faith communities.

Part 3 describes the formal emergence of Protestant youth groups in America. It was a period of organization as national youth ministry programs shaped local youth groups. As the public high school carved out a distinct place for early and middle adolescents in society, and the Progressive Era built an air of expectation of the ability of the American experiment to improve all aspects of life, Protestant youth groups followed suit.

Chapter 8 captures the dramatic birth and growth of the Society of Christian Endeavor, in which Christian youth found an attractive way to focus their efforts to know God. Using Meredith Willson's musical comedy *The Music Man*, set in the summer of 1912 in River City, Iowa, the chapter sets the context for the second cycle of youth ministry as it arose and then began to stagnate.

For Rev. Francis Clark, adapting the juvenile temperance pledge and challenging his young people to pledge an endeavor to know God provided the kind of innovation that captured the imagination of church leaders across the nation and around the English-speaking world. A young person visiting churches from a different denomination or in another country would feel very comfortable in the local Society of Christian Endeavor. The program was substantially the same. Even songs were sung out of the Christian Endeavor hymnal.

Quickly the idea of spiritual accountability expanded into denominational accountability as denominational imitations of Clark's Christian Endeavor both expanded and fragmented the movement. Protestant denominations quickly responded. Chapter 9 describes denominational youth programs of the same period. Saturday night in River City in Willson's musical captured the local Methodist Epworth League, one expression of a denominational youth program. Baptists, Lutherans, and Presbyterians similarly had programs that encouraged youthful spirituality as well as denominational loyalty.

During the period of youth societies, church leaders embraced the idea that young people could lead and participate in activities that enabled them to develop leadership abilities for service in the church while keeping them focused on Christian disciplines until such a time as God "showed up" in their lives. Like the previous cycle of youth ministry, the movement started with a great deal of energy and flourished for about twenty years before gradually running aground on the shoals of social change. By 1925 it found itself struggling for direction. But the jazz of the period of youth societies altered the manner in which churches engaged young people in their faith communities.

8

Trouble in River City

The Period of Youth Societies (1881–1925)

There is hardly a high school in America that at one time or another has not produced Meredith Willson's musical comedy *The Music Man*. The delightful story describes how a traveling salesman who calls himself "Professor" Harold Hill arrives in River City, Iowa, on July 4, 1912, intending to sell band instruments and uniforms by forming a boys' band and teaching them to play. Hill does not expect to stick around the town of 2,212 people long enough to train the reluctant musicians. All he wants to do is make a quick sale and then skip town.[1]

Professor Hill's strategy was simple. First he found something in River City that he could portray as a threat to the youth of the city, then he connected it to other fears of moral corruption that Hill knew parents harbored, and when enough hysteria was whipped up, the "professor" presented the idea of a boys' band as an immediate solution to the problem. Of course this meant that the parents would have to buy band instruments and uniforms, but that was a small price to pay for saving their children from "the road to the Depths of deg-ra-day-tion."

In one of the most creative songs ever included in a Broadway musical, Harold Hill plays on parents' fears to describe the "trouble right here in River City," which was indicated by the presence of a pool table in their community. Hill's song gives a classic "slippery slope" argument for the way that young people slide into a life of sin. First their boys played pool; then they gambled on their games, which in turn led to betting on horse racing. From there it was all downhill: they became cigarette fiends, danced at the armory with libertine men and scarlet women, and listened to shameless ragtime music.

By the time the salesman finished with the song, the entire community was clamoring for a way to keep the young ones moral after school. Harold Hill's suggestion was the formation of an adult-sponsored youth movement in the form of a boys' band. Though Hill's motivation is purely selfish, the church-sponsored youth societies that arose during the second cycle of youth ministry and spanned this period around the turn of the century were sincere responses to similar concerns. Parents wanted to keep their children moral and wanted them to know God.

The second cycle of youth ministry in the United States had the most clearly marked starting point of the three cycles that span the nineteenth and twentieth centuries. It began on February 2, 1881, in Portland, Maine, when Francis E. Clark formed the Young People's Society of Christian Endeavor. With a growing economic middle class in America, a spirit of optimism in the air, and a rising fear of foreign influences, the evangelical church was ripe for a new method of doing youth ministry. Response to Clark's ideas was enthusiastic and this support for an evangelically based philosophy of working with young people continued until the Scopes Monkey Trial made a mockery of Bible-believing Christians in 1925.

The Progressive Era

By the time Harold Hill arrived in fictitious River City, America had undergone a fundamental change. Cities had become the focal point of expansion. The value of manufactured goods had surpassed that of farm products in the United States. Whereas 53 percent of the labor force in 1870 were engaged in farming, by 1920 73 percent held nonagricultural jobs. If the first cycle of youth ministry was associated with the social dislocation caused by the movement of people from the east to the west, the second cycle is related to a mass movement from rural to urban America. Educational historian Lawrence Cremin refers to the period from 1876 to 1980 as the "metropolitan experience."[2]

The flood of people into American cities was a result of the Industrial Revolution and the jobs, especially in factories, that were available in the cities of the land. Some workers came from rural areas and settled in the cities looking for a better living than was available in agricultural communities, but more than twenty-five million entered the United States from Europe, and after the turn of the century a majority of these newcomers settled in cities.

The nation was optimistic. Despite occasional recessions the American economy grew at an amazing rate, and the United States became the world's foremost producer of manufactured goods. Railroads stretched from coast to coast carrying products over nearly a quarter of a million miles of track by 1910. Technical innovation, as evidenced by new patents, propelled the economy forward. Educational institutions were captured by the progressive flavor of the national psyche, and John Dewey emerged as a champion of teaching methods that centered on the child and were responsive to her or his needs.

The Christian church was affected by the spirit of the day. "In almost every major American denomination, sometime between the late 1870s and World War I, serious disagreements broke out between conservatives and liberals."[3] The more liberal elements deemphasized historic Christian doctrines in favor of interdenominational unity, whereas the conservatives stressed holding to the fundamentals of the faith and living in a manner that reflected traditional evangelical values.

One person who straddled the conservative/liberal divide was William Jennings Bryan. Bryan was best known in the contemporary world as the fighting fundamentalist who, according to the national media in general and H. L. Mencken in particular, made historic Christian orthodoxy look foolish at the trial of John Scopes in Dayton, Tennessee. While the trial was about Scopes's violation of the state law forbidding the teaching of evolution in public schools, defense attorney Clarence Darrow made the credibility of the Christian worldview the primary issue. Press accounts belittled conservative Christians as anti-intellectual. The resulting scandal left young people wondering if their endeavor to know the God of the Bible was intellectual suicide.

William Jennings Bryan died just days after the end of the trial. Yet removed from the shadow of the events in the last few days of his life, an examination of the contributions of "The Great Commoner" to American life in the twentieth century suggests a profound and progressive agenda. Though he failed to be elected president of the United States as the Democratic nominee on three occasions, Bryan's contributions to American political and social history far exceed those of most presidents. For example, Bryan is credited with early championing of the following: graduated income tax (16th Amendment), direct election of US senators (17th Amendment), women's suffrage (19th Amendment), workmen's compensation, minimum wage, eight-hour workday, Federal Trade Commission, Federal Farm Loan Act, government regulation of telephone/telegraph and food safety, Department of Health, Department of Labor, and Department of Education. Yet like most American politicians of his day, Bryan had a distinctively unprogressive view of race issues.[4]

Bryan's concerns for social issues were not those of the ordinary church member. The parents of River City better typified the values of the average evangelical church member at the turn of the century. They were more concerned with issues of conventional morality than national progress. Sloth, drinking beer from a bottle, reading dime novels, memorizing jokes out of Captain Billy's Whiz Bang, and using words like "swell" and "so's your old man" alarmed the people of Meredith Willson's comedy, and they were urged to maintain a discrete distance from those who practiced such moral indiscretions.

To help protect young people from the evil influences present in the changing culture at the turn of the century, youth societies came into being, first within the church and then independent from ecclesiastical controls. Before Harold Hill arrived in River City, the Methodist Church already had a chapter of the Epworth League. Each of the other Protestant denominations had similarly formed youth societies during the closing years of the nineteenth century. After the turn of the century Boy Scouts and Girl Scouts, 4-H Clubs, Future Farmers of America, Future Homemakers of America, and Camp Fire Girls would become agencies of socialization based on a Judeo-Christian ethic.

Francis E. Clark and the Society of Christian Endeavor

On February 2, 1881, the second cycle of youth ministry was born. It was revolutionary in its simplicity and yet profound in its impact. What Francis Clark did on that Sunday afternoon set the stage for youth groups around the world. Yet that was not his intent. Rev. Clark's immediate purpose was to respond to the concerns he had for the youth of his church.

Like many pastors across the nation, the twenty-five-year-old pastor of Williston Church in Portland, Maine, had been looking for a way to assist the young people of his church to continue in their Christian faith after an initial salvation experience. Unclear to church leaders was where young people fit into congregational life. Church membership was at the heart of the discussion. When would young people be ready for full church membership? If they were admitted to membership prematurely and they strayed from the faith, the idea of membership would be meaningless. If discouraged from joining too long, young people might turn from the church. Then what would become of the next generation and how would the church sustain itself?

As far as pastors were concerned this "youth problem" had to be addressed. Some blamed parents for failing to insist that their children attend church services or to provide religious instruction in the home.

Others pointed out that Sunday schools were full of children and youth but that the instruction received did not bridge the gap between childhood and adult membership. Still others admitted that methods used in church services and prayer meetings failed to interest anyone except those who led, and it was questionable if even they were fully engaged when not speaking or praying.[5]

The "youth problem" extended beyond youth ceasing to attend church. Economic prosperity made alternative forms of activities far more appealing to youth than church services, which appealed primarily to the cognitive powers of listeners. Alternatives abounded—roller skating, bicycle rides, picnics, socials, theater attendance, watching spectator events such as baseball, visiting amusement parks, even visiting a neighborhood saloon or its temperance alternative, the newly invented soda fountain. Not only was the church losing her youth; they had begun to "worship" elsewhere.

Young people, in the era before public high schools, typically engaged in business by age fifteen. To them Sunday school seemed childish. For even the most fervent youthful church attendees, few other options were available. Singing, literary, temperance, missionary, and social societies provided little to nurture their Christian faith. Prayer meetings for young people proved boring to most attendees. Yearly revival meetings failed to sustain Christian commitments. As the nineteenth century came to a close, increased attention was given to the needs of young people.

Rev. Clark was not alone in his search to solve this "youth problem." Virtually every Protestant denomination recorded efforts in local churches to address the "youth problem" as they saw it. John H. Vincent, reflecting on the growth of denominational youth societies, wrote in 1892, "There never has been a time in the history of the church when so much attention has been given to the organization and discipline of young people until now."[6] Much of this visibility of youth ministry came from national programs, the first of which was the Society of Christian Endeavor. Yet, as Joseph Kett pointed out, "Such rapid growth was possible only because of the prior existence of young people's societies in churches, societies now federated into national organizations."[7]

Nor was Francis Clark trained in youth ministry. His was the standard preparation for pastoral ministry, but during his formal education there were hints of the effective ministry to come. While at Dartmouth College (class of '73) and Andover Seminary (class of '76), the young man manifested both writing and oratorical skills. Though chosen one of the student speakers at his college graduation, Clark had an equal love for journalism and vacillated between the Christian ministry and a writing career until three months before graduation. Clark's collegiate journalistic experiences included being an editor of *The Dartmouth*

Magazine and serving as a correspondent for the *Boston Globe* and *The Congregationalist*. The latter provided a contact that later brought his fledgling youth society to public attention.

For five years Clark's ministry to youth at Williston Church seemed ineffective. Though the church grew from fifty in attendance to over four hundred in its first five years, Clark expressed frustration at the bottleneck that parents provided to allowing young people to join the church. Writing to his father in the fall of 1879, he reported:

> Tonight a new prayer meeting is started which we shall hold through the winter. It is especially for the young people, and I want to make it very informal and familiar where we shall sit around, talk, ask questions, etc. It is something of an experiment, but I hope it will succeed, for there are many young people whom we can't quite seem to reach by the existing meetings.[8]

Six months later, the experiment appeared to be a failure. From Clark's perspective, the apathy of parents was at the heart of the problem. He lamented:

> There is no reason in my judgment why thirty or forty [young people] should not come into the church [on] the first of May, but I find an unaccountable indifference and reluctance on the part of the parents of the church and I am afraid I shall receive but a few of them. Their parents acknowledge that [their children] are different from what they were, . . . and even they think they are converted, but [parents] will not encourage or even allow them, in some cases, to go any farther.[9]

To overcome the spiritual apathy of parents, Francis Clark realized he would have to find a way of attracting young people in spite of parental influence. Clark's wife had been somewhat successful with the girls of the church through a foreign missions oriented group that she called the "Mizpah Circle," but this was not enough. Like pastors of his day, Francis Clark sought for ministry ideas in the publications. An article by Theodore Cuyler, pastor of Lafayette Avenue Church in Brooklyn, captured his attention. Further contact with the Brooklyn pastor as well as exposure to the writings of Horace Bushnell's ideas on Christian nurture, to the YMCA, and to the "class meeting" used by the Methodists all contributed to his thinking, but still something was missing.

Then, after a week of prayer and special meetings in January 1881, an idea came to him. The concept would demonstrate to parents, church leaders, and the community the capacity of young people for sincere spiritual commitments.

The idea was accountability. Clark created a society whose primary purpose was to reinforce the desire of young people to grow in their walk with God—to strengthen their Christian endeavor. Accountability took two forms—a pledge to endeavor to know God and a commitment to serve in a weekly responsibility.

The pledge required two commitments. Every member was expected, "unless detained by some absolute necessity," to be present at every meeting and take part, "however slight" in each meeting. Then, once a month, an "experience meeting" was to be held, at which "each member shall speak concerning his progress in the Christian life for the past month." Failure to do so for three consecutive months meant removal from "active" status in the society.[10]

The idea of a pledge was not new. The temperance movement employed various forms of a pledge to help temperance society members abstain from alcoholic drink. The difference between the two pledges was that the temperance pledge was negative, designed to restrain members from indulging in "spirits," while the Christian Endeavor pledge was positive, intended to assist members to know God better. It could be said that Endeavorers pledged to indulge in the Spirit of the triune God.

Though the language of the pledge was masculine, the society was comprised of young people of both sexes. Harriet Clark balked at the idea of girls speaking in front of the boys when her husband first suggested it, but soon affirmed the wisdom of the mutual accountability.

The second type of accountability took the form of committee assignments. Soon after the initial meeting, every society member was assigned to a committee and was expected to perform tasks that made Christian Endeavor work. As the society grew, additional committees were formed so that every member had specific tasks he or she was expected to perform. Initially society officers formed a central committee while a "Lookout Committee" was constantly looking for new society members and the "Prayer Meeting Committee" prepared and led the weekly prayer and monthly experience meetings. As societies grew, committees proliferated. Everyone needed a place to serve.

The actual formation of the Society of Christian Endeavor took place in the pastor's home. Over sixty young people heard the constitution read, but when asked to sign the pledge they hesitated.[11] Then one young person who had helped the pastor convene the group signed his name. Two others followed. Within a few minutes fifty-seven people registered as active members while six more signed on as associate members. Officers were elected with Grandville Staples as president. By the end of the year, the society grew to one hundred twenty-seven members, thirty of whom joined the church. By the end of the third year, a hundred and eighty young people listed themselves as active and associate members. A new chapter of youth ministry had begun.

Henry B. Pennell, a boy of eleven, led the first prayer meeting. After an afternoon of preparation, Henry read Scripture, announced hymns, led in prayer, then somewhat timidly, yet with confidence, he expressed his thoughts about endeavoring to live as a Christian. Others followed. The hour filled with childlike, yet prompt, earnest, and devout expressions of Christian faith. Pledges were fulfilled. The Society of Christian Endeavor had launched successfully.[12]

The Spread of the Society of Christian Endeavor

Word of the new society spread rapidly. In October 1881 a second society was formed by Rev. C. P. Mills at Newburyport, Massachusetts. A third formed on St. Lawrence Street in Portland, Maine.

Propagation of Christian Endeavor societies resulted from two factors. Eager to share his experience with other pastors, Francis Clark published an article about his initial success in the August 1881 issue of *The Congregationalist*. A second article by Clark appeared in the *Sunday School Times* a short time later. Almost immediately, letters began flooding the study of the young pastor. After answering as many as he could, Clark decided to provide a more complete rationale for and description of the Society of Christian Endeavor in book form. The book, entitled *The Children and the Church, and the Young People's Society of Christian Endeavor, as a Means of Bringing Them Together*, was the first book published exclusively for youth ministry. Just as the Sunday school had spread as a result of newspaper coverage and printed training materials, Clark used the media of the day to spread the Christian Endeavor idea.

Probably just as significant to its spread in the early days was the relocation of society members to other parts of the country where they reproduced Christian Endeavor societies in churches into which they settled. Edmund T. Garland and his bride moved to Lincoln, Nebraska, while Charles B. Newton organized a society in South Hadley, Massachusetts. Mary Simpson married Rev. Edward Noyes and moved to Duluth, Minnesota, where she began a Society of Christian Endeavor. Early reports indicated societies beginning in Tacoma, Washington; Crewe, England; and Foochow (Fuzhou), China, as these people in their young adult years moved around the world.[13]

In June of the following year, six societies were known to exist. Interest was such that Clark held a conference at Williston Church for anyone who wanted to learn more about the society. When the second conference for Christian Endeavor was held on June 7, 1883, at Payson

Memorial Church in Portland, Maine, sixty-seven delegates gathered from fifty-six societies in fourteen states, representing 2,870 members. Representatives from seven denominations were present. These included Congregational, Baptist, Free Baptist, Presbyterian, Methodist, Dutch Reformed, and "Christian" churches.[14]

Annually thereafter conferences gave evidence to the growth of the movement. In 1884 at Lowell, Massachusetts, delegates represented 156 societies and 8,905 members. The following year in Ocean Park, Maine, delegates represented 253 societies and 14,892 members. In 1886, the conference moved out of New England to Saratoga Springs, New York, hosting delegates representing 850 societies and over fifty thousand members. Delegates at the annual conventions dramatically highlighted the multiplication of the movement. When the convocation returned to Saratoga Springs in 1887 it enrolled over two thousand delegates. The Philadelphia convention in 1889 brought together sixty-five hundred delegates; the Minneapolis convention of 1891 registered over fourteen thousand Endeavorers, while the Boston conference of 1895, only fourteen years after the first meeting of the society, saw 56,425 persons attend.[15]

By 1892, the *Southern Presbyterian* journal reported, "There is scarcely a land on the face of the earth without its societies of Christian Endeavor. The last year has been the year of greatest growth in the history of the movement. Almost every evangelical denomination in America has either adopted the society as its own or allows its existence without opposition. There are now at least 22,000 societies with a million and a quarter members in all parts of the world."[16]

Leadership Development and Stimulating Creativity

The health and vitality of youth organizations as they grow usually is measured by their ability to stay close to the grass roots and develop new leadership. Two tools used by Christian Endeavor, especially in the early days, reflected these twin essentials. The first was Christian Endeavor Unions that required local leaders to take regional responsibility and develop their skills. The second took ideas from across the nation and around the world and published them in *The Golden Rule*, a weekly newspaper that proved to be both a source of fresh ideas for local leaders and a means of tying the movement together.

Christian Endeavor Unions were both essential and problematic. Unions consisted of area rallies for Christian Endeavor societies. Though the annual conference hosted by Francis Clark provided the first union-type meeting, it was the local, regional, and state unions that provided the greatest venue for leadership development and mutual encouragement.

Unions were essential because they brought together members from various regions of the country to stimulate their endeavor to live as Christians. While the stated reason was mutual encouragement, the side effects were equally important. Weaker societies learned from stronger societies. Society officers and committee chairs gained insights from others doing the same job. Vision was cast for making a Christian impact on the world. Evangelistic appeals allowed nonmembers to begin their journeys to love and serve Christ.

Unfortunately unions provided a point of tension for pastors and denominational leaders. In an age when denominational loyalty was held precious, Christian Endeavor Unions diluted that allegiance through interdenominational contact. Doctrinal distinctives blurred in these public rallies. Denominational mission loyalties and subscriptions to denominational publications were threatened as young people found new options through union activities.

Perhaps inspired by denominational unions such as the Young People's Baptist Union and the Methodist Episcopal Young People's Union of Brooklyn, New York,[17] the first local Christian Endeavor Union was formed in New Haven, Connecticut, in 1886 under the leadership of Rev. J. E. Twitchell.[18] As described by Francis Clark a few years later, the four results of a union meeting were conversion, inspiration, instruction, and sociability. Smaller union meetings began with a supper and socialization. Next, young people led in a half hour of praise, Bible reading, and prayer. Then ten minutes of business, announcements, and planning, followed by a twenty-minute address (usually by an Endeavor member) and twenty minutes of devotional activities (public testimony of pledges made to God or their fulfillment).[19] Larger gatherings reached three to five hundred participants, requiring the omission of the meal.

Union meetings required active participation by youthful leaders. In order to maintain interest, variety was essential. Reports from societies, while essential for cross-pollinating ideas, had strict time limits. Featuring new and improved methods stimulated further local innovation. Perhaps most importantly, unions featured "home grown talent" so that local society leaders would have their day in the spotlight. Occasional outside speakers or union consecration meetings brought added variety to the mix, but union meetings primarily aided the leadership development of the young people themselves.

Interest grew. Each morning at nine o'clock, the office boy brought bags of mail into the Bromfield Street office of the United Society of Christian Endeavor in Boston. Frequently he left fifty to seventy-five letters on Rev. Clark's desk. Some landed in the office of the business agent.

Hundreds more received the attention of the general secretary. And that was only the first mail of the day. Clark estimated the number of letters at seventy-five thousand per year in 1890.[20] Many of the correspondents wished for advice and help with their societies and unions. Answering letters became a time-consuming and expensive task. Yet if the movement was to remain vibrant, these people needed to be served.

At the same time, one of the most frequent requests from Christian Endeavor officers at local, state, and national gatherings focused on establishing a newspaper to serve the movement. Yet Christian Endeavor operated on a very thin budget. To start a newspaper was an expensive proposition. Hearing the need expressed, five gentlemen purchased *The Golden Rule*, a struggling paper with a rather poor reputation and allowed Christian Endeavor to use it as its house organ. The cost of the weekly subscription was one dollar per year. By the second year two hundred thousand subscriptions spread the word about Christian Endeavor. From 1889 to 1898 the paper served the movement with news, curricular ideas, and training suggestions. In 1898 Christian Endeavor brought the communication function in-house and *The Christian Endeavor World* assumed the legacy of the *The Golden Rule*.

Between the unions and the newspaper, a constant flow of Christian Endeavor news and fresh ideas bypassed denominational leaders and local pastors, landing in the hands of the loyal and dedicated leaders of local societies. While this gave vibrancy to the movement, it also created tensions for denominational loyalists and contributed to youth society clones in virtually every major denomination.

Christian Endeavor Essentials

"How is it [i.e., a Society of Christian Endeavor] differentiated from the old type of young people's meetings that made so manifest a failure?" asked Amos R. Wells in *The Officers' Handbook*, published in 1900.[21] A century later the question remains relevant since Christian Endeavor societies continue to function in pockets of America and internationally. Answering his own question, Wells suggested six features.[22]

First was the pledge, which was described as essential to a Society of Christian Endeavor. Wells suggested that a society member should express a willingness to live in accordance with certain demands that Christ desires for his followers and should be willing to enter into an open covenant for that purpose. Officers, especially, should commit themselves to defending and advocating the practice. For anyone objecting to the practice on the basis of losing their freedom, Wells pointed out that Christian freedom consisted of doing the will of Christ, and the real question that should be asked was whether the pledge represented Christ's will.

The pledge changed over time (see chapter 3). By the time the Society of Christian Endeavor was twenty-five years old, the pledge had taken on the form of a litany, with public pledges made at least once a year. A form of the pledge prepared by Rev. W. H. G. Temple read as follows:[23]

OUR PLEDGE
The distinctive feature of the Christian Endeavor movement, to which
we have all given our loyal assent, and by which we have promised to
stand,
PROVIDES FOR
DAILY DEVOTIONS.
I promise . . . to pray and read the Bible every day.
WEEKLY TESTIMONY.
To be present at and to take some part, aside from singing, in every
Christian Endeavor prayer meeting.
MONTHLY CONSECRATION.
And, if obliged to be absent from the monthly consecration meeting, to
send, if possible, at least a verse of Scripture to be read in response to
my name at the roll-call.
CONSTANT LOYALTY TO CHURCH AND CAUSE.
To do my duty, support, and attend regularly the Sunday and midweek
services of my church.
DOING ALL
In the name and strength of . . .
. . . the Lord Jesus Christ.
BY FAITH. AMEN.

While changing forms, the pledge remained the focal point of the society. Individual accountability and the supporting structure of the society's meetings and committee work enabled young people to find a relevant means of staying connected with both God and their church.

The second essential feature of Christian Endeavor was the weekly prayer meeting and the monthly roll-call meeting. Sometimes the latter was called the "experience meeting" or the "consecration meeting." The weekly prayer meeting called for every member of the society to participate in some manner. But it was the monthly gathering that required a public expression of progress in a young person's endeavor to live as a Christian. Wells called it a test of fidelity to the pledge.[24] As suggested by its name, the roll-call meeting required each member of the society to give some evidence of his or her Christian endeavor during the previous month as each person's name was called. But the roll-call meeting served another purpose. This public accountability allowed "profitless" members to be weeded out and dropped from the rolls.

In order for public participation and accountability to take place, Dr. Russell Conwell of Philadelphia's Grace Baptist Temple urged that groups split when they reached sixty in membership.[25] This could result in two or more societies in the same church. Conwell's church had as many as fourteen or fifteen separate societies in order that everyone could participate both in the experience meetings and in various forms of service.

Systematic, definite, regular committee work proved to be a third essential of Christian Endeavor. Francis E. Clark explained the relationship between prayer meetings and committee assignments:

> It is a prayer-meeting society, but not only a prayer-meeting society. It is a society for Christian service, but not only for Christian service. It unites prayer and work. It combines frequent confession of Christ with constant service for Christ.[26]

Because the main purpose of the society was to train young Christians for participation in the church, officers and committee assignments provided venues for developing leadership skills. At the same time, the assignments supposedly bonded society members to their church. This hypothesis was never verified by the society, though the theory seems reasonable.

In his original description of Christian Endeavor, Francis Clark provided assignments for three officers (president, vice president, and secretary) and seven committees consisting of five members each. The Prayer Meeting Committee had charge of the Friday evening prayer meeting. The Lookout Committee brought new members into the society and helped them get involved. The Social Committee helped members get acquainted by planning occasional "sociables." The Missionary Committee raised money for missionary efforts by contributions or entertainments and occasionally sponsored missionary meetings. The Sunday School Committee sought to bring children and youth into the Sunday school who did not attend elsewhere, which it seems was the evangelistic expression of the local society. Relief and Flower Committees aided members who were sick and provided flowers to them or for the pulpit on Sunday morning.[27]

Individual societies functioned as effectively as did their president. Usually the presidents were male, and usually they were among the older youth involved in the societies. While pastors oversaw Christian Endeavor societies and frequently attended the prayer or roll-call meetings, presidents were responsible for the activities of their societies.

By the turn of the twentieth century, more officers and committees appear in the materials provided by the United Society of Christian Endeavor publishing house. A corresponding secretary and treasurer provided new officer roles, while an Executive Committee included the pastor of the church and Information, Calling, Music, Temperance, and Good Literature Committees provide new niches for members to serve.[28]

The fourth essential aspect of Christian Endeavor societies was daily prayer and Bible reading by the members. This private aspect provided the Christian core of the movement. Though the public aspects gave structure to a society, the private devotional functions provided the substance. Amos Wells commented:

> It is impossible to maintain in power the outer exercises of religion unless we maintain with fervor this private communion with God, and by course of Bible-study, and by the Quiet Hour pledge of at least fifteen minutes in the early morning for meditation and prayer, the Society is constantly reminding its members that their only strength for any work comes from on high, and must be drawn from reservoirs of prayer.[29]

Denominational loyalty was the fifth feature of Christian Endeavor. Though not included in the original design by Francis Clark, the rapid growth of the society and its spread across denominational lines forced the national leaders to affirm the priority of the local church in which a society was located and the denominational ties of that church. Christian Endeavor saw itself as a servant of the church and honored the authority of the local pastor. Some pastors viewed Christian Endeavor Union meetings, which brought together societies from various churches in a community, and national Christian Endeavor conferences as efforts to break across denominational lines. Though the effect of these gatherings was ecumenical, the purpose was the encouragement and training of local leaders and, at times, evangelization.

Leaders of the movement consistently reminded denominational leaders that Endeavorers became good church members. They contributed to denominational missionary efforts and subscribed to denominational periodicals, two of the most sensitive issues in sustaining denominational distinctives. Even when denominations formed their own youth societies, Christian Endeavor did not resist their utilizing the youth ministry strategy they had pioneered.

Yet Christian Endeavor was unapologetically an interdenominational fellowship. This was the sixth of the essential aspects of the movement. The system of unions produced gatherings of young people at city, county, state, national, and international levels. These rallies and conferences were essential to the movement. They captured the idealism of youth while serving as venues for the cross-pollination of ideas and the training of leaders. It was on this level and through his prolific writing that Francis Clark retained his greatest influence.

The Role of Francis E. Clark

More than in any other Christian youth movement, the growth and impact of Christian Endeavor were intricately tied to its founder. Although Francis E. Clark proved effective as a pastor while in his twenties, his great passion focused on young people. When he settled on a strategy that proved effective in sustaining the Christian commitments of the youth associated with his church, he immediately utilized his writing skills to share what had happened at Williston Church.

The mail brought a flood of inquiries from people who wished to replicate his ideas in their churches. Pastors who started their own Societies of Christian Endeavor deferred to Clark, and in turn the founder embraced some of their ideas while growing in his convictions of what the society should do and be. As mentioned above, both the Christian Endeavor union idea and the need of a newspaper to bind the movement together came from others and were quickly championed by Clark.

The rapid growth of the society forced a decision on the young pastor four years after he moved to lead Phillips Church in South Boston. The trustees of the Christian Endeavor Society, sensing the need for Clark's full-time leadership, unhindered by parish duties, asked the founder to accept the presidency of Christian Endeavor as his primary vocation. In his letter of acceptance on September 4, 1887, Clark set down six conditions that became the platform of the society. These convictions shaped the growth and development of Christian Endeavor.[30]

First, the society would be an integral part of the local church. He saw Christian Endeavor as a tool to be used by the pastor to bring young people into productive membership no matter what the denominational affiliation. Loyalties of society members were to be to the pastor, not the movement.

Second, the society would be "undenominational" in character. No denomination would have exclusive rights to the movement. The movement would serve all denominations as long as members could comply with the pledge. No doctrinal statement protected theological boundaries. The sacraments and mode of baptism were not matters with which the movement would concern itself. While denominations adopted Christian Endeavor as their official youth ministry, no communion served as the base for the movement. It demonstrated an ecumenical spirit that few movements have been able to emulate.

Third, the purely religious features were to be paramount. While social, musical, and literary activities were wholesome outlets for young people, they would not be the central focus of Christian Endeavor. Even moral issues such as temperance would not be allowed to take center stage in local societies. The pledge focused the energy of the movement on living as Christians.

Fourth, the movement would sympathize with all true moral reforms. It would not be captured by a narrow piety that paid attention to only personal issues. The Christian had an obligation to live as salt and light in the world. The word "sympathize" seemed well chosen, for just as wholesome activities enjoyed by young people were not to become the focal point, neither would the movement become a moral crusade of one sort or another. This was a delicate balance in the era of progressive reforms.

Fifth, the society would be managed economically, without a large number of paid agents or missionaries. Perhaps this stipulation, more than any other, flattened out any bureaucratic pyramid that might have developed and forced the movement to stay close to the grass roots. The primary source of income was the publishing wing of the movement. Newspapers, books, and supporting materials funded most of the society's professional staff. This meant that the bulk of the efforts to service societies in local churches would be provided by volunteers.

Finally, the officers, Dr. Clark included, would have the sympathetic support of state and local unions. As much as he was the visionary who kept the movement focused on its purpose, he realized that he needed to remain vitally in contact with the volunteers who provided most of the training and encouragement needed by society leaders in local churches. So seriously did he take this conviction that in 1898 he convinced the board to expand and include presidents of state and territorial unions to ensure an adequate and accurate flow of information from those most involved in local leadership of Christian Endeavor.

Based on these principles, Francis Clark spent the rest of his life keeping the movement focused on the vision he had established. Though quite a good communicator and writer, biographer W. Knight Chaplin commented, "He . . . did not claim to be ranked as an orator, and did not attempt flights of rhetoric. His power was in his winning personality, the transparent sincerity which touches and holds even the most prejudiced hearers, and the intense earnestness which is always more effective in the oratorical art."[31]

The Roman Catholic Church never adopted Christian Endeavor nor did Protestant Episcopal communions, yet in many denominations, and in all countries where nonconformity was strong, the movement flourished. Clark served as ambassador at large, traveling over a million miles around the world to promote the society. Funded by over five thousand articles he wrote, his travels promoted the society worldwide and brought him in touch with leaders in virtually every walk of life around the world.[32]

Growth and Decline of Christian Endeavor

Christian Endeavor peaked in international membership around its twenty-fifth anniversary in 1906 with nearly four million members spread across sixty-seven thousand societies in eighty denominations and fifty countries. This number remained fairly constant through the middle of the twentieth century though members in North America may have been a quarter of that number.[33] The numbers after the twenty-five years may be misleading for there seemed to be no mechanism for removing members who no longer could be considered youthful. The aging factor and with it the suggestion that fewer and fewer young people were joining the society masked the fact that Christian Endeavor, in its later years, had become more of an institution than a movement.

But it was the growth in the first ten years of the Society of Christian Endeavor that shaped modern youth ministry. From that group of about fifty young people in one church to over a million members in close to thirteen thousand societies, Christian Endeavor expanded around the world. Tireless work by the founder, a well-focused strategy, willingness to allow local adaptations, a constant flow of articles describing the growth and innovation, and a profound sense of ownership by volunteer workers and people of financial means allowed the movement to not only grow but to spawn denominational youth societies.[34]

New applications of the basic Christian Endeavor idea were quickly incorporated into the expanding society. Amos R. Wells described societies among American Indians, in prisons, among sailors, railroad men, station agents, telegraph operators, in life-saving stations.[35] Adaptations for large churches, accommodations for age groupings, incorporation of emphases such as missions and temperance, and translation of materials into as many as fifty languages allowed Christian Endeavor to remain relevant to the lives of those who would pledge their desire to live as Christians in their worlds.

For all the expansion of Christian Endeavor, ambiguity as to the essential mission of the movement limited its development. The pledge essentially bred an individualized form of Christian piety. Missing were missional aspects of the Christian faith. About the only outward aspect of the society focused on loyalty to the church, and even that was hard to quantify. Early in its development, Christian Endeavor shifted from stimulating piety to training for church involvement and leadership. Most churches, however, failed to connect the training process with church leadership. Christian Endeavor became an agency of the church with its internal need for structure and leadership. Like the Sunday school before it, Christian Endeavor became an add-on to the church.

It became a holding tank from which a few church leaders were drawn, while most members continued to swim.[36]

As times changed, Francis Clark failed to make the necessary adjustments. His travels took him away from youth ministry. Though the organization remained in capable hands, the "youth problem" addressed by Clark in the last decades of the nineteenth century was not the "youth problem" of the first decades of the twentieth century. Nor had the family or community structure remained the same. As Paula Fass observed, "The problem of youth was connected to changes in family nurture, education, sex roles, leisure habits, as well as social and behavioral norms. Above all, youth had become a challenge to an older social order."[37]

Conclusion

While the second cycle of youth ministry began with a spirit of optimism, an emerging economic middle class, and a fear of foreign influence, it started to fade in the 1920s with a growing spirit of skepticism on the part of young people toward the authority figures in society. World War I shattered the optimism of the Progressive Era. The Roaring Twenties gave birth to a rejection of traditional values by young adults, especially of traditional sexual mores. Though young people who still lived under the care of their parents retained values taught by parents and church, the growing influence of peers in the public high school began eroding the influence of that sanctuary.

Instead of being insulated from the influences of society, young people came in contact with influences foreign to their way of life on a daily basis. Kids from "the other side of the tracks" (as in River City) daily mixed with adolescents from the economic middle class in the public high school. Radio went commercial in the early thirties and quickly began to shape both family life and the economic habits of listeners. Veterans, barely out of their teenage years, returned from World War I and brought a new worldliness to their communities. Economic boom and then depression left the world of the early twentieth century a very different place from Portland, Maine, in 1881.

Katherine Evelyn Niles came to similar conclusions about the decline in relevance of the society after studying eighteen Christian Endeavor societies in Portland, Oregon. In an article published in 1929 she concluded, "Their forms and techniques, which remain much the same as they were in the beginning [i.e. the last decade of the nineteenth century] are no longer suited to modern society."[38]

9

Saturday Night in River City

Denominational Youth Societies (1889–1935)

Saturday night was Epworth League night in River City, Iowa. Zaneeta Shinn, the mayor's daughter, and most of the young people ages ten through thirty-four from respectable families of the town attended every meeting. The league was divided into three sections: the Junior Division for children ages ten to twelve; Intermediates included youngsters ages thirteen to seventeen; and the Senior League grouped everyone from age eighteen to thirty in a young adult fellowship. The Saturday night meeting was a "sociable." It was held only once a month and was designed to provide a good time for Methodist young people in a healthy environment.[1]

For Mayor Shinn and his wife, a healthy environment meant being surrounded by young people from the correct part of town. Of course, respectable families of River City whose children attended Epworth League provided the target market for "Professor" Harold Hill and his boys' band scam. Adding to the urgency of the situation was the fact that Zaneeta Shinn was infatuated with Tommy Djilas, whose father was a day laborer living south of town. Despite the fact that Tommy showed creativeness in building a music holder for piccolo players in Hill's band, he was still an undesirable person in the minds of the Shinns. As Professor Hill boldly stated, the Shinns had trouble, right here in River City.

By 1912, the Epworth League, along with young people's societies from the major Christian denominations, had taken on a broader function in their churches than was evidenced when the societies were formed during the last two decades of the nineteenth century. The desire to prepare young people for church membership, and to help them demonstrate efforts to live as a Christian should live, broadened into a type of protective society.

Stimulated by the dramatic success of the Society of Christian Endeavor, denominational youth programs started from grassroots efforts and consolidated in the formation of national youth societies. Fearing the loss of denominational distinctives and a diffusion of denominational loyalty while seeing the potential for what they were already doing, most religious bodies formed their own youth societies and began generating program materials. Though most of the denominational societies retained a pledge associated with membership similar to that of Christian Endeavor, the contents of the pledges changed and focused much more on denominational priorities and less on issues related to accountability in one's endeavor to know God and live as a Christian.

The Epworth League, formed from a merger of five district Methodist youth societies in 1889, created the earliest denominational youth program in the United States. Baptist Young People's Union followed in 1891 and was quickly followed by denominational youth programs in the other major Protestant denominations—Westminster League (Presbyterian General Assembly) in 1891, Walther League (Missouri Synod Lutheran) in 1893, Young People's Christian Union (United Brethren) in 1894, Young People's Christian Union (United Presbyterian Church) in 1895, Keystone League (United Evangelical Church in America) in 1895, and Luther League (Intersynodical Lutheran) in 1895.

Though denominational historians focus on the uniqueness of their tradition's experience in dealing with the needs of youth and addressing the "youth problem" as they defined it, each national society drew on the experience of local church experiments. Most efforts remained local. But others, like the experience of Christian Endeavor, spread by word of mouth and then through publications. It was the local effectiveness in addressing the youth problem that eventually forced denominational leaders to place their stamp of approval on the idea of local and national youth societies.

Epworth League

Attempts to respond to the needs of young people in Methodist Episcopal churches go back at least until 1872 when Rev. T. B. Neely organized a

Church Lyceum in the Fifty-first Street Methodist Episcopal Church of Philadelphia. The Lyceum encouraged the systematic reading of approved books by young people. Nearby churches copied the idea, stimulating youths' intellectual lives and fostering a taste for "pure and upbuilding" literature. The Lyceum idea remained relatively local and many churches discovered that the organization did not meet the needs of their young people.[2]

By 1883 in the youth ministry hot bed of Brooklyn, enough Methodist Episcopal young people's societies had formed to allow a Methodist Episcopal Young People's Union to be created. The union symbolized a fresh approach to dealing with the issues facing youth by having "friendly intercourse" with the Young People's Baptist Union, formed six years earlier.[3]

The Epworth League grew out of five regional youth societies on May 15, 1889, in Cleveland, Ohio. Even though the parent body, the Methodist Episcopal Church, remained divided North and South since before the Civil War, the Epworth League gathered delegates from the North, South, and Canada in a convocation held in Chattanooga, Tennessee, in 1895.[4] In so doing, the league provided a glimmer of hope of denominational unity that would not be realized until the beginning of World War II.

The original five youth societies provide a glimpse of the diverse means by which youth societies came into being. The earliest was the Young People's Methodist Alliance, established on August 25, 1883, at a meeting on the Des Plaines campgrounds near Chicago, Illinois. At the conclusion of a camp meeting at which Dr. and Mrs. Asbury Lowrey preached the Wesleyan doctrine of complete sanctification, many young people responded, seeking a fuller baptism of the Holy Spirit. According to Joseph F. Berry, the impact on the lives of these young people was quite dramatic. As the week continued, two of the young people, Winnie S. Benjamin and Lillian E. Date, decided to take some of their free time to pray and talk about their experiences. The next day others joined them. Toward the end of the week, John E. Farmer, a student at nearby Garrett Biblical Institute assumed responsibility for leading the group. Frank McCluney, a young bookkeeper from Chicago, suggested they sign a covenant in an attempt to keep alive the "holy enthusiasm" of their experience. Four days later in the Evanston church cottage on the camp meeting grounds, the Young People's Methodist Alliance was formed. Eighty young people joined before the end of the camp meeting.[5]

The formation of the Young People's Methodist Alliance was an example of a youth-led movement. Using their Methodist tradition of class meetings and solemn pledges, which dated back to the time of John Wesley, they formed the alliance that helped to sustain their commitment and within two years founded *The Alliance Herald* to promote their activities across the nation. The pledge to which members committed themselves demanded great discipline in their attempt to live holy lives (see chapter 3).

Within four years of the Des Plaines camp meeting, fifty societies with over two thousand members had joined the alliance. Several districts and camp meetings adopted the alliance, providing increased visibility for the youth society in an era when the idea was still new. By 1889 this number increased to 410 local societies and seventeen thousand members.

The second of the five initial Methodist youth societies was the Oxford League, formed in 1884. The league was the brain child of Dr. John H. Vincent,[6] chairman of the International Lesson Committee of the Sunday School Union, who still saw value in the Lyceum but wished to add a spiritual dimension that the older form of youth work had lacked. Proposing that the league provide a symmetrical spiritual and intellectual culture, he modeled it after Wesley's "Holy Club" at Oxford University in England.[7]

Probably because of the stature of Dr. Vincent, who was a bishop in the Methodist Episcopal Church, the Oxford League received prompt approval from the Centennial Conference held in Baltimore, Maryland, in December of the same year. Perhaps because of the pretentious sound of the name and lofty ambitions of its purpose, the growth of the league was slow. Not until the denomination's Sunday School and Tract Society threw its weight behind the league and began promoting the idea did growth begin. Then, within sixty days, five hundred chapters enrolled in late 1889. However, there was less evidence of young people joining than of pastors registering their churches with the league. This second form of youth society appears to be a top down attempt to solve the "youth problem" in the Methodist Church.

The Young People's Christian League, led by Rev. J. H. Twombly, represented the third type of Methodist youth society. In 1864 Twombly formed a young people's society in his church and led the General Conference in approving the organization of young people's societies in Methodist churches. Little progress was made, however, until after the establishment of Christian Endeavor in 1881. Though Twombly was old in years, he was said to be young at heart, and once again he stepped forward in 1887. Concerned about Methodist youth, he proposed to the Boston Methodist preachers meeting that a conference be held for young Methodists. The second convention attracted three hundred and fifty young people and brought about an apparently unexpected result—a league of Methodist young people's societies. Already in existence throughout New England were young people's societies such as he had established years earlier. How many of these were a product of the Society of Christian Endeavor's influence in the region cannot be determined. These regional meetings allowed existing Methodist groups to come together and share ideas.[8]

As the societies gathered, the idea of the Young People's Christian League emerged. Its purpose was to unify the existing societies, Lyceums, guilds, and bands. It was a loose confederation of youth societies that allowed local groups to retain their distinctive purpose while promoting mutual encouragement and cross-pollination among leaders. As with the other forms of Methodist youth societies, the idea spread to states as far away as Texas and Georgia by means of columns in denominational publications. This third approach allowed denominational structures to serve local youth societies. The long-term success of the strategy was never tested because within a year of the first meeting, the denomination-wide Epworth League was birthed with the aid of the Young People's Christian League.

A similar approach formed the Methodist Young People's Union in Detroit, Michigan. This was the fourth of the initial Methodist youth ministry efforts. A meeting was called by the Methodist Conference to discuss methods and materials for working with young people in December of 1887. Fifty churches and young people's societies responded. As in New England, youth ministry was already under way in Michigan. The union primarily united efforts. Again, columns in the conference's publication, the *Michigan Christian Advocate*, spread the idea and aided local societies.[9]

The final of the original societies, formed in northern Ohio, had hardly begun before the Epworth League replaced it.[10] Similar to the Michigan initiative, leaders focused on multiplying what was already going on in local churches. Local churches responded to the needs of youth, and denominational structures were built in Ohio to support those efforts.

Epworth League gave clarity to the approach the Methodist Episcopal Church would take in ministering to its youth. While methods used on the local level and effectiveness of efforts varied greatly, mission became the national emphasis of the league. Study programs stressed national and international projects. Charity work and public stands on moral issues like lynchings resulted in aid being sent to the families of victims. Local missions tended to focus on "orphanages," "old folks homes," and "shut-ins." Peer evangelism rarely was stressed. Frequently even the Saturday night sociables had a missionary flavor as money was raised for a Methodist outreach activity.[11]

The normal Epworth League met on Sunday nights during the school year. Since "youth" included people from age ten to thirty four, the league had little need for professionalized leadership. Young adults provided leadership and continuity. The Epworth League lasted for fifty years. In 1939, when the various Methodist church bodies merged forming the Methodist

Church, the Epworth League became the Methodist Youth Fellowship, and membership was restricted to adolescents, ages twelve to twenty-four.[12] The change from a society to a fellowship suggested a change in the nature of youth ministry as it moved into its third cycle.

Baptist Young People's Union

The Baptist Young People's Union provides a different pattern of how a national denominational youth program began. The first stage was the spontaneous efforts of local churches to meet the needs of their youth. Most of the records of these are lost. Yet the existence of the United Society of Young Men in Baptist Churches in 1803 indicates some sort of youth ministry in multiple Baptist churches shortly after the American Revolution.[13] References to youth ministries in the First Baptist Church of Rochester, New York (1848); under D. E. Holtemann in Marengo, Illinois (1858); and at First Baptist Church in Troy, New York (1863), under the leadership of George C. Baldwin, DD, suggest early efforts to respond to the spiritual needs of church youth.[14]

Brooklyn gave birth to the first Young People's Baptist Union. In late 1876, Abel Swan Brown, president-elect of the Young People's Association of the First Baptist Church in Pierrepont Street, expressed a desire to gather Baptist young people from the various Baptist young people's associations to discuss how they might cooperate in their efforts. He had helped found the first Baptist Young People's Association in Brooklyn two years after the Civil War, and with nine years of experience in his church he felt others could benefit from similar associations. The city of Brooklyn was a growing community with thirty-three Baptist churches. While records show Sunday schools in virtually all of these churches, young people's associations were not as common. By the second year of the union's existence, representatives of only fourteen Baptist churches participated.[15]

Judging by the initial activities of the Young People's Baptist Union in Brooklyn, the union appeared to have two purposes: social interaction, by which young men and women from different churches could become acquainted with each other, and a sharing of ideas through impromptu speeches. Objectives for the union, defined in October 1877, called for

1st. An increase in our Christian usefulness, which will result from more perfect acquaintance and fellowship.
2nd. The urging and encouraging of churches to form organizations to develop the spirituality and power of our young people.
3rd. The endeavor by mutual assistance to increase the interest and efficiency of our Young People's prayer meetings, to the end that souls may be saved.

4th. The development of the social feeling of Christian fellowship, which is so frequently set forth in the New Testament of Our Lord and Saviour, Jesus Christ, as essential to our spiritual growth and the welfare of His Church.[16]

It is quite likely that associations in individual Baptist churches had similar purposes. Young people's prayer meetings were at the heart of what local associations did. Perhaps begun in response to the Prayer Revival of 1857–59, which began across the East River in New York, their gatherings brought together young working people[17] and allowed them to give attention to their spiritual lives in an increasingly pluralistic society. Concerns about the influx of "tens of thousands who came to Brooklyn from foreign shores" with their "superstitions and ignorance" increased a sense of urgency for young people to give attention to their Christian lives.[18]

The Baptists, as was common in the mid-nineteenth century, understood *youth* to be what people would consider *young adults* today. Some had served in the military during the Civil War and thereafter. Many were married. All were employed. Rev. Henry Ward Beecher, speaking in the fifth year of the union's existence, reminded the gathered delegates that it had not been long ago when no man under twenty-five was ever called on to lead in prayer. Now swarms of young men were coming from farms and towns in the country to seek work in the city. Given their new freedom from parental control, these young people were easily enticed by corrupting city influences and selfish desires. Consequently Baptist churches were responding to this "youth problem" by allowing young men and women to create new means of reaching their peers.[19]

The work of both the union and Baptist church–based associations was accomplished through elected officers and committees. Constitutions prescribed the manner in which they functioned. Members took their leadership roles seriously. Committees sometimes included a dozen or more members and since there were six or eight committees, the number of young people involved sometimes reached a hundred.[20]

First Baptist Church in Charlottesville, Virginia, may have established the first Baptist Young People's Union in a Southern Baptist Church. There the name *union* referred to both the local church association and the cooperative efforts among Southern Baptist Churches. On November 23, 1884, Dr. John B. Turpin, pastor of the church, obtained permission from the deacons to organize a young people's society for the purpose of training youth in Bible study and Christian activities. Seventeen young people gathered. Pastor Turpin suggested the group associate with Christian Endeavor. Yet by a vote of nine to eight, the decision was made to form a society that was "strictly Baptist," so they formed the first Young People's Baptist Union in Virginia and perhaps in the South.[21]

With the period of reconstruction following the Civil War having ended only fourteen years earlier as Virginia was readmitted to the Union on January 28, 1870, resistance in the South to anything Northern remained strong.[22] Thus it may have been that the choice to start a "strictly" Baptist society was as much a choice to begin something that was "strictly" Southern. The forms of Baptist youth societies in the South appear to be less influenced by the "prayer meeting" model of Christian Endeavor than were Baptist churches in the North.

The second stage began when manuals were developed in order to spread the ideas across a state or throughout the nation. Oliver W. Van Osdel, DD, began the "Loyalist Movement" in Ottawa, Kansas, in 1886. Though the motto called for "Loyalty to Christ, in all things, at all times," the object of the movement was "to encourage the doctrinal study of the Bible, the adoption of direct proportionate giving, and missionary work." The denominational character was clear. Quickly Van Osdel developed and published a comprehensive plan for organizing Baptist young people. Two years later the plan was adopted by Kansas Baptist State Convention.

Dr. Alexander Blackburn wrote about the "Loyalist Movement" in a national Baptist publication and soon other pastors became interested. About the same time Rev. J. M. Coon of Whitewater, Wisconsin, published "The Self-Help Handbook for Young People" and urged its use in Wisconsin Baptist churches. The manuals enabled the "technology" of youth ministry to spread.

The third stage happened when the grassroots and regional ideas formalized into a national program. The Baptists put their organizational wheels into motion in 1889 and the following year a committee was set up to assist churches, associations, and states to establish Baptist young people's groups. By the end of 1890, fourteen states had held young people's meetings or had provided for such gatherings.

On April 22, 1891, a national Baptist young people's organization was established that was broad enough to include all Baptist youth groups, no matter what their name or constitutional structure. This inclusiveness was an attempt to embrace groups like Christian Endeavor that were already established in Baptist churches and to incorporate them into the national organization. Yet all societies were urged to subscribe to *Young People at Work*, the Baptist national publication, in order to provide continuity within groups with Baptist distinctives.

Walther League

Not every denominational group saw an organization for young people in the local church as a positive development. The Lutheran Church–Missouri

Synod demonstrated the tensions felt by immigrants as they attempted to establish themselves in America while still maintaining their ethnic identity. Other synods formed youth leagues as well.[23] Most remained small. As with many ethnic groups, their children became a source of anxiety for parents and church leaders of these German immigrants. Americanization threatened to lure their children away from the customs (Christian and otherwise) of the homeland.

C. F. W. Walther saw the American experience differently than many of his Lutheran friends who immigrated to America in 1838. Nine years later, adapting to the spirit of volunteerism in America he began the "German Evangelical Lutheran Synod of Missouri, Ohio, and Other States," now the Lutheran Church—Missouri Synod. Three years later, on May 7, 1848, Trinity Lutheran Church in St. Louis, Missouri, pastored by Dr. Carl Walther, founded the "Juenglingsverein," or young men's society. Assistant Pastor Johann Buenger justified the purpose as "giving support to needy students preparing for the ministry." No one could resist such a society.

By 1855 twenty-three such young men's groups organized, some joining a synodwide federation. Societies appeared in New York; Cleveland; Cincinnati; Fort Wayne, Indiana; and Monroe, Michigan. In Alterburg, Missouri, "Junglingsuntersutzungsverein" (youth support societies) formed in the congregation of Georg Albert Schieferdecker. Then, as rapidly as they appeared, they vanished. Elmer N. Witt observed, "Young men's groups were permissible but they worked 'best' in and for their own congregation only."[24] In 1881 there was another attempt to create a federation of young men's societies in Buffalo and Detroit as Luther Leagues in the East; leaders tried to establish an all-Lutheran young people's union, yet without success. Not until 1893 was a national Walther Liga (Walther League) established.

Churches in other synods took similar initiatives to form youth societies. All appeared to have common purposes. Commenting specifically on the Augustana Luther League, Clarence Peters noted, "Primarily [their purposes] were spiritual in nature. They were to assist youth in spiritual growth."[25]

Unlike the Methodists and Baptists, Lutherans were reluctant to allow young people to organize. For the most part it had to do with control or the loss thereof. Jon Pahl suggests three reasons. The most common reason related to the immaturity of young men and the complaint that they would create congregational disharmony because of conflicts within their society. The second objection had to do with discontinuity with their country of origin. Youth societies were an American creation and German immigrants faced too much change already without confusing their religious life as well. They had "Christenlehre," their own way of teaching young people. But perhaps the most telling concern had to do with worldliness: "Would the society promote smoking, drinking, playing pool, and other worldly pursuits? Would young men and women get together and . . . speak English?"[26]

There were exceptions. The Walther League, like the Society of Christian Endeavor, was born in a local church, First Trinity Evangelical Lutheran Church in Buffalo, New York. On March 9, 1875, Rev. Carl Gross asked the young men of the congregation to stay after the service for a few minutes. Only eight stayed. Not discouraged, Gross held the first meeting four days later and eighteen young men attended. The stated purpose was to "bring closer together Christian minded young men through Christian and academic pursuits."[27] Officers were elected. Attendance grew to twenty-six men between ages sixteen and thirty. Within a year, those in attendance included women.

With the proliferation of denominational youth societies, the Walther League formed nationally in 1893 with sixteen delegates from twelve societies representing 693 members. Still growth was slow. What youth ministry there was remained local. Resistance continued among many, and without congregational support Walther League societies did not exist in local congregations. At the end of World War I, only 310 Walther League societies existed.[28] Not until five years after World War I did the number of societies in the United States exceed the one thousand mark.[29] By 1929 the league had 1,607 societies.[30]

Though the Walther League continued in existence until 1989, two events occurred around 1930 that indicated changes in the direction of the league. Most significant was the beginning of professional denominational leadership for youth ministry in the 1920s and the assumption of leadership as general secretary by Otto Paul Kretzmann in 1934. Recognizing that much of the energy of the league had been focused on the issues of Lutheran experience of the late nineteenth century, O. P. (as he was called) reorganized the national office into two departments. One dealt with knowing and the other with doing the Christian life.[31] The second event involved the merger of Lutheran youth federations and leagues into larger organizations as synods merged between 1917 and 1935. Though the Walther League was not one of the mergers, changes in Lutheran youth ministry, including the Missouri Synod, attempted to respond to the post–World War I environment. Like other denominational responses to the changing world of adolescents, Lutheran youth ministry began moving into the third cycle of youth ministry.

Presbyterian Youth Fellowship

While Rev. Theodore L. Cuyler's Young People's Association at Lafayette Avenue Presbyterian Church in Brooklyn, New York, provided a pioneering structure for youth ministries in the latter part of the nineteenth century, his was far from the only effort among Presbyterian churches. Franklin B. Gillespie cites efforts to start parochial schools (1853), academies (1864), cooperation with YMCA programs (1877), and of course Sabbath Schools, one of which enrolled a reported 1,650 pupils.[32]

Concern for Presbyterian youth manifested itself early in the American experience. In 1799, during the presidency of John Adams, a committee of the General Assembly urged ministers to "lecture on the scriptures, and . . . endeavor where it is prudent and practicable to institute private societies for reading, prayer, and private conversations. Above all . . . be faithful in the duties of family visitation, and catechetical instruction of children and youth."[33] Sunday schools adapted from Robert Raikes's English model gained acceptance in some Presbyterian churches over the next few years and would continue through the nineteenth century. Records show nine hundred thousand Presbyterian Sunday school pupils in five thousand Sunday schools in 1889.[34] Still young people appeared lacking in biblical understanding.

In 1816, the General Assembly again expressed its concern for the biblical ignorance of younger parishioners. Parents were failing to properly train their children in the Christian faith. Ministers had to pick up the slack and were urged to give more time to educating youth. For the most part the means of doing this was left to the individual pastor, but the Assembly recommended that "the most effectual means of promoting the knowledge of the Holy Scriptures [would be that] classes be formed of the youth, to recite the Scriptures in regular order; that the recitations, if convenient, be as often as once a week, and from two to five chapters be appointed for each recitation."[35]

Fathers were seen as the ones primarily responsible for instructing their children in personal and religious matters, but periodic revivals were also seen as important because people of all ages in the same congregation were "brought together at the feet of Jesus." It was pointed out that two thirds of all who professed their faith in revival meetings were products of Sunday schools.[36] For the majority of the nineteenth century, Presbyterians relied on this pattern of instruction at home, supported by Sunday schools, the local efforts of ministers, and periodic times of revival to bring about the conversion and instruction of young people.

Sunday school literature and the publishing of Christian books dominated Presbyterian efforts to help children and youth grow up exhibiting Christian virtues. Even in the South during the Civil War, Presbyterian publishers found ways to overcome wartime shortages and provide Christian educational materials to churches.[37]

The advent of Christian Endeavor provided a new direction for Presbyterian churches. A vast majority of Presbyterian churches embraced the movement because "it provided the first opportunity in most churches for young people to be able to ask questions about their faith, to plan and lead in worship, and to have a part in developing their own programs."[38]

The response to Christian Endeavor by Presbyterian denominations varied. An 1884 report to the General Assembly of the Presbyterian Church in the USA (Northern Presbyterian) described the presence of young people's societies in many local Presbyterian churches. Yet it was not until 1906 that the General Assembly established a youth promotional department. This was followed by the creation of the Department of Religious Education, in which the Department of Young People's Work was a subdivision, in 1912. Still no denominational youth program was established until the Westminster Fellowship was organized in 1943.[39] Camps and conferences for young people provided a sense of cohesion among youth.

The United Presbyterian Church in North America took a different approach. Rev. James McFarland of Allegheny, Pennsylvania, proposed the formation of the Young People's Union, and on April 30, 1889, the new youth organization was launched. Modeled after Christian Endeavor, some thought it would be the Presbyterian branch of the older organization. But Francis Clark did not favor denominational branches, and so a separate organization was established.[40]

In the South, the Presbyterian Church in the United States traveled a different trail to youth ministry. While the liberation of African slaves was long overdue, the Civil War had a devastating impact on the youth of the white population. A quarter of a million Confederates died (out of a white population of less than eight million), a majority of whom were young. The economy of the South was in shambles. For churches in the South, youth ministry was not a high priority. Merely sustaining churches and Sunday schools was a stretch. With men at war, women assumed leadership positions in churches. Those men fortunate to return home after the war found their time consumed with rebuilding homes, businesses, and the Southern infrastructure. Consequently women retained a higher profile in church ministry than was evident in the North.

Attempts were made to create the Westminster League for the Southern Presbyterian Church in 1895. The league was a denominational creation formed in reaction to Christian Endeavor. Apparently the league knew better what it was not (Christian Endeavor) than what it was, though. It died after a long and often bitter struggle with Christian Endeavor.[41]

Miss Katherine Heath Hawes of Richmond, Virginia, is credited with beginning Presbyterian youth ministry in the Southern Presbyterian Church. After Hawes returned from boarding school in 1895, the pastor of Second Presbyterian Church, Dr. Moses Drury Hoge, asked Miss Hawes to teach either a boys or girls Sunday school class. She chose the boys class (they were ages eight to ten). Seeing how few boys attended Sunday school, Miss Hawes opened her home to them on Friday evenings for games and music, to provide them a place for fellowship with their peers. The following March, Company No. 1 of the Covenanters was born. Officers were elected, and a badge, watchword, and flag provided symbols of the Covenanters. Reports from and offerings for missionaries proved to be a focal point of the group. They eventually developed a choir and orchestra, then a fife and drum corps, followed by an emphasis on service projects.[42]

As the boys grew older, their enthusiasm for the Covenanters brought about a desire in other Presbyterian churches to have such a ministry. By 1900, Presbyterian churches in nine other states and the District of Columbia registered as Companies of Covenanters. Soon Miriams, a companion group for girls, was added.

Yet as a movement this new type of youth ministry was stillborn in the South. By 1920, Christian Endeavor dominated Presbyterian youth programs. Mary-Ruth Marshall reported that there were 1,125 Christian Endeavor societies with a membership of 32,929 in the denomination. At the same time, there were fifteen Westminster Leagues, fifteen Covenanter Companies, and twenty-four Miriam chapters whose composite membership totaled 1,059. While the average membership was just under thirty for all reporting youth groups, local churches clearly preferred Christian Endeavor.[43]

Impact of Denominationalism

From the last decade of the nineteenth century onward, denominational allegiances became primary factors in the development of youth ministry. Youth groups of different Protestant affiliations may have maintained relationships with other youth societies in their community, but increasingly they isolated themselves on the regional and national levels. This organizational separation was instrumental in the rapid spread of youth ministry. Rather than having only one youth ministry organization (Christian Endeavor), by the end of the century the United States had close to a dozen church-based youth ministry agencies, two of which rivaled the mother organization in size. Though some pastors still had doubts regarding even their denominational youth society participants' understanding of religious living and ecclesiastical control, denominational control and loyalty seemed safer than the nondenominational approach of Christian Endeavor. Also, denominational youth societies were safer places for young people to socialize and prepare for leadership in the local church and the national denomination.

By the end of the twentieth century's third decade there was a mood of optimism about what was being accomplished in youth programs sponsored by the major denominations. Summer conference attendance, money raised for missionary projects, publication of comprehensive programming materials for high school students, and leadership development were cited by denominational publications as reasons for confidence.[44]

Reports such as these were justified. Denominational involvement in ministry to young people increased dramatically from the humble beginnings of a few years before. Community, state, and national organizations developed, and many were staffed with capable and concerned adult leaders, the majority of whom were paid for their efforts. The place most likely for youth specialists to be employed, however, was in the denominational publishing houses.

A blizzard of printed materials swept from denominational presses. Following the example of Christian Endeavor they marketed training materials that provided step-by-step descriptions of every aspect of the youth program. Program materials quickly followed, allowing a local youth society to put together a variety of Sunday evening meetings with a minimum of work on the part of students or adult leaders.

With this direct link between youth societies and denominational headquarters, programs became increasingly generic. It was simply impossible to be in touch with the local needs of thousands of young people's societies and tens of thousands of adolescents. The consequence was that denominational youth workers, influenced by denominational priorities, began establishing the agenda for youth societies rather than local pastors or adult sponsors. World missions, stewardship, social issues, and denominational distinctives dominated the topics for weekly meetings. Encouragement toward personal encounters with God lagged.

Recognizing that the youth society idea, complete with constitutions, pledges, committees, and formal expectations, had run its course, the leadership established youth fellowships as the norm. Much more peer oriented, youth fellowships drew their leadership from fellow high school students, while adults served as sponsors. Gone were the memorization of Scripture and catechism; present were discussions and programs prepared by a rotated leadership. Pioneered by the Congregational Christian Church in 1936, youth fellowships became the norm in the early days of the third cycle of youth ministry.[45]

Published youth programming materials were to youth ministry what sheet music was to jazz. Rather than create effective youth ministry with youth, publishers enabled adults who loved kids to create a youth ministry "sound" by merely following the score. A few youth ministry musicians did develop from the discipline of playing the notes, but for increasing numbers of young people, the routine became as boring as playing scales in performance settings.

Activities in which denominational youth workers participated were effective. Camps, conferences, and area-wide meetings were too great an effort for volunteer youth workers to accomplish by themselves, so into this vacuum stepped professional youth workers. Two campgrounds in North Carolina, Montreat for Presbyterians and Ridgecrest for the Southern Baptists, were examples of locations where specialists assumed responsibility for national and regional programming.

Despite the growing superstructure in the young people's society "industry," there is little evidence that local church programs shared the excitement or dynamic of denominational or interdenominational efforts. Robert and Helen Lynd in their classic study of one Midwestern town published in 1929 concluded that the young people's meeting had remained "fundamentally unchanged since the nineties" while high school extracurricular activities had become conveyers of social prestige.[46]

The clearest indicator that church-based youth societies were losing their influence over economic middle-class young people was the rise of certain youth associations that emphasized wholesome activities designed to build character in boys and girls. These agencies, such as Boy and Girl Scouts, Camp Fire Girls, 4-H Clubs, and Boys Clubs of America, had little to do with the church but shared an ethic based on a Judeo-Christian heritage. These activity-oriented clubs required young people to have enough free time to participate in the club functions and sufficient financial resources to pay for the uniforms, equipment, and activities. Free time and discretionary cash were not available to the poorer classes of people, so the youth movements of the second cycle remained solidly within the middle class.

United Christian Youth Movement

One last gasp for air from the Christian youth ministry establishment in the early 1930s came from the United Christian Youth Movement. For those concerned with the spiritual nurture of young people, a vacuum existed. Christian Endeavor appeared incapable of providing either organizational or inspirational leadership. Christians concerned about the spiritual journey of young people began to look elsewhere. Denominational programs still using the youth society model existed but they languished in the doldrums of the depression era.[47]

Into this setting came two new strategies for youth ministry in 1933 and 1934. One started with support from denominational leaders, the Federal Council of Churches, the International Society of Christian

Endeavor, the National Council of the YMCA, the National Board of the YWCA, and the Boy Scouts of America. The other was a grassroots movement that spread initially by word of mouth.

The two organizations, the United Christian Youth Movement and the Miracle Book Club, were a study in contrasts. The former was the vision of men; the latter, the dream of a woman. The United movement had immediate national publicity through a variety of magazines and journals; the Miracle Book Club was around for more than two years before articles written by the founder were at last published in one magazine. The one began at a conference launched by the International Council of Religious Education; the other, in a classroom at the request of a handful of teenagers. The first was built on the assumption that young people could change the world; the second on the premise that young people themselves needed changing. The United Christian Youth Movement faded with the coming of World War II; the Miracle Book Club spread rapidly across the United States and, while disappearing during World War II, spawned a host of parachurch youth agencies. We will examine the Miracle Book Club more closely later.

"Christian youth building a new world" was the modest slogan of the United Christian Youth Movement. Shaped by a social gospel orientation, leaders fashioned a response to the youth movements of Hitler's Germany, utilizing national and regional conferences as well as a series of program helps for local youth groups of all denominations. Despite the difficulties of the Great Depression, the movement's progressive agenda sought to shape society into a just kingdom.

Regional conferences highlighted United Christian Youth Movement activities in 1935 with 9,152 young people attending sessions held in twenty-four cities from Seattle to Boston. The participants represented 2,017 churches, demonstrating a significant base of support.

Though national conferences continued into the next decade, the high point of the United Christian Youth Movement appears to have been the June 1936 gathering of "931 young people and adult leaders, representing nearly every state in the Union and many of the Provinces of Canada."[48] Seventy-one denominations and other agencies were represented, again suggesting a breadth of support. The schedule provided for two major addresses each day. Ten hours in the first three days were designated for young people to spend working on commissions dealing with topics such as "Developing a Personal Christian Life," "Building a Warless World," "Christian World Outreach," "A Christian Use of Leisure Time," and "A Christian and the Use of Beverage Alcohol."

The primary emphasis of the movement appears to have been closely akin to that of the Society of Christian Endeavor, especially in the latter days of Francis E. Clark. The theme of "youth building a new world" was stressed to the extent that certain local groups even staged parades for world peace and consequently were accused of being communists.

Other issues of concern for the United Christian Youth Movement were issues of spiritual development, a Christian economic order, race, and concerns for homes and families. In keeping with the progressive education orientation of the *International Journal of Religious Education*, which was the chronicler and primary precipitator of the movement, the group emphasized doing service projects as an expression of Christian living. To know was not enough; it was essential for participants to put their knowledge into action.

Despite the lofty-sounding ideas of the movement, how much was done in local churches and communities is another matter. From studies sympathetic to the movement the conclusion was drawn that the activities were not a priority at the local level. More interesting is the conservatism of the young participants in the 1936 conference. Some of the statements prepared by youth at the conference sounded more like calls for revival than expressions of progressive religious education:

- The first step . . . must, of necessity, be conversion, because we must first have experienced the new birth ourselves before we can change others.
- We long to do right, yet we crave the pleasures of sin, expecting forgiveness, and a reward of eternal life. We want unselfishness, yet we are selfish. We are our own hindrance to the happiness we seek. Is Christ the answer to this problem? We believe he is.
- We recommend that Christian people refrain from drinking and the handling of alcohol in any form.
- We believe it necessary to create a new order. An ideal for which to work, a goal toward which to achieve, is necessary for proper motivation of our work in creating the new order, which we hold must be based upon the principles of Christ.[49]

Nevin Harner's conclusions about the decade of the thirties were best exemplified by the United Christian Youth Movement. "It seems clear that during this period the emphasis upon social action climbed higher and higher above the horizon, reached its zenith, and began to decline." By 1941, the theme of the conference in Estes Park, Colorado, had retreated from changing the world to changing a part of the world. With the coming of the Second World War, expectations had become decidedly more modest.[50]

In 1947 the United Christian Youth Movement attempted to merge with the International Society of Christian Endeavor, but the effort was never consummated. Yet as Howard A. Worth reviewed the decade of the 1940s in *Religious Education*, the United Christian Youth Movement is distinctly absent. Even the themes of the movement had vanished. In its place, though stated in a derogatory fashion, is the Youth for Christ movement, which would continue as a visible option in the years to come.

Crisis: The Scopes Monkey Trial

While youth societies remained static in what they did and how they did it, the public high school made radical changes by the 1920s. Schools were larger. In the 1929–30 school year nearly five million students were enrolled in secondary schools. This was 51.3 percent of the age group between ages fourteen and seventeen.

High school curriculums changed as well. Instead of concentrating exclusively on the old liberal arts curriculum, high schools of the twenties included courses that were socially relevant such as business education, agriculture, household arts, music, and physical education. Along with this "progressive" education came a decrease in the influence of religion and an increase of the sway that science, and specifically the concept of evolution, had upon the curriculum.

The most important change was the role that the high school played in the community. The school, rather than the church, became the focal point of community life. Education functioned as the religion of the day. Salvation from life's problems (no longer viewed as sin) was acquired through knowledge applied to life. Teachers served as priests. Science was the Bible.

Even in Meredith Willson's River City in *The Music Man* the change was evident. The community "sociable" at the conclusion of the musical was set, not in a church, but in the high school assembly room. The changing nature of the public high school had set the stage for the decline of the youth society and with it the decline of the second stage in youth ministry.

It is fitting that the crisis that brought to a conclusion the second cycle of youth ministry found its context in the high school science education in Tennessee, with the key role being played by an aging William Jennings Bryan. The three-time presidential nominee of the Democratic Party, and Secretary of State under Woodrow Wilson, represented a blending of Christian piety and ideals of progress and American democracy. While maintaining an unshakable faith in the authority of Scripture and advocating a lifestyle based on that conviction, Bryan also stood for progressive ideas that would "protect the people in their social, economic and political rights, and promote the general welfare of the country."[51] The populist Democrat was a staunch opponent of the teachings of evolution and in his waning years he traveled extensively addressing the issue.

When the state of Tennessee, influenced by a groundswell of support from fundamentalist Protestants, passed a law that forbade the teaching of evolution in public schools, the American Civil Liberties Union offered publicly to finance a test case of the law. Even though school was already out for the summer, John Thomas Scopes, a substitute science teacher, agreed to be charged with the violation of the law in Dayton, Tennessee. The stage was set for one of the most highly publicized trials of the twentieth century.

Clarence Darrow, the foremost criminal lawyer of his day, and Dudley Field Malone were the lawyers for the defense financed by the ACLU. Bryan, at the urging and support of the World's Christian Fundamentals Association, agreed to act as one of the prosecuting attorneys. For eleven days in the heat of July 1925, the nation followed newspaper accounts of the drama in what came to be known as the Scopes Monkey Trial. The trial climaxed when Darrow called Bryan to the witness stand. The aging statesman, wearied by his many years of crusading and slowed by diabetes, proved no match for the younger attorney. Wilting in the summer heat, Bryan was made a laughing stock by the media that covered the trial, and along with Bryan, the belief in the authority of the Bible became a scandal.

Though John Scopes was convicted and fined $100 by the jury, his conviction was later reversed by the State Supreme Court on a technicality. The credibility of Bible-believers across the nation seemed to have been destroyed. Fundamentalists were relegated to the intellectual scrap pile, and science as taught in the public school replaced the Bible as preached in the church. Christian Scripture, which had served as the backbone of youth societies, found itself in the cross-hairs of the media in America. The very existence of Christian youth ministry was in jeopardy.

Conclusion

The people of River City, while being the creation of a playwright, were typical of the environment in which the second cycle of protestant youth ministry flourished and then floundered. The Epworth League, which had been stimulated by Christian Endeavor and put down roots in River City, was part of the wave of church-based young people's societies that had swept the nation starting in 1881. But by the summer of 1912 in River City, after thirty years of helping young people learn skills of church leadership and personal piety, the denominational youth societies had passed their prime and parents were looking for something else to keep their children "moral after school."

The boys' band that "Professor" Harold Hill proposed filled that need and captured the dynamics of the youth associations that came into being during the early years of the twentieth century. It was nonsectarian and yet shared the values of church people. The band was limited to children whose parents could afford uniforms and band instruments or who were motivated enough to earn money and pay for the required equipment themselves.

If there was a tether that held young people's movements to the church, it was the desire by parents to have their children avoid the evils of their day by discovering God and the truths of the Bible. Scouting organizations and 4-H Clubs were excellent activities, but they were not active in teaching the Bible or calling young people to Christian conversion. And when the Scopes Monkey Trial made a scandal out of the evangelical faith, it appeared as if the era of Christian youth ministry had come to an end. Now it was time for the public education system to assume the responsibility for building the character of the nation's youth.

part 4

Modern Jazz

The Period of the Relational Outreach (1933–89)

One of the big differences between New Orleans jazz and the cool jazz of the 1960s was who was creating the music. No longer was the pain of the blues and the black experience in America the soul of jazz. While undoubtedly still including these themes, cool jazz added new musical elements from a host of musicians who created their own forms of jazz. Chet Baker, Stan Getz, John Coltrane, Archie Shepp, Sun Ra, and others gained new audiences and used a modern sound to express their creativity.

Youth ministry in the mid-twentieth century saw the need to make better connections with young people if their journey to know and experience God was to succeed. New themes and forms needed exploring. The rigid forms of youth societies lost their ability to attract and hold young people, especially young men. The old way just wasn't cool anymore.

The answer came in the proposal to transform youth societies into youth fellowships and limit membership to high school or junior high school age. Young people could be participants, while adults receded into the background. This more appealing form of jazz gave new life to the social aspects of youth groups. Yet the inability of churches to find adults who would put up with the social immaturity and unreliability of student leadership caused churches to move toward employing youth specialists, first part time and then as full-fledged church staff members. This, in turn, moved young people into a more passive role.

While youth societies initially increased the participation of young people in youth groups, the jazz they were playing did not appeal to their high school peers. With the center of adolescent society no longer in the church, the high school society began to trump church activities on virtually every front.

Taking on a missional posture, parachurch agencies stepped into the breech. Using relational strategies to earn the right to be heard by unchurched high school students, adults found ways outside the church to engage teenagers and help them find a place where God would show up.

Together the fellowship group and parachurch outreach approaches formed the period of the relational outreach (1933–89) that dominated the middle of the twentieth century. Many youth groups in the twenty-first century are still shaped by the last vestiges of this type of youth ministry.

Part 4 captures the rise of the American teenager, the transition to a relational approach to youth groups, and the evangelical attempt to reach youth for Christ. Fellowship with Christian peers and friendships with unchurched friends shaped Christian formation, just as proclamation of the gospel reshaped the Protestant youth group.

The novel *The Great Gatsby* depicted the issues faced by mainline denominational youth ministry following World War I. The Roaring Twenties and the Great Depression isolated adolescents from the workforce and gathered them in public high schools. A new cycle of youth ministry became necessary. Chapter 10 captures the response as youth fellowships replaced the more rigid youth societies. Youth fellowships began in 1936 in the Congregational Christian Church and ended when the World Council of Churches called for an end to "youth programs" in 1965. Conferences and denominational resource materials shifted their focus from personal religion to bringing a holistic Christian gospel into contact with the imperfections of the world they would soon inherit.

Chapter 11 utilizes the musical *Grease* to capture initiatives taken by parachurch agencies in the evangelization and spiritual formation of high school youth. The reunion for Rydell High class of '59 in Jim Jacobs and Warren Casey's show takes place at about the high point of the third youth ministry cycle. This cycle stretched from the founding of the Miracle Book Club in 1933 through 1989 and primarily featured

Young Life, Youth for Christ, and Fellowship of Christian Athletes as Protestant youth ministry moved from the church to the high school campus.

Pleasantville is an allegory about a town where uncertainty is not an option and change is frightening. The Gary Ross movie, set in the era of black and white television, captures the tension local churches in the emerging evangelical movement felt as they came to grips with the fact of "teenagers" living in middle class communities but influenced by the sounds of the city. The tensions parents and churches felt set the stage for the next cycle of youth ministry. Chapter 12 traces the responses of evangelicals and others in smaller denominations within the broader Protestant ethos during the period dominated by parachurch youth ministries.

In chapter 13 *Friday Night Lights* captures a short period of youth rallies beginning at the end of the Depression era (1938) but exploding upon the public awareness in the latter days of World War II, before fading from public view and finally disappearing in 1967. Yet shortly thereafter rallies took on a new life in local churches, primarily in seeker-driven churches. If football games characterized high school societies on Friday nights, Youth for Christ rallies provided high visibility for one form of missional youth ministry on Saturday nights. As church youth groups and later parachurch clubs fed the rallies, their stated role was evangelistic. When youth evangelists like Billy Graham shifted their attention to adults, the rallies faded into the sunset.

Cool jazz in Protestant youth ministry both helped and hindered the search for knowing God that young people experienced. Relational youth ministry, when done well, built authenticity into the youth groups, addressed the hurts and vulnerability in the teenage experience, and allowed caring adults to be active participants in the world of adolescents. Youth ministries became vulnerable, however, when the God they sought to encounter became more a product of their collective relational values than the God of the Christian Scriptures.

10

The Great Gatsby

Youth Fellowships in Mainline Denominational Youth Ministry (1936–65)

n 1974 Francis Ford Coppola released his version of F. Scott Fitzgerald's novel *The Great Gatsby*, which told the story of Nick Carraway, a young Midwestern man in his twenties living on Long Island, New York. Nick becomes fascinated with the mystery and lavishness of his neighbor, Jay Gatsby, who is part of the new-rich and lives a lifestyle in stark contrast with Carraway's value system.

The movie, like the novel, focuses on the death of the American dream. Some would see the dream as the Protestant work ethic and others associate it with economic middle-class values and morality. Though not explicit, it is apparent that the wealthy Gatsby gained his fortune through dealings with organized crime and that he had not adhered to the American dream guidelines. This creates tension for Carraway, who passes judgment on all the rich characters in the story. Why is it the immoral people who have all the money and by implication, all the fun?

The book from which the movie was made produced quite a scandal when it was released in 1925. For many it was repudiation of not only Midwestern values but of middle-class values in general. Historian Paula Fass suggests that Fitzgerald's novel compares and contrasts old and new American values. Nick Carraway, the son of a Midwestern minister, reflects the stability of middle America. Jay Gatsby, by contrast, offers a youthful idealism that is the product of wealth and leisure, however obtained.[1]

The Roaring Twenties during which Fitzgerald wrote was a watershed era for youth in America. Using flappers, jazz, and gin to epitomize the new freedoms experienced by young adults, Fitzgerald pictures sexual freedoms experienced by young women from the right side of the tracks, music that appealed to the emotion more than to the head, and the central place alcoholic beverages played in the new social whirl, despite the fact that Prohibition was the law of the land.

The social impact of Gatsby's world challenged the established social order and especially the manner in which Protestants viewed their children's process of maturing into adulthood. Times were changing. For parents and ministers from Protestant churches, the changes required countermeasures, but the existing approach to youth ministry no longer appeared adequate.

Social changes popularized for young people during the Roaring Twenties lost their hold on the youth of the nation during the Great Depression. But President Roosevelt's New Deal and the specter of war in Europe provided a changing perspective for young people. The thirties temporarily delayed a new interpretation of what it meant to be a young person in America. By the time World War II ended in 1945, however, the whole understanding of what it meant to be an adolescent had changed again. In the years between the midthirties and the late seventies, mainline denominational youth ministry went through a series of changes as leaders attempted to see youth ministry through the eyes of teenagers.

The affluence tasted in the twenties and then blossoming in the forties allowed the benefits of wealth and leisure to trickle down to middle adolescents, who came to be known as *teenagers*. The experiences of young adults in Fitzgerald's novel became an option to teenagers, with one very significant exception. Unlike Gatsby's friends, teens were still living in the homes of their parents and were still dependent upon them.

Impact of the Roaring Twenties

Paula Fass's critique of American youth in the 1920s provides a masterful look at the changing social fabric of college and university students at the time. She succinctly critiques the situation in her opening comment: "Youth suddenly became a social problem in the 1920's. Part myth, part reality, the youth problem was for contemporaries a symbol for the strains of a culture running headlong into the twentieth century."[2]

With a growing number of young people leaving home in their late teens to attend tax-supported universities, a distinct culture emerged. No longer under the watchful eye of parents and communities that shared their parents' values, university students found themselves within a society of peers. University officials retained varying interpretations of *parentis in loco*, the philosophy that the university assumed the responsibility of parenting the students entrusted to their care. Yet as universities grew larger and more diverse in the cultural background of students, shared understandings of standards for student behavior became foggy.[3]

In the place of rules and customs handed down from their parents' generation, the university students of the twenties developed a new set of norms guided primarily by peers on campus. Traditionalists, as Fass designated people associated with social values of the nineteenth century, expressed alarm. Pessimism and despair filled their descriptions of the direction of society. Progressives applauded the changing mores, expressing hope for a new order in society unencumbered by the values of a bygone era.[4]

In retrospect the activities of university students met neither set of critiques, though they altered both. These students were both a product of changes in society already under way and a governor on the engine of change. While changes in family nurture already diminished the aloof authoritarian parental roles associated with some European cultures, university students never gave up on the ideals of marriage and family. New expectations for family life resulted in a more democratic expression of the nuclear family. Yet the White House Conference on Child Health and Protection concluded that "no single home pattern or childrearing environment existed in the United States. Rather, there were large differences along racial, ethnic, religious, and class lines."[5]

Economic middle-class families, from which a majority of university students came, gave special evidence of a harmonious relationship between generations. Fass commented, "On all the criteria—number of children, kinds of discipline and punishment, involvement of father as well as mother in child-rearing, the use of child-rearing literature, educational opportunities, diet, play, and extra-familial activities—the economic middle class families emerged as developing most consistently and rapidly the kinds of families in which democracy, affection, and child consciousness predominated. And it was this pattern that appeared to produce the best adjusted, best satisfied, and most emotionally stable adolescents."[6]

Despite the increase in family compatibility, the greatest social change in the 1920s was the rise of the peer group. Between 1900 and 1930 college and university attendance tripled, the largest proportion happening in the twenties. This concentration of late adolescents on campuses was a new phenomenon in the American experience. Public universities were, for the most part, coeducational. Freed from parental supervision, the new habitat changed the manner in which young men and women related. Extracurricular activities occupied the spare time of students, some of whom appeared to have been majoring in leisure-time activities. Fraternities and sororities provided a pecking order in the collegiate social life. Status became the currency of the day.

Sexual norms, perhaps the greatest concern of the traditionalists, changed as well, but not as much as progressives thought probable. Fass commented, "Students of modern sexual behavior have quite correctly described the twenties as a turning point, a critical juncture between the strict double standard of the age of Victoria and the permissive sexuality of the age of Freud."[7] Peers, movies, and popular music, especially jazz, became the arbitrators of morality on campus. Family, church, and community appeared to have lost out in the struggle for sexual purity. Despite a wide increase in noncoitus sexual activity (called *petting*) as well as more frequent intercourse engaged in by coeds, what many observers "failed to see was that older controls were being supplemented or supplanted by newer controls."[8] Marriage and family remained a cherished, though somewhat altered, value to university students.

Coupled with the concern over changing sexual norms, the absence of spiritual convictions and practices concerned Protestant traditionalists the most. Attempts to wed Darwinian evolution and Christianity in the late nineteenth century produced a liberal hybrid that satisfied neither scientists nor theologians, while university students increasingly sat on the sidelines. An optimistic worldview that viewed Christianity as the key to an enlightened era of peace and prosperity shattered as a result of World War I, when Christian nations fought Christian nations. University students drifted away from Christianity. Protestant churches and agencies turned to social services and entertainment to lure students back to the church building, if not to the faith of their youth. The religion of the day became leisure activities, primarily sports, dating, and song.[9]

Yet the degree to which the changing social milieu on university campuses trickled down to students in the rapidly expanding high school system is questionable. Without a doubt, many of the collegiate extracurricular activities became normal parts of high school life. Marketers promoted the collegiate look in clothing for high school students. The radio brought the musical sounds popular on college campuses to high school students. Dating replaced the older courting system which was closely controlled by parents. Yet at the end of the day, high school students went home to eat and sleep under their parents' roofs. While the peer group increased its influence, family rules and norms still shaped the values of middle and younger adolescents.

For Protestant churches, one reality became apparent: youth societies as formulated in the last two decades of the nineteenth century were no longer relevant to the lives of adolescents. On the university campus, denominationally sponsored houses and parachurch organizations like the YMCA and YWCA were more likely to be marginal to campus life than at the center of the social and intellectual whirl. On the high school level, the school replaced the church as the location where young people gathered.

Protestant youth ministries languished. The youth society structure was no longer the only entertainment in town. A drift from historic Protestant views on doctrine and the Bible left many young people, parents, and church leaders with a lack of clarity on what to affirm. A spiritual malaise influenced the youth associated with the major Protestant denominations.

In her insightful critique of mainline denominational youth ministry, Kenda Creasy Dean asked, "What happened to passion?" The passion to know and experience God that had been associated with Christian Endeavor in the late nineteenth century had faded. Dean concluded that attempts by

> the Religious Education movement—Liberal theology's brief but massive program of educational reform in the early twentieth century—cheerfully pilfered the progressive education movement and imposed an often unwelcome degree of professionalism on the chaotic landscape of mainstream Protestant education. . . . By the 1920s and 1930s the goals of the nascent field of youth ministry in mainline churches had become virtually indistinguishable from the goals of professional educators and public education—a realm wholly indifferent to the influence of Christian theology.[10]

When twenty-four-year-old John Scopes was put on trial for teaching evolution in violation of Tennessee law during the summer of 1925, the bottom dropped out of youth ministries that affirmed a historic Protestant view of Scripture. The young teacher who had been hired more to coach the football team than to teach science became the poster boy for attempts by the American Civil Liberties Union to remove a creationist perspective from public high schools.

The team of defense attorneys, the most notable of whom was Clarence Darrow, faced a team of prosecutors, including William Jennings Bryan, the man whom journalist H. L. Mencken snidely called the "Fundamentalist Pope." Bryan, lacking in theological training but well-versed in the vulnerability of the dark side of evolutionary reasoning—including the pro-eugenics position taken by the textbook being used in Tennessee—was outmaneuvered by the younger Darrow. The national press covering the trial made a scandal of both Bryan and conservative Protestant Christianity.[11]

If denominational youth societies had not been inclined to make changes in their youth ministry strategies, the Scopes trial was a rude awakening. The following years saw a revolution in how churches approached the nonformal training of youth for active participation in the church and the world.

The society in which adolescents lived changed as well. The public high school became the gathering place for teenagers. With the isolation of students from most adults five days a week, for six or more hours a day, new concerns arose. The size of schools increased, leaving minimal adult supervision on campus and an increased influence of the peer society. Extracurricular activities created different types of peer pressure, for good and for bad. The currency of the high school culture became status among peers. Juvenile delinquency worried the public. Youthful fads alarmed the sensibilities of the older generation.

While the Depression and World War II created a type of cultural parenthesis around the changes young people were experiencing, one conclusion was evident to the informed observer. Older forms of church ministry to youth were no longer appropriate or effective. While youth ministry had always been relational, the teenagers who found their voices in the American culture as they approached the middle of the twentieth century needed places where they could experiment with life's experiences and questions without being preached at by their parents' generation.

The Rise of the Youth Fellowship

At the instigation of the International Council of Religious Education, denominational youth leaders began asking how youth ministries could be done better. With fifty years of experience with young people's societies, they began asking how the two aspects of religious education (Sunday school and youth society) could be made more effective. Schooling had become the model for religious education and efficiency the standard by which it was judged. Youth societies with their committees and pledges simply did not match up to the educational standards of the mid-1930s.[12]

Into this gap stepped youth fellowships. The concept tied together the Sunday school and a new kind of Sunday evening meeting designed to foster fellowship with both God and peers. Luke 2:52 provided the cornerstone for young people who were to grow as Christ had, "in wisdom and stature and in favor with God and [people]."

In 1936, the Congregational Christian Church announced the formation of the Pilgrim Fellowship for its high school youth. The designation *fellowship* picked up on the rising influence of the peer group and shifted the focus of their youth group from the fragmented remains of the system of accountability initiated by Christian Endeavor to an ideal of Christian collegiality, especially for high school students. By the mid-1940s fourteen mainline denominations had adopted the approach.[13]

The new approach to youth ministry was closely associated with the United Christian Youth Movement. Though the movement failed to materialize as a means to rally young people to match the theme of the first conference in 1934, "Christian Youth Building a New World," the youth fellowship idea introduced by the movement provided a significant change in how churches approached the needs of their adolescent parishioners.

In consultation with denominational youth ministry leaders associated with the Federal Council of Churches, the United Christian Youth Movement identified five emphases for youth fellowships in local churches.

- Christian faith—to help youth grow in a vital Christian faith and life;
- Christian witness—to help youth make known to others the way of Christ by all they do and say;
- Christian outreach—to help youth know, and accept their responsibility in, the world-wide mission of the Church;
- Christian citizenship—to help youth understand community needs and, on the basis of Christian convictions, work to meet these needs through personal influence and group action;
- Christian fellowship—to help youth experience in all their relationships the bond of Christian fellowship which comes from their common faith.[14]

Sara Little, professor of Christian education emerita at Union Theological Seminary in Virginia, described her personal experience transitioning from the older Christian Endeavor approach to the newer strategy of youth ministry.

During the late '30s I was quite involved in the youth group at my church, Amity Presbyterian in Charlotte, North Carolina. On one occasion, I am not sure exactly when, I clearly remember going to downtown Charlotte on a drizzly Saturday night to march in a candlelight parade for Christian Endeavor. I was an officer in the county association. The next day, a Sunday afternoon, I went to a meeting of the Mecklenburg Presbytery Youth Council, in which I was also an officer. That was the last memory I have of

Christian Endeavor, partly because of the depressing parade, mostly because activities in our presbytery youth group grew rapidly and simply took up all the time I had. . . . I was present at the demise of Christian Endeavor and the growth of the Presbyterian Young People's League.[15]

Youth fellowships differed from youth societies in two very significant ways. First, they were under the complete control of the local church. Usually this meant being accountable to the church committee or commission on religious education. Area, state, regional, and national gatherings were designed to support and promote local church activities. Youth fellowships were tied exclusively to the local faith community. Though this ideal would be compromised from time to time, looking a bit more like union and national denominational conferences, for the most part the local ties of youth fellowships were primary.

The second difference from youth societies had to do with the ages of the members. Because there had been no age limitation on youth societies, people well into their adult years maintained leadership positions and in effect froze out younger leaders. The older members often made membership unappealing for younger people and limited the growth of these societies. To solve this problem, youth fellowships were open to every person in the church between the ages of twelve and twenty-four. Attendance for three consecutive weeks qualified a person for membership. Youth fellowships were further divided into intermediates (twelve to fourteen), seniors (fifteen to seventeen), and older youth (eighteen to twenty-four). The primary focus, however, was on the high school age group.

While Sunday school and youth fellowship meetings were at the heart of the new youth ministry concept, youth choirs, scout meetings, service projects, outings, and recreational activities also contributed to the newly developed educational concept. Usually a youth council of adult sponsors coordinated efforts. There were no professional youth workers on the local church level. Between 1936 and the end of World War II, the youth fellowship concept was adopted by most mainline denominations.

Methodist Youth Ministry

The formation of the Methodist Youth Fellowship at the Watch Night Service, December 31, 1941, served two purposes. The Epworth League no longer appealed to Methodist youth, at least as it once had. In its place came a new expression of the church's concern for youth.

The youth fellowships of the Methodist churches provided a breath of fresh air in ministry to high school students. World War II had just begun and while not a factor in the decision to change approaches to working with young people, the war changed the primary audience of Protestant youth ministries. Men of draft age enlisted in the military by the millions. Their sisters and girlfriends entered the workforce to support the war effort, but without boys of their age present at youth group activities, their attendance dwindled. This left high school students as the primary participants in Methodist youth ministries. While older youth remained a part of the Methodist Youth Fellowship, their participation decreased.

The second purpose for the newly-formed Methodist youth ministry was to engender loyalty to the Methodist Church. Two years before the formation of Methodist Youth Fellowship, the Methodist Protestant Church, the Methodist Episcopal Church, South, and the Methodist Episcopal Church had merged at their Uniting Conference in Kansas City, Missouri. Prior to the merger the official youth program of the Methodist Protestant Church had been Christian Endeavor, while the other two Methodist denominations had their own forms of the Epworth League. Methodist Youth Fellowship provided a new beginning.[16]

The purposes stated for the MYF reflected Methodist priorities. Unlike the more ecumenical Christian Endeavor, the newly-formed youth fellowship envisioned the formation of distinctly Methodist young people. The official purposes included:

- To live clean lives following the highest that we know;
- To give our loyalty and service through the Methodist Church of which we are a part, working with others that she may more perfectly follow the Master and more worthily bless mankind;
- To hold the ideals of unselfish service ever before us, striving continually for human betterment, placing the welfare of others above our own;
- And in simple trust, to follow Jesus as our Saviour and Lord.[17]

Officers elected annually provided the leadership. Working in cooperation with youth group sponsors, officers were responsible to develop and lead Sunday evening programs. Though materials were available to assist officers in preparing for meetings, no "prefabricated" forms were provided. Experience, however, suggested five areas associated with the Christian life that would provide themes for their gatherings: Christian faith, witness, fellowship, outreach, and citizenship.[18]

With the introduction of MYF, the pledge concept used by Christian Endeavor and the Epworth League disappeared. The focus had shifted over the years from purely endeavoring to know God to a more peer-oriented society. The transition to a youth fellowship approach formalized that change and placed the emphasis on membership and the benefits of fellowship with Christian young people. While MYF included Sunday school, the Sunday evening meeting was under the control of teenagers and became the heart of the new approach. A typical Sunday evening meeting included four parts—a forty-five minute program, thirty minutes of recreation and socializing, another half hour of food and refreshment, and occasionally a twenty to thirty minute business meeting.[19]

MYF came to resemble a high school club. Extracurricular activities for secondary schools grew in importance starting in the Depression era. In many ways these activities reflected the influence of the university campus, where leisure time was filled with social and recreational pursuits.

By 1953, MYF claimed a membership of 1,217,479. Identifying a rapidly growing population of teenagers, denominational leaders encouraged young members to claim four million, six hundred thousand for Christ by 1960.[20] Yet the challenge seemed predicated on the assumption that high school students would evangelize their peers. Of course many of those peers were Protestants of other denominations, but there appears to have been little response to the challenge. In part this was because the Methodist Youth Fellowship was not focused on evangelization. The program area emphasizing Christian witness tended to be project-oriented with responsibility for planning left to committee chairmen and adult sponsors. Christian Witness Projects, as suggested in denominational literature, looked more like a community visitation program, canvassing teenagers with whom the students had contact. The strategy looked more like a plan conceived in an editor's office than growing from evangelistically oriented MYF groups.

Instead of reaching millions of their peers for Christ, MYF found little increase of attendance nationally, peaking in 1961 and then beginning a prolonged decline. In his analysis of the annual reports of the Youth Department for the Board of Education of the Methodist Church for the decade of the 1950s, Charles Webb Courtoy reported,

> One begins to sense a growing concern of the youth staff that all is not well. Year after year there is a notation that older youth (18–23 years of age) are dropping out of MYF. . . . Even though the "Annual Reports" remained positive during the 1950's about the MYF for (high) school age youth, as the decade drew to a close a hint of the unrest to come began to be reflected in the reports.[21]

The focal point of Courtoy's concern was the Sunday evening fellowship meeting. A general malaise blanketed MYF groups. Methodist youth ministry was coming to the end of a cycle of ministry. His analysis left little doubt that Methodist youth ministries were no longer relevant to teenagers.

Lutheran Youth Ministry

Lutheran youth ministry varied widely depending on the synod and more specifically, the country of origin. Two names of Lutheran national youth organizations predominated—the Missouri Synod's Walther League and the Luther League, whose name and structure was shared by many of the other synods. While widespread local youth societies existed through the nineteenth century and into the early twentieth century, significant changes took place in the 1920s and 1930s. For most synods, the change was that they created national organizations or merged with other synods to create new youth organizations.[22] For the Missouri Synod, the Walther League continued to exist but reinvented itself. The process was a case study of Lutheran youth ministries.

While the Walther League did not change its name, the Missouri Synod youth society began changing its strategy in the 1930s. World War I forced a revision of both the Synod churches and the Walther League. When America went to war against Germany, the land of Luther, the American reaction against anything German forced the churches to shed much of their loyalty to their country of origin. Instead of perpetuating the German language and continental customs, the church moved toward the American mainstream. The Walther League became one of the key vehicles in that process.[23]

For local youth ministries the changes became a means of survival in American society. While some churches elected to provide parochial schools up through high school and thus retain historic Lutheran values, the majority of Lutheran teenagers attended public high schools and found themselves influenced by both academic content and, more importantly, their American peers. Jon Pahl commented, "The [Walther] League grew rapidly after World War I, when leaders adopted English as their official language."[24] Instead of standing against the dominant culture because of the language barrier, the Walther League used English to teach Lutheran values in an informal manner. Between the end of the war and 1960 the league grew from 310 to over five thousand local societies across the US.[25]

While Americanization of the Walther League was undoubtedly a factor in the growth of the league, attention paid to youth ministries by Lutheran leaders produced great dividends as well. The Missouri Synod hired a series of Field Secretaries starting with F. A. "Pap" Klein who published materials and manuals to assist local church leagues and promoted camping ministries to bring Lutheran youth together for teaching and fellowship. The volume of literature was impressive. As Lutheran churches paid attention to their youth, their young people responded.[26]

Changes in the content of the Walther League meetings were a third factor in the growth in the number of societies. While never influenced to any significant degree by Christian Endeavor, the league, under the leadership of Executive Secretary Otto Paul Kretzmann, started in 1934 to focus on two themes—knowing and doing. The more devotional themes drawn from Lutheran pietism gave way to applied forms of Christian living.[27]

"Change was the life-style; struggle was the methodology," summarized Elmer N. Witt, executive director of the Walther League from 1953 to 1967.

> Examples abounded: the change from all male to female and male youth societies . . . the switch from German to English . . . the movement from keeping youth within the church to getting youth to live and witness outside the church . . . the slow-but-sure change from lecture/preaching/didactics to group process/involvement/learning-by-doing . . . the development from relying solely on print to training which depends on person-to-person, eye-to-eye contact . . . the evolvement of periodicals suited to the times . . . the inevitable transition on the "burning question" of social dancing . . . the revolution from young adult to high school leadership.[28]

The struggle over changes produced tensions with pastors and parents. Local youth ministries had been safe places where Lutheran youth could be buffered from the changes in society. Expectations were that the local Walther League provided a place where Lutheran kids could meet, date, and eventually marry. Sexual purity was expected. That is one reason why dancing was frowned upon, for it was considered unhealthy physical contact between boys and girls.

The turbulence of the 1960s—related to the Vietnam conflict and the civil rights movement—resulted in a counterculture among college-age youth. The ferment further exaggerated the changes happening in Protestant youth ministries including the Walther League. When denominational youth leaders addressed justice and race issues at national conventions, local churches began pulling back from their involvement in the league. Youth ministries became increasingly localized. In 1977, the Walther League folded as an institution.[29]

Presbyterian Youth Ministry

Presbyterian youth ministry continued to be dominated by Christian Endeavor until almost the middle of the twentieth century. Presbyterians whose lives had been influenced by the New England–based Christian Endeavor movement were influential in the local Presbyterian churches, where denominational leaders sought to create youth ministries with a distinctly Presbyterian flavor.

The Presbyterian Church in the United States (Southern Presbyterian) went through a series of efforts to develop a denominational youth ministry to their liking. After the demise of the Westminster League (see chapter 9), the General Assembly named Walter Getty as the first director of the Young People's Division in 1924 and commissioned him to create the Presbyterian Young People's League. The desire was to merge all existing youth ministry organizations under an umbrella organization that paralleled the larger denominational program.[30] Like so many decisions made at the denominational level, the league never became a reality at the local church level.

Denominational leaders could see the problems the aging Christian Endeavor societies were presenting in local churches, but they appeared to have no viable alternative. Since Christian Endeavor leaders had no age limits, high school students found themselves mixing with people their parents' ages at church while operating in a peer society at school. As Kett suggests, adolescents started voting with their feet and participation declined.[31]

John Fairly was the next person called upon to help the PCUS address their staggering youth ministry. A pastor who had enjoyed some success in working with young people, Fairly was named to head the denomination's Religious Education Department. This included youth work. In 1930, he launched the Kingdom Highways Program, designed to help local churches develop youth ministries that coordinated all aspects of ministry to adolescents while allowing students to participate in organizing and leading their spiritual journeys. The framework allowed local churches freedom to utilize the creativity of their people and respond to local needs of their youth while providing a shared journey for youth within the denomination.[32]

The name *Kingdom Highways* was never associated with local youth ministries; instead the local youth ministries chose their own nicknames for the Young People of the (insert name) Church. While Christian Endeavor was allowed to retain their name and remained strong in PCUS churches through the 1930s, the tide eventually began to shift. Christian Endeavor became more of a memory than a vital force. Kingdom Highways served youth ministries in the PCUS through the Depression and World War II years, but with the new mood in society following the war, something more in keeping with the emerging teenage culture was needed.

The Presbyterian Church in the USA (Northern Presbyterian) and Cumberland Presbyterian Church followed a similar pattern in their development of youth ministries. Like it did in the Presbyterian Church in the US, Christian Endeavor provided the backbone of PCUSA youth ministries. As was true of their southern sister denomination, leaders struggled with coordination of their educational efforts when Christian Endeavor was not entirely under their administrative leadership.[33]

In each Presbyterian denomination, the issue appeared to be a matter of denominational control more than a conflict of philosophy of how best to address the needs of young people. Few fresh ideas were offered to counter Christian Endeavor. Only as the culture in which young people lived changed did Presbyterian churches reach out for a fresh strategy of youth ministry. As the youth society approach dominated by young to middle-age people became irrelevant to teenagers living daily in a peer society, Presbyterians embraced the newly introduced youth fellowship approach to youth ministry.

Shortly after the United Christian Youth Movement introduced the youth fellowship concept, the Presbyterian Church USA formed Westminster Fellowship (1943) and the Presbyterian Church in the US initiated the Presbyterian Youth Fellowship (1946). Teenagers were viewed as an essential part of the church. Yet youth fellowships were more of a ministry to young people than a ministry with them. While these youth fellowships were envisioned to be a coordinated effort utilizing parents, pastors, directors of religious education, adult advisors, departmental superintendents, Sunday school teachers, and youth choir directors, by the middle of the 1950s youth fellowships focused on Sunday evening activities and the role of the youth advisor, who served as a coach to high school students in a context that they could plan and structure. Sunday evening meetings became the time when Westminster Fellowship or PYF met.

By the end of the 1970s, the youth fellowship idea appears to have run its course in Presbyterian churches. Sara Little commented,

> I don't know what to say about the '60s and '70s. Denominations lost their sense of direction, with few clues as to what to do structurally. The great moment of insight that came in the '50s, when youth were proclaimed as part of the church *now*, was true and good, but did not adequately recognize they were struggling to find their own identity and direction for life. All the cultural forces that we know about—the counterculture, new life movements, neoconservatives—are to be noted. So is the increasing influence of the para-church groups, which, though many had emerged in the '40s (Young Life, in 1941; Youth for Christ, in 1944), now assumed greater visibility.[34]

Kenda Creasy Dean, associate professor of Youth, Church, and Culture at Princeton Theological Seminary, commented, "The hemorrhage of adolescents from mainstream Protestantism began in the late 1950s, and by century's end had swelled to a full-fledged ecclesial crisis."[35] Again, young people were voting with their feet. As Dean concludes, they had lost both the passion of Christ and their passion for Christ.

Baptist Youth Ministry

The mainline Baptist conventions marched to a different drum than did their sister Protestant denominations. From the beginning they resisted being absorbed into Christian Endeavor by creating the Baptist Young People's Union in 1891.[36] Four years later the Southern Baptist BYPU was organized in Atlanta, Georgia.[37] In both the North and the South the initiatives were based on the conviction that youth programs needed to be strictly Baptistic and under the sole authority of the local church without interdenominational affiliation. Initially BYPU admitted only young people seventeen years of age and older.

Baptist youth ministry followed the youth society model pioneered by Christian Endeavor. More than in any of the sister denominations, programming materials for Southern Baptist churches were assigned to the Sunday school board with its enormous publishing capacity. Responsibility for BYPU, however, remained at the local Baptist church level and widely varied in effectiveness.

The social dynamics that affected Methodists and Presbyterians, and to a lesser extent the Lutherans, challenged the Southern Baptist convention to change its approach to youth ministry. The high school peer society began redefining youth ministry as young people gathered in public high schools. A good portion of high school youth were younger than seventeen and still in a formative period of their lives. Southern Baptists responded by creating the Baptist Training Union in 1934, which included a specific section for "intermediates" ages thirteen to seventeen.[38]

While designed to be part of a larger strategy for training the future leadership of the church, the intermediate section of BTU took on the flavor of youth fellowships, meeting on Sunday evenings before the evening church service and offering social events at other times. Programming was built around a group-committee approach that divided the youth group into four planning groups who worked together to present programs once a month. Materials published in Nashville helped Southern Baptist Training Unions organize and raise the quality of weekly meetings. Yet the quality of youth group meetings was seldom very high. In many cases adults planned the programs when students failed to do their jobs.

By the 1950s many churches across the convention began calling for major changes in the training union program. In 1964 training union enrollments began to drop and continued downward for the next two decades.[39] The Sunday school board responded in 1970 with a name change and new program suggestions and materials. The new name, *Quest*, alarmed the messengers (delegates are called "messengers" in Southern Baptist terminology) at the convention in New Orleans, and the new youth ministry idea was rejected, leaving individual churches to bring about innovation. Without a mandate to change, the training union limped on throughout the 1970s.

Opinions differ over why the messengers felt alarm about the suggested changes. W. L. Howse argued that the messengers had been taught that if they trained their youth in a certain way, they would get predictable results.[40] The sudden change appeared to be a contradiction to the system with which they had been raised.

This may have been complicated by two events in which churches began to feel the Sunday school board was pushing racial desegregation. Though the board had been given the responsibility to teach Christian ethics, the inclusion of an offensive book by black author James Baldwin in a training union bibliography and the insertion of a picture of a black male with two white female college students in the training union periodical, *Becoming*, suggested an agenda offensive to the conservative Southern constituency.[41]

Whatever the cause, leadership of youth ministry passed from the Sunday school board to local churches. Where churches depended on Southern Baptist publications for programming suggestions, the continuation of an increasingly ineffective approach to youth ministries was problematic. Into this gap moved a growing number of youth pastors who shaped Baptist youth ministry at the grassroots level.

While the first Southern Baptist church to employ a full-time staff member to serve as church youth director was Third Baptist Church in St. Louis, Missouri, in 1927, the practice of employing youth ministers did not become a common practice in Southern Baptist churches until the 1970s when the training union approach had become irrelevant to most teenagers. Even then Southern Baptist youth ministers were for the most part trained as Christian educators tied to church educational structures far more than they were as evangelists or spiritual directors.

One innovation to increase involvement of youth in the church was the youth choir. Adapting popular musical styles of the 1960s and 1970s, these choirs attracted youth and gave them a voice in ministering to their churches and beyond. Publishing houses responded by publishing youth musicals, and youth ministries took on a new look.[42]

Camps for Southern Baptist teenagers changed during the 1970s as well. They became far more relational, with decentralized leadership. Moving away from schooling-type specialization, counselors became guides for a weeklong spiritual journey. Phillip H. Briggs commented:

Perhaps the most significant change in Southern Baptist youth camping was the development of "Centrifuge." Centrifuge camping is a diversion from the traditional youth camp of Bible classes, extended preaching services, and long, emotional invitations.[43]

The rise of the youth minister marked the end of the youth fellowship era in Baptist churches. In its place came an emphasis on Christian discipleship. Symbolic of the change was *Disciple Life*, developed by R. Clyde Hall and Wesley O. Black. The youth training curriculum incorporated a taxonomy of youth discipleship learning objectives for students in grades seven through twelve.[44] Youth ministry in the Southern Baptist convention had become highly intentional.

Two youth movements that developed in Southern Baptist churches had a national impact on youth ministry. The movement for sexual purity before marriage called True Love Waits was conceived and popularized by Jimmy Hester and Richard Ross in conjunction with LifeWay Christian Resources; it resulted in over three million purity pledges by the end of the twentieth century. Similarly the Southern Baptist–generated See You at the Pole has impacted approximately three million middle and high school students each year as they gather around the flagpoles at their schools on a September day to pray for their fellow students. Yet youth group attendance and baptisms of adolescents in Baptist churches continued to decline as the twenty-first century began.[45]

Conclusion

The promise of the United Christian Youth Movement in the midthirties to empower young people to "build a new world" never caught hold as a youth movement. Yet it served as a catalyst to rethink church youth ministry. Concluding that the era of youth societies was over and influenced by the call of progressive educators for organization and efficiency, mainline denominations attempted to incorporate youth ministries into departments of youth that spanned the ministries of the church to adolescents.

Accepting the facts that *youth* now meant *teenagers* and that teenagers lived much of their lives shaped by peers in the public high school, fellowship among Christian young people became the central attraction of youth ministries. Pledges to abstain from alcoholic beverages or to know God were a thing of the past, though a pledge of sexual purity would later emerge. Youth fellowships focused on helping teenagers address the issues Christians needed to address—faith, witness, outreach, citizenship, and fellowship. In practice, however, the Sunday evening meetings called *youth fellowship* came to emphasize fellowship with only a veneer of the other issues thrown in to justify its existence in the church.

While there were benefits in youth fellowships as Christian peer groups were created to counter high school peer pressures, Charles Webb Courtoy concluded:

> The weaknesses of the fellowship era are legion. The youth fellowship was too institutional. Vast amounts of time and energy were spent on organization and "programs," and too little on God's mission to the world. Salvation became identified with membership in the fellowship. Christian witness too often was translated into membership recruitment. By having their own organization, the congregation tended to think in terms of youth as the church of tomorrow rather than to incorporate them into the life and mission of the church as fellow Christians. The youth fellowship was too often program centered rather than person centered. . . . Too often what happened on Sunday did not help with what happened on Monday in the young person's life.[46]

Even with the weaknesses of Protestant youth ministries, the world of the American dream, as depicted in *The Great Gatsby*, persisted into the middle of the twentieth century, though in a significantly modified form. Values shaped by a Protestant world and life view persisted. While imperfect and constantly being modified, the Protestant youth group provided for teenagers a laboratory for experimentation with the real life connection between their Christian faith and the social milieu of the peer society of their high school experience.

By the 1960s, the forms of church youth ministry formulated in the thirties had run their course. Kenda Creasy Dean concluded:

> In 1965, the World Council of Churches called for an end to the balkanization of young people into isolated "youth programs," urging congregations to integrate youth into the total mission of the church. Financially strapped denominations responded by amputating costly youth departments—yet, as staffs and budgets shriveled, no mechanisms emerged to help local churches absorb young people into their larger ministries.[47]

Concurrent with the efforts of mainline Protestant churches to gain greater control and provide increased educational sophistication to their youth ministries, another approach to Protestant youth ministry had begun to happen. Drawn primarily from the evangelical wing of Protestantism but not directly under ecclesiastical control, several independent efforts to reach youth for Christ grew into a movement that in the long run shaped Protestant church-based youth ministry.

11

Grease

Parachurch Club Programs (1933–89)

elcome Back: Rydell High, Class of '59," read the large sign trimmed in green and brown. It could have been a class reunion anywhere in the United States and looked very much the same. Former cheerleaders, honor society students, and former athletes along with that majority of average students gathered to see if life after high school had been kind to their classmates.

But the Rydell High School reunion is different. Instead of focusing on the leaders of the student body, Jim Jacobs models the story after his experience as a "greaser" at Chicago's Taft High School and uses the musical *Grease* to tell an idealized story about the people who never bothered to show up for a class reunion. Or, if they did, their primary purpose was to show the "jocks" and "rah rahs" that they had been a success after graduation even though they had been viewed with disdain for their mode of dress, choice of friends, or selection of interests during high school years.

The movie version, released in 1978, depicted a flashback to their senior year. It featured John Travolta as Danny, the leader of the Burger Palace Boys and the archetype of a '50s greaser, and Olivia Newton-John playing the role of Sandy, a sweet, wholesome, "Gidget" type of girl who has just arrived in the community and is about to identify with the high school's "in crowd" but instead is attracted to Danny's charm.

The setting for *Grease* is the apathy of the fifties. A nation wearied by a world war and the Korean conflict had enjoyed the security and conservatism of the Eisenhower years. High school students were divided into three groups. The first was student body leaders, which consisted of athletes, cheerleaders, and student officers. The second was a collection of people called "greasers," who flaunted their rejection of the symbols of status in the high school community. Though the two groups varied from school to school, the combined groups seldom exceeded 30 percent of the student body.

The last and by far largest group in the public high school of the fifties was a nameless group that existed between the two cliques that have been stereotyped so often in movies like *Grease*. These average students were like Sandy, who merely wanted to have friends and a place to belong in the social structure of Rydell High. These students were the primary participants in the third cycle of youth ministry. Though Young Life, and to a lesser extent Youth for Christ clubs, attempted to attract student body leaders (they seldom targeted the "greasers"), the ordinary participant was drawn from the middle section of the student body.

The late fifties to the late sixties was the high point of the parachurch contribution to the third cycle of youth ministry. As in the previous two cycles, ministry agencies came into being in the context of social disruption and solidified as one—or in this case two—organizations moved to the front, until eventually their strategies were imitated by the church and their cutting edge of effectiveness waned.

Secularization of the Adolescent World

Rydell High School was a product of two major events of the twentieth century—the Great Depression and World War II. The high school experience was a relatively new episode in the lives of the youth of America when the stock market collapsed on "Black Thursday," October 24, 1929. The number of young people enrolled in secondary education had doubled each decade of the century, with 4.4 million high school students filling publicly financed classrooms that fall day.[1]

The twenties had been a period of social liberation for young people, but just when adolescence began to be fun, the Depression came. Life was no longer filled with a multitude of options. Survival became the concern of both parent and child. In some industries unemployment ran as high as 30 to 40 percent. Banks closed. Homes, farms, and businesses were lost to foreclosure. With a scarcity of jobs, young people stayed in school longer and by the end of the decade, high school enrollments had increased by another 50 percent to 6.6 million.

The quality of high school education improved as the adolescent population increased. One trend concerned conservative Protestants, however. Religion in general and Bible teaching more specifically were systematically being removed from the classroom. By 1941, twelve states, mostly in the East, required Bible reading in the public schools, while an equal number in the West and Midwest had outlawed the practice. This trend was finalized when the United States Supreme Court, in the *McCollum v. Board of Education* decision of 1948, held that a program that permitted religious instruction within public schools during school hours and excused students from a part of the secular school schedule was unconstitutional.

A similar process of secularization took place in organizations originally designed to include a Christian witness in their ministries to American youth. The YMCA provided a classic example of the trend. Throughout the second half of the nineteenth century the organization shifted from addressing merely the spiritual needs of young men to an effort to address social issues. As the movement grew, various expressions of Christianity, including Catholic perspectives, became part of the conversation. By the end of the century the evangelical and pietistic aspects of the YMCA began losing out. Religious activities became more difficult to describe in annual reports due to the lack of agreement on what the spiritual impact of the organization should be.[2]

Evelyn McClusky told of a similar transition in the YWCA. In 1935, while she was teaching Bible classes for the organization in a high school in Portland, Oregon, a representative of the national organization called the volunteers together and informed them that the emphasis of the organization in the United States had become loyalty to Jesus. References to salvation were to be scaled back since the YWCA now included women of other religious groups, not all of which were Christian.[3]

The dual movements of students out of the home and into the high school while religious instruction was being removed from the public school and youth organizations left a vacuum of religious and moral instruction. Though the effectiveness of such instruction for religious purposes was questionable, concern expressed by Protestant parents and clergy increased. These trends gradually escalated during the period and set the stage for a response by Christian adults.

World War II was the second disruption of the social order in the nation. The attack on Pearl Harbor brought the United States into the war and rallied the nation around one massive task—a military victory on two fronts. Fifteen million service men and women went to war. With a shortage of men on the home front, thousands of women went to work in defense plants. The economy, though military in focus, was functioning at or near capacity. There was not much time to relax or socialize except as a means to prepare for the war effort.

The impact of the war on youth ministry was twofold. From the popularization of church youth ministries under Francis E. Clark in 1881 until World War II, leadership for youth societies had come from young adults within church youth ministries. Societies included people in their early and middle twenties who served the role that later became known as sponsors for the younger groups. When the transition to youth fellowships began in the mid-1930s, young adults frequently served as adult sponsors though teenagers assumed greater leadership roles. Then the war came and when many from this pool of leaders enlisted in the military, the church had to find a new group of adults to reach young people for Christ.

The war created a crusade spirit. Young Americans who entered the war discovered their abilities to lead and drew on the resources of their homeland to rid the world of the fascist threat of Germany and Italy as well as the imperialist ambitions of Japan. With victories on both fronts American service personnel returned home convinced they had saved the world. Soon Christian young adults were ready to participate in another crusade—a campaign to change the spiritual convictions of the nation and the world. No longer closely bound by provincial perspectives on their Christian faith, the worldly-wise young believers returned home to lead the church in cooperative efforts of evangelism.

Into this setting came the Youth for Christ movement, a scattered assortment of young adults who took as their task the evangelization of their peers and those a few years younger than themselves. Only later, as the war was drawing to a close, did one group of these youth evangelists band together and call themselves Youth for Christ International. Yet reaching teenagers for Christ through new forms of parachurch organizations was already a decade old.

Incarnational Strategy: High School Clubs

In apparently unrelated settings across the country, adults who shared a concern for young people began experimenting with a form of youth ministry based in or near high school campuses, a type of ministry that came to be known as relational evangelism. If youth ministry jazz was a combination of improvisation and syncopation (or timing), the incarnational club programs that sprang up in a variety of forms in the thirties and forties illustrate both.

In Chicago, for example, as one glanced through the pages of *Schurzone 1941*, the annual yearbook of Carl Schurz High School, page 112 was distinct. Pictured were twenty-one students and two faculty sponsors of the Miracle Book Club. The description of the club called it a "strictly nonsectarian" organization, which met on Friday afternoons in a conveniently located church. This club, however, was not an isolated phenomenon. It was a chapter of a national club program based in Oakland, California, that had been founded eight years earlier.

Even earlier, Noel Palmer of Canada's InterVarsity Christian Fellowship began a ministry to high school students that was modeled after an Australian group called Crusaders. At the suggestion of Howard Guinness the work was started in Victoria, British Columbia, and Toronto in 1931, to evangelize high school students and channel them into InterVarsity chapters on university campuses.

Across the continent, John Miller began High Light Clubs for high schoolers in Washington, DC, in 1942. The reason was simple. Some kids he knew wanted to grow in their Christian faith. Apparently something was missing in their family and church experience. Soon others heard about the idea and wanted clubs in their schools as well. In time four clubs met in homes on weeknights to study the Bible. There was little outreach to students who did not share their spiritual convictions, but along with his friend Wade Seaford, Miller led the clubs and helped students bring meaning to their faith.[4]

"Ever attend a meeting on a bus?" asked Kansas City's Al Metsker in a 1949 *Youth for Christ Magazine* article. Most people have not. Yet for Bible clubbers in Kansas City the experience was common. Following the Supreme Court's *McCollum* decision, most school districts removed religious instruction from public schools. In Kansas City innovative measures were employed by those Christians who wanted to maintain a Christian presence on the high school campus. Consequently, a school bus was bought for four thousand dollars and fitted like a club house for the "Youth on the Beam" clubs of the city.[5]

The common denominator among these stories was an innovative spirit that began in conservative Protestant youth work during the 1930s and 1940s. Youth ministry jazz emanated from the hearts of young adults still passionate to reach teenagers for Christ. High school–based Bible clubs began springing up with the express purpose of becoming an incarnational presence for Christ on the public high school campus.

Without ecclesiastical roots, the clubs came to be known as "parachurch" agencies from the Greek preposition "para" which means "alongside." Club leaders considered themselves to be alongside, and thus complementary to, the church. Many clubs were started as the response of one person to a perceived need.

Others were initiated by local committees or people affiliated with agencies whose primary function was to conduct Saturday night rallies. In these cases, innovations were most frequently copied from club ideas employed in other cities. For the most part church members began these Bible clubs outside the domain of the church. Yet the methodology and curricular approach would influence church youth ministry for years to come.

Evelyn McClusky and the Miracle Book Club

In a movement as diverse as that which spawned these innovations in the second third of the century, and in a nation as sprawling as the United States, it would be folly to suggest that one club gave birth to the other Bible clubs that dotted the land. Yet one high school club did originate earlier than any other in the United States, was widely publicized in the *Sunday School Times*, and can be found in the records of club programs like Young Life, Youth for Christ, Chicago's High School Crusaders, and the Detroit-based Voice of Christian Youth. This foundational association was the Miracle Book Club, founded by Evelyn McClusky in 1933.

While living in Portland, Oregon, Mrs. McClusky, who was in her forties and whose husband had divorced her, was asked by a friend to teach the Bible to a class of high school students meeting in her home. The daughter of a Presbyterian minister, McClusky consented and for the next two years taught the Washington High School Bible class.[6]

Enthusiasm for the class spread to other schools. By June of 1935 six other schools had chapters of what had come to be known as the Miracle Book Club. The *Sunday School Times* ran an article entitled "Winning High School Students for Christ" and two well-crafted stories by Mrs. McClusky about individuals to whom she had witnessed.[7]

The effect was much the same as the article written by Francis E. Clark in *The Congregationalist* over fifty years earlier. Within a year more than a hundred chapters of the Miracle Book Club were in place as the founder continued to promote the club. In 1937 McClusky's book, *Torch and Sword*, explained the purpose for the club's structure. By then chapters had been formed in every state of the Union and various foreign countries. Though the exact count of clubs is suspect, the *Sunday School Times* proclaimed that the number of chapters chartered by the organization, which had moved its headquarters to Oakland, California, was over one thousand by the end of the year.[8]

The growing club movement attracted quality people into leadership positions. Edith Schaeffer along with her husband, Francis, became the Pennsylvania State Directors in 1939. Mrs. Charles J. Woodbridge served as the State Director for North and South Carolina while Jim Rayburn served in a similar position for Texas in 1940.

Located in neutral locations near public high schools and taught primarily by women, the chapters of the Miracle Book Club had four goals. They wanted to invite young people first to salvation in Christ, then to realize that Christ lived in them, which in turn enabled them to be victorious in Christian living, followed by becoming Christian "conversationalists." Mrs. McClusky was convinced that young people could be taught to weave a Christian witness into any conversation without alienating the listener. Today this might be referred to as lifestyle or relational evangelism.[9]

A typical meeting was divided into two parts. Student officers led the first fifteen minutes, which included singing, some club rituals, and "minutes" from the previous meeting. This was followed by forty-five minutes of teaching from a book of the Bible given in a lecture/story-telling format. Such invitations for salvation as were given were low-key and were never stated in a manner in which a student might be embarrassed.[10]

Evelyn McClusky developed a tight set of distinctives to which all teachers were expected to conform. First, the founder was a gifted storyteller and as a result the lecture was usually cloaked in biblical stories or reports of her current experiences related to the theme of the lesson. Questions were to be saved for private discussions after the club meeting. Even calls for public Christian commitments were considered inappropriate. Club meetings were not to be perceived by students as attempts to "convert" people, though in reality the lessons moved in that direction. Teachers were expected to follow her script.

Second, the lessons used the Bible (the Miracle Book) to bring high school students to experience the supernatural working of God. McClusky avoided the extremes of legalistically calling for Bible reading, prayer, personal witness, and regular church attendance, as had characterized the Christian Endeavor, or for social engagement, as encouraged by the United Youth Movement of the 1930s. In so doing, McClusky wanted to avoid the rhetoric of Protestant Fundamentalism or Modernists that raged following the Scopes Monkey Trial over teaching evolution in public schools. She fully expected God to show up to teach and guide young people.

While the Miracle Book Club was accused by some of being too feminine, Evelyn McClusky loved having "wild young people" attend chapter meetings. This was a third distinctive. She was not afraid of confrontation. Her firm conviction was that the Miracle Book, when taught in a creative manner, would overcome all resistance on the part of even the most disruptive of kids.

A fourth distinctive involved the leadership of the club, which mostly consisted of women. Perhaps reflective of the juvenile temperance movement, even area and state co-coordinators were most frequently women.

In 1938, 67 percent of the teachers mentioned in letters to the editor of *The Conqueror* were women. The following year the figure rose to 80 percent before dropping to 73 percent in 1940.[11]

Jim Rayburn, the founder of Young Life, was the most effective of the Miracle Book Club teachers. His chapter in Gainesville, Texas, built around his own communication skills rather than McClusky's materials, grew from three to 123 members in thirteen months and by the spring of 1940 reached 170 students. He later became the Texas State Director of the Miracle Book Club before forming the Young Life Campaign in 1941 and enfolding the Texas chapters into his newly-formed organization.[12]

Al Metsker and Jack Hamilton, who were the founding fathers of the Youth for Christ club program, got their start in Kansas City's first Miracle Book Club chapter. It was during his term as chapter president in 1941 that Metsker first expressed his desire to see a group started near every high school and college in greater Kansas City, a dream which he realized in cooperation with his former Miracle Book Club vice president, Jack Hamilton, after Metzger founded Kansas City Youth for Christ. From these beginnings grew the national YFC club program.

Though Mrs. McClusky's organization was the first parachurch organization in the United States to focus on high school youth, it faded from sight soon after Jim Rayburn took the Texas chapter and founded Young Life. McClusky's publications continued for many years, as did her demand as a speaker among the many who loved and respected her, but youth ministry passed on to others who became leaders especially in Young Life and Youth for Christ. Evelyn McClusky became known as the mother of parachurch youth ministry in the middle of the twentieth century.

Jim Rayburn and Young Life Clubs

If Evelyn McClusky set the stage for the parachurch high school club program, Jim Rayburn forged the high school club methodology that would be perfected in the Young Life movement in the 1940s and 1950s. A nearly identical strategy was adopted by the Youth for Christ International club division in the 1960s and then found its way into church youth ministries during the 1970s. Rayburn's contribution was at the heart of the parachurch contribution to church youth ministry.

Jim Rayburn's split with the Miracle Book Club in 1941 was awkward but necessary. While a student at Dallas Theological Seminary, Rayburn was asked to become the Texas State Director of the Miracle Book Club. Already leading one of the clubs, the young seminarian agreed and soon recruited men from the seminary to lead other clubs. Quickly the Miracle Book Clubs in Texas took on a much more masculine flavor with Rayburn's style replacing Evelyn McClusky's more flowery approach to communication.[13]

Following a fund-raising banquet in Dallas for the Miracle Book Club in the spring of 1941, Rayburn made the tough decision to incorporate the clubs under the name of Young Life Campaign. The decision did not sit well with Mrs. McClusky or the many women who previously had hosted or taught Miracle Book Clubs, but there was nothing they could do about it. Rayburn had both recruited the leaders and obtained the much-needed financial backing of Chicago-based Herbert J. Taylor, chairman of Club Aluminum.

Rayburn's approach to youth ministry was fundamentally different from anything that had preceded it. Unlike Miracle Book Club, it was not designed for Bible study, and distinct from Baptist Young People's Union, Epworth League, and Walther League, it claimed no denominational ties. Nor was it based in the local church like the Christian Endeavor Society had been, and it was focused exclusively on high school students unlike YMCA efforts. Rayburn's approach to youth ministry was essentially a missionary effort by Christian adults to win uncommitted high school students to a personal relationship with God through Jesus Christ. Young Life was Rayburn's improvisation, a new sound of youth ministry jazz.

There are five distinct contributions that Jim Rayburn and the Young Life movement made to youth ministry. The first and perhaps most significant was that clubs were leader centered. From the first training manual produced in 1941, it was evident that the adult leader would be in charge of the weekly club meeting and would be the primary speaker:

> The Leader is it! A Young Life Club does not begin and grow by [having] a group of young people sending for materials and methods. It gets results as the LEADER meets his qualifications and is HIMSELF effective in conducting the meeting and teaching young people to do so.[14]

Even the singing was led by adults in most meetings. Students participated in the club "minutes," which were usually skits or humorous announcements.

The philosophy of adult-led meetings was an extension of McClusky's approach and stood in stark contrast with the approach of church youth ministries, which at the time were moving to student-led youth fellowships. Jack Hamilton's strategy for Youth for Christ clubs and the InterVarsity-influenced Inter School Christian Fellowship in Canada depended on student initiatives and leadership. Both of these club systems viewed the adult leader as a trainer and coach who taught students how to lead meetings and do the work of evangelism on the high school campus.

A second distinctive of Young Life was that it was evangelism focused. Rayburn was influenced by his father, who was a Presbyterian evangelist, and later by Rev. Clyde Kennedy of the First Presbyterian Church in Gainesville. When Kennedy asked Rayburn, then a student at Dallas Theological Seminary, to minister to students in Gainesville, his concern was outreach oriented. "Jim," the minister explained, "I'm not particularly worried about the kids who are in [church]. They're safe. As far as they're concerned I don't need your services. To you I entrust the crowd of teen-agers who stay away from church. The center of your widespread parish will be the local high school."[15]

Perhaps the best known contribution of Rayburn's Young Life Campaign was its emphasis on "winning the right to be heard" by secular high school students.[16] By this slogan Young Lifers meant that they needed to gain the friendship and respect of students before expecting them to listen to the claims of Christ. The Christian gospel was relationally authenticated, and on the young person's own turf—football games and practices, high schoolers' hangouts such as soda fountains, school events and, when permitted by school authorities, the high school cafeteria.[17]

It was not enough, however, for the staff person or volunteer leader to merely establish contact with students and build relationships. The whole process, which came to be known as "incarnational theology," led to a point at which the Christian gospel was presented. The club meeting was the initial place to call for commitments to Christ, but with the purchase of resort camps starting in 1945, a second and even more *effective delivery system* was discovered. Clubs became the vehicle to get high schoolers out of their own context and to a fabulous resort where they would have the best week of their lives and at the same time be presented with the Christian gospel. Students came from across the nation for a week at a time and found the gospel not only spoken but lived out twenty-four hours a day.

Jim Rayburn's *conversational approach* to public speaking was a fifth distinctive of Young Life's ministry. He was different from the preachers of his day. He did not shout or pound the pulpit. He just talked. Fellow staff member George Sheffer described Rayburn's style:

He really wowed kids. He had such a shy, quiet approach. He was marvelous building up to a punch line. Like, "High school isn't so bad, is it? It's just the principal of the thing." Kids would cheer and whoop and howl. . . . He was corny as could be [for] the first half. Then he'd talk about the fact that our nation was based on the Christian faith and there was a heritage in our country that a lot of kids didn't know anything about. "You're doing yourself a disservice," he'd say, "if you don't at least find out what you're missing.[18]

This style was perpetuated by leaders who followed Rayburn.

Young Life clubs spread from Texas to the Pacific Northwest, the Chicago area, and Memphis, Tennessee. From there the movement branched out into other areas of the nation with strongholds in affluent communities near major cities. Statistics were not well kept under Rayburn's leadership. It is clear that by the time Bill Starr followed Rayburn as executive director of the movement in 1964, there were over four hundred clubs in existence. This number grew to the one thousand mark by 1973, and continued to grow until efforts were made to expand the clubs by increasing the capacity of the movement's summer camps in the nineties.

The impact of Young Life was rather astounding considering the fact that the number of clubs was so small and the number of communities in which the clubs were located was even smaller. Rayburn's organization held no rallies, had no radio broadcasts, had no strategic plan, and the only magazine was designed for internal use. The ministry was distinctly missional and as such gained the hearing of influential people like Herbert J. Taylor, Christian philanthropist and chairman of the Board of Club Aluminum, and attracted the attention of theological educators at places like Wheaton College and Fuller Theological Seminary who in turn spread the word.

Jack Hamilton and Youth for Christ Clubs

Judy Raby was a homeless girl who lived with a high school friend. Loaded with talent and creative energy, she would be a senior in a Kansas City High School during the 1946–47 school year. Already active in the highly popular Saturday night Youth for Christ rallies (see chapter 13), she decided to attend the Second Annual Youth for Christ Convention with rally director Al Metsker. At the Medicine Lake conference near Minneapolis, Metsker shared an idea with Judy, "Maybe we could get some Bible clubs going and challenge kids to bring their unsaved friends to the rally. If you're interested in this sort of thing, let me know when we get back."

Shortly after school started, Judy showed up at Metsker's office wondering when the clubs would get started. For the next several weeks the idea was presented at the rallies. Twelve high schoolers from ten high schools responded and the club program was under way. One problem existed, however. Metsker was far too busy with his other responsibilities to head up a club program.[19]

The leadership problem was solved when Jack Hamilton, Metsker's vice president from Miracle Book Club days, walked into the Youth for Christ office and volunteered for full-time Christian ministry. The director "hired" his friend on the spot with the stipulation that Hamilton would raise his own salary. Thus began the Youth for Christ club program, known first in Kansas City as Youth on the Beam, and according to Hamilton's corny humor, "They had a 'YOB' to do."

The Kansas City club experimentation provides an example of a youth ministry jazz ensemble. Metsker, the lead player, improvised a new sound. Raby, a teenager, picked up on the new progression and engaged peers in the jam session. Hamilton, as an adult volunteer, brought his talent to the session and quickly became the major promoter of YFC club ministry jazz. This Kansas City "sound" then spread, first informally and later intentionally within the YFC movement.

Unlike Young Life clubs, Youth on the Beam's stated purposes were not evangelistic. Christian fellowship among the students, spiritual growth through Bible study, higher Christian living as a means of fighting juvenile delinquency, and interclub activities were their purposes. Yet all of this was part of a larger delivery system intended to encourage Christian students to bring their non-Christian friends to the Saturday night rallies.

By the spring of 1947, twelve thriving clubs had been established. The number swelled to twenty by the end of the following school year. Kids planned and led the programs. Everything from special music and skits to emceeing and selecting speakers was left for them to do. The large number of traveling evangelists and performing artists on the circuit just after World War II made it easy for the student leaders to obtain speakers. Some would speak in the Saturday night rally and then address club meetings during the week. Pastors, businessmen, and missionaries were also available for club meetings.

In time the club program began to influence YFC rallies. Bible quizzing, which originally was designed to help new believers grow in their Christian faith, became a fixture in the rallies and made the club-rally delivery system even more effective. Students from various high schools came to the rallies to cheer for their school's quiz teams and in the process made or renewed spiritual commitments.

By 1950 it was obvious that Youth for Christ International needed to develop a nationwide club program. Torrey Johnson, the first president of YFCI, had seen the success of Miracle Book Club and Hi-C (High School Crusaders) from Chicago's Carl Schurz High School because both groups had met in the building of the church that he pastored. But it was the organization's second president, Bob Cook, who brought Jack Hamilton from Kansas City and gave him the mandate to start a national club program.

Hamilton went first to Detroit to get a program rolling, then to Portland, Oregon, and later to San Diego, all the while spreading the word through *Youth for Christ Magazine*. By the summer of 1951 the high-energy Hamilton reported that seven hundred clubs had been established. By year's end a thousand were reported and that number stretched to 1,956 by the time of the annual convention in 1955. Though some insiders question the accuracy of the annual reports, the official record shows that the club program reached a peak of 3,073 clubs in 1962 before declining along with the Saturday night rallies.

Campus Life Strategy of Youth for Christ

During the middle of the decade of the sixties, Youth for Christ International made a bold shift in philosophy. Clubs were severed from the rallies and redesigned to stand entirely alone. Rallies were discontinued in most places. Bible quizzing and national music competition, which were both related to the rally concept, were phased out. New staff members were recruited to minister on two or three campuses instead of coaching student leaders in twenty-five or thirty schools. The primary leadership of the clubs switched from student leaders to trained Youth for Christ specialists.

Three factors made the change possible and even necessary. "Baby boomers" had come of age as high schoolers. They were living in the Benjamin Spock–post Sputnik era in which the emphasis in education was on dialogue and understanding rather than the older educational idea of lecturing and retention. A second generation of Youth for Christ leaders who were not married to the rally idea took a hard look at the scope and effectiveness of the ministry and concluded that changes had to be made. At about the same time, the organization's structure changed, making the decision-making process much more functional.

At issue in Youth for Christ was an understanding of the religious makeup of the American teenage population. It was "discovered" that only about 5 percent of American adolescents claimed to have had a Christian conversion experience, while another 35 percent claimed to have some sort of religious affiliation. This left 60 percent of the high school population "unchurched," as YFC staff described them, meaning that they claimed no regular contact with a church or synagogue.

The new generation of leaders took these findings and asked a hard question: "Which of these groups are we reaching?" The answer was most disconcerting. Most of the teens identified with YFC clubs were in the first category—students who already claimed to have had a conversion experience. The next largest group were those associated with a church or synagogue, followed by a very low number of students who claimed no active religious affiliation.

A readership survey of those who subscribed to *Youth for Christ Magazine* in 1960 supported this finding. Of those responding to the nonscientific poll, 96 percent said that their church had a youth group of some kind while 85 percent indicated they attended that group regularly. Only 6 percent said they never attended a church youth group at all. Later research done in cooperation with the Human Learning Research Institute at Michigan State University further validated these findings.[20]

If these findings were true, then something was very wrong with the YFC ministry philosophy. The very people whom the organization was claiming to reach were remaining outside of the program's influence. This realization helped to usher in the Campus Life philosophy of ministry.

Salt Lake City was an unlikely place for the meeting in 1962 at which six club leaders discussed a club philosophy that could reach beyond students already committed to Jesus Christ to the unchurched, non-Christian student. Bill Eakin, Willie Foote, Jack Hamilton, Bob Kraning, Ken Overstreet, and Bruce Washburn spent two days together and conceptualized a new shape for campus ministry.[21]

This brainstorming session illustrated youth ministry jazz in action. Only Hamilton worked out of the Wheaton, Illinois, national office. The others brought local club improvisations to the jam session. A new YFC club sound soon filled the air. Still realizing that the teenagers themselves were the key to high school evangelism, the leaders drafted a teen-to-teen philosophy whereby the Christian teenager could properly and successfully communicate in action and words his or her personal faith in Jesus Christ to her friends, her campus, and her world.

Over the next several years innovative approaches to club ministry were field tested. A "2-plus-2" format emerged. Two meetings each month would be focused on outreach while the other two meetings would concentrate more on biblical content. In San Diego under the leadership of Ken Overstreet, Jim Green and Mike Yaconelli pioneered ways to attract and hold non-Christian youth at club meetings. This included limiting a club leader to a few campuses in order to allow him (the vast majority were male) to meet and build relationships with campus leaders in a manner similar to that employed by Young Life leaders. The outreach meeting came to be called Campus Life Impact.

In Fresno, California, and Arlington Heights, Illinois, Larry Ballenger and Clayton Baumann explored methods for aiding students who wanted greater spiritual formation. This discipleship aspect came to be called Insight. Impact and Insight together came to be known as Campus Life. At about the same time, the organization's magazine changed its name from *Youth for Christ Magazine* to *Campus Life*.

Insight meetings were the first to be initiated. Though designed to attract the YFC club crowd, the adult leader was now in charge. He guided the meeting to address three questions: "Who am I in relationship to God?" "Why should I communicate my faith to others?" and "How can I best carry out my responsibility for Christian witness?" The format for each session as described in the Insight/Impact Manual, first published in 1968, included four components: instruction (biblical and psychological insights from the leader related to needs of Christian students), inspiration (prayer, challenges from leaders or students), involvement (discussions and testimonies), and initiative (gentle but firm encouragement to put his or her faith to work on the high school campus).

The second part of the Campus Life strategy was the Impact meeting. It was designed to be

> an informal evening meeting of one hour centered around a YFC Campus Life Director. It contains a significant amount of involvement by students who participate in both informal preliminaries of the meeting (ice breakers and games) and in the discussion/talk-to before the wrap-up.
>
> The make-up of the audience should comprise at least a one-to-one ratio of non-Christian to Christian, and the meeting should be at a comfortable place for the non-Christian to be.[22]

The reception to the Campus Life strategy in those places that adopted the ideas was outstanding. Special relational skills were needed to implement Insight/Impact. Some of the staff had these naturally. Others were trained in interpersonal and small group dynamics. But some leaders simply could not master the new style of doing youth ministry. Nationally the average attendance at Campus Life clubs remained about the same as the older YFC clubs. For the next two decades the number of Campus Life clubs hovered at about the one thousand mark, though both the number of clubs and average attendance dipped significantly as the eighties drew to a close.

The rapid movement from creating youth ministry jazz in Salt Lake City to establishing the new sound across the nation was both successful and counterproductive. In all likelihood it was the only way the new strategy could have been put in place. The publication of new club materials took the Utah jazz idea, field-tested and expanded it through local improvisations by the most creative "musicians" in the movement, and provided a type of sheet music to even the least creative club leaders. Quickly the new sound reached local high schools.

The process employed to publicize the Utah jazz sound, while efficient in replacing the older club philosophy, standardized the Campus Life sound. In the process it prevented innovation. Campus Life became the face of Youth for Christ. The creation of fresh youth ministry jazz outside the sounds of Campus Life clubs was not encouraged. In the long run, the jazz sound flourished, but the creative process that produced it languished. Some would even say it died.

Fellowship of Christian Athletes

The one organization ministering to high school students that sustained its growth pattern into the last decade of the twentieth century was Fellowship of Christian Athletes. Established in 1954 by Don McClanen with the blessing and financial support of Branch Rickey, then the general manager of the Pittsburgh Pirates, and a group of Pittsburgh businessmen, the organization immediately began to fashion a ministry to and among professional athletes and coaches. National conferences starting during the summer of 1956 quickly gave the organization visibility and credibility within the sports fraternity.[23]

Actually the idea of a ministry focused on high school students was not formalized until 1966 when the name "huddle" was given to the growing numbers of groups springing up among young men in the high schools of the nation. From the beginning huddle groups were a grassroots movement. Led by coaches, other faculty members, or parents interested in sports, huddle groups included singing, announcements, and a talk or Bible study led by the adult sponsor or a guest from the world of sports.

Huddle groups were not an end in themselves. FCA provided very little training for huddle group leaders but supplemented their impact on students through area rallies and weekend and week-long summer conferences. Thus the huddle groups became a delivery system for getting student athletes, many of whom knew very little about Jesus Christ, to attend conferences where they met well-known athletes and coaches as well as received instruction in the truths of the Christian faith.

As with most other parachurch ministries, numerical records in the early days of the movement were more like guesses than accurate data. Reports show a thousand huddle groups in 1969, a figure that, if accurate, placed the FCA high school program numerically on par with Young Life and Campus Life after just three years in existence. The figure is a bit misleading, however, because some of these huddle groups were on college campuses. Yet the sudden growth was impressive. By 1972 there were fifteen hundred huddles and in 1977, two thousand.

The March 1990 report from Richard F. Abel, president of FCA, called 1989 a "miracle year." According to Abel, 18 percent of the high schools in the nation had FCA huddle groups during the past year. The August

1990 report on high school huddle groups showed 3,357 chartered units on the campuses of the nation. Total high school membership in FCA was just over 19,500 for the same period of time, an increase of 53 percent over the previous year.

Growth in the 1990s sustained the pattern. Despite internal problems connected with the National Service Center in Kansas City during the midnineties, growth at the huddle level continued. In the 1994 annual report, President Dal Shealy reported 3,702 high school huddle groups even though high school membership fell to 16,425, primarily because of a more precise means of counting members. Similarly junior high/middle school huddle groups increased from 581 in 1990 to 864 in 1994, with the number of members growing from 2,460 to 3,071.

The question could be asked as to why the high school ministry of Fellowship of Christian Athletes appears to have grown so rapidly while all of the other high school–based ministries were going through a period of malaise. Four factors should be considered. First, FCA had just completed its first twenty-five years of ministry to high school students and historically that period is the time of most rapid growth in all parachurch ministries. Second, the whole concept of a huddle group has a built-in point of contact for adults with students. Whereas most other ministries have to find a way to enter the student's world and build relationships, the huddle-group leader already had that contact through his or her role as coach, faculty member, or parent with a common love for athletic competition.

A third reason for the growth of FCA's high school ministry was the niche to which the ministry was targeted. Unlike church and other parachurch youth ministries who felt it incumbent upon them to reach every student in their church or high school, FCA made no such claims. Student athletes and peers interested in sports were the organization's audience. The fascination these young people had for successful athletes, and the willingness of Christian men and women in highly visible positions in the sports world to give of themselves at camps, conferences, and even at the huddle-group level, enabled FCA to stay on task with its target audience.

The last reason may be the cement that holds together the other explanations for FCA's growth. It is finances. Since huddle groups were staffed by volunteers, most of the fund-raising activities went into the very types of projects to which donors like to give—highly visible activities and facilities. Though finances weighed heavily on the shoulders of the professional staff, volunteer leaders' pay was simply the joy of serving in the lives of the high school students to whom they ministered.

Two problems with FCA should be noted, however. The organization was very weak in providing training for huddle-group leaders, which led to an unevenness in how effectively Christian truth was taught. Though camps and conferences help correct some of this randomness, much more needed to be done to raise the methodological and theological effectiveness of the lay leaders. FCA, however, was not a learning culture; it was a *doing* culture. Even though most of coaching has to do with breaking skills down into teachable components and then bringing about changes in behavior, it appears that FCA has struggled to learn what coaching means when training huddle leaders.

A second problem grew out of the training deficiencies of FCA. The organization may have imported the American mystique into its ministry, claiming that "winning isn't the most important thing, it is the only thing." A constant emphasis on sharing the victory, and on "no pain, no *gain*," tended to teach impressionable high school students a value system that was contrary to the concepts of yielding, sacrifice, and humility that are major themes in biblical teachings.

Recognizing these leadership weaknesses in FCA, Kevin Harlan initiated a Leadership Institute in an attempt to provide training for key leaders in the group. Invitations were sent out to people with two or more years of supervisory experience in FCA, and twenty-one people were accepted. The group met six times over two years at the national training center in Indiana, with each training session lasting four days. Built around a selection of books, the training explored the implications of the books to FCA leadership. The Leadership Institute strategy envisioned these leaders taking the training process back to their regions and reproducing it among their leaders.

Other Club Programs

To keep the parachurch club movement in proper perspective, it's important not to leave the impression that the four organizations mentioned in this chapter were the only shows in town. In reality there were probably hundreds of localized club programs, but only a few spread widely enough to merit mention.[24]

High School Bornagainers (Hi-BA), founded by Brandt Reed in metropolitan New York in 1938, was designed to train Christian students in the know-how of personal evangelism on the high school campus. Like Young Life, all meetings were led by adult staff members, but a staff person in Hi-BA may have led as many as ten meetings each week and as a result did not have much time to spend on the campus "earning the right to be heard." For Hi-BA this was no problem because it was the trained student who was to be the evangelist anyway.

Two other distinctives set Reed's organization apart from the others. Staff people were placed in an area only at the invitation of the local churches. They were seen as an extension of the churches' training ministry. This was further enhanced by including a world missions emphasis in every meeting. In addition, a high school missionary conference was held as one of the two or three major events planned for clubs throughout an area.

The ministry remained a regional high school agency operating primarily in the New York/New Jersey metropolitan area but with a missionary extension in Japan. Kenn Clark, who led the ministry in Japan for years, took over the leadership of the organization in 1982 after the death of Brandt Reed.

High School Crusader clubs (Hi-C), sponsored by Christian Teacher's Fellowship, were an outgrowth of the Miracle Book Clubs in Chicago. When, in 1943, the teacher's group felt they were no longer being serviced by Mrs. McClusky's organization, the new organization was formed utilizing primarily Moody Bible Institute and Wheaton College students to lead the clubs. Though Hi-C was also a regional organization, students returning home after college planted clubs as far away as Hampton Roads, Virginia, and Portland, Oregon.

When the group moved away from the Miracle Book Club affiliation, board member C. Stacey Woods suggested the name *High School Crusaders* after an organization he had seen in Australia. With the new name came new concepts of ministry. Instead of merely focusing on Bible studies, Hi-C clubs, under the leadership of Gunner Hoglund and later Daniel Ankerberg, began to sponsor activities that would build bridges to other teenagers. Basketball leagues that were formed in various parts of the city, Saturday morning radio broadcasts aimed at Christian teenagers, and area-wide social activities such as banquets added to the list of outreach activities. The most spectacular event, however, was the formal concert given each year by the 125-voice Hi-C Chorale in Chicago's Civic Opera House. At its high point Hi-C had seventy-eight clubs in the Chicago area.

Hi-C remained a vital part of youth ministry in the Chicago area until 1959 when Bill Gothard Jr. became the director. A product of the club program, Gothard felt that significant changes needed to be made both in club strategy and in the organization's approach to fund-raising. The idealistic young man refused to depend on promotional letters to generate financial support, choosing instead to "trust the Lord to provide." Funding sources began drying up and the whole program started to deteriorate rapidly.

With Hi-C in decline, Chicagoland Youth for Christ began establishing its own clubs in high schools. Competition developed. At one point, Schurz High School had both a Hi-C and YFC club with cousins Arnold Mayer and Alan Aiger serving as presidents of the respective organizations. The final demise of Hi-C did not come until the late sixties when Chicagoland YFC absorbed the once-dynamic club program.

Dunamis Clubs were the creation of Dawson Trotman for high school students in the Los Angeles area beginning in 1939. Tired of what he described as the "take-it-easy" philosophy of ministry, the founder of the Navigators decided to set up a new system that would lay out stiff requirements and make membership a privilege. What students did between meetings was the key to the weekly gathering. When the boys gathered (later there was a similar group for girls called Martures), there was spirited singing and then an "oral check-out" on Bible portions that they were to memorize during the week. This was followed by reports on TNT (Tackle 'n Trust), assignments in which fellows told their peers about their Christian faith. The meeting was concluded by a Bible study or challenge from the leader.

By 1941, thirty-five clubs were sprinkled across Southern California. Lorne Sanny, a student at Biola College, was given responsibility for the clubs, which boasted as leading members Ralph Winter, who later directed the United States Center for World Mission, and Dan Fuller, best known as Professor of Systematic Theology at Fuller Theological Seminary. The organization did not last long under Sanny's leadership primarily because the young man's skills were soon needed in the broader leadership of the Navigators.

Campus Crusade for Christ started a high school extension of its rapidly growing college and university ministry in 1966. Bill Bright, the founder of Campus Crusade, observed college students who had made commitments to Christ on campus returning home and starting high school versions of the college ministry. While consulting with his seminary friend, Carl Wilson, Bright conferred with Bill Starr of Young Life and Sam Wolgemuth of Youth for Christ International to see if there was room for another high school ministry in the United States. Starr's response cut to the heart of the matter. "We are reaching perhaps one percent of the high school students of America. It would be naive of us to say there is no room for Campus Crusade for Christ to reach high school young people. We just ask that you cooperate with us, that you work with us, that you move carefully into what you are doing so as not to make unfortunate mistakes."[25]

Student Venture, as the ministry came to be known in 1982, mirrored the college strategy. It included personal evangelism by staff members, small-group discipleship groups, periodic evangelistic blitzes by staff evangelists including Pat Hurley, Bill Reif, and Dawson McAllister. Major training conferences or ministry projects during vacation periods were likewise part of the ministry.

As the decade of the eighties drew to a close, Student Venture had two hundred fifty full-time staff serving in eighteen metropolitan areas nationwide, with the largest staff teams in Minneapolis and Houston. Though staff members stressed evangelism, their emphasis on discipleship was underscored by the fact that sixty-five hundred students were engaged in discipleship groups during the 1988–89 school year. The ratio of students to staff, twenty-six to one, placed the movement squarely within the range of average size youth ministries in the nation.

While parachurch ministries to high school students were the most influential club programs of the third cycle of youth ministry, churches also staffed and sponsored club activities with the help of a different type of parachurch agency. Most of these groups were an extension of children's club programs. Christian Service Brigade, established by Joseph Coughlin in 1937, was an evangelical alternative to the Boy Scouts. Brigade's sister organization, Pioneer Girls (now Pioneer Clubs) came into being under the leadership of Betty Whitaker two years later. Awana Youth Association, incorporated in 1950 with roots in the urban setting of Chicago, was the product of Lance Latham and Art Rorheim. In each case the children's portion of the program was much more successful at attracting and holding members than was the high school version.

Jack Wyrtzen established church-based Word of Life clubs for high school students in the church. The program has been most successful in churches where lay leadership needs a curriculum to follow and high schoolers want a youth group that reaches beyond the church's youth club. In the first decade of the twenty-first century there were over one hundred missionaries and associates servicing over twelve hundred Word of Life clubs across North America. The total weekly attendance of about thirty-three thousand young people placed the clubs just under twenty-eight in average attendance and on par with the optimum size of Protestant youth ministries, at thirty students per week.

There were other club programs as well. The Oakland, California–based Key to Life Clubs in 1940 had an emphasis on reaching the student who did not seem to fit anywhere else. King's Teens, founded by Mike Martin in 1944, spread throughout the Pacific Northwest and up into Alaska in the decade following World War II. But most of the smaller regional clubs were eventually absorbed by the national parachurch club programs.

Conclusion

As the decade of the 1990s began, Taft High School, the model for *Grease*'s Rydell High, was without a Christian parachurch ministry. No Campus

Life club, no Young Life club, no Fellowship of Christian Athletes huddle group. Nothing. Unlike 1959, when a Christian presence was at least felt by some students, today there is little possibility that the Jim Jacobs of the student body will be exposed to the Christian gospel.

Why the demise of incarnational witness at Taft High School and the other secondary schools of the nation? One answer is that, like the end of the period influenced by Christian Endeavor, society had changed. While high schools remained the last tribal experience of teenagers, they no longer had the same simple social structure of the fifties and before. Entitlement programs robbed jocks of their elite status. There was no longer a defined social structure and, as a result, ministry approaches had to change.

12

Pleasantville

The Evangelical Church Discovers Teenagers (1933–89)

Pleasantville, in the 1998 movie, is, well, pleasant. Boringly pleasant. Nauseatingly pleasant. Black and white (with tones of gray) pleasant. In the fairy-tale town of black-and-white television created by Gary Ross, there was no need for toilets; married couples slept in separate beds and had no knowledge of sex; every basketball shot swished; the study of high school geography terminated at the end of Elm Street; and dinner was always on the table when father came home. Life was ideal—no rain, no hatred or tears, no flat tires, not even a passionate kiss. Uncertainty was not an option. Emotion was suppressed. Everything was predictable.

Predictable, that is, until Mary Sue and Bud found themselves transported from their normal teenage angst in the 1990s to the stupefying pleasantness of Pleasantville. Bud qualified as a card-carrying geek whose week's highlight was watching the Pleasantville marathon, a twenty-four-hour rerun of the fifties television show. Mary Sue, by contrast, came across as a boy crazy, C minus, Barbie-doll type who, by her own confession, never read a book or entertained a serious thought.

Had Bud entered Pleasantville by himself, very little would have changed. He knew all the plots of all the shows. Embracing the characters as friends, he would have sheltered them from the intrusion of the enlightened 1990s. Unfortunately, for Bud and for Pleasantville, no such insulation could be maintained because of Mary Sue. When she brought her attitude with her, the cultures clashed. The movie cleverly portrayed a conflict of worldviews by using black-and-white pictures to represent predictability and control and using color to express uncertainty and emotion. Gradually the whole town was colorized. Even the mayor, a symbol of stability, succumbed to feelings of anger and was drawn into the world of color.

Yet in a surprising twist, Pleasantville transformed Mary Sue even as she contributed to the transformation of the town. In her nineties world of hormones and emotion, Mary Sue lived only for the moment. She was caught up in the attention of guys, and critical thinking hovered near the low end of her value scale. While in Pleasantville, reading became for Mary Sue a form of rebellion against pleasantness, but as she read, she discovered a world of ideas that liberated her from her world that had been guided exclusively by the passions of the moment.

"Nothing's Gonna Change My World"

Youth ministry in the 1930s became a search for Pleasantville. "Nothing's Gonna Change My World," the Randy Newman song sung as the credits rolled at the end of the movie, captured the determination of evangelical churches in North America. Everything else appeared to be uncertain. World War I dealt a blow to the optimism of the progressive era. The Great Depression shook confidence in the economic system of America. Media coverage of the Scopes trial for teaching evolution in a Dayton, Tennessee, public school challenged the worldview of Christians who viewed the Bible as the cornerstone of their faith and lives.

The cultural changes in America between the time of the establishment of the Society of Christian Endeavor in 1881 and the 1925 Scopes trial extended to nearly every aspect of a young person's life. Christians who placed biblical Truth (capital "T") at the center of their worldview resisted the cultural trend toward a modern way of understanding science and religion. Parents, feeling the cultural sands shifting right under their feet, looked in alarm at the impact the changes were having on their children. Though a similar concern had led Theodore Cuyler and his peers to move from the danger of New York to the safety and homogeneity of suburban life in Brooklyn, now the sounds of the city were beginning to invade their suburban and rural safe havens.

Entertainment for young people created the most visible clash of worldviews between Christian adolescents and their parents. Paula Fass analyzed the clash more broadly, pitting the "damned" against the "beautiful," traditionalists against progressives. The youth problem of the 1920s, while in evidence primarily among young adults who had left home to attend college or seek employment, alarmed parents with traditional values who distrusted "changes in family nurture, education, sex roles, leisure habits, as well as social values and behavioral norms."[1]

The new medium of radio brought the sounds of the city to every community in America. KDKA in Pittsburgh received a commercial license in 1920, and by 1930, every state in the nation had commercial stations. The creation of the NBC network in 1926, followed by CBS, ABC, and Mutual networks raised the caliber and popularity of the new medium of news and popular culture. The record industry broadened beyond the sounds of Enrico Caruso and John Phillips Susa to jazz and big band performances. Bypassing theaters, schools, and churches, popular culture came straight into the homes and radio became a focal point of family activity.

Churches and Christian leaders quickly took advantage of the new medium. Church services were first broadcast on New York's WJZ in January of 1922. Later that same year, "The great commoner, William Jennings Bryan, broadcast a sermon from Point Breeze Presbyterian Church in Pittsburgh over KDKA."[2] By 1932, Moody Bible Institute had its own station, WMBI, dedicated to broadcasting Christian content, primarily sermons and music. Despite this growing access to the airwaves, traditional Christians became increasingly uncomfortable with the manner in which radio brought popular culture into the home.[3]

At about the same time, comic books (or funny books as they were known in the early days) brought inexpensive entertainment into the homes of American people. Initially found in pulp magazines, *The Funnies*, published by Dell Publishing, appeared on newsstands in tabloid-sized books. Early stories featured ordinary heroes like Popeye, Dick Tracy, and the Shadow fighting crime. Others were essentially humorous such as Mutt and Jeff and Krazy Kat. Most reinforced American values of right and wrong.

By the 1930s, the comic book industry reached its Golden Era with three essential types—science fiction (Flash Gordon), detective stories (Dick Tracy, Secret Agent X-9), and jungle adventures (Tarzan, Jim of the Jungle). Soon to follow were superheroes (Superman, Batman, Wonderman). While the essential storylines harmonized with middle-class values, the visualization of force and violence alarmed some parents and Christian leaders. This visualized adventure in the form of violence with a touch of sex appeal was available to children and youth on newsstands and at the corner drugstore in every community.

The rapid growth of comic book popularity concerned many Americans. Sterling North, literary editor for the Chicago Daily News, writing in 1940, expressed the concern of many readers:

> Badly drawn, badly written, and badly printed—a strain on the young eyes and young nervous systems—the effects of these pulp paper nightmares is that of a violent stimulant. Their crude blacks and reds spoil the child's natural sense of color; their hypodermic injection of sex and murder make the child impatient with better, though quieter, stories. Unless we want a coming generation even more ferocious than the present one, parents and teachers throughout America must band together to break the comic magazine.[4]

Popular magazines *Time* and *Look* joined in the criticism of comics. With support based on research by psychiatrist Frederic Wertham, who had provided expert testimony that helped end school desegregation, the United States Senate Subcommittee to Investigate Juvenile Delinquency investigated links between the more violent forms of comic books and the rising tide of adolescent crime. Chaired by future vice-presidential candidate Estes Kefauver, the hearings forced comic book publishers into a form of self regulation.[5] People connected with conservative Protestant churches shared the media's concern over the possibly negative influence comic books were having on adolescents.

The impact of motion pictures on young people similarly concerned many Americans. In 1907 Chicago became one of the first cities to censor movies, setting strict controls over what could be shown in theaters. When the racially-charged D. W. Griffin film *Birth of a Nation* was released, Chicago banned its showing.[6] In 1910 *Good Housekeeping* charged that the movie theater was fast becoming "a primary school for criminals."[7]

In 1930, the Motion Picture Producers and Distributors of America established a Production Code to fend off criticism and city-by-city censorship. Administrated by Will Hays, a prominent Republican and Presbyterian, the code was hard to manage until pressure from the National Legion of Decency, created in 1934 by the American Catholic archbishops, brought the industry in line with its thirteen points. The code remained in effect until 1968 when it was replaced by an industry-imposed film classification system.

Protestants benefited by the initiatives of the Catholic Church, but continued to express concern about the content of movies. On a more local level, Protestants responded similarly. Stephen W. Paine, the president of Houghton College in New York state, exemplified one of the more conservative voices when he wrote a series of articles for the *Wesleyan Methodist* that was later published in a pamphlet entitled "Why I Do

Not Attend Movies."[8] The reasons given had to do with concern that movies were not helpful for living holy lives. Concerns focused on assertions that movies fostered crime, served as propaganda for the liquor industry, and debauched Christian ideals of sex.

Changing Direction of National Youth Societies

In addition to social concerns shared by much of the economic middle class, church leaders, committed to the fundamentals of the Christian faith, found the direction of denominational youth ministries as well as the emphasis of the Christian Endeavor at their national and international conferences to be a problem. The themes of the keynote addresses for the International Society of Christian Endeavor represented a shift from the original emphasis on endeavoring to know God to a focus on Christian citizenship and loyalty to Christian Endeavor. By 1894 at the Cleveland convention the slogan suggested the change—"Strike for our principles, for good citizenship, for missions." Two years later in Washington, DC, the message was stronger. "Fidelity and Fellowship, one and inseparable; Loyalty and brotherhood, one and inseparable; Obedience and independence, one and inseparable; Christian citizenship and Christian mission, one and inseparable." The 1903 theme in Denver suggested the influence of the progressive movement when the slogan was "Advanced Steps in Increase and Efficiency."[9]

By the last years of Francis Clark's leadership of Christian Endeavor, presidential addresses focused on sustaining the movement. "New Victories from Old Ideals" (1919), "Christian Endeavor Foursquare" (1921), and "A Campaign of Fidelity to Principles" (1925) suggest the typical themes of a movement more concerned with retaining its place in the larger church than in bringing about evangelization and personal spirituality. While "ideals" and "principles" carried a biblical as well as an organizational meaning, the latter had become the predominant theme.

While many evangelicals at the beginning of the twenty-first century would affirm the holistic message of Dr. Clark, convention themes represented at least a turn from the original emphasis on prayer and encountering God. The new emphasis may have indicated a drift toward a social gospel that focused on institutional change rather than the personal holiness emphasized by local pastors from Cotton Mather through Jonathan Edwards to Theodore Cuyler.

While the social gospel appeared to be the culprit to many pastors and theologians, challenges to the piety of young people from evangelical Protestant homes concerned parents even more. Without a doubt modern thinking and modern lifestyle were joined at the hip, but parents were far more concerned about what would happen below the waist than above the shoulders. They wanted to raise their children in Pleasantville.

Mainline denominational youth ministries followed a similar pattern to Christian Endeavor. The Lutheran's Walther League illustrates the change. Summarizing the changes in the league in the middle of the twentieth century, Jon Pahl concludes,

> Over the decades, then, the leaders of the Walther League had shifted the content and form of the Christian knowledge they conveyed to Lutheran youth. In the thirties, the league communicated to youth teachings based on traditional Lutheran piety and dogma, and moral lessons encouraged personal purity. By the sixties, both content and form had diffused, focused less on personal piety and purity and more on ecumenism, social justice, and international understanding.[10]

Addressing the Youth Problem of the Thirties

When Will H. Houghton became president of Chicago's Moody Bible Institute in November 1934, he left the pastorate of Manhattan's Calvary Baptist Church with its thriving youth ministry under the leadership of Lloyd T. Bryant. Seeing a need to address the needs of young people, in September 1935 Houghton initiated "Youth's Page" in the widely read *Moody Bible Institute Monthly* magazine (shortly later changed to "Youth Page"). This contribution to youth ministry continued until June 1942 when World War II concerns changed the column to address "Soldiers, Sailors and Marines."

A study of the "Youth Page" over the seven years of its existence captures the concerns for young people expressed by conservative Christians. For the first year the column was attributed to President Houghton and thereafter to Elizabeth Andrews Houghton, the president's wife. In his first column Houghton provided four ways in which the column could be used:

1. It may be given over to Bible study for youth.
2. It can be devoted to plans for the successful operation of young people's work.
3. It can provide information concerning what Christian young people are actually doing.
4. It may discuss the important problems which you [i.e., young people] are facing.[11]

A survey by the author of the 161 articles published in the seven-year span of "Youth Page" suggests that evangelical readers were primarily interested in dealing with the problems faced by young people of the day. While one quarter of the articles dealt with evangelism, virtually all the rest focused on social issues of concern to conservative Christians.

This concern for successful operation of young people's work by Moody Bible Institute was symptomatic of evangelical concerns in the 1930s. In the next two decades parachurch youth ministries would spring up to help the Protestant church evangelize high schoolers (Miracle Book Club, Young Life, Youth for Christ, Hi-BA, Hi-C, Fellowship of Christian Athletes) and collegians (InterVarsity Christian Fellowship, Campus Crusade for Christ, Navigators).

While the youth ministries of mainline Protestant denominations moved toward a more socially progressive agenda, efforts to minister to teenagers (as they would be called after World War II) in smaller evangelical Protestant denominations remained focused on matters of personal piety, doctrinal purity, and evangelism. Still driven by local youth issues, few churches felt the need or desire to conform to national Christian youth ministry programs.

Youth ministries in the emerging evangelical denominations varied widely. Characteristics sometimes combined to aid or resist youth ministry formation. Those churches with roots in rural America, where attendance was small, often resisted fragmenting the church by providing special programs for adolescents. The young people were needed to participate as adults might in teaching Sunday school, singing in the choir, and maintaining the church properties. Some examples of these evangelical denominations were the Wesleyan Methodist Church and the Church of God (Cleveland, Tennessee).

Churches with strong foreign mission emphases expected their young people to prepare for Christian service at home and abroad. For these evangelical traditions, youth ministries led young people to conferences featuring missionaries and speakers who inspired those attending to serve the Lord. In some cases these meetings preceded and aided the formal process of the churches becoming a denomination. The Evangelical Free Church of America and the Christian and Missionary Alliance share some of these missional characteristics.

Newly forming evangelical church groups (some of whom resisted the idea of becoming a denomination), showed distinctive features central to their identity. Holiness or supernatural spiritual gifts, for example, provided an emphasis so important that youth ministries were sometimes considered distractions. The Church of the Nazarene and various charismatic groups fit into this collection of churches.

Ethnic churches provide a fourth category of evangelical denominations where youth ministry emerged in the twentieth century. Traditional adult authority structures clashed with the desires of the next generation to integrate into the mainstream of American society. While African American denominations were well established in the nineteenth century, the development of youth ministries came in the twentieth century. Immigrant Christian churches from China, Korea, Scandinavian countries, and later from Hispanic countries shared similar characteristics.

While each of the newer Protestant denominations was distinct and could validly argue for the originality of their youth ministry experiences, the last part of this chapter will attempt to illustrate how representative denominational churches responded to their unique perspectives of their youth problem and how they improvised a response in anticipation that God would show up in the lives of their teenagers. While the issues related to the popular culture and growth of peer pressure in public high schools remained constant concerns, no educational theory or theological perspective other than their common respect for the authority of the Bible drove the development of their youth ministries. Yet the youth ministries ended up looking very similar by the 1960s.

The Church of the Nazarene

The Church of the Nazarene formed in 1908 as a merger of three regional groups of churches concerned about matters of holiness that were grounded in the teachings of John Wesley. While young people's societies existed in the Church of the Nazarene in the West, they were virtually absent in the Pentecostal Association of Churches in the East or in the Holiness Church of Christ in Texas. The young people's societies that did exist included people ages twelve to forty. Since the average life expectancy at that time was 51.1 years of age, for many churches it may have been redundant to form a youth society since at the time of the merger the average church had fewer than fifty members.[12]

Yet shortly after the merger, the General Assembly established a Committee on Young People's Societies and charged them with giving "adequate attention to the needs of our young people." The committee responded by producing a manual to guide local churches in their efforts to form local societies. In keeping with their shared emphasis on holiness, the committee reported,

> We believe that our young people will find their greatest joy in God's glad service, and hence we feel that no provision of a social aspect need be introduced. . . . Let our young people strive by every legitimate means to enlist the interest of others, endeavoring to win them for God and holiness.[13]

The first report of a local youth society was the Young People's Nazarene League at the Utica Avenue Pentecostal Church of the Nazarene in Brooklyn, New York, in 1912. It met on Thursday nights and, using the manual as a guide, focused its meetings on deepening spirituality and seeing "souls saved, sanctified and reclaimed."[14]

At Kansas City First (Nazarene) Church two years later, Will T. McConnell wrote of the advantages of having a young people's society. Some included providing Christian activity, preventing worldliness, and strengthening and keeping young people on fire for God.[15] Earle Wilde of Los Angeles First Church wrote three articles for the denominational magazine, *Herald of Holiness*, calling for creativity, organization, and leadership. Challenging young men and women to lead in a manner as effective as business or military leaders, Wilde called for attractive meetings that would win the attention of young people. Using an analogy that was not uncommon among evangelical Christians before World War II, Wilde commented, "As I sit here, I see nearly all the young people of this town hurrying off to the ball game. Why? Because the Devil makes the ball game popular and attractive."[16]

As a diehard Chicago Cubs fan, I sometimes agree with Wilde that the Devil made me root for them. The Cubs have not won a World Series since before he wrote his article, but winning was not the point. The emphasis in young people's societies on the local level was on personal holiness, and a growing list of entertaining activities was seen as detracting from a life of walking with God.

The first gathering of a young people's district league was held in Brooklyn, New York, in 1915. Soon followed by district conventions in Southern California, Chicago, Pittsburgh, Western Oklahoma, Arkansas, and the Northwest, these conferences elected officers who challenged every church to have a young people's society that was youth-led. Personal evangelism and the distribution of Christian literature were seen as their way of helping the church succeed.[17] These gatherings appeared to be similar in form and effect to the union meetings of the Baptists and Methodists that also began in Brooklyn and union gatherings of Christian Endeavor.

While the Nazarene young people's societies began two decades after the youth societies of mainline denominations, the need to redefine *youth* came at about the same time. Society was changing, and by the 1930s a majority of youth under the age of twenty attended high school. The Church of the Nazarene recognized this change and in 1932 formed the "Intermediate Society" or "High School Nazarene Young People's Society." Four years later it was renamed Hi-NY. Yet the emphasis on holiness remained the same. A pledge expected of society members read,

> Realizing my duty to God and His church I promise by His grace to seek the New Testament standard of heart purity; to strive always to live

consistently for my Master; to make it the rule of my life to read the Bible and pray daily; to attend faithfully all services of N.Y.P.S.; and to take an active part in the services as opportunity affords me.[18]

Personal holiness and piety remained a consistent emphasis of the youth ministry of the Church of the Nazarene through the middle of the twentieth century. For Nazarene youth, living their Christianity was closely tied to Bible reading and prayer. Purity of heart evidenced its existence in holiness of life and separation from worldly activities.

Evangelical Free Church of America

Immigrants from the Scandinavian countries settled in clusters across the United States and Canada during the late nineteenth century. Three church affiliations they brought with them were Lutheran, Baptist, and Evangelical Free. Each transplanted both ethnic and denominational forms of worship in their adopted land.

Evangelical Free Churches derived their name from their twin desire to proclaim the Christian gospel (the evangel) and to be independent (thus "free") from the state church, which in Scandinavian countries was the Lutheran church. In October of 1884, Swedish free churches formed an association in Boone, Iowa, while about the same time two Norwegian-Danish groups formed associations in Boston, Massachusetts, and Tacoma, Washington.

Very quickly young people's societies formed in these fiercely independent churches. The Swedish Evangelical Free Church reported such groups as early as 1888. By 1924, reports indicate societies in seventy-nine churches with a total membership of 2,692 young people, or an average of about thirty-five per church. Archival pictures suggest the young people to be in their twenties and thirties, much like other youth societies in the nineteenth century.[19]

Young people's conferences brought youth society members together in gatherings, first in Iowa and later in Illinois, Minnesota, Nebraska, Colorado, California, and Washington. While reports of the activities of these conferences for youth societies are sketchy, two functions are apparent. Speakers at the conferences provided the youth with inspiration and direction related to Christian ideals and work. At the same time, funds from the conferences went to support missionaries outside the United States. The constitution of the Minnesota Free Church Young People's Conference in 1912 further clarified these two foci, stating, "The purpose of this conference shall be to execute the Lord's work in bringing salvation to the unsaved and edifying all young people in this, our State of Minnesota."[20]

Reports from other state young people's conferences in 1923 indicate a similar pattern. The Minnesota conference raised eight thousand dollars in pledged giving and commissioned seven young men and women for foreign missionary service. The Illinois conference reported voting to support Miss Anna Hall for seven years as she went to China. Over fifteen hundred dollars was subscribed. Similar patterns of mission interest were reported in young people's conferences in Iowa, Nebraska, and Colorado. The intent of the reports was that local young people's societies would carry the continued load of fulfilling the subscriptions and praying for the missionaries.[21]

The significance of these reports of young people's societies and conferences in the Evangelical Free Church is threefold. First, the function of the young people's societies was highly missional but not necessarily evangelistic. The focus was on the spiritual encouragement of youth and on the support of missionaries and ministries outside their home community. Second, the structure of the young people's societies seemed more closely related to the ethnic traditions of the Evangelical Free Church than connected to the larger youth movement begun in New England. Third, the movement appears to be led by Free Church young people in the heartland of America more than the inspiration of moneyed people in the major cities.

The pattern of centering youth conferences and youth group activity around international missions commitments survived the Great Depression and continued into the 1940s and 1950s. Part of the reason why the Swedish Evangelical Free Church and the Norwegian-Danish Church merged in 1950 to form the Evangelical Free Church of America was because of the productivity of the youth conferences in supporting missional efforts. Statewide and national youth conferences contributed to increased feelings of trust and collegiality among the fiercely independent Scandinavians who relished their freedom. Yet their commitment to evangelical efforts exceeded their suspicions of each other, and their young people led the way.

Free Church Youth Fellowship began on June 6, 1941, in Denver, Colorado. The idea of a national organization for Free Church youth had been under discussion by youth group leaders for several years, but with the election of Mel Larson of Minneapolis and the formulation of a constitution, FCYF gave young people in the movement a voice at the national level. As a journalist, Larson would later chronicle the Youth for Christ movement with books and articles.

The first national FCYF conferences drew upon the Youth for Christ movement even as local youth ministry attempts formalized into the

Youth for Christ organization. Gil Dodds, winner of the Sullivan Award for amateur athlete of the year in 1943 and popular speaker at YFC rallies, along with future president of Youth for Christ, Bob Cook, and the first paid staff member of YFC, Billy Graham, spoke at the national FCYF conferences in the early years.

Yet the Free Church Youth Fellowship groups in local Free Churches were the places where youth ministry happened from week to week. When the United States entered World War II in 1941, the leadership of local groups changed dramatically. Young adult males entered the armed services, leaving high school students to provide the leadership for FCYF. To support these novice leaders, mimeographed programs, written for the most part by Elmer Sandberg, were mailed to high school leaders and their adult sponsors. In 1948, Mel Larson published a book containing fifty-two programs, one for each Sunday of the year, to aid local leaders.[22] The era of the youth fellowship had come to this small Scandinavian denomination.

While the national FCYF conference remained the domain of young adults as the Swedish and Norwegian-Danish Free Churches merged in 1950, local groups were changing. Because of their close association with Youth for Christ, FCYF began to resemble club programs related to the movement. Teams of high school students used the program materials to involve teenagers in ministering to their church peers, while adult sponsors bridged the generations and used the programs as a natural means of getting to know students and helping them formulate Christian values.

In 1960, a few years after YFC began using Bible quizzing, FCYF did so as well, starting in Minnesota and spreading to Illinois. By the end of the 1960s, Bible quizzing and music contests were parts of local Youth Fellowship programs across the nation.[23] This mushroomed into national arts festivals where high school students competed in categories from preaching and drama to creative writing and all types of music. The national program shaped the energies of local FCYF groups. The increasing energy needed on the local level led to a professionalizing of youth ministry as youth pastors took responsibility for leading local church youth ministries.

By the end of the 1970s, the festivals had taken on a life of their own, and youth pastors began asking what youth ministry was all about. Competitions did not seem to be creating followers of Jesus Christ. Both national and local leaders began reassessing the essential nature of youth ministry. What had been good in the fifties and sixties seemed strangely irrelevant to the needs of high school and middle school students in the seventies and eighties.

Church of God (Cleveland, Tennessee)

In the mountains on the boarder between Tennessee and North Carolina, a holiness movement developed during the last quarter of the nineteenth century that would become the Church of God. Influenced by tent revival meetings led by charismatic speakers in the highly illiterate Appalachian region, and with a heavy emphasis on the coming of the Lord, a group of people gathered in a farmhouse in 1886 to set in motion a Pentecostal movement. The movement claimed over six million members in one hundred and fifty countries by the first decade of the twenty-first century.

Despite the fact that families in the mountain region were much larger than elsewhere in the nation, attention to educating these children lagged far behind the rest of the nation. Similarly, Sunday schools were sparse with forms of youth ministry developing much later than in other sections of the country. Because Pentecostalism was a noncreedal movement, the need for Christian education was secondary to encounters with God generally experienced in adult gatherings, whether at church or in camp meetings. The primary concern for youth was the same as for adults. These were mountain people, living and ministering within a rural culture prone to domestic violence, "corn liquor," fornication/adultery, and thievery.[24] Sanctification was needed for everyone. Consequently there seemed to be no need for ministries distinctly directed to young people.

While many churches had Sunday schools, they were more like poorly constructed lectures or sermons than opportunities to capture the spiritual interest of young people entering their adolescence. Despite concerns expressed by the General Overseer and others in 1913 that the movement would disappear if the hearts of the youth were not won, as late as 1923 fewer than 5 percent of the 740 churches reported services specifically for youth.[25]

A year later matters began to change. As the denomination expanded beyond the Appalachian region of its origin, new voices were heard. Mrs. Lettie Cross of Detroit addressed the assembly of 1924 expressing concern that young people be sober-minded. Concerns about youth in the Roaring Twenties moved the Church of God to action on behalf of their youth.[26]

On the very Thursday the stock market crashed in 1929, Young People's Endeavor was officially born in the Church of God. Though not specifically related to the crash, the step proved fortuitous. Though still embedded in the tradition of preachments and prohibitions, young people of the Church of God began having a place of their own.

The primary thrust of the Young People's Endeavor was training youth to become mature Christian leaders. The "endeavor" was not so much a path to know God (though that was desired) as had been the case of the Society of Christian Endeavor; it was more of a pathway to holiness. Alda B. Harrison served as the creative voice and inspiration for the denominational youth program for nearly two decades, publishing a pamphlet in about 1938 entitled "How to Organize and Conduct C. of G. Y. P. E." (Church of God Young People's Endeavor).[27] Yet the "pathway" clearly included the Pentecostal experience. In the pamphlet, Harrison avers, "The greatest need of the church today is for God-called leaders. Leaders filled with the Holy Ghost who have given up the frivolous things of the world and launched out for God."

While the Church of God youth ministry paradigm was very much about education and leadership development, it was operated as an addition to the regular (i.e., adult) worship service functions. The local church was the primary place that young people met God. Richard Castleberry comments,

> In these services they were expected to encounter God in the same manner as their adult contemporaries. . . . It is intergenerational with the youth and even children participating in the services alongside one another. . . . The witness of God's work among their parents and mentors had a dramatic effect on them.[28]

Structured like the youth societies of other denominations, YPE officially included youth in their thirties until the 1950s when the changing youth culture made it wiser to create age groupings in line with public school. Though slower than other denominations to incorporate the youth fellowship idea, the Church of God rapidly absorbed many of the programs made popular by Youth for Christ International. In 1958, Bible quizzing and talent contests began at the local level and culminated at national youth conferences. Mission education and local projects supporting denominational missionaries became common for youth ministries.

Like other evangelical denominations, Church of God youth ministries were more shaped by the Youth for Christ movement than by the Society of Christian Endeavor. Encounters with God as understood through the Pentecostal experience were expected in church services, at camp experiences, and at national youth conferences. Youth ministries served as a feeder system to these events. Yet, Castleberry commented, "The development of youth groups tended to segment youth from the life of the church. Youth ministry became a sub-category of the church's mission, not an integrated part of it."[29]

While denominational growth exploded during the second half of the twentieth century, youth ministries developed in a highly entrepreneurial fashion. Local youth ministers drew upon their creativity and resources in the broader evangelical movement to shape their ministries. National leaders provided conferences that influenced church-based programs. Training conferences were more like Youth Specialties conferences than any attempt to shape a denominational philosophy of youth ministry. It was not until the beginning of the twenty-first century that formal youth ministry degrees were established at Lee College and the Church of God Theological Seminary.

Mennonite Church

The peace tradition and simple lifestyle of the Mennonite tradition shaped youth ministries in the Mennonite Church. Seeking to follow their Savior as a community of faith, Mennonite churches valued the intergenerational nature of their churches. The simplicity of their dress and disciplined way of life symbolized their desire to live as Christians in the modern world.[30] Yet Mennonite youth ministries developed in a pattern similar to that of newer denominations that formalized their fellowships following the First World War.[31]

Following the Dutch reformer Menno Simons, the movement was rooted in the Anabaptist tradition, which placed them at odds with Lutherans and Catholics in Germany. Seeking freedom of religious expression, Mennonites sought the tolerance of Pennsylvania and the farm country of Manitoba and from there spread throughout the heartland of the United States and Canada.

Like other nonmainline denominations, efforts to provide distinctive ministries to youth were resisted by church leadership well into the twentieth century. Young people's meetings began in the last decade of the nineteenth century just as the Society of Christian Endeavor swept the nation, but they were local initiatives in churches like Prairie Street Mennonite Church in Elkhart, Indiana, in 1885.[32] Over the next twenty-five years the idea spread from church to church. Meetings generally were held in homes with Bible study the primary focus. As early as 1911 a handbook was published for those working with these meetings. Yet, little organization connected the various young people's meetings.

In 1921, the Twelfth Mennonite General Conference formed the Young People's Problems Committee to address the spiritual life of youth ages fifteen to twenty-seven. The committee surveyed the grassroots efforts to respond to the needs of youth and published articles to assist the broader Mennonite constituency. Regional institutes and conferences in the 1930s helped pave the way for the rise of youth ministries.

In 1942 efforts to encourage Mennonite distinctives among high school youth took on the form of formal education when Lancaster Mennonite School opened its doors to high school students. Though two schools opened earlier in the century, the initiative in Lancaster led to the establishment of a dozen more by 1960. This form of youth ministry made youth ministries marginally relevant where Mennonite schools existed.

World War II and later the Korean and Vietnam conflicts heightened the urgency for developing youth ministries in Mennonite churches since a high percentage of youth left the peace tradition of the movement to join the armed services. Mennonite Youth Fellowship was formally launched during the summer of 1948. In 1953 the *Youth Fellowship Manual for Local Youth Groups*[33] was published to assist local leaders. The manual provided tools for encouraging the distinctives of the Mennonite heritage, including efforts to win others to Christ.

By 1951 approximately 30 percent of the Mennonite congregations were affiliated with MYF, with notable exceptions in more conservative communities. Starting in 1958, national conferences encouraged the development of local MYF groups. Over a thousand attended the 1959 meeting in Orrville, Ohio.

Camps for youth and national conferences were the primary places where Mennonite youth encountered God. Schools and MYF served as the social settings that provided training in Mennonite values, but it was at camp that God showed up most frequently. As youth ministries went to camp and later did work projects in the name of Christ, spiritual encounters occurred.

The 1960s were a period of turbulence in the American culture and in an attempt to face into the issues confronting Mennonite youth, the Mennonite Youth Fellowship cabinet was discontinued at the end of 1968. In its place the church named Art Smoker to serve as churchwide Secretary for Youth Ministry, a position he held until 1974. With professional leadership the mood of Mennonite youth ministry changed from a rural, "protect our youth" mind-set to a more activist perspective addressing peacemaking and justice issues.

At the same time, there was a shift in the educational patterns of Mennonite youth. When MYF was launched in the late forties, few Mennonite young people went to college. Most remained on family farms, and their churches served as the social hubs of their world. By the 1970s a large percentage of Mennonite young people went to college or enlisted in voluntary service, leaving a vacuum in leadership for MYF groups.[34]

Like so many other denominations, local Mennonite churches began employing youth ministry specialists. With the option of attempting to create a national Mennonite youth program primarily through publications or developing and supporting local youth workers, Mennonites chose the latter. In 1967 the MYF cabinet officially dissolved itself, effective in 1968. It was replaced by the MYF Youth Council, which was an expansion of the MYF Advisory Council. Three staff members (one from the Mennonite Board of Education, one from the Mennonite Board of Missions and Charities, and the Secretary of Youth Work from the Mennonite Committee on Christian Education) were in charge of implementing the Mennonite youth program.

Resisting the temptation to create a niche for young people, Mennonite churches wanted to incorporate their youth into every aspect of church life. Some even wanted young people included in denominational offices and as elders in local churches. The desire for inclusion left youth ministries with an unclear role in local churches.

Despite their best efforts, the shifts left other gaps at the local church level. The desire to respond to the gospel in addressing justice issues engaged many Mennonite youth, but in matters related to the expectation of spiritual encounters with God, Christian spirituality took a back seat. At the same time, the rise of Youth Specialties and *Group* magazine began providing program materials and leadership training that appealed to many youth group leaders, with the result that substantive Mennonite values were in danger of being lost on high school students.

Like youth programs in other denominations, the era of the fellowship group ended with the rise of professionalized youth ministry. Both at the national level and in local churches, part-time and then full-time paid youth workers assumed leadership in guiding and overseeing Mennonite youth ministries.

The Youth Specialties/*Group* Magazine Phenomenon

The demise of effective youth ministry in the first two cycles of youth ministry was closely associated with the co-opting of the parachurch agency's ministry technology by the church and denominational structures. In both cases the methodologies were adapted for use in the church while the core rationale was either discarded or significantly modified. Once incorporated into the church's program the Sunday school became a spiritual nursery for church families rather than remaining an evangelistic arm of the congregation. When denominational bodies imitated the Society of Christian Endeavor, the result was a watered-down pledge that required little accountability from individual members.

The same pattern emerged as youth ministry neared the end of its third cycle. Once again the church copied the technology of parachurch agencies, this time Young Life and Campus Life, and employed their methods to maintain youth ministries of Christian adolescents in church settings while practically ignoring the vast majority of young people who had not made a commitment to the Christian faith. The primary agents for providing that transfer of information were Youth Specialties and *Group* magazine.

Youth Specialties arrived on the youth ministry scene in the fall of 1968. Campus Life had just launched its Impact/Insight strategy, while Young Life was recapturing some of the momentum it had lost when its founder, Jim Rayburn, became ill and new leadership took over the reins of the organization. Though there was a growing host of youth pastors, no one seemed to be aware of how many there were and what their needs happened to be.

Wayne Rice and Mike Yaconelli worked together for several years on the staff of San Diego Youth for Christ. Both were active in formulating the Campus Life strategy for Youth for Christ before resigning to finish college. To support their education the two men served as part-time youth ministers, Wayne at San Diego First Church of the Nazarene and Mike at Lemon Grove First Baptist.

To further supplement their incomes Rice and Yaconelli took some of their programming ideas, which they had generated both in their Youth for Christ days and later in their church ministries, and published a fifty-two-page youth program manual that they cleverly called *Ideas*. To market their product they rented a booth at the Greater Los Angeles Sunday School Convention and sold their initial run of two hundred copies. Quickly another five hundred copies were printed, which was followed in 1969 by *Ideas No. 2*. Thus Youth Specialties was launched.

One of the awkward aspects of the early days of Youth Specialties was the fact that many of the ideas that were published and copyrighted by the young entrepreneurs had been developed while they were still associated with Youth for Christ International. YFC leaders felt the organization owned the material though it had never been copyrighted. Consequently, Campus Life leaders found themselves in the touchy position of having to secure permission from Youth Specialties to use programming ideas they had helped generate.

By 1970 there were four *Ideas* books and the two men took a major risk by sponsoring an event that came to be known as the National Youth Workers Convention. Primarily using old YFC buddies like Jay Kesler, Bill McKey, and Ken Overstreet, the conference attracted approximately three hundred people, and even though the company lost money, a youth ministry training tradition had begun.

The following year they picked up an underground Christian newspaper called *The Wittenberg Door*. Published by two youth workers from the Los Angeles area, Paul Sailhamer and Gary Wilburn, the paper's motto was "There is no public reform that was not first private opinion." The satire and humor as well as the dissatisfaction with the local church were an appropriate match for Rice and Yaconelli's perspectives on the current state of ministry. Youth Specialties acquired the publication for its debts and six hundred dollars' worth of unfulfilled subscriptions and promptly misspelled the name of the expanded magazine. Sticking by their mistake, the new name became *The Wittenburg Door* when it was issued in June 1971.

The fledgling organization gained national attention because of the 1971 convention, which attracted six hundred fifty people to hear such speakers as Francis Schaeffer, Hal Lindsay, Lyman Coleman, Larry Richards, John MacArthur Jr., and others. The following spring the two men and their new associate, Denny Rydberg, went on the road with what they called "National Youth Programming Seminars." These seminars became a way to take youth ministry "ideas" to the people and at the same time market *Ideas*.

Though Yaconelli and Rice continually fought against the inconsistencies of the religious establishment, their visibility, creativity, and insights in the world of youth ministry soon made them part of a newly established power block. *Ideas* were their commodities. Consistently they generated programming ideas that had once been the domain of the parachurch agencies and marketed them to every church youth worker in the nation. The net effect was a rapid and broad distribution of parachurch ministry technology to people who were more interested in methods for keeping students active in youth ministries than in full cycle discipleship. The final phase of the third cycle of youth ministry had begun.

During the summer of 1974, Thom Schultz, a youth pastor in Loveland, Colorado, became frustrated with the lack of programming ideas for church youth ministry available in magazine form. *The Wittenburg Door* had settled on a diet of humor, issues, and renewal-oriented interviews. *Campus Life* magazine, the publication of Youth for Christ International, focused on the individual high school student and his or her world. Sunday school materials were, well, Sunday school materials.

Finding a niche in the post–Jesus Movement church youth ministry market created by Youth Specialties, Schultz created *Group* magazine, which masterfully gathered the youth ministry technology from any source available and sold it first in article form and later in books compiled from the best pieces in the magazine. The circulation grew from four hundred fifty in 1974 to twenty thousand in 1979 and fifty-four thousand in 1984. Growth then leveled off at fifty-seven thousand subscribers in 1989.

With the growth of the magazine leveling off, Schultz's organization increased its emphasis on book publication and events for youth ministries. Unlike Youth Specialties, which focused on adult leaders, Group Publishing attempted to reach the student leaders in the church youth ministries. A "Colorado Flood Disaster Recovery Camp" in 1977, followed by the "First National Christian Youth Congress," which convened in Estes Park, Colorado, in 1978, were the first steps in that direction. By the end of the eighties it was estimated that over fifteen thousand young people were involved in Group-sponsored events during the year.

Thom Schultz's organization had found a way to provide services to the local church similar to the manner in which Youth for Christ had served local YFC clubs and rallies in the fifties and sixties. "Youth Congress"–type events were a throwback to the old Winona Lake (Indiana) Conventions of Youth for Christ, which ceased in the early seventies. The work camps provided for church youth ministries what "teen teams" of young musicians had previously supplied within Youth for Christ.

Some might conclude that the Youth Specialties/*Group* phenomenon had breathed life back into church youth ministry. Rather than facing the end of a cycle of youth ministry, the church had become the rallying point, with youth ministry publishing house conglomerates as the catalyst. A new generation of youth ministry had already begun. The contention might further be supported by the rise of the two Sons—Son City (later called Student Impact) and Sonlife Ministries, with their broad followings in youth ministry circles (see chapter 15).

Unfortunately the conclusion was far too optimistic in face of the facts. The entire publishing/training system was based on one factor: money. Youth ministry as defined by Youth Specialties/*Group* or exemplified by a growing number of large churches was built around the assumption that church youth ministries will have professional youth ministers, volunteers, and interns who would have the discretionary funds available to buy materials, attend seminars, and take young people halfway across the nation to attend conferences or participate in work projects. The market was stratified within an economic middle- and upper-middle-class clientele from which women and minorities were functionally excluded from leadership.

While the bulk of the youth population in the nation was found in urban settings or in communities that had little contact with Christian youth work, the vast majority of youth ministry took place in groups of thirty or fewer kids located in a range of middle-class suburban settings. The Youth Specialties/*Group* phenomenon had merely allowed an increasing number of youth ministers to communicate more effectively to an ever decreasing percentage of the youth population. It was the last gasp before the death of the third cycle of youth ministry.

National Network of Youth Ministries

In 1979, toward the end of the third cycle of Protestant youth ministry in America, twenty-five youth workers came together at a Colorado mountain retreat to compare notes. The agenda was simple: talk. Find out from some of the more experienced youth workers in America what they felt was happening in their shared desire to minister to the youth of America. The question being asked, according to Paul Fleischmann, was "How well are we doing in reaching our nation's teenagers for Christ?" Their conclusion: "Not very well."[35] This concerned the group and especially Fleischmann, with his background in Campus Crusade for Christ.

With all the activity generated by national conferences and parachurch programs, the overall impact on the teenagers of America was negligible. Protestant youth ministries were inwardly focused. While the continued emphasis on Christian discipleship was a positive trend, little energy was being expended on reaching the vast majority of high school students who knew little about the Christian gospel. A vision was born during the meeting. If these leaders built a network of youth workers who would combine their energies, perhaps significant headway could be made in helping youth come to know and love God.

Though the National Network was initially conceived of as an unstructured meeting place for youth workers to gather and fellowship, leaders such as Barry St. Clair, Dennis Miller, and Paul Fleischmann soon saw a need for structure and focus. Influenced by their concern for world evangelism and continued contacts with Campus Crusade for Christ, Fleischmann and St. Clair attempted to mobilize local networks of church-based youth workers into evangelistic units.

For the next three years the networking process begun in Colorado continued. In the fall of 1982, the name *National Network of Youth Ministries* was invented and eighty-six youth workers joined by donating a seventy-five dollar fee.[36] (The membership fee was later discontinued.) Calling the annual gatherings *forums*, the network's nature changed to a conference format with leading youth workers addressing the annual gathering. By 1988 membership had grown to over eleven hundred, with members coming from forty-three states and five other countries, representing fifty-four denominations and twenty-five organizations. Nearly half of the major metropolitan areas in the United States had networks of youth ministers. Attendance at their annual forum in Colorado reached about 245.[37]

The theme of evangelization and discipleship of teenagers held the network together. Driven by their continuing realization that youth ministry had hardly penetrated America's high schools, the NNYM cajoled and encouraged youth workers not to be bound by the walls of their individual churches or denominational affiliations and to cooperate in addressing the spiritual needs of students before they left home for college or careers. Networks, however, were extra work for already busy youth ministers and so most evidences of networking came in the form of events that youth workers could fold into their existing programs.

Conclusion

By 1989, with the fall of Communism, times had changed. Pleasantville no longer existed. The world of Protestant youth ministries in America had changed. Broadcast television with three major networks exploded into hundreds of cable and satellite delivery systems, followed by on-line streaming TV with thousands of channels. MTV pioneered reality programming. MP3 players personalized listening habits. Pornography on demand invaded kids' bedrooms.

At the same time, families and communities were fragmented. If, as the African proverb suggested, "It takes a community to raise a child," child rearing had become the challenge of the new millennium. Complicating the situation was the loss of authority in American culture. Young people, more than ever before, challenged everything, as did the media, educators, political leaders, and church leaders.

To compensate for these difficulties, a new class of specialists in the form of professional youth workers stepped into the gap. Although they were equipped with degrees in youth ministry from Christian colleges and seminaries, or trained on location by large Protestant churches with reputations for effective youth ministry, the gap was impossible to fill, even for the most gifted of youth workers.

The third cycle of youth ministry had ended, and it became uncertain how the challenges faced by Protestant youth ministries in America would now be met. The transition to a new form of youth ministry was under way.

13

Friday Night Lights

The Youth Rally Era (1938–67)

*F*riday Night Lights, the movie-turned-television series, captured a phenomenon that became central to the high school experience after World War II. The movie depicts the 1988 Permian High School Panthers football team as they made a run toward the state championship only to lose in the semi-finals. Yet the story could have been virtually any high school from the late forties on.

In the fifties, the quarterback and other starters on the football team were the most popular people on most high school campuses. Nearly everyone seemed to follow the football players. So when people associated with Youth for Christ or Young Life wanted to get students to attend their clubs or youth rallies, they found ways of connecting with the athletes.

For Youth for Christ the weekly event was the rally on Saturday night. Since Friday nights or sometimes Saturday afternoons in the fall were sacred on the high school calendar, Saturday night became a natural alternative. Teenagers wanted something to do on weekends, and many parents viewed these rallies as wholesome activities even though they were religious. In the mid-twentieth century culture that had grown more religious during and shortly after World War II, the Saturday night rally was a type of party.

Going Public with the Gospel

For Washakie High School in Worland, Wyoming, November 22, 1952, was an exciting day. Led by halfback Dick Harkins's four touchdowns, the Worland squad downed rival Douglas, twenty-six to thirteen, to become the state class A football champions.

The thrill was even greater for Wendy Collins, Youth for Christ director for southern Montana and northern Wyoming. The night before the victory, fourteen of those gridders had gathered in the home of their team physician, Dr. L. S. Anderson, for a time of Bible study and prayer. Then on the evening of the championship victory, sixteen newly crowned state football champions lined the platform at the Worland Youth for Christ rally to give testimony of their personal relationship to Jesus Christ.[1]

An isolated occurrence? Not really. By 1952, thousands of communities, large and small, felt the impact of the Youth for Christ movement. *Newsweek* reported on the most dramatic evidence of the movement's success when it described the 1944 Memorial Day Youth for Christ Rally, attended by a reported sixty-five thousand "sweater-topped bobby soxers, adult civilians and servicemen" at Chicago's Soldier Field. By 1949, there were similar rallies covering as many as 1,450 cities across the nation.[2]

As World War II moved dramatically toward a worldwide Allied victory, America was ready to celebrate. Ten years of economic depression followed by six years of war had put a damper on the nation's capacity to enjoy itself. All that was needed was an excuse and a bit of organizational know-how. The Youth for Christ movement provided both.

The excuse was captured in the "Youth for Christ" slogan, as enthusiastic young ministers from a Protestant fundamentalist tradition became concerned about the moral and spiritual condition of America's youth. Where the phrase was first used is difficult to determine. According to the movement's earliest historian, Mel Larson, the motto was first used in 1934 when Paul Guiness, a young Australian evangelist, used the title at a Sunday night youth meeting held in a theater in Brantford, Ontario.[3]

Oscar T. Gillian apparently was the first person in the United States to use the slogan in any official manner. In 1938, Gillian's Detroit-based "Voice of Christian Youth" used "Youth for Christ" as their motto. The year 1940 found Jack Wyrtzen, an insurance man turned evangelist, using the phrase for rallies in New York's Times Square. By 1943 Roger Malsbary had launched regular "Youth for Christ" evangelistic meetings in Indianapolis. Soon St. Louis, Chicago, and a legion of other cities picked up on the theme and the idea of Saturday night rallies.[4]

As the war wound down, the response to the Youth for Christ meetings increased. Thirty thousand crowded into Chicago Stadium for a "Victory Rally" in the fall of 1944. Twenty thousand packed Madison Square Garden for one of Jack Wyrtzen's "Word of Life" rallies as another ten thousand people were turned away. Minneapolis drew seven thousand to Municipal Stadium on two occasions, while Kiel Auditorium in St. Louis seated five thousand people to hear the gospel, with a focus on bringing youth to Christ.[5]

The movement spread so effectively and rapidly that one might look for a master strategy formulated by a few people and implemented by others in their organizations. But such was not true. The youth rally idea was a grassroots movement which spread like a grass fire on a parched August day. It was youth ministry jazz. Improvisation. Timing. God's jam session.

Youth rallies, however, were neither new nor the unique domain of Youth for Christ. Juvenile temperance rallies in the nineteenth century had many of the same dynamics, though a different message. Baptist Union rallies in Brooklyn and Christian Endeavor union meetings across the nation in the latter half of the nineteenth century brought young people together with the intent to encourage greater loyalty to Jesus Christ.

Yet for a twenty-year period starting near the end of the Great Depression, various forms of youth rallies captured the attention of the American media and catapulted youthful evangelists into the public eye. While Billy Graham was the most well known of these evangelists, hundreds of others preached the Christian gospel of personal salvation to the groups who would become known as teenagers.

The advent of radio shaped the rhythm of the rallies. Realizing that their youthful audiences were accustomed to the pacing of radio programs where each feature was short and to the point, and where dullness would be deadly, rallies followed the same precision. Very tight instructions were given to every participant, from those on the platform to the ushers. The message was short and direct, seldom lasting more than twenty-two minutes. If the rally was broadcast on the radio, there would usually be a "radio message" that lasted only six or seven minutes followed by the twenty-two minute message after they were "off the air."

It was the firm conviction that the Christian gospel could be presented with all the necessary content to allow a precise altar call to draw young people to make spiritual commitments. The messages presented resembled evangelistic messages preached by George Whitfield, Charles Finney, D. L. Moody, and Billy Sunday, except that they appealed specifically to youth. Little, if any, attention was paid to the fuller implications of the gospel. Rally presentations focused on sin and personal repentance.

A message by Torrey Johnson, the first president of Youth for Christ, illustrated the youth rally message. Not concerned with gender-inclusive language, his 1944 radio message entitled "Problems Not Solved by Science" made an evangelistic appeal by declaring:

> There are still three problems today that are not solved by science. The first is the problem of SIN, the second is the problem of the SOUL, and the third is the problem of ETERNAL DESTINY.
> I am glad that I can say that the problem of sin was settled nineteen hundred years ago when Jesus Christ died for sin on the Cross of Calvary. With outstretched hands, He says tonight, "Him that cometh unto me, I will in no wise cast out." "I am the way, the truth, and the life: no man cometh unto the Father but by me."
> The second problem is the problem of the soul. I testify to you that all the research and all the good things that science has brought to us can never satisfy the soul of man. But Jesus *can* satisfy the soul, as you heard from the testimonies of these three friends a few minutes ago.
> Then I think of the problems that come to us day by day. I am glad that Jesus not only saves, He not only satisfies, but He also solved all the problems that we meet along life's way.[6]

Using a much more conversational tone, Jim Rayburn, founder of Young Life, reduced the gospel to very simple terms for his high school audience. Though taken from a 1952 club talk rather than a rally, there were three or four hundred students present, and the message more directly addressed issues faced by high schoolers in their Colorado Springs school. Then Rayburn spoke of conversion:

> There is a mysterious thing that happens when you get properly related to Jesus Christ through this trusting business, believing on him the way the Bible says. Then something happens inside of you, something God does. You don't have to struggle with it. It comes from God. It makes new life because it actually is new life. It makes new life possible for you because it's a new life in you.[7]

Both Youth for Christ and Young Life were parachurch organizations that attracted students from a wide cross-section of denominational churches. Consequently, both movements attempted to reduce the Christian message to its essential core and allow the various churches to which their converts would go to fill in the fuller implications of the gospel as understood in their traditions. This then left these movements, like earlier evangelistic movements, vulnerable to the criticism of presenting a gospel message that was too simplistic. Yet, despite the criticism, the movements saw a growing impact upon the lives of teenagers.

The primary years for Saturday night youth rallies stretched between 1938, with the Detroit rallies of the Voice of Christian Youth, to 1967, when Youth for Christ discontinued the Saturday night rallies in favor of a club-based approach to evangelization. The peak years came at the end of World War II, between 1944 and 1950, and continued strongly in many places through the 1950s. The youth rally tradition both preceded and followed this period in different forms, but the golden era of youth rallies took place from late in World War II to the beginning of the Korean conflict.

Lloyd T. Bryant and Youth Centers

Lloyd T. Bryant of New York City appears to have been the originator of a youth-targeted mass evangelization effort in the United States. After graduating from New York's National Bible Institute in 1932, Dr. Will Houghton of Manhattan's Calvary Baptist Church, future president of Moody Bible Institute, named Bryant as the church's first full-time minister to youth. Bryant's motto was "training through participation" and student involvement in evangelistic efforts was the key. His young people, ages twelve through the midthirties, were involved in hospital visitation, radio work, literature distribution, and open air preaching. Bryant used just about any means to get high school and college-age youth under the sound of the Christian gospel. Popular speakers, symposiums, debates, dinners, conferences, and retreats were all part of his strategy. A decade later, Bryant would be so innovative as to open the nation's first "Christian Youth Theatre" in the Times Square district of New York.[8]

Youth centers were at the heart of Bryant's approach to youth ministry. Using his own New York Youth Christian Center on West Fifty-seventh Street as a base, Bryant was instrumental in developing fourteen or fifteen youth centers throughout the east by 1936. When their number reached forty, Bryant founded the Association of Christian Youth Movements of America to spread the ministry.[9]

Starting in the late twenties Bryant sponsored three evangelistic meetings every week for seven years in Manhattan's Christian and Missionary Alliance Tabernacle. He held the gatherings on weeknights so as not to conflict with normal gatherings of churches in the community. Outstanding speakers and gospel musicians were featured along with "unusual" testimonies from young and older people who witnessed to God's saving and keeping power. Lively singing as well as a youth choir and orchestra added to the appeal of the meeting to young people.

There was another factor contributing to the success of Bryant's youth centers. The Depression had left young people few options for social life after school. Youth center evangelistic meetings were a socially acceptable manner to get out of the house during the week. Thus Bryant's ministry met both social and spiritual needs of adolescents.

Percy Crawford and Radio

More than anyone else, Percy Bartimus Crawford influenced the style of youth evangelists during the thirties and forties. Reacting against the boring religious meetings he had attended in his childhood, Percy came to be described as the "master of the seven minute sermon," and insisted on a fast-moving, lively service. Every rally was entertaining. Even the quartet that traveled with the evangelist knew to laugh on cue in order to stimulate audience response, even though they had heard the same joke in scores of previous youth rallies.

Crawford's background, like many of those who led the Youth for Christ movement, was economically deprived. Abusiveness on the part of Crawford's father caused the teenager from Minnedosa, Manitoba, to leave home to seek his fortune in Southern California. Instead of material wealth he discovered a spiritual dimension to his life and by 1931 had made his way through the Bible Institute of Los Angeles (now BIOLA University), University of California at Los Angeles, Wheaton College, and Westminster Seminary in Philadelphia.

When the Missionary Board of the Presbytery of Philadelphia asked the recent seminary graduate to assume the responsibility for the dilapidated Albert Barnes Memorial Presbyterian Church, the young visionary took to the streets in order to reach the community. Outdoor meetings held on the steps of the downtown church drew hundreds of people. Then building upon his radio experience, gained during undergraduate days in Los Angeles and Chicago, the young pastor began the "Young People's Church of the Air" in 1931. Youth ministry jazz adapted to the newest force in popular culture. The ministry multiplied rapidly and soon the broadcast had a network of 275 stations.[10]

As mentioned earlier, the use of radio forced a discipline on public meetings. Competition from variety shows and radio drama forced the rapid pacing of the rallies. "Dead air" would weary listeners, so meetings moved with the precision of a Swiss clock. The response to Crawford's evangelistic appeals suggested the validity of this new concept in youth ministry.[11]

Invitations to speak at evangelistic rallies followed. Crawford's staccato speaking style became a standard on the rally circuit. As Youth for

Christ evangelistic meetings multiplied during the forties, he traveled and spoke on a regular basis. Mel Larson suggests that "unconsciously many Y.F.C. speakers patterned their messages after Crawford's preaching."[12] Among those influenced were a budding evangelist named Billy Graham and a New York insurance man named Jack Wyrtzen.

Jack Wyrtzen and Saturday Night Rallies

If there was one person at the eye of the Youth for Christ storm, it was Casper John Von Wyrtzen, better known as Jack Wyrtzen. The assessment of Gil Dodds, the world class miler and 1943 Sullivan Award winner who gave his testimony at rallies across the nation, was that there would have been no Youth for Christ movement as it was known in the midforties without Jack Wyrtzen. In all probability he was correct.[13]

Born in 1933, Jack spent his childhood in Brooklyn where he developed the musical interests that provided the setting for his involvement in the Jamaica High School dance band. His interest in horses and sports combined with the trombone talent were instrumental in Wyrtzen's joining the 101st Cavalry Band. It was there as a young adult that the personable young man met George Schilling, who would later be instrumental in Wyrtzen's spiritual conversion.[14]

Though his parents were Universalists, young Wyrtzen did not associate with any church consistently. Thus, when a spiritual turbulence aroused him during his late teenage years and a Christian conversion took place, Jack turned not to the church but to a group of friends. Together they sought to discover and serve God. Chi Beta Alpha, they called themselves. From this group came Word of Life Fellowship (Wyrtzen's organization) and Brandt Reed's High School Evangelism Fellowship in the late 1930s as well as a director for the already existing Pocket Testament League in the person of Alfred Kunz. Young men, disenchanted with the current sounds of youth work, created fresh sounds.

Though all of the young men enjoyed preaching, Jack Wyrtzen emerged as the most effective in attracting and holding audiences. Like his conversion experience, his audiences were not conventional. Prisons, rescue missions, open air meetings, and evangelistic banquets were all sounding boards for the budding youth evangelist. Stimulated by Percy Crawford, Jack and the "fraternity" began radio broadcasts beamed at youth on Tuesday mornings over Brooklyn's WBBC in 1940.[15]

The boldest steps in those early days were twenty-eight-year-old Wyrtzen's twin decisions to try Saturday night rallies in New York's bustling Times Square and to broadcast the evangelistic messages over fifty-thousand-watt WHN, one of America's most powerful independent radio stations. Two hundred and fifty people attended the first "Word of Life" broadcast. Within four months the numbers would swell to a thousand each Saturday night. From that point on Wyrtzen's efforts to evangelize youth grew in intensity.[16] While jazz music would never be tolerated at a Wyrtzen rally, youth ministry was the jazz with which he was experimenting.

Within five years the Saturday night rally broadcasts were packing the major auditoriums of New York City and the nation. Twenty thousand jammed into Madison Square Garden; Carnegie Hall was packed with youth and adults each week; three thousand gathered in Chicago; four thousand came to rallies in Philadelphia; and five thousand attended in Boston. Three thousand boarded a ferry boat for a ride up the Hudson River. At the conclusion of each meeting an invitation was issued by the youthful evangelist for young people to "come to Christ." Weekly scores, even hundreds, responded, walking forward to be counseled by a battery of volunteer youth workers.

Wyrtzen's ministry expanded after World War II. Evangelistic tours to Mexico and the British Isles were followed by the purchase of a resort for young people in upper New York State. Word of Life camps at Schroon Lake attracted a national clientele and included facilities for children (the Ranch), youth (the Island), and adults at the Inn.[17] These were followed by international camps, Word of Life Bible Institute, and a church-based Bible club program with over twelve hundred North American clubs. Yet it was the Saturday night rallies that were most frequently imitated by youth workers across the nation.

Jim Rayburn and Young Life Campaigns

Jim Rayburn stood in stark contrast to Jack Wyrtzen. Whereas Wyrtzen was raised in Brooklyn, Rayburn's home was Newton, Kansas, or wherever in the West his evangelist father planted his tent for meetings. Wyrtzen's parents were Universalists; Rayburn's were Presbyterians. Wyrtzen began evangelistic work at age nineteen, while Rayburn was weaned on his father's evangelistic meetings and imitated his father as early as age two and a half. Wyrtzen had to drop out of high school during the Depression; by contrast, Rayburn was a graduate of Kansas State University and Dallas Theological Seminary. The most evident difference was in speaking styles. Wyrtzen used a rapid-fire delivery while Rayburn pioneered a conversational approach to evangelistic communication. Yet as different as the two men were, Wyrtzen and Rayburn serve as bookends for the movement to evangelize youth in the 1940s and following.[18]

Though Jim Rayburn is best known for the incarnational club strategy that he pioneered, his early efforts utilized a mass evangelism approach to youth ministry. The name of the organization he founded, Young Life Campaign, was borrowed from the National Young Life Campaign of Great Britain after founders Rev. and Mrs. Frederick Wood visited Dallas Seminary and described their British ministry. With their permission, the thirty-year-old Rayburn used the campaign motif to promote week-long evangelistic efforts in the Texas towns of Galveston, Houston, Dallas, Fort Worth, and Weatherford. On February 25, 1941, a Dallas newspaper proclaimed "Young Life Pep Rally Draws 2,000." Rayburn's approach was beginning to look like the efforts of Bryant, Crawford, and Wyrtzen.[19]

The ingredients of these Texas rallies were similar to those in the East—large auditorium, enthusiastic music, and preaching appealing to young people. Yet there were three differences. Rayburn's rallies were attended nearly exclusively by young people, whereas meetings addressed by the others had an adult population as high as 50 percent of the audience. Without the adults and the donations made through campaign offerings, rallies never became a means to provide financial support for the movement. This fact alone may have given Rayburn the freedom to scrap the mass approach to youth evangelism in favor of a club- and camp-based strategy by the midforties.

The second difference was that radio was never a significant part of Rayburn's ministry. Whether this omission was by design or by oversight is not clear. Rally-based youth ministries needed radio coverage to spread the news of meetings and events. Rayburn seldom used the media in that manner. It was not part of his vision. Instead he preferred to feature what was happening in Young Life clubs. His form of youth ministry jazz played an intensely relational motif. Consequently the Young Life campaign rallies peaked in 1943 and thereafter played a secondary role to the blossoming club program and the camping ministries that became part of the movement with the purchase of Star Ranch in 1945.[20]

Perhaps as a consequence of not following the youth rally approach, Rayburn differed from his northern evangelical counterparts. His approach involved creating a team of missionaries to high schools who communicated in a conversational manner. None of them used the staccato rhythm of the radio preachers. Rayburn and the people he brought onto the Young Life team spoke to groups of teenagers in a manner similar to a conversation at a family reunion when stories were recalled and told to a new generation. This storytelling style of communicating the Christian message carried over into the camping ministry, allowing kids unaccustomed to Protestant preaching to listen with interest to the story of the Christian gospel.

Rayburn's approach allowed him to travel under the radar of the critics of the Youth for Christ movement. He and the Young Life staff did not sound at all like the stereotypical "hell-fire and damnation" preachers whom the press loved to stigmatize. Consequently, a Young Life approach to youth ministries was adopted in many mainline denominational churches, even though the core message of Christian salvation communicated by the movement differed very little from the rest of the Youth for Christ movement in those early days.

Torrey Johnson and the National Vision

A person who taught Greek at a seminary would not seem the most likely candidate to serve as a leader in the Youth for Christ movement, and yet Torrey Maynard Johnson, who had taught the Greek language at Northern Baptist Seminary, became the first president of Youth for Christ International. At age thirty-six Johnson was a product of Chicago— Carl Schurz High School, Northwestern University for two years, then Wheaton College, and Northern Baptist Seminary. During the early forties he became the pastor of Midwest Bible Church, which claimed to be the fastest growing church in Chicago.[21]

Though Johnson was an evangelist in his own right, his contribution to the movement was his national vision for evangelizing youth. This dream began in Chicago where he originated a radio program that became "Songs in the Night" and was later turned over to a young pastor in suburban Western Springs named Billy Graham. Evangelistic boat cruises similar to those sponsored by Jack Wyrtzen were hosted by Midwest Bible Church. Twenty-two hundred young people crowded on board. Invitations to speak at evangelistic meetings flooded his desk. One of these invitations was to speak at Roger Malsbary's Indianapolis Youth for Christ rally. "This can happen in Chicago," was the guest speaker's thought.

Happen it did. For twenty-one weeks in the spring of 1944, Chicago's Orchestra Hall was packed with over two thousand young people of all ages. WCFL, Chicago's powerful "Voice of Labor," broadcast the Saturday evening extravaganza. Then on October 21, 1944, Chicago Stadium hosted a "Victory Rally" sponsored by Johnson's Chicagoland Youth for Christ. Twenty-eight thousand people attended to witness the same type of high-powered program as Wyrtzen would sponsor in Madison Square Garden a little over a year later.

Like a snowball rolling downhill, the movement gathered size and momentum. Torrey Johnson and Robert Cook's book, *Reaching Youth for Christ*, did for Youth for Christ what Francis E. Clark's book, *The*

Children and the Church, had done for Christian Endeavor sixty years earlier: it took what was happening in one location and briefly explained how it could be done elsewhere. Letters again covered Johnson's desk. The need for a national organization seemed apparent. A new sound of youth ministry jazz was spreading.

At the invitation of Arthur W. McKee, director of the Winona Lake Bible Conference Grounds, Roger Malsbary, Torrey Johnson, and a half dozen other youth leaders met in August 1944 to plot a strategy. By November the group had expanded to include thirty-five men from twenty-one cities who elected Torrey Johnson chairman of a "Temporary Youth for Christ International Committee." Offices were set up in Chicago to promote the first Youth for Christ International Week at Winona Lake during the last week of July 1945.[22]

When July 22, 1945, arrived, forty-two delegates representing different rallies were present at the Winona Lake Conference Grounds. A roll call of those attending read like a who's who of the leadership of evangelicalism for the years to come. Most prominent among those present was a young pastor/evangelist named Billy Graham, who had already become the first nonclerical employee of the fledgling organization.

It should be noted, however, that none of the other evangelists mentioned in this chapter were present. Reasons varied. Wyrtzen distrusted structures other than his own. Crawford was headed in a different direction as he prepared to found the King's College. Rayburn had already left the rally emphasis in favor of club and camp work. The net result was that, although Youth for Christ International was voted into being on July 29, 1945, and a structure was provided for the movement that would provide a tidal wave of missionary and evangelistic ministries focused on young people, organizational unity was not and never would be achieved. Perhaps the very entrepreneurial nature of the movement proved to be its strength.

Though Torrey Johnson was an outstanding evangelist in his own right, the contribution he made to the movement was more visionary and political in nature. It took a skilled hand to bring together such a diverse group of Protestant fundamentalists who still had the tendency to distrust bureaucratic structures, which many of them viewed as being one of the factors that brought about the slide of mainline denominations into theological liberalism a generation earlier.

A Sense of Revival

As the decade of the fifties began "revival" was the dominant theme of the evangelical church, in general, and the Youth for Christ movement, in particular. *Youth for Christ Magazine* released a quotation from the president of the United States under the caption, "Truman Longs for Revival." The president was reported to have said, "Many times during the past decade the conviction has come to me with increasing force that a revival of the spirit of old-fashioned religion is what the world needs most."[23]

Dr. Harold J. Ockenga, pastor of Boston's Park Street Church, told the 1949 midsummer Youth for Christ convention that it was time for a spiritual revival. By the following March, Ockenga reported in *Christian Life Magazine* that "America's Revival Is Breaking," followed by the proclamation in April that "Revival Is Here."[24]

With youth evangelists in the forefront of the spiritual awakening, the revival took two forms. The best known aspect had to do with the response to the evangelistic preaching of such people as Billy Graham (in Los Angeles and Boston), Bob Jones (Vancouver, British Columbia), Merv Rosell (Des Moines), and others. The response to the invitations for spiritual commitments was so great that the word "revival" was appropriate.

Billy Graham's eight-week campaign sponsored by "Christ for Greater Los Angeles" in the fall of 1949 brought the revival to national attention. More than a third of a million people flocked to hear the youthful evangelist in a tent that seated 6,280 people. Thousands responded including people from the movie industry. The resulting publicity was spectacular. *Time, Life, Newsweek, The Associated Press, The United Press, The International News Service, London Daily Mail*, and many local papers carried reports of the hand of God working in Los Angeles. The reports were instrumental in the spread of the midcentury awakening.

At the same time a different type of revival was happening on the campuses of the nation. The best known was the spiritual movement that took place at Wheaton College for thirty-eight hours between 7:00 p.m. on Wednesday, February 8, 1950, until 9:00 a.m. on Friday, February 10. In a quiet and at times unemotional manner, students stood to give testimony of God's working in their lives. Many confessed sin and asked for forgiveness from friends and fellow students. There was no preaching and a minimum of singing as students and faculty members waited their turns to witness to the working of the Holy Spirit in their lives. God had showed up and the impact was felt across the country.

Huntington College, Greenville College, Pasadena College, North Park College, John Brown University, Houghton College, Asbury College, and Northern Baptist Seminary experienced similar workings of the Spirit. Revivals were also reported on the high school level at Wheaton Academy (near Wheaton College) and in Columbus, Ohio, where under the encouragement of Hi-BA (High School Bornagainers) several hundred junior and senior high school students met before school twice a week to pray.

This passion for revival contrasted with the emphasis on Christian nurture that dominated the youth ministry strategies found in mainline Christian denominations. The redefinition of nurture begun by Francis E. Clark evolved during the second cycle of youth ministry to a point where teenagers were being called upon to change the social systems of the world without addressing the personal spiritual issues dealt with by both Horace Bushnell and youth ministry pioneers like Theodore Cuyler and, before him, Jonathan Edwards. The revised nurture marched to the beat of a liberal theological agenda discredited by two world wars among enlightened nations.

Yet the new revival emphasis did not revert to the exclusive dependence on the sort of radical conversions that Horace Bushnell reacted against a century earlier. Not simply a call for piety, this was a call to mission. Bushnell would probably have viewed the events of 1949–50 as one of the periodic corrections that God uses to refocus the church on living as Christians in the world.

The revival of 1950, especially as it related to youth ministry, was short-lived, though its impact continued for years to come. By the fall of 1950 all that the Christian periodicals reported were evangelistic meetings, which continued to be described as revivals but lacked the spectacular dynamics of the previous year. Yet no one whose life had been touched by a special working of the Spirit of God could return to life as usual. From the ranks of young people involved in the revivals of 1950 came leaders for the youth and missionary movements that emerged in the following years.

More significant for the Protestant youth ministry of America was the fact that few high school or junior high youth ministries felt the direct effect of these revivals. Testimonies of the college revivals were retold on high school retreats and in weekly meetings, but few reports can be found of similar prolonged experiences involving young people who still lived with their parents.

Where Did All the Rallies Go?

Youth for Christ rallies were most effective in the late forties. As the social stability (some would say apathy) of the Eisenhower years took hold of the culture, the weekly Saturday evening evangelistic effort went through a period of decline. The rallies were revived briefly by student participation in a national quizzing program and talent contests in the late fifties and early sixties before being discontinued as part of the national strategy in the late sixties.

If the *Minneapolis Star* report that 1,450 cities had Youth for Christ rallies in 1949 was accurate, the decrease to 255 chartered rallies reported to the organization's 1958 Midwinter Convention was dramatic. Even granting the difference between newspaper "hype" and the conservative numbers that may have resulted from an official chartering procedure, which was resisted at the grassroots of this entrepreneurial type organization, the decrease was significant.

The next five years saw a reversal of the number of chartered Youth for Christ rallies reported until the numbers peaked in 1963 with 327. Then the slide began again with the number reported in 1967 reaching a low of 232 before the rally concept was discontinued in all but a few cities such as Kansas City; Evansville, Indiana; and Lancaster, Pennsylvania. Some of these rallies later left Youth for Christ to form the Youth Evangelism Association.

While the number of rallies decreased, the number of people attending the Saturday night meetings similarly declined. A look at the charter applications for the Hampstead, Maryland, Youth for Christ International program provided further statistical documentation for the decline of the rally. The Hampstead program in most ways would be considered a model program. Hosting fifty-two rallies each year, the regional vice president and local director, Earl W. Schultz Jr., developed both junior high and high school clubs that actively participated in the national Bible quiz program, placing second at the Winona Lake Convention in 1963. Rally attendance in Hampstead increased from 1952, when about 150 attended, until 1963, when 304 could be expected to attend the weekly gathering at North Caroll High School Auditorium. Then the slide began. By 1968 crowds were averaging 235 per week, the same as 1957. Saturday night evangelistic rallies were not the attraction they once were. Times had changed and so would the methodology of youth workers.

In-Church Youth Rallies

Just as the rallies officially disappeared from Youth for Christ USA, two young men reinvented the rally and placed it squarely in the local church. David Holmbo, the youth minister and associate music minister at South Park Church in Park Ridge, Illinois, and his friend from Camp Awana, Bill Hybels, saw youth ministry as a vehicle for reaching kids and their "seeking" friends with the gospel of Jesus Christ. Instead of utilizing a rally or union meeting bringing together teenagers from many churches, Holmbo and Hybels created the same dynamics within their church on Tuesday nights.

Son City Spectacular launched the new concept of youth ministry in 1973. Using virtually every method previously associated with youth rallies (primarily contemporary music, drama, testimonies, media, preaching highly relevant to kids' lives) and adding club dynamics adapted from their experience with the Awana club program (creatively-designed competitions among teams of high school students), the duo quickly saw students bring their "seeking" friends by the busload. Dropping the "Spectacular" after the first month, Son City became everything the Youth for Christ rallies had ever been, except that it was based in South Park Church in Park Ridge, Illinois, with a distinctly seventies flair. The impact was immediate and the response far more effective than Youth for Christ rallies had been.

Dave Holmbo created the music and drama. Bill Hybels became the dynamic communicator. Together they generated and sustained a vision for evangelization seldom seen in youth ministry. Within six months attendance passed three hundred each week. During the summer of 1974 Son City moved into the church auditorium to accommodate five hundred, and still attendance grew. By 1975, attendance somewhere between a thousand and twelve hundred forced Son City to meet on two nights. While Holmbo and Hybels brought variations to the old youth rally themes, the fresh sound of youth ministry jazz came from teenagers themselves.

Students believed in what was happening. They knew they would not be embarrassed if they brought their best friends. Soon friends brought their friends. The message Bill Hybels preached was hard-sell Christianity done in a manner that would offend teenagers only with the gospel of Jesus Christ, never with the cultural encumbrances of their fundamentalist background at Camp Awana.

When Son City became Willow Creek Community Church, the in-church contemporary rallies continued. Students from as many as thirty or forty high schools gathered for midweek seeker-targeted meetings. The Son City rally strategy appealed to the baby boomer generation. The programmatic formula was simple. Team competition was the key. Teams were formed according to high schools, and student leaders led teams. Teenagers came because of relationships with their friends who modeled servant leadership within the team context. Competition among the teams heightened enthusiasm.[25]

With youthful energy flowing like a fifties pep rally, the teams moved into the auditorium where winning teams were announced amid cheering and a rock band. Then sometimes drama transitioned into a talk by Don Cousins or, later, Dan Webster and Bo Boshiers. When the invitation was given, student leaders urged their peers to respond and frequently led them to Christ.

In time the intensity of Son City (later called Student Impact) burned out the high school leaders and required that young adults (primarily college and seminary students) assume team leadership. The system reflected the linear thinking of a modern mind-set and as long as Willow Creek Community Church continued to grow, Student Impact grew with it.

All across America and the world, churches imitated the in-house youth rallies of Willow Creek Community Church. The total number of young people presented with the Christian gospel in Willow-like settings far exceeded those reached in the Youth for Christ rallies. Yet even the in-church rally strategy began to fade as modernity gave way to a generation of postmodern youth. The high school social structure that enabled Son City/Student Impact to flourish gave way to an in-church social construct attracting an ever increasing number of teenagers from church families and fewer of the high school seekers for whom the ministry was built.

By the first decade of the twenty-first century, youth ministry at Willow Creek Community Church shrank to a few hundred attendees. Competition between teams from various high schools escalated to imitate the television program, American Gladiator, and then disappeared as teenagers looked more for communal experiences than for conquests.

As the third millennium developed, the in-church rally still existed but the evangelistic impact diminished. The dynamic performances of musicians, media, drama, and effective preaching still attracted teenagers to the show. But the pool of seekers in such settings decreased consistently. New venues for rallies created a new kind of youth ministry jazz. Shaped by MTV's *Spring Break* and extreme sports, youth evangelists in the early twenty-first century set up their stages on beaches in order to engage the sun seekers and bring them into contact with the Son their hearts seek.

Conclusion

While Friday night lights and Saturday night rallies appealed to jocks and their friends, there was another social set that seldom showed up at either of these events. This group was the "greasers," with their successors known as "heads" (potheads) and burnouts. It is questionable if the rally approach to youth ministry ever reached them. For that matter, with a few highly publicized exceptions like future Olympic decathlon champion Rafer Johnson and the football team of Washakie High School, not many student body leaders were included in the thousands of young people who attended the rallies. Most were just average teenagers, who were by far the majority of the high school population.

By the sixties, the Saturday night youth rally had run its course. Many other options for social activities had become available. Besides, the financial burden for sustaining these rallies fell on the adults who attended, and with a growing alienation between generations culminating in the late sixties, the idea of spending Saturday night with their parents and other adults became unappealing. Only in places like Willow Creek, where teens could gather with few adults present, did the rally survive, and usually this was no longer on Saturday night.

Nearly as quickly as the rallies came into being, they disappeared. Once again the focus of youth ministry reverted to churches and parachurch clubs. Even through the rally era, Young Life focused on clubs held on weeknights. Fellowship of Christian Athletes started with summer camps but by 1956 formed weekly clubs called Huddle Groups. With the end of the rally era, Youth for Christ similarly focused on weeknight club meetings with a new approach they called Campus Life.

Perhaps the rallies, more than any other single aspect of youth ministry in the middle of the twentieth century, defined how the Christian gospel was presented to teenagers. Rally after rally, the emphasis was placed on sin and repentance. Speakers defined sin in terms of personal holiness. Little attention was paid to the social implications of the gospel.

part **5**

Jazz Fusion

Combining Old and New (1990 and Beyond)

Jazz fusion combined styles of jazz music with a wide variety of musical genres as diverse as rock, country, R&B, hip-hop, Latin salsa, and forms indigenous to other parts of the world. Toward the end of the twentieth century, jazz became an expression of the musicians of the world.

In much the same way, youth in America morphed into a mosaic very different from the world in which rock and roll was born. With Caucasians moving toward becoming a minority, sexual preferences and activity challenging historic Judeo-Christian standards, erratic weather patterns battering previously safe havens, and economic institutions changing rapidly, assumptions about life after high school and college appeared highly uncertain during the first decade of the twenty-first century. Though few high schoolers read the writings of Thomas L. Friedman, their world had become hot, flat, and crowded.[1]

Youth ministry became a fusion of the Christian church worldwide. Historic expressions of Christian spirituality from Roman Catholic, Orthodox, Protestant, and charismatic perspectives began shaping Protestant youth groups. Asian and Hispanic expressions of youth ministry challenged the vitality of North American youth groups. Evangelicalism came under criticism from Emergent elements of churches, much of which was formed by youth ministry in the last third of the twentieth century.

At the same time youth ministry agencies formed after World War II struggled to reinvent themselves in a youth culture that viewed the world far differently than did their founders. Church-based youth ministries that attracted imitators across the nation found themselves in a continuous scramble to revitalize their core strategies.

The final chapters of the book look at the now-faltering youth ministry establishment, not in a desire to lay to rest ministries that proved spiritually forceful in many lives, but to suggest that, as Christianity continues spiraling toward the culmination of history, a new wave of youth ministry will shape young people and the church communities in which they find their significance.

14

Into the Woods

Reinventing Youth Ministry

tephen Sondheim's musical *Into the Woods* uses fairy-tale characters Little Red Riding Hood, Jack (of beanstalk fame), Rapunzel, and Cinderella to create a sequel to the original story of "Jack and the Beanstalk." In a clever scene, the characters are threatened by the wife of the giant who was slain in the original story. Panicking, the characters offer the narrator of the story as a sacrifice to the giantess in order to save their own lives. Then realizing how lost they would be in the story without a narrator, the group recants their offer only to have Witch, who precipitated the whole problem, throw the narrator into the arms of the giantess, and he subsequently is killed. Still the play goes on.

In some ways, youth ministry at the beginning of the twenty-first century is like Sondheim's musical. The narrator is dead and yet the play goes on. Some have suggested that there never was a narrator or that everyone has become his own narrator. Many in Protestant youth ministry desired for the cast to return to their original stories and not be hampered by the current dilemma. Yet the play goes on.

Protestant youth ministry in America is in transition. The desire of youth workers to help teenagers connect with the God of the Bible remains constant. Experiencing pressure to increase youth group attendance numbers or report ever increasing numbers of conversions, the leaders of youth ministries find themselves in a setting where changes in the world have forced them to change how they go about their ministries. Yet the direction in which they should move remains unclear.

Having pioneered market-sensitive ministry for most of the youth culture era that began in the midfifties, youth ministers very quickly learned to follow the lead of Jim Rayburn and earn the right to be heard by young people. This missional approach of entering the world of high school students included asking questions, listening to their music, reading their magazines, and identifying with their problems. In its most basic form, this is cultural exegesis. Yet the Christian gospel did not change; salvation was still offered by the grace of God through faith in Jesus Christ plus nothing. Youth for Christ in the 1940s had a phrase for their strategy: "Geared to the times, but anchored to the Rock."

As the twentieth century drew to a close, it was apparent to many observers that youth ministry had to face this world of dramatic change. The author's previous historical sketch, *The Coming Revolution in Youth Ministry*,[1] merely placed in written form information that youth workers closest to the customers (adolescents) already knew. Parachurch youth ministry had grown stagnant. If changes were not made, the major parachurch ministries were in danger of becoming minor contributors to the spiritual journey of young people.

One option was for parachurch agencies to close up shop and allow churches to assume the role they should have been playing all along. None of the parachurch agencies in the United States or Canada opted for this approach. Nor should they have done so.

The opposite approach to youth ministry in the twenty-first century centered on strategies to reinvent the existing ministries. Young Life accomplished a brilliant metamorphosis in the last decade of the twentieth century then flattened out their growth midway through the first decade of the twenty-first century. YouthFront, the former Kansas City Youth for Christ program, similarly morphed into a ministry more responsive to teenagers seeking to experience God's presence. Other church and parachurch agencies enjoyed moderate success, while still others withered, producing only occasional evidences of the life they once enjoyed.

Pluralism and the High School Campus

The racial composition of teenagers in America changed. Statistics for the fall 2005 school year identified 16,275,000 high school students in the United States,[2] 14,909,000 of whom were attending public high schools. The other 1,366,000 high schoolers were enrolled in private secondary schools. An analysis of the racial or ethnic composition of public schools (K–12) in the fall of 2005 showed this growing diversity. While 64.8 percent of students were white in 1995, only 57.1 percent of the school population was white in 2005. The black population increased slightly (16.8 percent in 1995 vs. 17.2 percent in 2005), while Hispanics increased much more rapidly (13.5 percent in 1995 vs. 19.8 percent in 2005). Asian or Pacific Islanders increased from 3.7 percent to 4.6 percent of the student population, while the population of American Indian or Alaskan Native students increased from 1.1 percent to 1.2 percent of American students.[3]

High school dropouts disappear from the radar of most youth workers. While the status high school dropout rate decreased in the decade and a half between 1989 and 2005, 9.4 percent of high school students sixteen through twenty-four years of age stopped attending school without graduating. The dropout rate among white students has decreased from 9.4 percent to 6 percent in the period. The rate for blacks fell from 13.9 percent to 10.4 percent, while Hispanic dropouts dipped from 33 percent to 22.4 percent.[4] Yet one in ten students in America failed to graduate from high school. Missiologists would view high school dropouts as hidden peoples as far as youth ministry is concerned.

The demographics of the high school campus changed as well. By the end of the second decade of the twenty-first century half of the high school students in America will be nonwhite. No longer will people concerned with reaching youth for Jesus Christ expect to have a single program or strategy that is attractive to all of the high school population. The ethnic factor alone has made it impossible. Nor can program ideas gathered from national conferences dominated by white middle-class youth workers or traditional educational institutions serve as the basis for attracting and holding high school students in local communities unless those settings compare favorably to the circumstances from which the trainers came.

As the new millennium began, National Network of Youth Ministries hosted a conference for network coordinators at Circle-C Camp outside Kansas City. Following an extended time of worship music led by a group from YouthFront (formerly Kansas City YFC), Fred Lynch, the African American coordinator of urban networks, gave a report of his newly-established ministry. His first comment was as insightful as I have heard on the issue of the diversity of styles necessary in youth ministry. "That's not our kind of worship music," he said half jokingly, but with penetrating honesty. The worship music, profoundly meaningful for the predominantly white audience at the conference, did not connect with our black brother. Diversity illustrated.

"What will the U.S. be like when whites are no longer the majority?" asked the cover story of *Time* magazine as the final decade of the twentieth century began.[5] At the beginning of the new millennium white children in the public school systems in California, the District of Columbia, Hawaii, Louisiana, Mississippi, New Mexico, and Texas accounted for less than half of the student populations. Nonwhite students in Arizona, Florida, Georgia, Maryland, New York, and South Carolina are but a few percentage points from surpassing their Anglo peers.[6]

Major cities have long been the habitat of minority groups but with the growth of world-class cities within the borders of the United States two major factors created a migration of ethnic peoples toward the suburbs. Gentrification of urban real estate along with the elimination of major public housing projects forced many lower-income residents to find cheaper housing inconveniently located in less affluent suburbs and in rural communities. On the other end of the income scale, the upward mobility of people of color allowed increasing numbers to achieve the American dream in communities where funding of public schools ensured university admissions and a broad spectrum of extracurricular activities. America has in fact begun changing colors. If immigration patterns and birth rates continue as expected, youth ministry will behold an entirely new face by 2020.

Educational entitlement programs begun in the 1970s created a new climate on campus. "Equal access" became a way of life. No longer could a few talented or popular people dominate the life of a high school. Athletics were no longer the exclusive domain of a few well-coordinated seniors, nor were they dominated strictly by males. Women's sports came into their own in the late twentieth century. The overwhelming popularity of soccer star Mia Hamm and the 1999 World Cup champion team as well as Danica Patrick's success and popularity in the male-dominated sport of Indy car racing demonstrated the point. In some schools female athletic teams surpassed the popularity of traditional male sports. Complete competition schedules for freshmen and sophomores in both major and minor sports brought about a greater breadth of participation.

Money invested by school boards and booster clubs into music, drama, cheerleading, pom-pom squads, speech teams, and other extracurricular activities altered the perception of what matters in the lives of high schoolers. Regional, state, and national competitions as well as summer camps for just about every specialty gave activities once perceived as the domain of "losers" an improved schoolwide status.

Music also expressed the pluralism of the high school society. Instead of attempting to "blast" everyone else with one's preferred music, students were likely to be found wearing headphones, listening to stations of choice or a favorite musical selection downloaded to MP3 players from performers who may have never released a traditional CD. No longer was there a tyranny of one particular musical style. Alternative music epitomized the diversity. The hip-hop culture captured the fancy of large white audiences. Choice became the fashion of the day.

After-school jobs produced another type of pluralism in the high school society. A majority of suburban high school students now have a steady source of income that lessens their dependence on parents, community, or church agencies for entertainment. Young people discovered the financial freedom to be selective in the way they used their time. Yet because of work schedules, they did not have as much free time to use.

For a number of years students from Trinity Evangelical Divinity School canvassed high school students in the Chicago area to discover how they described social groups on their campuses. Writing in 1976, Ralph Keyes identified two basic groups that he called the "innies" and the "outies,"[7] but as the century came to an end, Trinity students identified a bewildering array of clusters, all of which have ever-changing forms of in-groups and out-groups. The following designations came from the high school students. Many are not very flattering. All suggest a system of social segregation.

> Actors, bandies, band members, blacks (African Americans), blonds, brains, bullies, bummers, burnouts, cheerleaders, computer people, cool people, crew (wearing black, peace symbols), debaters, dorks, drama people, druggies, Filipinos, floaters, fobs (fresh off the boat), friendlys, gangs (gang bangers), geeks, gothic, "the group," grunge, hairspray/makeup people, headbangers (heads), hippies (groovey), Hispanics (Puerto Rican, Mexican, Cuban, etc.), housers, in crowd, japs (Jewish American princesses), jocks, Koreans, loners, lost people (losers), metal heads, mommy boys, nerds, new wavers, nice crowd, nobodies, normal, others, overly violent, partiers, peace freaks (granolas), pom poms, popular group, preppies, punks, rap music, residents, richies, scum bags, six pack, skater punks (skaters), sluts (rough girls), smart people, smokers, snobs (snobby girls), social climbers (yuppies), squids, stoners, thick (lovers), tide, trendies, waivers, wannabes, and weirdos. Our Canadian friends have added some that you may recognize: alternatives, artsies, B-boys, bushers, environmentalists, freaks, jirts, mod, retro, rockers, thrash, wankers.

Canada is even more diverse than the United States. In 1986, Donald Posterski and Reginald Bibby reported Canadian youth ages fifteen to twenty-four have come from British (37 percent), French (27 percent), and other (36 percent) backgrounds.[8] The intentionally-bilingual culture honors cultural pluralism, making American patterns of youth ministry nearly irrelevant except in pockets of British influence. The 1996 census reported 1,956,115 young people in the fifteen- to nineteen-year-old age bracket. A wave of immigration from Asia and in particular from Hong Kong in preparation for the return of British dependency to the People's

Republic of China in 1997 contributed to the increased diversity of Canadian high schools.

The new pluralism—or more accurately, fragmentation—of the high school society profoundly affected youth ministry in North America. In some places the impact has been coming for a long time. In others, its arrival has been a shock. If the world of teenagers has simply changed, how well are church and parachurch youth ministries adjusting to the change? The jury is still out. In the next few pages I will provide critiques of several youth ministries and their attempts to stay current with the emerging youth culture.

Youth for Christ USA

"I believe we're in a crisis of youth ministry," stated Mike Yaconelli, cofounder of Youth Specialties and resident gadfly of the profession before his untimely death in 2003. "Most of our models of parachurch youth ministries were developed in the 40s, 50s and 60s and are out of touch. When I talk to their staffs they get angry and defensive. I'm sorry. I wish I could say it's a golden age and everything's going great—but it's not. We must focus on how kids really are today—not dwell on what we were or did in the past."[9]

Whether Yaconelli's words were appreciated or not, people within parachurch agencies expressed similar concerns. When Bill Muir returned to Youth for Christ USA to become the vice president of the ministries division in the spring of 1989, he discovered the once-dynamic organization to be "only two or three bricks from becoming a monument." The national staff were holding on to ministry models formulated in the midsixties but without the creative minds at the grassroots level that would enable the organization to constantly renew itself.

The yearly comparison of statistics compiled by the organization suggested that stagnation had beset the once-dynamic movement. A financial crisis following the move of YFC USA offices to Denver, Colorado, forced difficult decisions. Under the leadership of Roger Cross, YFC began a decade-long process of reinventing itself. This resulted in a new leadership team headed by Dan Wolgemuth.

A closer look at the difficulties faced by YFC USA provided a perspective for understanding why changes had to be made. In 1975–76 reports showed 1,021 high school clubs in the United States. The number grew gradually to 1,276 in 1985–86 and then declined to the 1,001 mark in 1987–88. By 1996–97 the number of clubs declined even further to 980. Then as Roger Cross led the organization in a renewal process called Future Search the number of school-based programs began growing again, reaching 1,309 in 2001. The figures for 2006 identify Campus Life as being active on 1,382 campuses. Ministries to at-risk youth and teen parents have seen increased growth recently under a strategy that seeks to tie the mission to key ministry outcomes more than to club meetings or professions of salvation.

It should be noted that the number of junior high clubs increased from 214 in 1985–86 to 585 in 1996–97. A few clubs were even reported in elementary schools (eighty in 1996–97). But overall the target audience in the club picture appears to be growing younger.

Field staff for Youth for Christ USA showed a similar decline. From a high of 821 during the 1979–80 school year the organization reported the equivalent of 549 club workers, with two part-time staff members counted as one full-time person. Some of the decline reflected the natural attrition that took place when a new leadership team was put in place by the organization. Rev. Dick Wynn followed Jay Kesler as president in 1985 and served six years until a financial crisis and other organizational factors caused him to decline the possibility of another term in office. Under Wynn's leadership the full-time staff (including headquarters staff) reached 887 in 1985–86. That number remained about the same under Roger Cross's leadership beginning in 1992 and continuing until his resignation in 2004.

Youth Guidance ministries of YFC evolved over the years. By the beginning of the twenty-first century Youth Guidance expanded to include Teen Moms and City Life and became known as community-based ministries targeting young people outside the main stream of the high school society. Though the number of young people with whom the staff has contact on a weekly basis doubled between 1980–81 and 1987–88 (4,900 to 10,014), the number of staff members has decreased in that same period (148 to 133), while the number of Youth Guidance programs have increased only slightly (eighty to eighty-eight). With the broader definition of community-based ministries and a surge of revitalization, 713 programs were reported in 2001. Juvenile Justice Ministries and City Life broadened ministry, seeking to blend the teaching of life skills with the Christian gospel for at-risk kids and other urban youth.

Conferences in Washington, DC, and Los Angeles (DC/LA) provided one (actually two or three) of the highest impact Christian conferences available to the youth of America in the late 1990s. Capitalizing on YFC's heritage of providing inspirational training events, which dates back to 1945 at Winona Lake, Indiana, DC/LA attracted over thirty thousand young people annually from the midnineties through the end of the century. Unlike the earlier YFC conventions, speakers and performing groups came from across a spectrum of youth ministry leadership. Most were not products of Youth for Christ. The dual emphasis on evangelism and training students to reach their peers attracted primarily church youth and their friends. In 2006 Youth Specialties began running DC/LA, and in 2008 ownership shifted to Zondervan/Youth Specialties in an attempt to enable YFC to focus on their core ministry.

To what can we attribute the decline in Youth for Christ campus ministry programs? Two primary events come to mind. When Mike Yanconelli and Wayne Rice formed Youth Specialties in 1969 and started the National Youth Workers Convention in 1970, they made available the YFC training and materials to a generation of church-based youth workers who began doing Campus Life in church contexts. Add to this the 1990 Supreme Court ruling (*Mergens v. Westside Community Schools*) upholding the Equal Access Act of 1984, permitting student-led clubs to meet on high school campuses. The decision altered the niche previously filled by some Campus Life clubs and set in motion a movement of student-led Bible clubs based on local leadership. In many ways, Youth for Christ had done its job so well that its niche in the ecology of youth ministry had been taken over by the very people it spawned.

Sensing a changed landscape, Youth for Christ USA moved its national office from Wheaton to Denver and in the process began rebuilding its national leadership team. President Dick Wynn and his colleague Bill Muir proposed investing two million dollars in "Video 390," a high-tech approach to small group ministries. At the same time they worked to establish the new headquarters facility as a national training center for youth ministry with the idea of finding and training one hundred thousand volunteers by the year 2000.

The financial condition of the organization made these dreams impossible. A recession and the consequent failure of a major donor to fulfill a financial commitment essential for the vision left YFC USA essentially bankrupt. The history of YFC repeated itself. Innovations initiated by the national office of YFC once again failed to result in permanent changes in ministry philosophy or direction.

In 1992 YFC USA elected Roger Cross president. For the previous year as interim president, Cross's unenviable responsibility required him to cut a million dollars out of the national budget just to keep the ministry afloat. Innovation ground to a halt, and the midnineties saw most of the organizational energy going into survival tactics while the youth culture drifted away from the movement. Innovation at the grassroots level either dried up or became disconnected from the national leadership.

As the new millennium approached, Cross presented a national strategy to the board of trustees that would double or triple the ministry in the next five years. Though the board bought the vision, the field staff, whose responsibility it was to implement the plan, did not. The crisis continued.

Recognizing that his leadership style worked better as consensus builder than prophetic visionary, Cross reversed his tactics. He accepted the distinct possibility that without major changes YFC would die, possibly with him at the helm, and he proposed a total reassessment of the movement. Dubbed "Future Search," the process began in August 1999 and brought together a wide cross-section of field staff to begin dreaming about what a new YFC could look like. For three days thirty-nine leaders representing the diversity of the movement's leadership asked, "What does Christ want YFC to be in the twenty-first century?" The five-step process they used sought to create a vision and consensus for reviving Youth for Christ USA.

Out of that, ten themes emerged that the group felt were important for the future. The themes, however, spoke to the hurt and distrust within the organization more than they painted a vision of a desired future.[10]

Cross then went on the road for three months, held fourteen twenty-four-hour regional forums around the country, had five to six hundred staff at those forums, and laid out these ten themes. Four additional themes emerged in these forums, suggesting lively input from the field. Yet the additional themes suggested continued mistrust of the national service center in Denver.[11] At the heart of the feedback from the regional forums appeared to be deep questions about money. Since fees paid by local programs funded the national office in Denver, the statement being made was that they were not getting their money's worth and felt powerless to do anything about it.

The process was not easy. People felt threatened and field staff read power issues into the process. Trust had yet to be rebuilt, but Cross persisted. The process, projected to be completed by January 2001, stretched into 2003 before a national consensus began to come together. At the midwinter Convention, a "Grand Goal" was adopted by the staff:

> With God's help and direction, we seek to engage 5,000,000 young people by the year 2010 in a lifetime journey to follow Christ. To do this, we will need to:
> 1. Pursue young people everywhere, especially the hard to reach.
> 2. Reach young people through 5,000 schools and community ministry sites.
> 3. Grow the ministry to 300 strategic towns and cities.
> 4. Resource and connect staff, churches, and community leaders.
> 5. Multiply our efforts through strategic partnerships with churches, kingdom organizations, and the worldwide movement of YFC.
> 6. Equip 300,000 young Christian leaders in evangelism and discipleship.
> 7. Create higher levels of organizational innovation and excellence.[12]

As the Future Search process moved forward YFC grew only slightly and continued to deal with financial challenges at the national level. The aftermath of the attack by Muslim extremists on September 11, 2001, and an intentional shift of DC/LA 2003 from evangelism to the exclusive training of students to do three-story evangelism (your story, my story, His story) further challenged the financial stability of the organization when attendance failed to reach even minimal expectations. The ethos of the organization appeared to shift toward an empowered grassroots movement being supported by the national service center in Denver. Yet, with this grand goal in place, Roger Cross resigned as president in 2004. On April 1, 2005, Dan Wolgemuth took the reigns of Youth for Christ USA. But whether the movement can reinvent itself remains to be seen.

Young Life

In the 1990s, for the first time in its history Young Life selected a president from outside the movement. In July 1993 Denny Rydberg assumed leadership of the fifty-two-year-old mission and with deliberate speed put into place three changes that would reshape the movement by the end of the decade. The organization Rydberg inherited was static but not especially healthy.

Upon his arrival, Rydberg found a mission with surprising consistency in staff effectiveness, plagued with islands of mediocrity, and experiencing an underlying climate of tension. During his first two and a half years, the new president addressed a variety of organizational health issues through a vigorous schedule of communication (written and in person), restructuring organizational systems and capturing the ethos of movement. At the same time he began reengineering the mission, starting the development of a well-focused leadership team.

Under Rydberg's guidance, the leadership team developed a ten-year plan, officially introduced at the 1996 All-Staff Conference in Orlando, Florida. The plan called for Young Life to move from 6 percent of the adolescent communities in the nation to 25 percent. That is a growth from fifteen hundred to sixty-four hundred clubs, a growth of over 400 percent, and it included twelve target communities underserved by Young Life. In order to make the growth possible Young Life would have to double the number of full-time field staff and quadruple the number of volunteer workers. The centrality of camp in the Young Life ministry approach required the mission to more than double its capacity of camping facilities, targeting one hundred thousand campers by the summer of 2006.[13]

For the mission to achieve these goals, a strategy called Recruit, Train, Deploy (RTD), which was begun in 1994 and implemented the following year, decentralized, focused, and expanded personnel work. Staff recruited staff, while volunteers recruited volunteers and committee people recruited more committee people. An expanded two-year training program required all new staff to take nine courses, five of which were provided at staff conferences, two in the field, and two through regional colleges and seminaries. All could be taken for academic credit. In his report to the board of trustees in November 1997, Rydberg reported a 34 percent increase in deployed staff in the two years since the start of RTD, and a 48 percent increase in the past three years.[14]

Through the RTD process, Young Life identified twelve target locations for the deployment of youth workers and the establishment of ministries. Rather than waiting for new areas to open up as they always had, Rydberg's team determined to identify underserved communities and find a way to innovate ministry. In 1996 they announced twelve locations. The target communities include: Boston, Southern California, Detroit Metro, Inner Mountain Rural, Ohio Valley, Valley in Texas, Long Island, Southwest Hispanic, Broward and Dade Counties in Florida, Arkansas and Mississippi Delta, fifty international schools, and twenty European countries of sizable populations.[15]

Young Life's niche in reaching young people for Christ was a bit more secure than that of Youth for Christ, primarily due to their youth ministry resorts, yet the mission appeared to have reached a plateau when Rydberg arrived. Statistics alone do not tell a story, but the annual reports of Young Life over the decade from 1978 to 1987 demonstrate a lack of momentum. The organization remained relatively stable in three areas: professional staff (479 vs. 476), volunteer staff (6,368 vs. 6,076), and the number of clubs (1,003 vs. 1,042). The only areas of fluctuation were in camp attendance, which was up (16,729 to 19,269), and average club attendance, which was down slightly (53 to 49). Factors such as these prompted one veteran regional director to suggest that the movement suspend all ministries during its fiftieth anniversary year (1991) and rethink its entire mission. Though the plea was ignored the suggestion made its point.

Under Rydberg and the implementation of RTD, changes were dramatic. As John Miller, one of the Young Life pioneers, exaggerated at the turn of the millennium, "Young Life [has grown] more in the last five years than it has in the last 50."[16] Yet the exaggeration was substantially true. The 1997–98 annual report showed 1,043 full-time US and international field staff, 10,374 volunteer leaders, 1,595 clubs or equivalents plus 357 junior high clubs, with 26,780 high schoolers attending camp. Two years later Denny Rydberg reported 3,200 full-time US and international field staff, 22,890 adult volunteers, 2,876 outreach locations (formerly called clubs), with 32,662 high school kids and 6,673 WyldLifers (a total of 39,335 teenagers) attending camp. Twenty camps and numerous alternative sites accommodated the growing numbers of teenage lives being touched by the ministry of Young Life. At the 2004 All Staff Conference, Rydberg reported that as best they could determine, Young Life had touched the lives of a million kids during the previous year.

Then midway through the first decade of the twenty-first century, Young Life's full-time staff growth leveled out and became essentially static while other ministry indices increased modestly. The 2007 report of ministry statistics reported 3,180 full-time staff, 28,159 US volunteers, 4,016 US schools/ministries (outreach locations), with 33,888 high schoolers and 12,508 WyldLifers (a total of 46,396 teenagers[17]) attending camp. The Capernaum Project, ministering to physically and mentally challenged teenagers in 110 locations; the Young*Lives* ministry, supporting teen moms in sixty-two locations; Multicultural Young Life, serving urban teenagers in 698 cities; and Small Town/Rural Young Life, serving single high schools in 831 towns with populations under twenty-five thousand were significant departures into underserved teenage populations and resulted in Young Life's growth primarily being in these new venues.[18]

The reinvention of Young Life resulted from a decision by the board of trustees to select a president from outside the movement and to support the new president as he guided and at times dragged the mission through a revamping process. Meanwhile the world changed. As Young Life returned to the basics with new personnel and facilities, teenagers themselves had changed. Relational youth ministry, done within the context of modernity, continued to appeal to some young people, but the growth of nonlinear thinking shaped by cable television, the Internet, cell phones, and MP3 players may force Young Life to rethink their essential assumptions about youth ministry again.

Staff members changed also. In 2008, second-generation Young Life staff member Jeff McSwain directed the Durham and Chapel Hill Young Life programs until he circulated a paper that called into question the manner in which the gospel was presented at Young Life camps and in clubs. In response, Young Life President Rydberg issued a paper entitled the "Non-Negotiables of Young Life's Gospel Proclamation." When McSwain refused to sign the hastily drawn up document, he and his staff were terminated. While ripples flowed through the movement, Young Life continued with about the same number of staff they had reported four years earlier.

What is yet to be determined is if the innovative changes of the past decade and the relational adjustments necessary to engage the current generation can be sustained by Young Life's financial base.

Fellowship of Christian Athletes

Fellowship of Christian Athletes, founded in 1954, quietly grew to be the most widespread evangelical presence on high school campuses in the United States. At the end of the decade of the eighties, FCA had regular contact with students on more campuses than the next three largest parachurch youth ministries combined (Student Venture—the high school division of Campus Crusade for Christ, Young Life, and Youth for Christ). In the decade-ending annual report in 1990, FCA reported 4,134 huddle groups scattered across 18 percent of the secondary schools in the United States.

Growth continued throughout the nineties with 7,160 officially sanctioned huddles reported in 1998 and 7,790 in 2003, but then dropped to 6,830 in 2007. Despite a financial crisis and a change of leadership in the national office in the 1993 school year, field staff numbers continued to grow from 191 in 1988 to 484 in 1998 and 580 in 2007. FCA-sponsored camps similarly increased from 6,778 campers at thirty-four summer camps in 1988 to 16,011 campers during 159 weeks of camp at seventy-six sites in 1998, and 42,001 at 240 summer camps in 2007. FCA remains the largest and most visible national Christian presence on the high school campus in America.

"One Way 2 Play—Drug Free" was one of the most visible aspects of FCA. Begun in 1991, the program tied together three cords to enable students to live a drug-free lifestyle: faith in Jesus Christ, commitment to say no to alcohol and other drugs, and accountability to one other person. Using the huddle group structure to facilitate the triple accountability, over one hundred thousand students signed commitment cards to live drug free as of the 1999 school year, but the numbers dropped to 67,462 in 2003 and 46,401 in 2007. In its early stages, this faith-based drug prevention method was viewed as such an effective tool that Barry R. McCaffery, President Bill Clinton's drug czar, named Carey Casey, the program's director, to the board of the National Drug Prevention League.[19]

The strength of the organization has been a dedicated core of volunteer huddle-group leaders who invest their spare time in the lives of student athletes. The link was a natural one. Coaches or people connected with high school athletic programs invited male and female jocks to participate in a group meeting where the "language" of sports is mixed with the Word of God. Though one need not be a member of a team to participate, the "language" was understood. Volunteerism appeared to have peaked in 1994 when 27,634 teammates helped lead huddle groups. While the increase in field staff enabled a better ratio to teammates, the number of volunteers fell throughout the remainder of the decade, suggesting some deficiencies in how volunteers were nurtured by FCA personnel.[20]

Like Youth for Christ and Young Life, Fellowship of Christian Athletes changed leadership during the eighties and again in the nineties. Richard F. Abel assumed the reigns of leadership from John Erickson in 1988 and proclaimed FCA to be the best-kept secret in America. The key to this secret was lay volunteers. The organization did not need to be highly visible in order to pay staff members to work on a particular campus because willing workers were already in place. The natural relationship between huddle-group leader and student, most frequently established on the playing field, enabled the adult leader to be aware of the issues that needed to be addressed. Huddle group talks reflected these insights.

In 1992 a financial crisis in the home office led to major staff cutbacks. The national office owed over three million dollars to field staff accounts, resulting in a crisis of confidence in the leadership. Dramatic steps reduced the internal debt to just over two million dollars by the end of the fiscal year. Nothing illegal was exposed, yet Abel wisely stepped aside and Dal Shealy assumed responsibility for leading FCA. By 1995 the debt was repaid, a new national leadership team was in place, and the home office in Kansas City was viewed by field staff as the national service center.

Like the president of Youth for Christ, Dal Shealy's role focused on reestablishing financial stability and public confidence in the fellowship. Responsibility for reengineering FCA rested on the shoulders of the staff and primarily Chief of Staff Kevin Harlan. The challenge was significant. With FCA huddles still increasing in number, the illusion that similar efforts would produce similar results may have stymied significant change. According to Harlan, FCA was growing most rapidly in rural America. This was good in two ways. Almost half of the high schools in America were located in rural communities, and few other parachurch agencies had made these smaller high schools a priority. FCA had an open field before them.

In addition, diversity issues growing prominent in urban and suburban areas were less of a concern in rural America. Sports teams still tended to be the kings and queens there. Thus, huddles could still use many of the traditional program activities pioneered by Young Life and Youth for Christ but only appearing in the *The Play Book: The Handbook for FCA Leaders* in the midnineties.

Like every youth ministry organization, weaknesses existed within FCA. It was a grassroots movement that gained its credibility from what local sportsmen and women did at the local level. The national office existed to facilitate ministry through volunteers. As Kevin Harlan saw it, the huddle leader and the student leader were the customers of the national office. The influence of the national office was measured by the services it provided. This tended to make the national office product driven. Program materials (including *One Way 2 Play—Drug Free*) and FCA team gear dominated product catalogs.

The FCA tension between *learning* culture and *doing* culture continued. FCA struggled to learn what coaching meant when applied to training huddle coaches. Camps were a severely underused tool for teaching huddle leaders. The "model huddle" idea used at camps wisely provided "training by demonstration," but nothing formal. If not in all camps, at least the leadership camps needed to spend as much time on teaching huddle-group leaders how to train students in spiritual and character disciplines as sports camps spent teaching athletic skills.

At the core of what FCA had to offer was an integrated view of the athlete as a person. Without careful leadership training, huddle-group leaders merely "stuck" Jesus onto their lives like buckeyes on an Ohio State helmet. Student athletes and coaches needed to learn that their significance comes not from their performance (on or off the field) but from who they are in the presence of God through Jesus Christ. Like champion athletes, ultimate success came not from the will to win, but from the will to practice to win. It was of urgent importance that FCA identify the drills that assist in character development and Christian spirituality and then begin training huddle leaders to incorporate these drills into their huddle groups.

Quality control remained the most pressing issue. Recruitment of field staff was still hit-or-miss. There remained little meaningful contact between volunteers and the local or regional professional staff. In 1988 the 3,961 huddle groups were supervised by 191 field staff, a ratio of twenty-one groups per staff member. By 1999 the ratio fell to seventeen huddle groups per field staff member (7,180 huddles to 484 field staff). In 2007 the ratio improved to about twelve huddles per field staff member (6,803 huddles to 581 field staff). Yet a majority of the field staff member's time went into area or regional activities rather than the development of lay leaders. The result was an uneven quality of huddle groups. Christian concepts may have been swallowed up in cultural interpretations of Christian living. In some places the gospel of success functionally replaced the concept of salvation by faith in Christ.

Following its fiftieth year celebrations, Veteran NFL coach Les Steckel became the seventh president and CEO of the Fellowship of Christian Athletes on March 1, 2005. Like the other parachurch youth ministries, the FCA national service center in Kansas City faces financial challenges and will be hard-pressed to develop field staff and volunteers as they seek to be a Christian presence contributing to the Christian nurture of student athletes and their friends as their athletic loves become a pathway for discovering God's presence in their lives.

Conclusion

As a new generation of youth ministry unfolded, most of the major players from the twentieth century seriously sought to reinvent themselves to renew their ministry to high school students. As in the Sondheim musical, they were eager to launch into the "woods." Although convinced that the Narration remained unchanged, their individual narrations were losing traction. For the most part, ministries that employed youth specialists remained locked within the white economic middle class. Agencies attempting to reach the entire student population with a single strategy ceased to grow. Churches and parachurch agencies that empowered leaders to identify niches of ministry and bring Christ to those within those niches struggled but were headed in an appropriate direction. Statistics suggest that each agency carved out a niche for ministry and settled within the safety of that stratum in the ecology of the youth culture.

Though the church had increased its participation in responsible evangelization of adolescents, the evangelistic inroad to the current generation had produced a negative growth factor. Even where the combination of church and parachurch agencies had been able to keep up with the increasing population of the public high school, conversions remained primarily within a homogeneous grouping compatible with the values of the Protestant church. Urban dwellers and minorities, though receiving increased attention, had been overlooked, as had the students on the fringes of the high school society in suburban and rural communities.

Parachurch youth ministries appeared to hold their own but lost market share. To maintain, in the current climate, was to fall behind. Each organization exerted major efforts to respond to the changing demographics and increased pluralism of the youth culture, yet the very assumptions upon which each major ministry was founded had changed and the adjustments made in response were slow in coming.

There is little doubt that the major parachurch youth ministries will continue to have significant ministries to America's youth for the foreseeable future. The financial stresses at the end of the first decade of the twenty-first century will no doubt force a retrenching of ministry strategies, but core strategies are so well established that few changes should be expected.

Reinventing youth ministry now may have passed back to local churches. The call for innovation from academics who provide training for the rising generation of youth workers may be voiced in the wrong places. No significant innovation in Protestant youth ministry has arisen out of seminaries or colleges. The jazz of youth ministry has always sprung from the streets, homes, and churches where youth workers have engaged a new generation of young people.

15

Mr. Holland's Opus

The Legacy of Youth Ministry

lenn Holland loved music and deeply desired to compose a musical piece of lasting significance. In the 1995 movie *Mr. Holland's Opus* the musician takes a job as a high school teacher in order to pay the bills but gradually discovers how little time he has to pursue his passion. Gradually he realizes the truth of the phrase from a Beatles' song, "Life is what happens to you while you are busy making other plans."

Initially his ambition to compose music causes Holland to view teaching as merely a job, and he is frustrated by the challenges he faces in the classroom, but over time he becomes both an excellent teacher and mentor to students. His life is further complicated at home when he discovers that his son is deaf and cannot enjoy his musical passion. The movie traces the emergence of the impact Holland has both in the classroom and at home.

The movie concludes at the climax of a thirty-year teaching career with a high school auditorium of former students, colleagues, and family honoring the retiring teacher for the impact he had on their lives. They were in fact Holland's opus. They were his legacy.

As youth ministry enters the second decade of the twenty-first century, youth workers are discovering a legacy they have left behind. In this closing chapter I will focus on that legacy.

Professionalization of Youth Ministry

The professionalization of youth ministry began with Young Life. Though early Sunday school teachers and Sunday school missionaries had been paid and YMCA workers received modest salaries, for the most part youth ministry was a volunteer-led operation until the middle of the twentieth century.

So adamant was Francis E. Clark that Christian Endeavor remain in the hands of volunteers that he made it a condition of his employment as the first president of the organization he founded. Publishing resource materials funded both Christian Endeavor and many of the denominational officials who contributed to the growth and spread of Protestant youth ministries in America.

When Youth for Christ burst on the scene a few years after Young Life, the organization quickly built poorly paid professional staffs brimming with passion to reach teenagers with the good news of Jesus Christ. As churches began to feel the need to respond to the challenges of the post-war baby boom, youth directors were employed by local churches and youth ministry began to move toward professionalization. By the midsixties, many churches dropped the youth director nomenclature in favor of youth pastor or youth minister. Ordination of this new class of clergy followed.

By the seventies, the early crop of church-based youth workers had begun to age (at least in youth ministry terms) as had the Young Life and Youth for Christ staff before them. Churches tended to treat even the most successful youth ministers as novice adults and expected them to soon grow out of this fun-and-games period of their lives and move on to their life's work. Youth ministers reacted against this criticism, though, because many of them saw their ministry as a lifelong calling and not just a first stage in ministry.

An article on the professionalization of youth ministry in *Christian Education Journal*, along with its rejoinders, articulated the argument. On one side certain youth ministers saw youth ministry like the law, medical, and educational professions where professional standards controlled the practice. The other side suggested that youth ministry was like professional athletics where performance waned as one aged and people were expected to move on to coaching or other professions associated with their sport.[1]

Some youth ministers remained in primary youth ministry working directly with kids, but most moved on to other careers. In the late seventies, as Bible colleges, Christian liberal arts colleges, and seminaries recognized that students would like academic preparation for youth ministry, educational institutions turned to some of these "aging" youth ministers to teach classes and develop majors and programs in various aspects of youth ministry. Most of these instructors found it desirable and necessary to earn a terminal academic degree in order to remain within the academic fraternity.

For the most part these academic programs grew out of the Christian Education programs of schools. The National Association of Professors of Christian Education (NAPCE, later renamed North American Association of Professors of Christian Education) provided a forum for youth ministry professors to gather and hone the knowledge and skills of youth ministry education.

Youth ministry majors proliferated in the eighties and nineties. The next step was to initiate a professional organization dedicated to the field of youth ministry education. Mark Cannister reported:

> In the spring of 1994, *Youthworker Journal* published an article by Dennis "Tiger" McLuen, Bethel and Luther Seminaries, that featured profiles of colleges and graduate schools which offered youth ministries majors. Intrigued by the article and the growth of the youth ministry professors networking group at the NAPCE conferences, Ken Garland, teaching at the time at Talbot School of Theology, took it upon himself to call for a gathering of youth ministry educators which quickly became the Association of Youth Ministry Educators (AYME). Since the 1994 NAPCE Conference was to be held in Southern California, Ken wrote all of the people that he knew from NAPCE and the *Youthworker Journal* article who were teaching youth ministry and personally invited them to participate in a youth ministry education symposium to be held at the Talbot School of Theology in October 1994, two days prior to the NAPCE Conference.[2]

By the end of the first decade of the twenty-first century the association had a membership of 176 and published a refereed journal, the *Journal of Youth Ministry*. Along with this came a proliferation of books addressing aspects of the field of youth ministry. Introductory books were highly redundant, with professors needing to publish and a variety of publishers wanting to get their foot in the market.[3] As one critic suggested, there was really only one book published, just with different authors.

Among the youth ministry educators a debate developed as to whether youth ministry should remain within the field of Christian education or take on the character of pastoral theology. While the former consisted mostly of evangelical schools and the latter, those associated with mainline denominations, the discussion proved to be a very healthy process of examining the essential nature of youth ministry. Far from the instinctive responses by Protestant church leaders over the "youth problem" in their individual churches, youth ministry had become both an academic and a theological discipline.

Nonformal Youth Ministry Training

While many youth ministers chose the route of academia to train youth workers and perpetuate their legacies, an alternative route to developing youth ministry skills also developed. This was accomplished through training seminars. The decade of the eighties may have been the time when the torch was passed from parachurch agencies to local church ministries. It was also in the eighties that several nonformal training programs developed. Even as colleges and seminaries wrestled with youth ministry preparation as an academic discipline, far more people were entering the profession of youth ministry without formal training and being developed through self-directed learning that involved networking and seminars.

National Network of Youth Ministries

As the National Network of Youth Ministries expanded (see chapter 12), its mission came into focus. While networking was at the heart of what was happening, Paul Fleischmann, writing in the summer of 1986, outlined five key goals that had emerged from these gatherings: encouraging each other to develop spiritually, sharpening each other's skills in evangelism and discipleship of youth, implementing strategies to expose every student of every community to the Christian gospel, providing resources that would enable youth workers to "persevere for a lifetime," and organizing locally to reproduce models of evangelism and discipleship.[4]

By the winter of 2004, *Network Magazine* listed thirteen thousand network members who annually signed the NNYM covenant that reflected the key goals outlined by Fleischmann in 1986.[5] A year later the number of networks in the United States was reported at 560 with an additional fifty-seven internationally.[6]

The vision of establishing a ministry to every campus in America by the year 2000 came to be the focal point of NNYM. In 1996, at a gathering of eight thousand youth workers in Atlanta's Georgia Dome, the vision came to be called Challenge 2000 and targeted fifty-six thousand high schools, middle schools, and junior high schools in the United States and Canada, calling for a "measurable presence" on each of these campuses.[7] This effort resulted in a significant increase in evangelization of teenagers on the campuses that were adopted by church and parachurch agencies.[8] In 2001 NNYM reported, "We can now count more than 35,000 of the 56,000 public and private schools as 'adopted for Christ' by local efforts."[9]

Networks started rather naturally as community groupings of youth workers. As they spread, national leaders saw gaps in the manner in which groups of teenagers were being touched by the gospel. An adaptation of the networking idea came at the 1995 forum when a group described as "Dream Team" initiated the idea of other types of networks sparking follow-up action and ongoing initiatives. The networks envisioned by the "Dream Team" were then labeled Affinity Networks in 2000. Doug Tegner, National Coordinator of the Challenge Alliance, explored the issue further and found pockets of people claiming "Our kids are so different" that the networks from the dominant culture were simply irrelevant to their ministries.[10] In the Fall of 2006 NNYM reported Affinity Networks for middle school, youth missions, Native Youth, Rural, Urban Networks, Youth Ministry Women, and Youth Transition (dealing with "loss of faith" after high school).[11] This spirit of cooperation spread beyond affinity groups formed within NNYM to promote community-based services for teenagers such as Big Brothers and Sisters of America, Communities in Schools, and the National Mentoring Center.[12]

Modeling their spirit of networking in the context of the evangelism and discipleship of teenagers, NNYM promoted two movements that began in Southern Baptist circles. The most visible networking function promoted by NNYM was See You at the Pole, which drew three million students to the flagpoles in front of their schools in late September each year. The purpose was to pray that God would show up in a special way in their schools.[13] True Love Waits was present but less visible in NNYM as they asked students to pledge chastity until marriage. Other nationally featured networking events included Fields of Faith, an evangelistic outreach once a year on school athletic fields pioneered by Fellowship of Christian Athletes' Jeff Martin.[14] The student-initiated Revival Generation, which was the dream of high schooler Josh Weidmann, linked students in much the same spirit as NNYM.[15]

Networking became both youth ministry training and youth ministry survival for many youth workers. Evangelization and discipleship of youth remained the focal point of NNYM even as the organization adjusted to changing conditions in youth culture. While the value of networking remained the guiding vision of the organization, the constant turnover of youth workers at the grassroots level has made the ideal stronger than the actual delivery of ministry to youth.[16] But that may be as much the nature of networking in general as it is in NNYM. Like in the previous cycles, youth ministry appeared once again to be the healthiest and most effective when youth workers joined hands to achieve common goals.

Sonlife Ministries

Sonlife Ministries, founded by Dann Spader in 1979, had a vision for promoting a biblical youth ministry that would result in discipling and evangelizing students through church youth ministries. With the dream of assisting ten thousand youth ministries to adopt the strategy and model ministries in a thousand communities with five hundred active resource people servicing them, Spader forged a relationship with Moody Bible Institute's extension department and began providing training seminars across the nation.[17]

The core of Sonlife training expressed disciplemaking ministry as a four-stage process that Dann Spader gleaned from his chronological study of the life of Christ. To be effective in doing youth ministry, Spader proposed four sequential steps from Christ's ministry. *Building* teenagers in their love relationship with Jesus and his church established the ministry direction. *Equipping* people with skills for caring for peers moved the youth ministry beyond fun and games. *Winning* peers to Christ extended the influence of a youth ministry beyond the walls of the church building. Finally, *multiplying* prepared mature leaders (teen and adult) to reproduce themselves and thus extend the influence of the ministry.

By focusing on what Spader called a "Great Commission mind-set," youth ministries could be freed from program orientation and reoriented to specific characteristics of Christian living and service. Instead of expending the energy of youth pastors and volunteers on activities designed to be attractive and fun for even the nominal Christian and nonbeliever, Sonlife trained youth workers to become intentional about training students to follow the Great Commandment and engage in the Great Commission among peers, especially from school. The Sonlife training had many of the features of a well thought-out curriculum theory. While youth leaders needed to contextualize the strategy, youth ministry in local churches took on a scope and sequence in harmony with evangelical understandings of the Bible.

From its initial training of twenty-nine youth workers in 1980, the training multiplied. By the end of ten years, Sonlife reported that a cumulative total of 14,331 had received Sonlife training, with 3,864 leaders attending in 1989. Ten years later the total receiving Youth Strategy or Advanced Training from 1980 to 1999 mushroomed to 58,123 but the number trained in 1999 remained on par with 1989 at 3,932. Training enrollment peaked in 1992 with 5,075 and gradually decreased to 3,607 in 2002. For the most part these were church people who were either novices in youth ministry (lay and professional) or were receiving advanced training within the Sonlife system.

A close look at the products of the Sonlife system gave Spader and youth workers cause for concern. A survey was taken in 1986 of fifty people who had taken the Sonlife Advanced Training. The churches surveyed averaged 577 in attendance on Sunday morning. Though the youth workers reported an average of eleven volunteers working with them, they averaged only seven conversions to Christ per church per year. This was admittedly better than most youth ministries in the nation but by no means a tidal wave of response. The question could be asked, "Did this represent what Sonlife had in mind when seeking to establish a Great Commission mind-set?"

A similar Sonlife survey conducted in 1989 received eighty-nine responses. Though church attendance was slightly higher and the average number of volunteer workers was lower, the average number of conversions per church per year was only up to nine. These conversion figures were slightly lower than the numbers reported by Youth for Christ for the same periods—eight conversions per club in 1985–86 and twelve per club in 1987–88.

To address this problem and complement this training of adults, Sonlife created Students Equipped to Minister to their Peers (SEMP). Initially called the Sonlife Evangelism and Missions Conference, the ministry began directly training high school students to share their faith. From an initial 140 in 1986, SEMP grew to 7,226 teenagers in 1999 with a cumulative total of 30,460 having received SEMP training.

In its first ten years, eleven evangelical denominations had affirmed the Sonlife training system and had established a working relationship with Spader's organization.[18] By the close of the century the number grew to seventeen, and twenty-seven denominations pointed their youth leadership to Sonlife as a primary training tool. The idea of training youth workers within a church-based structure differed from providing program materials as denominations had done historically, or as independent youth-oriented publishers such as Youth Specialties and Group Publishing were doing currently. The strategy also varied from the earlier approach of creating new parachurch agencies that worked directly with pre-Christian young people, as Youth for Christ, Young Life, and Fellowship of Christian Athletes had done at midcentury.

As Sonlife approached its twenty-fifth anniversary, two factors converged calling for a rethinking of Spader's approach to discipleship training. As Sonlife's influence expanded within North America, people trained by Spader's organization took the ministry training materials to international settings, first in Australia and Eastern Europe, then expanding to forty-seven countries by the end of the twentieth century. As trainers prepared for working in non-North American settings, modifications had to be made to the materials and training. As missionaries had discovered for centuries, Western concepts of Christianity had to be contextualized.

The growth of the postmodern environment in North America similarly called for modifications in the Sonlife training. With Spader's blessing, work began under the leadership of staffers Dave Livermore and Steve Argue to update the training process. The revision, however, called into question Spader's core claim that the four stage process was "the strategy of Jesus." To Livermore and Argue, the strategy was more a product of modernity than of exegesis and as such was open for revision. Unconvinced, Spader pushed back, calling for incorporation of his core ideas into any strategic revisions.

With revisions seemingly at an impasse, Livermore and Argue, along with North American Director of Student Ministries Bill Clem, resigned from Sonlife. At question appeared to be the issue of contextualization. If in fact the Sonlife strategy was the strategy of Jesus, it could not and should not be changed. But if the Sonlife strategy was a modern paradigm supported by biblical ideas taken from the life of Christ, the training would not fare well as postmodernity increased influence on teenagers.

Dave Livermore was replaced as president by Chris Folmsbee, but Sonlife continued to wrestle with the relevance of the classic Sonlife model of training. Folmsbee, like his predecessors, saw a need to address the changing environment of the youth culture. On September 1, 2007, Sonlife merged with YouthFront of Kansas City, Missouri, the successor of Kansas City's Youth for Christ program, which had pioneered the national club program for YFC in the 1950s. YouthFront, under the leadership of Mike King, was actively reinventing their youth ministry in order to address the issues of the twenty-first century. Both Folmsbee and King sought to address the spirituality of teenagers in a manner that drew upon historic practices of the Christian church. The impact of this merger and its influence in reshaping Protestant youth ministries in America remains to be seen.[19]

Seeker-Driven Church-Based Youth Ministries

Perhaps the best known and most widely imitated church youth group in the 1980s was "Son City" (later called "Student Impact") based in the Willow Creek Community Church.[20] Son City continued the youth ministry begun by Dave Holmbo and Bill Hybels at South Park Church in nearby Park Ridge in 1973. Each Tuesday evening high school students made their way to the church located in South Barrington, Illinois, for competition, team activities, and a powerful program that culminated in an evangelistic or pre-evangelistic message.

Under the leadership of Dan Webster, Son City consistently attracted eight hundred students each week. Though the numbers were impressive, Webster realized that there was a problem. While the church continued to grow, exceeding twelve thousand at Sunday services, the youth ministry had plateaued. It was not merely a matter of demographics (fewer adolescents per capita); Son City had hit a barrier similar to that which hinders the growth of entire churches of a similar size.

Three minor changes were implemented. The name, which sounded more like a cult (Son Moon of the Korean cult called the Moonies) or a retirement community than a youth movement, was changed to Student Impact. Interestingly enough, this was the same name chosen by Youth for Christ in the midsixties when they revised their club program.

An additional person was brought on staff to assist Webster in staff development. "Bo" Boshers's responsibility was to train and disciple the young adults who in turn were to minister to and through student leaders on the thirty or so high school campuses from which Student Impact drew kids. It was a function that had become impossible for Webster to accomplish due to the pressures of preparing the weekly celebration.

Accompanying this second change was the addition of sixteen paid interns who served as team leaders and focused attention on individual high school campuses. Under Boshers's leadership these men made conscious efforts to evangelize and disciple high school students in Chicago's northwest suburbs. The majority of the discipleship training provided for the students focused on "taking their high schools for Christ." Within the first year, attendance at the midweek youth program jumped by nearly 40 percent, averaging over eleven hundred students. The target number under this new strategy was two thousand high school students each meeting and ministry on thirty high school campuses. Shortly thereafter the ministry peeked at sixteen hundred students weekly.

The philosophy of ministry looked very much like a combination of the best of the Youth for Christ rallies from the 1940s and the cream of the Campus Life club strategy from the late sixties. Two questions, however, needed to be addressed. The first was, "Could this approach be duplicated elsewhere?" Though the structure is relatively simple, the financial and leadership demands made the probability of successful clones highly unlikely except in very affluent communities. The second question candidly stated was, "Does it matter if the ministry cannot be duplicated?" The response should be a resounding "No!" Willow Creek's mission was to reach its own community. Other youth workers must discover tactics suited to their unique contexts.

When Webster resigned and began a church in Michigan, Bo Boshers took over the ministry. Building on the foundation established by Don Cousins and Dan Webster, the ministry remained at about sixteen hundred in weekly attendance. A constant emphasis on evangelism drove student leaders and adult interns to invite seeking students to their Tuesday night meeting.

Then tragedy struck. Pete Lampson, one of the most effective college student leaders, and two companions died in an automobile accident en route to California during the summer of 1995. The mission-oriented ministry failed to provide the nurturing structure necessary to support the leaders impacted by the crisis. Internal tension followed. While Willow Creek Community Church continued to grow, surpassing twenty thousand in weekend attendance, Student Impact numbers fell, plateauing well below a thousand and threatening to sink even further.

Leadership changes failed to remedy the decline. Teams and competition no longer proved to be the attraction they once were. A ministry model created for a boomer generation of teenagers no longer appealed to a changing generation of students and leaders. Yet another strategy failed to emerge. Jeff Vander Stelt brought a background in Sonlife training and attempted to respond to a postmodern call for spirituality. He shifted the weekly meeting to worship evangelism but the chemistry failed to reverse the trend. Additional Directors of Student Ministries came and went. Experimentation with a more relational and decentralized strategy followed but a clear direction failed to crystallize. Other ministers to students followed but the nature of youth ministry at Willow Creek had changed, as had the student population.

Willow Creek Association still sponsored well-attended Student Ministries Conferences, while Student Impact remained static and in search of direction. The youth ministry designed for baby boomers in the modern era had not transferred to a generation influenced by a postmodern mind-set. In the spring of 2008, the conference faced into the changing nature of American youth. Naming the conference Shift, the speakers explored Emergent themes applied to youth ministry and sought fresh understandings of adolescent spirituality. Future directions for local church youth ministry remained in doubt.

Purpose Driven Youth Ministry

Doug Fields entered youth ministry in the same way that many of the best youth workers of the 1970s and 1980s did: he volunteered in his home church. Two years later in 1981, he was offered an internship with Jim Burns at South Coast Community Church (now Mariners Church) in

Newport Beach, California, as he completed his undergraduate work at Vanguard University and began studying at Fuller Theological Seminary. Equipped with an infectious smile, an enormous ability to communicate with students, and a load of creativity, Fields took over the reins of the student ministry in 1985.

Southern California in the 1980s was a hot bed of youth ministry. Tic Long, at Youth Specialties, picked up on Fields's giftedness and invited him to become part of a creative team of trainers, including Duffy Robbins, Chap Clark, and Mike Yaconelli, who helped sharpen his thinking and understanding of youth ministry, even though Fields was the only church-based speaker on the team.

The ministry at South Coast Community Church was purpose driven. The purpose, however, was drawn from church growth principles, utilizing a funnel to illustrate how the ministry used large events to attract teenagers into the ministry. Fields taught his ministry team how to help young people move into medium-sized groups in order to find places to fellowship and learn about God and the Bible. His intent was to have each student settled into a small group of six to eight kids who would build mutual accountability for spiritual growth while being "loved-on" by a caring, adult volunteer. The strategy had been adapted from a former youth pastor, Chuck Miller, who had pioneered it at Fourth Presbyterian Church in Washington, DC, before bringing it to Lake Avenue Congregational Church in Pasadena.

In his book *Your Church Can Grow*,[21] C. Peter Wagner called the three parts of the funnel *celebration, congregation,* and *cell.* Adapting the ideas to youth ministry, Chuck Miller, Mike Risley, and others used the *celebration* to replace the Sunday school hour and challenged students to have an impact upon their high schools for Christ. *Congregations* took different forms. Sometimes they were discussion groups on Sunday morning. Others were ministry teams, such as bands, that performed on Sunday morning or at retreats. *Cells* were, for the most part, high school campus–based and were led by adult volunteers.

Fields refined the idea and used the words *expose, equip,* and *experience* to further focus the youth ministry. "*Expose* were our outreach events . . . both large and small. Basically anything that would serve as an 'open door' to unchurched or cultural Christians was incorporated in the ministry to reach these kids. The *Equip* programs included anything with Christian content that led to spiritual formation. This included, but was not limited to, small groups and various kinds of Bible studies. *Experience* were opportunities for kids to actually do ministry; that is, student leadership, ministry teams, campus pastors and such."[22]

In practice, the funnel worked from the bottom up. Small groups were located geographically, usually according to the high schools that the students attended. Some high schools had multiple groups. Many of the small-group leaders were college students, as Fields had been when he entered youth ministry. It was the responsibility of the small-group leader to shepherd his or her little flock of teenagers, helping them both to grow spiritually and to reach out to their peers and bring them into the ministry. Thus it became the collective responsibility of the small groups to increase the size of the top of the funnel.

With success at South Coast Community Church, Fields attracted the attention of Rick Warren at Saddleback Valley Community Church (now Saddleback Church) and in 1992 began fifteen years as youth pastor developing what came to be known as Purpose Driven Youth Ministry.[23] By then the funnel strategy had run its course and the youth ministry of thirty-five kids he inherited allowed Fields to reinvent his ministry from the ground up. His new pastor, Rick Warren, had written a book entitled *The Purpose Driven Church*[24] that simply took the five purposes most churches bury in their constitutions and placed them at center stage in their ministry. In his new ministry Fields found a coherent strategy for being the church and quickly began focusing all the energy of the youth ministry on those five purposes. Based on the Great Commandment (Matt. 22:37–40) and the Great Commission (Matt. 28:19–20), Fields determined that the youth ministry would focus on worship, ministry, evangelization, fellowship, and discipleship.[25]

Actually the funnel did not go away. Fields suggests the funnel is still there in Rick Warren's five concentric circles.[26] The circles are simply a topographical view of the funnel. So instead of three parts of the funnel, there were five: *community, crowd, congregation, committed,* and *core.* With the original funnel process, youth ministers assumed the *community* was the target for the funnel and not a specific part of the ministry. *Crowd* was similar to *expose. Equip* was broken into *congregation/committed* and *experience* was similar to a *core* student.

In a critique of churches that continually increase programs without disciplined purposefulness, Fields suggested that as a church's program commitment increased, attendance would usually decrease. It would be like looking down a funnel from the top end. Essentially Fields created a scope and sequence for the ministry based on purposeful activities tied to the five purposes of the church. While many of the elements appeared to remain the same as employed at South Coast Community Church, they were actually very different. Perhaps the biggest change was that all the kids and staff were not expected to satisfy all five purposes of the youth ministry in every youth ministry function. Biblical purposes were clear. Audiences differed. Though not spoken about, there were many funnels moving kids at various maturity levels to greater maturity in Christ.

Not everything came together all at once. Fields told his new pastor that it would take five years before the church could expect to see the youth ministry produce the desired fruit.[27] Though numbers of students involved increased significantly, it was not until 1995 that the midweek small groups clicked into gear, helping young people to connect with fellow believers, to be cared for and held accountable for their walk with God. These same-sex groups met in homes throughout the community. Led by adults who retained the purpose orientation, each group consciously developed student leaders. It took two more years before discipleship turned into service and a dedicated core of teenagers took on leadership responsibilities and, in turn, multiplied the impact of the ministry.

Though no pledge was used as in the days of Christian Endeavor, the Purpose Driven Youth Ministry sought to develop six spiritual habits in the lives of teenagers. Having seen kids graduate from high school without the ability to grow on their own, the HABITS idea was developed to help kids learn to grow on their own so that when the program was gone (small group) and the person was gone (their leader), they would have developed spiritual habits that would help in their connection with God. The habits included:

Hang time with God through prayer and Bible study
Accountability to another believer
Bible memorization
Involvement with the church body [not just the youth ministry]
Tithing commitment
Study Scripture—this goes beyond just reading the Bible.[28]

To accomplish these outcomes, adult leaders used a series of very well-designed materials and training opportunities to aid students in their spiritual journeys. These journeys differed because not every student started at the same point. For example, those Fields called *core* students were expected to serve peers and beyond. But students didn't necessarily wait until they were recognized as *core* students to begin serving. In fact it may have been service that attracted non-Christians into the ministry in the first place.

The Purpose Driven Youth Ministry, as evidenced by the six habits desired for the life of students, remained rooted in evangelical theology and pietism. Every element of the youth ministry was intentionally tied to the five purposes of the church. The core values placed relationships, both among students and between students and adults, at the heart of the ministry. While the curriculum was clearly defined, the old adage that more is caught than taught remained central to the ministry. As with other Protestant youth ministries, the expectation remained that students would encounter God in a meaningful way during their teenage years at Saddleback Church.

While the growth of the Purpose Driven Youth Ministry at Saddleback remained impressive, reaching over two thousand students weekly, the more significant contribution came from the training that Doug Fields provided for youth ministers, both in North America and beyond. Both Youth Specialties and Group Publishing, who sponsored the largest youth workers' conferences in North America, used Fields and the PDYM as a major training feature late into the first decade of the twenty-first century. Given all of this training plus his Purpose Driven Youth Ministry Student Leadership Conference, which attracted over a thousand student leaders to Saddleback Church, Fields is one of the major trainers of Christian youth workers. When viewing his Web site, which merged with Group Publishing, the nonformal educational influence of PDYM reminds the student of youth ministry history of the publications and conferences provided by Christian Endeavor under the leadership of Francis E. Clark that shaped youth ministry more than a century earlier.

Sustainable Youth Ministry

In 1986, Mark DeVries assumed responsibility for the youth ministry in Nashville's First Presbyterian Church. His eight years of experience equipped him to anticipate success in the church in which he still serves over twenty years later. Yet after the first five years, the ministry languished with very little evidence of the dramatic success in the church where worship services were attended by about a thousand parishioners. The youth ministry declined with only about thirty in weekly attendance.

In an attempt to reinvent youth ministry at First Presbyterian Church, DeVries divided the junior high and senior high ministries by grade levels and over the next eight years each grade level seemed to top out at thirty with an overall attendance of about a hundred and fifty. His efforts at family-based youth ministry helped refocus the ministry a bit but failed to give it the boost that he desired.[29] Other adjustments increased the attendance slightly as the ministry ran at a healthy 20 percent of the worship service attendance.

In the years that followed, DeVries continued to experiment. His book *Family Based Youth Ministry*,[30] first published in 1994, opened up doors for consulting with other churches, many of whom were from mainline Protestant denominations. Invariably what he found in a fairly wide cross-section of churches was that churches wanted to hire their way out of a slumping youth ministry. Churches would hire a youth minister, make virtually no other changes, and expect the youth ministry to turn around.

Gradually DeVries came to realize that what was required to develop sustainable youth ministries was to create and maintain ministry systems. He concluded that two key components were at the heart of sustainable youth ministry: youth ministry architecture and an atmosphere in which the ministry remains healthy.[31] The architecture would provide a ministry building plan that staff and volunteers alike could follow while the atmosphere dealt with matters like trust among leaders, clarity of expectations shared by staff and volunteers, and a sense of ownership shared by all involved. Essentially it was a systems approach to youth ministry requiring transparent and secure Christian leadership.

While not trained in educational or systems theory, Mark DeVries began building both his youth ministry and the youth ministries of churches with whom he consulted, improvising aspects of both. In the process he became an architect for youth ministries. In working with close to a hundred churches, he and a team of consultants began working with each church by doing a three-day assessment that enabled the Youth Ministry Architects to determine what type of ministry each church wanted to build. It really did not matter to DeVries what type or model of youth ministry each church wanted to build. His team responded by creating the blueprints and offering consultations as the ministry was built.

The atmosphere for ministry required community building. Youth minister, senior pastor, students, parents, volunteers, church leaders, and parishioners needed to be on the same page. All stakeholders needed to share the same vision for youth ministry in the church. The mission statement had to have a long-term perspective. Goals needed to be revisited every three years and should reflect a shared understanding of the ministry. Values similarly needed to be explicit so everyone would know where to go for help in times of need. There could be no lone rangers.

More than anything else, DeVries facilitated community among those interested in teenagers. Good youth ministers have always done this. Effective systems flow out of community. But DeVries made the components of the youth ministry system explicit. Sustainable youth ministry, discovered DeVries, consisted of designing an educational plan and assisting churches to remain on the same page as they worked their plan.

Like Fields, DeVries was a trainer. His training, however, came through his consulting work, his books, and his Web site. Calling his ministry Youth Ministry Architects, DeVries recognized that few churches had the financial commitment to hire people who could provide what he called "stable, durable infrastructures." So he and his team consulted with small- to medium-sized mainline denominational churches to facilitate viable youth ministries. Building nonformal educational strategies in conjunction with youth ministry teams in a wide variety of churches, the Youth Ministry Architects aided churches to prepare young people for those times in their adolescent years when God becomes a meaningful part of their lives.

Two Lingering Criticisms

The most strategic criticism of Protestant youth ministry even in the first decade of the twenty-first century was that it remained too white. Since much of the available funding for youth ministry came from the economic middle class, a vast majority of the youth ministry energy remained within the dominant culture. Young Life and Youth for Christ continued their efforts in underserved and ethnically diverse areas. But the history of youth ministry in America suggests that innovation, the jazz of youth ministry, would come from within the various communities of color. Some innovations have happened. Fernando Arzola Jr., writing from his Puerto-Rican American experience in the Mott Haven section of the South Bronx, proposes a holistic form of youth ministry that he calls "prophetic." With transformation as central to his call for action, Arzola calls for ministry that begins from the teenager's experience in the city, followed by a group analysis of the situation, and then uses their faith tradition to establish a course of action. Implementation followed by reflection/evaluation establishes a pattern of youth ministry that grows out of the context and is sustainable by youth ministers in urban America.[32]

Perhaps the dominant theme of the African American community is the hip-hip culture. Efrim Smith and Phil Jackson address the connection between Christianity and the black community by proposing the establishment of hip-hop churches. Based on their experiences with such churches in Minneapolis and Chicago, the African American writers show an appropriately edgy response to their urban cultures. At The House in the Lawndale section of Chicago, this expression of youth ministry uses the four basic components of the hip-hop culture to express the Christian gospel—deejayin', emceeing, breaking, and graffiti. While suburban wannabes come to visit, the expression of youth ministry is growing out of the urban hip-hop culture.[33]

Sam George, speaking for Asian Americans, writes of the "coconut generation," which he describes as tan on the outside and white on the inside. Writing from the context of the Indian experience in America,

George proposes how Asian Indian youth ministry might look within the American experience.[34] Chinese, Japanese, Korean, and Filipino youth workers address similar challenges as they seek to honor their cultures and embrace their Christian faith in America.

Perhaps the most frequently repeated criticism of Protestant youth ministries at the beginning of the twenty-first century was the accusation that they were merely fun and games. Describing the era just prior to the start of Christian Endeavor in 1881, Francis E. Clark said, "That was the era of church entertainments and religious amusements."[35] The perception and the reality in some places was that youth ministries were no longer places to meet God or for that matter even to gain any substantially Christian knowledge or experience. Youth ministries had become a church-based babysitting service for teenagers. The fun activities used to attract young people to youth ministries so that evangelistic appeals or discipleship training could follow became synonymous with an increasing number of youth ministries.

While Char Meredith's story of Young Life was entitled *It's a Sin to Bore a Kid,*[36] the story was missional in nature describing how the movement earned the right to be heard by high school students. Current critics of the fun-and-games approach charge that much of youth ministry has settled for nothing more than entertainment. Mark Yaconelli called this approach "a Nickelodeon approach to youth ministry that seeks to appeal to kids' propensity for fun and recreation."[37] Steve Wright reminds youth workers that "Paul's desire for Timothy was not about fun and games; he wanted to develop him to be grounded and be able to defend his faith."[38]

Two sources made youth ministries vulnerable to the fun-and-games criticism. Despite the fact that the number of Christian colleges and seminaries offering sophisticated majors in youth ministry increased rapidly throughout the second half of the twentieth century, many youth workers entered Christian ministry solely based on their relational skills with teenagers. The lowest common denominator between teens and youth workers was fun. Thus they started there and sometimes did not progress to engaging Christian content, much less experiencing God in their collective experience.

The easy accessibility of programming materials from a wide range of sources both in book, magazine, or subscription form as well as resources accessed over the Internet fed the downgrading of quality of Christian content, leaving youth ministries vulnerable to the criticism of being Christianity-lite. The sad reality was that the quality for some youth ministries whose leaders depended on published materials may have increased as a result of these sources. But for most, the criticism of dumbed-down Christianity applied. The problem was not so much with the publishers as with inexperienced youth leaders.

The second reason the fun-and-games criticism may be true found its roots in the pressure youth ministers felt to generate numbers of students attending youth group functions. In many churches this pressure was tied to expectations of conversions and baptisms. With these relentless pressures in place, youth pastors had to find ways to lure new kids to their youth ministries. A culture of superficiality developed in which entertaining activities predominated while the gospel was watered down to an easy believism and forms of cheap grace. The types of Christian disciples produced in these youth ministries looked like those in John 6:66 who drew back and no longer followed Jesus when the Master expressed the hard sayings about being the bread of life.

The fun-and-games criticism, combined with the conviction that the family (and more specifically the father) should provide spiritual instruction to young people, led to a call by the Family Integrated Movement to eliminate youth ministries as well as Sunday school all together. Closely associated with Christians in the American homeschooling movement, the movement goes beyond Horace Bushnell in returning Christian nurture to the Christian home. For homes where this strategy is employed, a delicate balance is needed with the instructional role of the Christian community as the extended family of God.

The criticism should be tempered a bit. Fun is part of a healthy maturation process. Play is the work children engage in to make sense of their world. Young people need laughter to buffer the challenges of the world around them. Youth ministry without any fun and games would be a dreary place to be. Just as happy families laugh together, youth ministries need opportunities to enjoy life in God's family. For the entire history of Protestant youth ministries in America, fun and games have been part of the mix. The problem comes when they become the dominant features of what youth ministries do.

Conclusion

As a professionalized youth ministry has matured, there is both good and bad news. A plausible argument could be made (but that is another book) that youth ministry in the twentieth century has shaped the Protestant church of the twenty-first century. Especially in newer churches and church movements, the expectation that God will show up is still based on an evangelical interpretation of Scripture and a modified pietism that addresses the new issues current in American culture. That is the good news.

The bad news is that youth ministry in the twentieth century has shaped the Protestant church of the twenty-first century. Many of the flaws of youth ministry in the twentieth century are showing up in a wide variety of churches in the twenty-first century. Doctrinally thin, ethically tolerant, and consumer oriented, many churches have lost their passion for the hard sayings of the Christian gospel.

The time has come for the creativity of youth ministry jazz. Jam sessions are needed at every level, from national service centers to local groups of volunteers. New sounds of ministry are needed. Continued modifications of the current system simply will not keep up with the changes in the world in which we live. Youth ministry has grown conservative, and too many leaders have become protectors of treasured memories. Ownership of property, advanced degrees, and successful youth ministry business ventures have minimized risk-taking and cultivated a desire for respectability.

The open questions that must be faced as youth ministry progresses in the twenty-first century are: who will improvise, and what will the resulting forms of youth ministry look like? Looking at the history of youth ministry enables us to pursue answers to those questions, for history demonstrates that concerned Christians have come to this point not once, but twice before in the short annals of ministry focused on youth.

Epilogue

A
dmittedly there are gaps in the history of Protestant youth ministry in America provided in this book. Christian music, for example, has been a major contributor to the lives of young people. From the time of Jonathan Edwards on, the music found meaningful by young people has contributed both to evangelization and nurture. Songbooks from the juvenile temperance movement, Christian Endeavor, Word of Life, Young Life, and Youth for Christ all witness to the presence of music in youth ministry. With the advent of radio and records, gospel themes presented in musical styles similar to the popular music of the day shaped not only youth ministry but the church of the next generation.

Little has been said about African American youth ministry. More than perhaps any other church's form of youth ministry, the black church has resisted the temptation to place young people in their own little silos. Many reasons may be given and yet the effect is that little documentation is available for the history of ministry to black youth in America. Jon Pahl's chapter "Forging Freedom: African-American Youth Ministries, 1930–Present" provides a useful snapshot of Bethel A. M. E. Church in Baltimore as an excellent start.[1] A similar approach was taken by William R. Myers in *Black and White Styles of Youth Ministry: Two Congregations in America*.[2] But much more attention needs to be given to the issue.

The same can be said about virtually all ethnic Protestant American youth ministries. People from the United Kingdom were early adopters of the forms of youth ministry described in this book, as were most Asian Protestants, many of whom have strong presences in America. Hispanic youth ministry has a shorter history and, due to the family structure and language factors, looks different from that of the dominant culture.

Youth ministry to at-risk kids similarly drew the short straw in the book. While the Sunday school initially targeted this population, including slaves and Native Americans, the stories need further exploration for an objective assessment. The histories of ministries to kids in the juvenile justice system, gangs of all varieties, as well as runaway and throwaway kids are worthy of books of their own.

The impact of parochial schools in providing a place where God shows up is an extremely important part of Christian nurture in certain denominations and movements. In addition, much could be said about families who school their children at home. All of this could be included in Protestant youth ministry, but has received little attention in this book.

Women's issues are virtually absent from the book. Christian camping is nearly ignored. The development of student missionary trips and, before that, service projects, deserves attention. Youth ministry in Pentecostal and charismatic churches barely appears. The young people in urban churches gradually faded from the book in the twentieth century. Church-based club programs, though more focused on children, have significant roles for Christian nurture of youth in some locations.

All of these areas of research and writing are needed to gain a fuller picture of Protestant youth ministry in America. The author would love to see these and other issues addressed in future books on the subject.

So Where Do We Go from Here?

In *The Coming Revolution in Youth Ministry*, I attempted to be a futurist. I was right about one thing—youth ministry was about to change. I have tried to remain in the role of a historian in this book, but as I conclude, I would like to venture several questions for those who would minister to youth in the second decade of the twenty-first century and beyond.

1. Youth ministry in America totally misses close to three quarters of the adolescent population in America. How will Protestant youth ministry change to meet that challenge?
2. Much of youth ministry claims to function as a part of local churches, yet many students have no meaningful relationships with adults outside the youth ministry context. How can the faith community be restructured so that adolescents become vital parts of the Christian fellowship?
3. With its history of pietism in the Protestant tradition, much of youth ministry has become atheological, at least in a formal sense. How can churches systematically train children and youth in the essentials of their faith traditions?

4. With research continuing to show the family as the most important factor in Christian nurture, how should Protestant youth ministry change to better utilize the most natural part of the discipleship process?

5. Historically Protestant youth ministry has been grounded in nonformal educational aspects of the church. For the most part it has assumed that for youth to experience God, they need to have supplementary theological education, with prayer and Bible study considered the essential parts. With so little instruction about the triune God available elsewhere in society, how should youth ministry change?

6. Protestant youth ministry in America has had a mixed history of dealing with social and justice issues. How should these issues be addressed to provide a prophetic voice in society?

7. What can Protestant youth ministry in America learn from other Christians in America and from Christians from other lands?

8. What does Protestant youth ministry contribute to theory of learning?

9. How will Protestant youth ministry relate to classic Christian spirituality?

10. Where does youth ministry find its theological grounding?

Notes

Series Preface

1. James W. Fowler, *Faith Development and Pastoral Care* (Minneapolis: Fortress, 1987), 17.
2. Scott Cormode, "Constructing Faithful Action," *Journal of Religious Leadership* 3 (1/2), (Spring/Fall 2004): 267.

Chapter 1 *Newsies*

1. Joesph F. Kett, *Rites of Passage: Adolescence in America 1790 to the Present* (New York: Basic Books, 1977), 3–7.
2. Robert H. Bremner, ed., *Children and Youth in America: A Documentary History*, vol. 1, *1600–1865* (Cambridge, MA: Harvard University Press, 1970), vii.
3. Kett, *Rites of Passage*, 38.
4. Thomas Hine, *The Rise and Fall of the American Teenager* (New York: Perennial, 2000), 59.
5. Bremner, *Children and Youth*, 1:69, 818.
6. Ibid., 20–21.
7. Walter Isaacson, *Benjamin Franklin: An American Life* (New York: Simon and Schuster, 2004).
8. Eugene Francis Clark, *A Son's Portrait of Dr. Francis E. Clark* (Boston: Williston, 1930), 3–20.
9. William Revell Moody, *Life of D. L. Moody* (New York: Macmillan, 1930).
10. Gerald L. Gutek, *Education and Schooling in America* (Englewood Cliffs, NJ: Prentice-Hall, 1983), 15.
11. Ibid., 17; H. Warren Button and Eugene F. Provenzo Jr., *History of Education and Culture in America* (Englewood Cliffs, NJ: Prentice-Hall, 1983), 31–33.
12. Bremner, *Children and Youth*, 1:5, 23–26.
13. Ibid., 172–74.
14. Gutek, *Education and Schooling*, 13–14; Button and Provenzo, *History of Education*, 34–36.
15. Bremner, *Children and Youth*, 1:89.
16. Button and Provenzo, *History of Education*, 37–38.
17. Bremner, *Children and Youth*, 1:6–9.
18. Ibid., 9; also see Hine, *Rise and Fall*, 60–61.
19. Bremner, *Children and Youth*, 1:330–35. For a survey of the African experience in America, see Lerone Bennett Jr., *Before the Mayflower: A History of Black America*

(Chicago: Johnson, 2003); Edgar A. Toppin, *A Biographical History of Blacks in America Since 1528* (New York: David McKay, 1971).

20. Walter Edgar, *South Carolina: A History* (Columbia: University of South Carolina Press, 1998), 102.

21. Button and Provenzo, *History of Education*, 52.

22. Ibid., 77–82; David B. Tyack, *Turning Points in American Educational History* (New York: John Wiley and Sons, 1967), 51–58; Kett, *Rites of Passage*, 127–28.

23. Edward A. Krug, *The Shaping of the American High School: 1880–1920* (Milwaukee: University of Wisconsin Press, 1969), 5, 11; Gerald L. Gutek, *A History of the Western Educational Experience* (New York: Random House, 1972), 368.

24. Robert H. Bremner, ed., *Children and Youth in America: A Documentary History*, vol. 2, *1866–1932* (Cambridge, MA: Harvard University Press, 1971), 601, 605–6.

25. Glen H. Elder Jr., "Adolescence in Historical Perspective," in Joseph Adelson, ed., *Handbook of Adolescent Psychology* (New York: Jon Wiley and Sons, 1980), 28.

26. Button and Provenzo, *History of Education*, 89.

27. Bremner, *Children and Youth*, 1:346–47.

28. Tyack, *Turning Points*, 119–77; Button and Provenzo, *History of Education*, 84–134.

29. Kett, *Rites of Passage*, 112.

30. Krug, *Shaping*, 174n5.

31. Kett, *Rites of Passage*, 143.

32. Krug, *Shaping*, 127.

33. Bremner, *Children and Youth*, 2:628.

34. Edgar, *South Carolina*, 173, 176, 297–99.

35. Krug, *Shaping*, 129–30.

36. Bremner, *Children and Youth*, 2:601.

37. Button and Provenzo, *History of Education*, 115–16.

38. "What is the Nineteenth Ward," *Chicago Tribune*, February 13, 1898, 25.

39. Bremner, *Children and Youth*, 2:611–13.

40. Daniel J. Levinson, *The Seasons of a Man's Life* (New York: Knopf, 1978).

41. Hine, *Rise and Fall*, 1–10.

42. Paula S. Fass, *The Damned and the Beautiful: American Youth in the 1920's* (New York: Oxford University Press, 1977), 7.

43. Mary T. Martin Sloop and Legette Blythe, *Miracle in the Hills* (New York: McGraw-Hill, 1953), 68.

44. Tyack, *Turning Points*, 358–61; Fass, *Damned and the Beautiful*, 211.

45. Fass, *Damned and the Beautiful*, 212.

46. Ralph Keyes, *Is There Life After High School?* (New York: Little, Brown, 1976).

47. Fass, *Damned and the Beautiful*, 210–21; Keyes, *Is There Life?*

48. Bremner, *Children and Youth*, 2:607.

49. http://www.allcountries.org/uscensus/37_urban_and_rural_population_and _by.html.

50. William J. Collins, "When the Tide Turned: Immigration and the Delay of the Great Black Migration," *Journal of Economic History* 57, no. 3 (September 1997): 607.

Chapter 2 *Rebel Without a Cause*

1. http://www.filmsite.org/rebel.html.

2. Paula S. Fass, *The Damned and the Beautiful: American Youth in the 1920's* (New York: Oxford University Press, 1977), 271.

3. For a complete treatment of the "invention of adolescence," see Philip Graham, *The End of Adolescence* (Oxford: Oxford University Press, 2004), 25–43; Joseph F. Kett, *Rites of Passage: Adolescence in America 1790 to the Present* (New York: Basic Books, 1977), 215–44; Glen H. Elder Jr., "Adolescence in Historical Perspective," in Joseph Adelson, ed., *Handbook of Adolescent Psychology* (New York: John Wiley and Sons, 1980), 3–46; Richard M. Lerner and Lawrence Steinberg, "The Scientific Study of Adolescent Development," in Lerner and Steinberg, eds., *Handbook of Adolescent Psychology*, 2nd ed. (New

York: John Wiley and Sons, 2004), 1–43; John W. Santrock, *Adolescence*, 8th ed. (New York: McGraw-Hill, 2001), 5–30.

4. Lerner and Steinberg, "Scientific Study," 1.

5. Graham, *End of Adolescence*, 25.

6. Colin Heywood, *A History of Childhood* (Cambridge: Polity, 2001), 103–9.

7. Thomas Hine, *The Rise and Fall of the American Teenager* (New York: Perennial, 2000), 16.

8. Charles Bracelen Flood, *Lee: The Last Years* (Boston: Houghton Mifflin, 1981), 162.

9. Ibid., 215.

10. G. Stanley Hall, *Adolescence: Its Psychology and Its Relations to Physiology, Anthropology, Sociology, Sex, Crime, Religion, and Education* (London: Appleton and Company, 1904).

11. Graham, *End of Adolescence*, 26.

12. Lerner and Steinberg, "Scientific Study," 3; Hall, *Adolescence*, ix–xvii.

13. Garrison Keillor, *Lake Wobegon Days* (New York: Penguin Books, 1985), 17.

14. Robert H. Bremner, ed., *Children and Youth in America: A Documentary History*, vol. 2, *1866–1932* (Cambridge, MA: Harvard University Press, 1971), 666–749; H. Warren Button and Eugene F. Provenzo Jr., *History of Education and Culture in America* (Englewood Cliffs, NJ: Prentice-Hall, 1983), 210–14.

15. Lawrence A. Cremin, *The Transformation of the School* (New York: Vintage Books, 1964), 127; Edward A. Krug, *The Shaping of the American High School: 1880–1920* (Milwaukee: University of Wisconsin Press, 1969), 266–77.

16. Adriana Lleran-Muney, "Were Compulsory Attendance and Child Labor Laws Effective? An Analysis from 1915 to 1939," *Journal of Law and Economics* 45, no. 2 (2002): 404–6.

17. Bremner, *Children and Youth*, 2:502–4.

18. William H. De Lacy, "Juvenile Courts," in *The Catholic Encyclopedia* (New York: Robert Appleton, 1910), 8:586–87.

19. Graham, *End of Adolescence*, 31–32, 35–38.

20. Hine, *Rise and Fall*, 8–9; Graham, *End of Adolescence*, 26.

21. *Moody Monthly*, July 1942, 652.

22. Fass, *Damned and the Beautiful*, 221, 254–55.

23. Jean Piaget, *The Child's Conception of the World* (Paterson, NJ: Littlefield, Adams, 1960); Lev S. Vygotsky, *Thought and Language* (Cambridge, MA: MIT Press, 1962); Lawrence Kohlberg, "The Development of Modes of Moral Thinking in the Years 10 to 16," PhD diss., University of Chicago, 1958; Carol Gilligan, *In a Different Voice* (Cambridge, MA: Harvard University Press, 1982); James W. Fowler, *Stages of Faith* (New York: HarperCollins, 1981); John Westerhoff, *Will Our Children Have Faith?* (New York: Seabury, 1976); Mary Wilcox, *Developmental Journey* (Nashville: Abingdon, 1979); Bruce Powers, *Growing Faith* (Nashville: Broadman, 1982); B. F. Skinner, *About Behaviorism* (New York: Knopf, 1974); Albert Bandura, *Social Foundations of Thought and Action: A Social Cognitive Theory* (Englewood Cliffs, NJ: Prentice-Hall, 1986); Urie Bronenbrenner, *The Ecology of Human Development: Experiments by Nature and Design* (Cambridge, MA: Harvard University Press, 1979); S. E. Dragastin and Glen H. Elder Jr., eds., *Adolescence in the Life Cycle* (New York: Halsted Press, 1975).

24. Hine, *Rise and Fall*, 266–67.

25. Walter Kirn, "Will Teenagers Disappear?" *Time*, February 21, 2000, 60–61.

26. Christian Smith and Melinda Lindquist Denton, *Soul Searching* (Cambridge: Oxford University Press, 2005).

27. David Elkind, *All Grown Up and No Place to Go* (Reading, MA: Addison-Wesley, 1984). The book was revised and updated in 1998.

28. http://www.census.gov/Press-Release/www/releases/archives/education/005157 .html.

29. Students from the author's class at Trinity Evangelical Divinity School, asked high school students they knew to identify and name the groups of students on their campus. The following groups were named by one or more respondents: academic/smart ones (honor

society/book-school obsessive/teachers pet); anime; atheists; band (band geeks/drum line/ flag corps/color guard); broadway company (theater/musical groups/artsy/emos); bulk girls; Christians; class clowns; computer people (tech kids/gamers); crazy people; cultural similarities (Asians/Blacks/Filipinos/Koreans/Latinos/Mexicans/Puerto Ricans); dance clubbers; DDR (Dance Dance Revolution/break dancers/ravers); diversity club; druggies (potheads/troublemakers/stoners/rap kids/metal heads/alcoholics); floaters; fusion guru; gander; gangsters; ghetto (black girls/hotties/black guys/white people who think they are black); gigolos; grade in school (esp: freshmen/lower classmen); halo; hunters; jocks popular (football players/boys basketball/soccer/cross country/field hockey/guys and girls volley-ball/wrestlers/sports groupies); jocks unpopular (girls golf/bowling/gymnastics/baseball/ girls basketball/tennis); marshal arts people (kung fu/tae kwon do); math and riddles; nerds (geeks/goths/wiggers/hip-hop/over-achievers/honor roll); normal; overall cool kids; politically active (Amnesty International); popular girls (including cheerleaders); preps (posers); promiscuous girls; punk people (punks/punk rockers); satanists; skaters; smokers; sporty popular (girly popular/hotties/style-obsessed girls); rich; student council (student council groupies); TOTC people; wallflowers (loners/quiet people); wannabes.

30. George Barna, "Research shows that spiritual maturity process should start at a young age." The Barna Group, November 17, 2003, http://www.barna.org/FlexPage.aspx ?Page=Barnaupdate&BarnaupdateID=153.

31. Kenda Creasy Dean, *Practicing Passion* (Grand Rapids: Eerdmans, 2005).

32. Smith and Denton, *Soul Searching*, 30–71.

33. Kett, *Rites of Passage*, 121.

34. Elliott West and Paula Petrik, eds., *Small Worlds: Children and Adolescents in America, 1850–1950* (Lawrence, KS: University Press of Kansas, 1992).

35. Fass, *Damned and the Beautiful.*

36. Hine, *Rise and Fall.*

37. Jon Pahl, *Youth Ministry in Modern America: 1930 to the Present* (Peabody, MA: Hendrickson, 2000).

38. Histories of high school education provide useful insights. See Krug, *Shaping of the American High School*; James S. Coleman and Thomas Hoffer, *Public and Private High Schools: The Impact of Communities* (New York: Basic Books, 1987); Elizabeth Hansot and David Tyack, *Managers of Virtue: Public School Leadership in America, 1820–1980* (New York: Basic Books, 1982).

39. Kett's description of Mather's meetings as being an example of a youth-led movement is stretched, for the groups he envisioned as a young person did not come into being until he was a pastor.

40. Frank Otis Erb, *The Development of the Young People's Movement* (Chicago: University of Chicago Press, 1917).

41. Kett, *Rites of Passage*, 86–87.

42. Glen H. Elder Jr. ("Adolescence in Historical Perspective," in *Handbook of Adolescent Psychology*, ed. Joseph Adelson [New York: John Wiley and Sons, 1980], 3–46) suggests that Kett's perspective is based on "commentaries of upper-class adults," which has some validity, though Kett cites many sources from other classes.

43. James D. McCabe Jr., *Lights and Shadows of New York Life* (Philadelphia: National Publishing Company, 1872), 413.

44. Kett, *Rites of Passage*, 233, 154, 215, 241.

45. Ibid., 115.

46. Ibid., 128–29, 152, 170.

47. Fass, *Damned and the Beautiful*, 15–25.

Chapter 3 *Bruce Almighty*

1. Christopher Lee Coble, "Where Have All the Children Gone? The Christian Endeavor Movement and the Training of Protestant Youth, 1881–1918," ThD thesis, Harvard Divinity School, 2001, 16.

2. Ibid., 16–70; Joseph F. Kett, *Rites of Passage: Adolescence in America 1790 to the Present* (New York: Basic Books, 1977), 79–84.

3. See Carol E. Lytch, *Choosing Church: What Makes a Difference for Teens* (Louisville: John Knox, 2004).

4. Michael F. Gleason, *When God Walked on Campus* (Dundas, ON: Joshua, 2002).

5. Dorothy Ross, *G. Stanley Hall: The Psychologist as Prophet* (Chicago: University of Chicago Press, 1972), 16.

6. W. R. Estep, "A Thousand Lives for China: Lottie Moon," in *More than Conquerors*, ed. John D. Woodbridge (Chicago: Moody, 1992), 56–62.

7. G. Stanley Hall, *Adolescence: Its Psychology and Its Relations to Physiology, Anthropology, Sociology, Sex, Crime, Religion, and Education* (London: Appleton and Company, 1904), 282–83.

8. Hall cites D. L. Moody, Bishop D. A. Goodsell, Rev. E. E. Abercrombie, Evangelist G. F. Pentecost, H. K. Carroll, Dr. J. L. Hurlbut, Editor J. M. Buckley, Evangelist M. S. Kees, President Thwing, Evangelist B. Fay Mills, Rev. Ichabod Spencer, Rev. Th. Simms, Rev. C. M. Hall, Dr. Davidson, and Dr. R. E. Cole (ibid., 288–89).

9. Kett, *Rites of Passage*, 87.

10. Ibid., 119–21.

11. Ibid., 195.

12. Paula S. Fass, *The Damned and the Beautiful: American Youth in the 1920's* (New York: Oxford University Press, 1977), 45.

13. Ibid., 45.

14. Ibid., 138.

15. Thomas Hine, *The Rise and Fall of the American Teenager* (New York: Perennial, 2000), 82.

16. Ibid., 83.

17. Robert S. Lynd and Helen Merrell Lynd, *Middletown: A Study in American Culture* (New York: Harcourt, Brace and World, 1929), 316–19.

18. Ibid., 393–98.

19. Robert S. Lynd and Helen Merrell Lynd, *Middletown in Transition: A Study in Cultural Conflict* (New York: Harcourt, Brace, 1937), 307–8.

20. August B. Hollingshead, *Elmtown Youth* (New York: John Wiley and Sons, 1949), 243.

21. Ibid., 246.

22. James W. Fowler, *Stages of Faith* (New York: HarperCollins, 1981), 151–73.

23. John Westerhoff, *Will Our Children Have Faith?* (New York: Seabury, 1976), 89, 94–96.

24. James Bryan Smith, "Spiritual Formation of Adolescents," in *The Christian Educator's Handbook on Spiritual Formation*, ed. Kenneth O. Gangel and James C. Wilhoit (Wheaton: Victor, 1994), 248–49.

25. Duffy Robbins, *This Way to Youth Ministry: An Introduction to the Adventure* (Grand Rapids: Zondervan, 2004), 408.

26. James E. Reed and Ronnie Prevost, *A History of Christian Education* (Nashville: Broadman and Holman, 1993), 260.

27. Richard F. Lovelace, *The American Pietism of Cotton Mather* (Grand Rapids: Christian University Press, 1979), 215–16.

28. Charles Arthur Boyd, *Young People at Work in Baptist Churches* (Philadelphia: Judson, 1928), 2.

29. Lovelace, *American Pietism*, 216.

30. Ibid., 217.

31. Richard F. Lovelace, *Dynamics of Spiritual Life* (Downers Grove, IL: InterVarsity, 1979), 38.

32. Ibid., 39.

33. Ibid., 40.

34. Lovelace, *American Pietism*, 201.

35. Anne M. Boylan, *Sunday School: The Formation of an American Institution, 1790–1880* (New Haven: Yale University Press, 1988), 6–7.

36. Paul H. Vieth, *The Church and Christian Education* (St. Louis: Bethany, 1947), 22; Boylan, *Sunday School*, 7.

37. Boylan, *Sunday School*, 16.

38. Robert W. Lynn and Elliott Wright, *The Big Little School: 200 Years of the Sunday School* (Birmingham, AL: Religious Education Press, 1980), 40–41.

39. Ibid., 44.

40. Robert L. Hampel, "Influence and Respectability: Temperance and Prohibition in Massachusetts, 1813–1852," PhD diss., Cornell University, 1980, 60–106; Wilhelm Liese, Joseph Keating, and Walter Shanley, "Temperance Movements," *Catholic Encyclopedia* 14 (New York: Robert Appleton Company, 1912), 17–19; Ian R. Tyrrell, *Sobering Up: From Temperance to Prohibition in Antebellum America, 1800–1860* (Westport, CT: Greenwood, 1979), 135–58.

41. Smith, "Spiritual Formation," 14–15.

42. Ibid., 23.

43. Coble, "Where Have All the Children Gone?" 16–21.

44. Ibid., 24.

45. Francis E. Clark, *The Children and the Church, and the Young People's Society of Christian Endeavor, as a Means of Bringing Them Together* (Boston: Congregational Sunday School and Publishing Society, 1882), 83.

46. Francis E. Clark, *Ways and Means* (Boston: D. Lothrop, 1890), 100. The pledge was revised in 1889. Amos R. Wells, *The Officers' Handbook: A Guide for Officers in Young People's Societies, With Chapters on Parliamentary Law and Other Useful Themes* (Boston: United Society of Christian Endeavor, 1900), 138–39.

47. Francis E. Clark, "A Familiar Letter from the President of the United Society," *The Golden Rule*, October 31, 1889, 74.

48. Amos R. Wells, *Expert Endeavor* (Boston: United Society of Christian Endeavor, 1911), 13.

49. Joseph F. Berry, *Four Wonderful Years* (New York: Hunt and Eaton, 1893), 10.

50. Boyd, *Young People*, 174.

51. Ibid., 207–8.

52. Clarence Peters, "Developments of the Youth Programs of the Lutheran Churches in America," ThD thesis, Concordia Theological Seminary, 1951, 209.

53. Gerald Jenny, *The Young People's Movement in the American Lutheran Church* (Minneapolis: Augsburg, 1928), 22.

54. Myron T. Hopper, "Young People's Work in Protestant Churches in the United States," PhD diss., University of Chicago, 1941, 264.

55. Kenda Creasy Dean, *Practicing Passion* (Grand Rapids: Eerdmans, 2005), 40n26.

56. Ibid., 8.

57. Nevin C. Harner, "A Decade of Youth Work in the Churches," *Religious Education* 38, no. 1 (January–February 1943): 29.

58. Dean, *Practicing Passion*, 44–45.

59. Charles Webb Courtoy, "A Historical Analysis of the Three Eras of Mainline Protestant Youth Work in America as a Basis for Clues to Future Youth Work," DMin project, Divinity School of Vanderbilt University, 1976, 65–72.

60. Sara Little, "Youth Ministry: Historical Reflections Near the End of the Twentieth Century," 1997, www.ptsem.edu/iym/research/lectures/downloads/1997/1997%20Little%Youth%20Ministry.pdf, 19.

61. Mendell Taylor, *Nazarene Youth in Conquest for Christ* (Kansas City, MO: Nazarene Publishing House, 1948), 48.

62. Michael Yaconelli, *Dangerous Wonder* (Colorado Springs: Navpress, 1998), 11.

63. Mark Yaconelli, *Contemplative Youth Ministry* (Grand Rapids: Zondervan, 2006) and *Growing Souls* (Grand Rapids: Zondervan, 2007).

Chapter 4 Whatever Goes Around Comes Around

1. Peter F. Drucker, *Innovation and Entrepreneurship: Practices and Principles* (New York: Harper and Row, 1985), 4–5.

2. Auther M. Schlesinger Jr., *The Cycles of History* (New York: Houghton Mifflin, 1986), 23–48.

3. Ibid., 29.

4. Ibid., 35, 44.

5. Michael Barkun, "The Awakening Controversy," *Sociological Analysis* 46, no. 4 (1985), 425–43.

6. See David O. Moberg, *The Church as a Social Institution*, 2nd ed. (Grand Rapids: Baker Books, 1984), 73–99.

7. Richard F. Lovelace, *Dynamics of Spiritual Life* (Downers Grove, IL: InterVarsity, 1979), 61–72.

8. S. N. Eisenstadt, *From Generation to Generation* (London: Free Press of Glencoe, 1956).

9. Mike Yaconelli, "Obituary," *The Wittenburg Door*, October 1971, 10.

10. Paul Eshelman, *The Explo Story* (Glendale, CA: Regal Books, 1972), i.

11. Voddie T. Baucham Jr., *Family Driven Faith* (Wheaton: Crossway, 2007).

12. Robert W. Lynn and Elliott Wright, *The Big Little School: 200 Years of the Sunday School* (Birmingham, AL: Religious Education Press, 1980).

13. C. Howard Hopkins, *History of the Y.M.C.A. in North America* (New York: Abingdon, 1951).

14. David M. Howard, *Student Power in World Evangelism* (Downers Grove, IL: InterVarsity, 1970).

15. Mark H. Senter III, *The Coming Revolution in Youth Ministry* (Wheaton: Victor, 1992).

16. Gilbert L. Dodds, "A Survey of Youth for Christ," MA thesis, Wheaton College, 1948, 18.

17. Char Meredith, *It's a Sin to Bore a Kid* (Waco: Word, 1978), 41–45.

18. Evelyn M. McClusky, "The Miracles Worked in 'Miracle Book Club,'" *Sunday School Times* 80, January 22, 1938, 62.

19. Amos R. Wells, *The Officers' Handbook: A Guide for Officers in Young People's Societies, With Chapters on Parliamentary Law and Other Useful Themes* (Boston: United Society of Christian Endeavor, 1900), 9–15.

20. Evelyn M. McClusky, *Torch and Sword* (Oakland: Miracle Book Club, 1937).

21. Correspondence from Ted Benson to Herbert J. Taylor, January 1, 1941. Herbert J. Taylor Papers, Archives of the Billy Graham Center, Wheaton College, Folder 7, Box 11, Collection 20.

22. Torrey Johnson and Robert Cook, *Reaching Youth for Christ* (Chicago: Moody, 1944).

23. Francis E. Clark, *The Children and the Church, and the Young People's Society of Christian Endeavor, as a Means of Bringing Them Together* (Boston: Congregational Sunday School and Publishing Society, 1882).

24. Harold John Ockenga, "Revival is Here!" *Youth for Christ Magazine* 7, April 1950, 8–13.

25. James E. Bennet, "The Revival in Our Midst," *Sunday School Times* 86, March 25, 1944, 218.

26. W. Knight Chaplin and M. Jennie Street, eds., *Fifty Years of Christian Endeavour* (London: British Christian Endeavour Union, 1931), 30.

27. Lynn and Wright, *Big Little School*, 150.

28. Edwin Wilber Rice, *The Sunday School Movement and the American Sunday School Union* (Philadelphia: Union, 1917), 67.

29. H. Clay Trumbull, *The Sunday School: Its Origin, Mission, Methods, and Auxiliaries* (New York: Scribner's, 1911), 67.

30. Randall Balmer, *Mine Eyes Have Seen the Glory* (New York: Oxford University Press, 1989), 149.

31. On December 5, 1977, the Young Life Campaign revised its articles of incorporation and among the changes was Article III, *Existence*, which states, "Young Life shall have perpetual existence."

Chapter 5 Tom Sawyer and the British Invasion

1. Joseph F. Kett, *Rites of Passage: Adolescence in America 1790 to the Present* (New York: Basic Books, 1977), 87–93.

2. "Cadets of Temperance," *The Cyclopaedia of Temperance and Prohibition* (New York: Funk and Wagnalls, 1891), 60.

3. Ian R. Tyrrell, *Sobering Up: From Temperance to Prohibition in Antebellum America, 1800–1860* (Westport, CT: Greenwood, 1979), 140–45.

4. Frank Otis Erb, *The Development of the Young People's Movement* (Chicago: University of Chicago Press, 1917), 1–32.

5. C. Howard Hopkins, *History of the Y.M.C.A. in North America* (New York: Association, 1951), 19–22; Kett, *Rites of Passage*, 40, 104.

6. Erb, *Development*, 21.

7. Charles Arthur Boyd, *Young People at Work in Baptist Churches* (Philadelphia: Judson, 1928), 2; Cotton Mather, *Religious Societies: Proposals for the Revival of Dying Religion by Well-Ordered Societies for That Purpose* (Boston, 1724); Kett, *Rites of Passage*, 194.

8. George M. Marsden, *Jonathan Edwards: A Life* (New Haven: Yale University Press, 2003), 155–56.

9. Edwin Wilber Rice, *The Sunday School Movement and the American Sunday School Union* (Philadelphia: Union, 1917), 43.

10. Jack L. Seymour, *From Sunday School to Church School* (Washington, DC: University Press of America, 1982), 28.

11. Anne M. Boylan, *Sunday School: The Formation of An American Institution, 1790–1880* (New Haven: Yale University Press, 1988), 7.

12. Ibid., 9.

13. Ibid., 10–11.

14. Ibid., 16.

15. Rice, *Sunday School Movement*, 196.

16. Clarence H. Benson, *The Sunday School in Action* (Chicago: Moody, 1932), 19.

17. Seymour, *From Sunday School*, 30.

18. Robert W. Lynn and Elliott Wright, *The Big Little School: 200 Years of the Sunday School* (New York: Harper & Row, 1971), 90–94.

19. Hopkins, *History*, 18.

20. Ibid., 45–46.

21. Ibid., 32.

22. J. Edwin Orr, *The Second Evangelical Awakening in America* (London: Marshall, Morgan and Scott, 1952), 21–26; Hopkins, *History*, 81.

23. Orr, *Second Evangelical*, 119.

24. Hopkins, *History*, 184.

25. Tony Ladd and James A. Mathisen, *Muscular Christianity: Evangelical Protestants and the Development of American Sport* (Grand Rapids: Baker Books, 1999); Clifford Putney, *Muscular Christianity: Manhood and Sports in Protestant America, 1880–1920* (Cambridge, MA: Harvard University Press, 2001); Hopkins, *History*, 245–70.

26. Hopkins, *History*, 272.

27. Ibid., 294–99; David M. Howard, *Student Power in World Evangelism* (Downers Grove, IL: InterVarsity, 1970).

Chapter 6 Cadets of Temperance

1. Robert L. Hampel, "Influence and Respectability: Temperance and Prohibition in Massachusetts, 1813–1852," PhD diss., Cornell University, 1980, 60–106; Wilhelm Liese, Joseph Keating, and Walter Shanley, "Temperance Movements," *Catholic Encyclopedia* 14 (New York: Robert Appleton Company, 1912), 17–19; Ian R. Tyrrell, *Sobering Up: From Temperance to Prohibition in Antebellum America, 1800–1860* (Westport, CT: Greenwood, 1979), 135–58.

2. Frederic Smith, *The Jubilee of the Band of Hope Movement* (London: United Kingdom Band of Hope Union, 1897), 14–15. Frederic Smith's work is the most comprehensive account of the juvenile temperance movement and serves as the basis for most other accounts.

3. Ibid., 15–17.

4. Ibid., 26.

5. Ibid., 38.

6. Ibid., 51.

7. Ibid., 97.

8. Ibid., 194–208.

9. Ibid., 208–23.

10. Ibid., 224–47.

11. Graham Warder, "Selling Sobriety: How Temperance Reshaped Culture in Antebellum America," PhD diss., University of Massachusetts Amherst, 2000, vii.

12. Theodore Ledyard Cuyler, *Recollections of a Long Life* (New York: The American Tract Society, 1902), 39.

13. Theodore L. Cuyler Archives, Princeton Theological Seminary, Special Collections—Luce #250, Box 1, Scrapbook 6, p. 6.

14. Francis E. Clark, *The Children and the Church, and the Young People's Society of Christian Endeavor, as a Means of Bringing Them Together* (Boston: Congregational Sunday School and Publishing Society, 1882), vi.

15. Francis E. Clark, *Ways and Means* (Boston: D. Lothrop, 1890), 4–5.

16. Ibid., 11.

17. Amos R. Wells, *The Officers' Handbook: A Guide for Officers in Young People's Societies, With Chapters on Parliamentary Law and Other Useful Themes* (Boston: United Society of Christian Endeavor, 1900), 40; Amos R. Wells, *Prayer Meeting Methods* (Boston: United Society of Christian Endeavor, 1916), 40.

18. Francis E. Clark, *Memories of Many Men in Many Lands: An Autobiography* (Boston: United Christian Endeavor Society, 1922), 73; William Knight Chaplin, *Francis E. Clark: Founder of the Christian Endeavour Society* (London: British Christian Endeavour Society Union, 1902), 19.

19. Asa Hull, *Hull's Temperance Glee Book* (Boston: O. Ditson, 1877).

20. Elisha A. Hoffman, *Songs of the New Crusade* (Chicago: Hope, 1876).

21. Anna A. Gordon, *The Temperance Songster* (Cincinnati: Fillmore Music House, 1904).

22. For a more complete treatment see George W. Ewing, *The Well-Tempered Lyre: Songs and Verse of the Temperance Movement* (Dallas: Southern Methodist University Press, 1977).

23. *Junior Carols* (Boston: United Society of Christian Endeavor, 1906).

24. *The Endeavor Hymnal for Young People's Societies, Sunday Schools and Church Meetings* (Boston: United Society of Christian Endeavor, 1901).

Chapter 7 *Gangs of New York*

1. Edwin G. Burrows and Mike Wallace, *Gotham: A History of New York City to 1898* (New York: Oxford University Press, 1999), 642.

2. Ibid., 733.

3. George M. Marsden, *Jonathan Edwards: A Life* (New Haven: Yale University Press, 2003), 126.

4. Ibid., 153–56.

5. Ibid., 81–84.

6. Theodore Ledyard Cuyler, *Recollections of a Long Life* (New York: American Tract Society, 1902), 86.

7. Thomas Hine, *The Rise and Fall of the American Teenager* (New York: Perennial, 2000), 147.

8. Joseph F. Kett, *Rites of Passage: Adolescence in America 1790 to the Present* (New York: Basic Books, 1977), 178.

9. Ibid., 90–93.

10. Cuyler, *Recollections*, 259–60; also see Kett, *Rites of Passage*, 88–89.

11. Francis E. Clark, *The Children and the Church, and the Young People's Society of Christian Endeavor, as a Means of Bringing Them Together* (Boston: Congregational Sunday School and Publishing Society, 1882), vi, 39.

12. Milford Sholund, "A Historical Survey of Youth Work," in Roy G. Irving and Roy B. Zuck, eds., *Youth and the Church: An Approach to Christian Education of Youth* (Chicago: Moody, 1968), 62.

13. Roy Zuck, "Sunday Evening Youth Groups," in J. Edward Hakes, *An Introduction to Evangelical Christian Education* (Chicago: Moody, 1964), 318–19; J. M. Price, James H. Chapman, L. L. Carpenter, and W. Forbes Yarborough, *A Survey of Religious Education* (New York: Ronald, 1959), 252.

14. Cuyler, *Recollections*, 4.

15. Theodore L. Cuyler, "A Symposium: What was the most potent influence of which you were conscious in your conversion?" April 28, 1892, Theodore L. Cuyler Archives, Princeton Theological Seminary, Special Collections—Luce #250, Box 3, Scrapbook 14.

16. "Rev. Theodore L. Cuyler, Lafayette Avenue Church, Brooklyn, U.S.A.," *The Christian*, July 5, 1889, 9. Theodore L. Cuyler Archives, Princeton Theological Seminary, Special Collections—Luce #250, Box 2, Scrapbook 12.

17. Ibid.

18. "Historical Discourse in Lafayette Presbyterian Church, Brooklyn, N.Y.," *Brooklyn Daily Union*, June 6, 1876. Theodore L. Cuyler Archives, Princeton Theological Seminary, Special Collections—Luce #250, Box 1, Scrapbook 8.

19. Cuyler, *Recollections*, 268–69. Cuyler Chapel, one of the auxiliary chapels of Lafayette Avenue Church, was established and financed by the Young People's Association, a practice not uncommon in Cuyler's day. The practice suggests an early form of youth ministry genesis in churches. Theodore L. Cuyler, "Cuyler Chapel," Theodore L. Cuyler Archives, Princeton Theological Seminary, Special Collections—Luce #250, Box 3, Scrapbook 14.

20. Theodore L. Cuyler, "Forerunners of the Christian Endeavor Society," Theodore L. Cuyler Archives, Princeton Theological Seminary, Special Collections—Luce #250, Box 3, Scrapbook 14.

21. Ibid.

22. Ibid.

23. Theodore L. Cuyler, "The Young People's Meeting," Theodore L. Cuyler Archives, Princeton Theological Seminary, Special Collections—Luce #250, Box 1, Scrapbook 3, p. 80.

24. Ibid.

25. Ibid.

26. Theodore L. Cuyler, "Temperance and Young People's Societies," Theodore L. Cuyler Archives, Princeton Theological Seminary, Special Collections—Luce #250, Box 1, Scrapbook 8.

27. Ibid.

28. "Rev. Dr. Cuyler's Church," Theodore L. Cuyler Archives, Princeton Theological Seminary, Special Collections—Luce #250, Box 1, Scrapbook 7, p. 82; "Rev. Theodore L. Cuyler, Lafayette Avenue Church."

29. Cuyler, "Forerunners of the Christian Endeavor Society."

30. Mary Bushnell Cheney, *Life and Letters of Horace Bushnell* (New York: Arno Press & The New York Times, 1969), 282.

31. Horace Bushnell, *Christian Nurture* (New York: Scribner's, 1886), 233, 248–49.

32. Cheney, *Life and Letters*, 4.

33. Ibid., 8.

34. Perry G. Downs, "Christian Nurture: A Comparative Analysis of the Theories of Horace Bushnell and Lawrence O. Richards," PhD thesis, New York University, 1882, 71.

35. Ibid., 72.

36. Bushnell, *Christian Nurture*, 10 (emphasis added).

37. Mark W. Cannister, "Youth Ministry's Historical Context: The Education and Evangelism of Young People," in Kenda Creasy Dean, Chap Clark, and David Rahn, eds., *Starting Right: Thinking Theologically about Youth Ministry* (Grand Rapids: Zondervan,

2001), 80–84; Mark W. Cannister, "Back to the Future: A Historical Perspective on Youth Ministry," *Christian Education Journal* 3, no. 2 (Fall 1999): 17–30; Perry G. Downs, *Teaching for Spiritual Growth* (Grand Rapids: Zondervan, 1994), 65–66.

38. Theodore L. Cuyler, "Pen-Pictures of Eminent Preachers, " Theodore L. Cuyler Archives, Princeton Theological Seminary, Special Collections—Luce #250, Box 3, Scrapbook 14.

39. Francis E. Clark, *Memories of Many Men in Many Lands: An Autobiography* (Boston: United Christian Endeavor Society, 1922), 78.

40. Ibid., 78.

41. Marsden, *Jonathan Edwards*, 298.

42. Clark, *Memories*, 39.

43. William Knight Chaplin, *Francis E. Clark: Founder of the Christian Endeavour Society* (London: British Christian Endeavour Union, 1902), 2–6; Dwight M. Pratt, *A Decade of Christian Endeavor, 1881–1891* (New York: Revell, 1891), 17–19; Clark, *Memories*, 28–41.

44. Clark, *Memories*, 47.

45. Ibid., 77.

46. Ibid.; Chaplin, *Francis E. Clark*, 21–38.

47. Clark, *Memories*, 85.

Chapter 8 Trouble in River City

1. Meredith Willson, *The Music Man* (New York: G.P. Putnam's Sons, 1958).

2. Lawrence A. Cremin, *American Education: The Metropolitan Experience, 1876–1980* (New York: Harper and Row, 1988).

3. George M. Marsden, *Fundamentalism and American Culture* (New York: Oxford University Press, 1980), 102.

4. Michael Kazin, *A Godly Hero* (New York: Knopf, 2006); "William Jennings Bryan Recognition Project," http://www.agribusinesscouncil.org/bryan.htm.

5. Christopher Lee Coble, "Where Have All the Children Gone? The Christian Endeavor Movement and the Training of Protestant Youth, 1881–1918," ThD thesis, Harvard Divinity School, 2001, 16–70.

6. John H. Vincent, "The Coming Church," *Independent* 44, July 7, 1892, 1, cited in Joseph F. Kett, *Rites of Passage: Adolescence in America 1790 to the Present* (New York: Basic Books, 1977), 190.

7. Kett, *Rites of Passage*, 190.

8. Eugene Francis Clark, *A Son's Portrait of Dr. Francis E. Clark* (Boston: Williston, 1930), 78.

9. Ibid., 79.

10. William Knight Chaplin, *Francis E. Clark: Founder of the Christian Endeavour Society* (London: British Christian Endeavour Union, 1902), 30.

11. The exact number varies from account to account: fifty-eight in Francis E. Clark, *Memories of Many Men in Many Lands: An Autobiography* (Boston: United Christian Endeavor Society, 1922), 80; sixty in Francis E. Clark, *The Children and the Church, and the Young People's Society of Christian Endeavor, as a Means of Bringing Them Together* (Boston: Congregational Sunday School and Publishing Society, 1882), 39; fifty-seven in Chaplin, *Francis E. Clark*, 33; sixty-three (fifty-seven active members and six associate members) in Dwight M. Pratt, *A Decade of Christian Endeavor, 1881–1891* (New York: Revell, 1891), 47.

12. Pratt, *Decade*, 54.

13. Ibid., 56–59.

14. Ibid., 67.

15. Clark, *A Son's Portrait*, 162–81.

16. Earnest Trice Thompson, *Presbyterians in the South*, vol. 3, *1890–1972* (Richmond: John Knox, 1973), 147.

17. The Young People's Baptist Union was formed in 1877, followed by the Methodist Episcopal Young People's Union in 1883. See Thomas Armitage, *History of the Young People's Baptist Union of Brooklyn* (New York: T. R. Jones, 1890), 1–18, 95–100.

18. Amos R. Wells, *The Officers' Handbook: A Guide for Officers in Young People's Societies, With Chapters on Parliamentary Law and Other Useful Themes* (Boston: United Society of Christian Endeavor, 1900), 138; Francis E. Clark, *Ways and Means* (Boston: D. Lothrop, 1900), 257.

19. Clark, *Ways and Means*, 261.

20. Ibid., 251.

21. Wells, *Officers' Handbook*, 9.

22. Ibid., 10–15.

23. Amos R. Wells, *Prayer Meeting Methods* (Boston: United Society of Christian Endeavor, 1916), 101.

24. Wells, *Officers' Handbook*, 11.

25. Francis E. Clark, *The Christian Endeavor Manual* (Boston: United Society of Christian Endeavor, 1925), 170.

26. Ibid., 99.

27. Clark, *Children and the Church*, 41–43.

28. Wells, *Officers' Handbook*, 22–23, 25, 39–41.

29. Ibid., 13.

30. Clark, *A Son's Portrait*, 102.

31. Chaplin, *Francis E. Clark*, 107–8.

32. His son, Eugene Francis Clark, mentioned among his father's memorable friends Presidents Taft, Wilson, Harding, and Coolidge; Christian leaders Billy Sunday, Dwight L. Moody, Henry Ward Beecher, and Phillip Brooks; and other leaders including William Jennings Bryan, G. Stanley Hall, William Gladstone, and many others. See Clark, *A Son's Portrait*; Clark, *Memories of Many Men*.

33. Christopher Lee Coble suggests there may have been one hundred denominations. Coble, *Where Have All the Children Gone?* 134. See also J. C. Willke, "Christian Endeavor, International Society of," *Encyclopedic Dictionary of Religion*, eds. Paul Kevin Meagher, Thomas C. Obrien, Sister Consuelo Maria Aherne (Washington, DC: Corpus, 1979), 746. *New Catholic Encyclopedia* cites membership as late as 1964 at about four million. T. Horgan, "Christian Endeavor Society," in *New Catholic Encyclopedia* (New York: McGraw-Hill, 1967), 3:639. Phyllis I. Rike places the total membership at three million in more than seventy-five countries and island groups, with approximately a million in North America. Phyllis I. Rike, "International Society of Christian Endeavor," in *The Encyclopedia of Modern Christian Missions*, ed. Burton L. Goddard (Camden, NJ: Nelson, 1967), 341.

34. Pratt, *Decade*, 75; Coble, *Where Have All the Children Gone?* 133–91.

35. Amos R. Wells, "A New Religious Force," *The New England Magazine*, June 1892, 519.

36. Kett, *Rites of Passage*, 195–98.

37. Paula S. Fass, *The Damned and the Beautiful: American Youth in the 1920's* (New York: Oxford University Press, 1977), 13–14.

38. Katherine Evelyn Niles, "A Survey and Critique of Young People's Societies," *Religious Education* (June 1929): 534.

Chapter 9 Saturday Night in River City

1. J. Warren Smith, "Youth Ministry in American Methodism's Mission," *Methodist History* 19, no. 4 (July 1981): 224–30.

2. Joseph F. Berry, *Four Wonderful Years* (New York: Hunt and Eaton, 1893), 3–4, 12–13.

3. Thomas Armitage, *History of the Young People's Baptist Union of Brooklyn* (New York: T. R. Jones, 1890), 95–100.

4. Smith, "Youth Ministry," 225.

5. Berry, *Four Wonderful Years*, 8–9; Wade Crawford Barclay, *The Methodist Episcopal Church, 1845–1939: Part Two* (New York: Board of Missions of the Methodist Church, 1957), 103.

6. Barclay, *Methodist Episcopal Church*, 98–100.

7. Berry, *Four Wonderful Years*, 12–16.

8. Barclay, *Methodist Episcopal Church*, 101–2; Berry, *Four Wonderful Years*, 16–21.

9. Berry, *Four Wonderful Years*, 21–24; Barclay, *Methodist Episcopal Church*, 103.

10. Berry, *Four Wonderful Years*, 25–27; Barclay, *Methodist Episcopal Church*, 103–4.

11. Smith, "Youth Ministry," 226–28.

12. Ibid., 228.

13. Charles Arthur Boyd, *Young People at Work in Baptist Churches* (Philadelphia: Judson, 1928), 3.

14. John Wesley Conley, *History of the Baptist Young People's Union of America* (Philadelphia: Griffith and Rowland, 1913), 16.

15. Armitage, *History*, 19–23.

16. Ibid., 6, 84–88.

17. The biographies of the presidents of the Young People's Baptist Union of Brooklyn describe them as ranging in age from their early thirties to their early forties. These would probably constitute the most mature members of young people's associations. Armitage, *History*, 19–222.

18. Ibid., viii.

19. Ibid., 72–73.

20. Ibid., 136, 141.

21. Elbert Joseph Wright, *Virginia Baptist Training Union History* (Richmond: Baptist Training Union, 1947), 13–14.

22. Southern Presbyterians shared a similar bias against Christian Endeavor in part because of it being from the North. "The *Southwestern Presbyterian* pointed out that Christian Endeavor was directed by Northern men, under no ecclesiastical control." See Earnest Trice Thompson, *Presbyterians in the South*, vol. 3, *1890–1972* (Richmond: John Knox, 1973), 148.

23. More than other Protestant traditions Lutheran churches proliferated youth societies. Beside the Walther League, Clarence Peters described the following: Luther League of the American Lutheran Church, Young People's League of the Evangelical Lutheran Church, Augustana Luther League of the Augustana Evangelical Lutheran Church, Luther League of America of the United Lutheran Church in America, Luther League Federation of the Lutheran Free Churches, Danish-American Young People's League of the Danish Evangelical Lutheran Church of America, The Luther League of the United Evangelical Lutheran Church, Slovak Luther League of the Slovak Evangelical Lutheran Church, Luther League of the Suomi Synod, as well as youth ministries in the Norwegian Synod of the American Evangelical Lutheran Church and Evangelical Lutheran Joint Synod of Wisconsin and Other States. See Clarence Peters, "Developments of the Youth Programs of the Lutheran Churches in America," ThD thesis, Concordia Theological Seminary, 1951.

24. Elmer N. Witt, "125 Youthful Years," in *Superservant: Resource for Youth Ministry* 4, no. 3 (Summer 1972): 11 (St. Louis: Board for Youth Services, The Lutheran Church—Missouri Synod).

25. Peters, "Developments of the Youth," 209.

26. Jon Pahl, *Hopes and Dreams of All* (Chicago: Wheat Ridge Ministries, 1993), 11.

27. Ibid., 13.

28. Witt, "125 Youthful Years," 11.

29. Gerald Jenny, *The Young People's Movement in the American Lutheran Church* (Minneapolis: Augsburg, 1928), 18–40.

30. Jon Pahl, *Youth Ministry in Modern America: 1930 to the Present* (Peabody, MA: Hendrickson, 2000), 19.

31. Ibid., 20.

32. Franklin B. Gillespie, "Youth Programs of the United Presbyterian Church—An Historical Overview," *Journal of Presbyterian History* 59, no. 3 (Fall 1981): 316–18.

33. Ibid., 310.

34. Ibid., 320.

35. Ibid., 311–12. The General Assembly suggested a long list of subjects in addition to knowledge of the Scriptures—history of the world, biographical studies of people known for their piety, doctrine, directions for acceptable worship, manifestations of the presence of the Holy Spirit in lives, and practical lessons to regulate conduct in various relationships in life. This list apparently had to do more with the preparation of ministers than with training the average young person in Christian living.

36. Gillespie, "Youth Programs," 314, 316.

37. Wallace McPherson Alston, "A History of Young People's Work in the Presbyterian Church in the United States (1831–1938)," ThD thesis, Presbyterian School of Theology, 1943, 50–52.

38. Gillespie, "Youth Programs," 330.

39. Peters, "Developments of the Youth," 43.

40. Gillespie, "Youth Programs," 345–48.

41. Mary-Ruth Marshall, "Precedents and Accomplishments: An Analytical Study of the Presbyterian Youth Fellowship of the Presbyterian Church in the United States, 1943–1958," EdD diss., Presbyterian School of Christian Education, 1993, 47–51.

42. Alston, "History of Young People's Work," 89–115.

43. Marshall, "Precedents," 51.

44. Mark H. Senter III, "The Youth for Christ Movement as an Educational Agency and Its Impact upon Protestant Churches: 1931–1979," PhD diss., Loyola University of Chicago, 1989, 96–97.

45. Sara Little, "Youth Ministry: Historical Reflections Near the End of the Twentieth Century," 1997, www.ptsem.edu/iym/research/lectures/downloads/1997/1997%20Little%Youth%20Ministry.pdf; Marshall, "Precedents," 34–91.

46. Robert S. Lynd and Helen Merrell Lynd, *Middletown: A Study in American Culture* (New York: Harcourt, Brace and World, 1929), 216–17, 398.

47. Pahl, *Youth Ministry*, 30.

48. Harold I. Donnelly, "A Brief Report of the Christian Youth Conference of North America," *International Journal of Religious Education* (September 1936), 6.

49. Harold I. Donnelly, "Christian Youth at Work," *International Journal of Religious Education* 12 (July 1936): 21–22.

50. Nevin C. Harner, "A Decade of Youth Work in the Church," *Religious Education* 38, no. 1 (January–February 1943): 26–27.

51. Paolo E. Coletta, *William Jennings Bryan: Political Puritan, 1915–1925* (Lincoln: University of Nebraska Press, 1969), 105.

Chapter 10 *The Great Gatsby*

1. Paula S. Fass, *The Damned and the Beautiful: American Youth in the 1920's* (New York: Oxford University Press, 1977), 25–29.

2. Ibid., 13.

3. Fass uses university newspapers, published by students, as a primary source to analyze student opinion. That these newspapers were an accurate voice for all, or even a majority of the university students, is a questionable assumption. Yet her careful analysis of editorials by students from a broad cross section of American universities expresses an important voice for an elite segment of students.

4. Fass, *Damned and the Beautiful*, 13–17.

5. Ibid., 112–13.

6. Ibid., 113.

7. Ibid., 260.

8. Ibid., 290.

9. Ibid., 42–46.

10. Kenda Creasy Dean, *Practicing Passion* (Grand Rapids: Eerdmans, 2005), 38, 40.

11. Michael Kazin, *A Godly Hero* (New York: Knopf, 2006), 262–95.

12. Charles Webb Courtoy, "A Historical Analysis of the Three Eras of Mainline Protestant Youth Work in America as a Basis for Clues to Future Youth Work," DMin project, Divinity School of Vanderbilt University, 1976, 65–72.

13. Sara Little, "Youth Ministry: Historical Reflections Near the End of the Twentieth Century," 1997, www.ptsem.edu/iym/research/lectures/downloads/1997/1997%20Little%Youth%20Ministry.pdf, 19.

14. *Handbook: Senior High Fellowship* (Richmond: John Knox, 1952).

15. Little, "Youth Ministry," 18.

16. *Handbook of the Methodist Youth Fellowship* (Nashville: General Board of Education of the Methodist Church, 1953), 11–13.

17. Ibid., 14.

18. Ibid., 66.

19. Ibid., 83.

20. Ibid., 158–59.

21. Courtoy, "Historical Analysis," 74–75.

22. The Evangelical Lutheran Church formed the Young People's Luther League from the Young People's Federation of the Hague Synod, the Young People's Association of the Norwegian Synod, and the Young People's League of the United Norwegian Church in 1917; the Lutheran Free Church had the first convention of the Young People's Federation of the LFC in 1920; in 1924 the Synodical Luther League Council was organized to govern the youth ministry of the Augustana Lutheran Church; when three synods merged to form the American Lutheran Church in 1930, their youth ministry was called the Luther League; the United Evangelical Lutheran Church formed its Luther League in 1935. "Lutheran Youth Organizations," in *The Encyclopedia of the Lutheran Church* (Minneapolis: Augsburg, 1965), 3:2548–53.

23. Jon Pahl, *Youth Ministry in Modern America: 1930 to the Present* (Peabody, MA: Hendrickson, 2000), 17–20.

24. Jon Pahl, "What's History Got to Do with It? Understanding the Roots of Youth Ministry in America," 2004, http://www.youthspecialties.com/articles/topics/pastpresentfuture/history.php, 2.

25. Elmer N. Witt, "125 Youthful Years," in *Superservant: Resources for Youth Ministry* 4, no. 3 (Summer 1972): 11 (St. Louis: Board for Youth Services, The Lutheran Church—Missouri Synod); W. G. Polack, "A Half Century of Organized Youth Work," in *Fifty Years*, ed. W. F. Weiherman (Chicago: Walther League, 1943), cited in Clarence Peters, "Development of the Youth Programs of the Lutheran Churches in America," ThD thesis, Concordia Theological Seminary, 1951, 92; Pahl, "What's History," 2.

26. Witt, "125 Youthful Years," 11–12.

27. Pahl, *Youth Ministry*, 17–20.

28. Witt, "125 Youthful Years," 15.

29. Pahl, "What's History," 2.

30. Mary-Ruth Marshall, "Precedents and Accomplishments: An Analytical Study of the Presbyterian Youth Fellowship of the Presbyterian Church in the United States, 1943–1958," EdD diss., Presbyterian School of Christian Education, 1993, 56–58.

31. Joesph F. Kett, *Rites of Passage: Adolescence in America 1790 to the Present* (New York: Basic Books, 1977), 246; Marshall, "Precendents," 61.

32. Marshall, "Precendents," 58–60; Little, "Youth Ministry," 18.

33. Charles Harvey McClung, "The Development of the Denominational Youth Program in the Presbyterian Church in the U.S.A., 1881–1954," PhD diss., University of Pittsburgh, 1957, 132–33.

34. Little, "Youth Ministry," 21–22.

35. Dean, *Practicing Passion*, 7.

36. Forrest B. Fordham, *The Baptist Youth Fellowship Handbook* (Philadelphia: Department of Youth Work, American Baptist Convention, 1951), 10.

37. Phillip H. Briggs, "Patterns in Southern Baptist Youth Ministry," *Baptist History and Heritage* 26, no. 4 (October 1991): 5.

38. Peters, "Development of the Youth," 33; Briggs, "Patterns in Southern Baptist," 6.

39. Steven Dewayne Beasley, "The Development of the Church Training Program of the Southern Baptist Convention: A Historical Review," EdD diss., Southern Baptist Theological Seminary, 1988, 154, 158–69.

40. W. L. Howse, "Reflections on the QUEST Episode," unpublished paper in the Church Training Collection of the Dargan Library at the Sunday School Board, 1, cited in Beasley, "Development of the Church Training Program," 1.

41. Beasley, "Development of the Church Training Program," 175–79.

42. Wesley Black, "Youth Ministry Comes of Age," *Search* 23, no. 3 (Spring 1993): 8; Briggs, "Patterns in Southern Baptist," 7–8.

43. Briggs, "Patterns in Southern Baptist," 9.

44. Ibid., 6–7.

45. Steve Wright, *Rethink: Decide for Yourself, Is Student Ministry Working?* (Wake Forest, NC: Inquest, 2007), 28–32.

46. Courtoy, "Historical Analysis," 78–79.

47. Kenda Creasy Dean, "The New Rhetoric of Youth Ministry," *Journal of Youth and Theology* (November 2003): 9.

Chapter 11 *Grease*

1. To put the 1929 high school enrollment into perspective, the number of students attending public secondary schools in 1989 was approximately 12.4 million or about three times the enrollment of 1929. Had the rate of growth continued from the first three decades of the century there would be more high school students today than there are citizens of the United States (318.4 million students).

2. C. Howard Hopkins, *History of the Y.M.C.A. in North America* (New York: Association, 1951), 402.

3. Evelyn M. McClusky, *Torch and Sword* (Oakland: Miracle Book Club, 1937), 46.

4. John Miller, *Back to the Basics* (Colorado Springs: Young Life, 1991); John Miller to Mark H. Senter III, February 24, 1988.

5. Al Metsker, "A Bus Did the Trick," *Youth for Christ Magazine*, June 1947, 26–28.

6. For biographical information see McClusky, *Torch and Sword*, 43–57.

7. "Winning High School Students for Christ," *Sunday School Times*, June 29, 1935, 432–33; Evelyn M. McClusky, "The Ruby in the City Dump," *Sunday School Times*, July 6, 1935, 447–48, 455; McClusky, "The Sailor Boy in the Greyhound Stage," *Sunday School Times*, July 13, 1935, 459, 463.

8. "Miracle Book Clubs for Young People," *Sunday School Times*, May 9, 1936, 327–28; "The Miracle Book," *Sunday School Times*, March 20, 1938, 201; Evelyn M. McClusky, "The Miracles Worked in 'Miracle Book Club,'" *Sunday School Times* 80, January 22, 1938, 61–62.

9. McClusky, *Torch and Sword*, 125.

10. For the general club format see ibid., 126–29.

11. Mark H. Senter III, "Mother of the Parachurch High School Movement in America: A Look at the Miracle Book Club and Evelyn McClusky," *Christian Education Journal* (Spring 1991): 73–85; Mark H. Senter III, "Look What You Started, Mrs. McClusky," *Youthworker Journal* 7 (Winter 1991): 66–68.

12. Jim Rayburn to Herbert J. Taylor, November 8, 1940, Herbert J. Taylor Papers, Archives of the Billy Graham Center, Wheaton College, Folder 26, Box 69, Collection 20; Ted Benson to Herbert J. Taylor, January 1, 1941, and March 2, 1941, Herbert J. Taylor Papers, Archives of the Billy Graham Center, Wheaton College, Folder 7, Box 11, Collection 20.

13. For a more complete discussion of the break between Young Life and the Miracle Book Club see Mark H. Senter III, "The Youth for Christ Movement as an Educational Agency and Its Impact upon Protestant Churches: 1931–1979," PhD diss., Loyola University of Chicago, 1989, 174–77.

14. "Young Life Leaders' Manual," 2, Herbert J. Taylor Papers, Archives of the Billy Graham Center, Wheaton College, Folder 26, Box 69, Collection 20.

15. Char Meredith, *It's a Sin to Bore a Kid* (Waco: Word, 1978), 20.

16. John A. Mackay is given credit for coining this phrase. See Emile Cailliet, *Young Life* (New York: Harper and Row, 1963), 62.

17. See Gary Willard Downing, "Incarnational Witness: A Model of Ministry Linking Young Life to the Organized Church," DMin project, Luther-Northwestern Seminaries, 1978; Ted Benson to Herbert J. Taylor, April 30, 1941, Herbert J. Taylor Papers, Archives of the Billy Graham Center, Wheaton College, Folder 7, Box 11, Collection 20.

18. Meredith, *It's a Sin*, 36. An example of a Rayburn talk is found in Jim Rayburn III, *Dance, Children, Dance* (Wheaton: Tyndale, 1984), 122–29.

19. For a more complete discussion of the Youth for Christ clubs see Senter, "Youth for Christ Movement," 196–202.

20. "The American Christian Teen-ager Survey," *Youth for Christ Magazine*, April 1960, 9.

21. *Campus Life Operational Manual* (Wheaton: Youth for Christ International, 1984), 4.

22. *Campus Life Impact* (Wheaton: Youth for Christ International, 1968), 1.

23. For a survey of the development of Fellowship of Christian Athletes, see Wayne Atcheson, *Impact for Christ: How FCA Has Influenced the Sports World* (Grand Island, NE: Cross Training, 1994).

24. For a more complete survey of the other clubs see Senter, "Youth for Christ Movement," 188–96, 202–9.

25. Bill Bright, *Come Help Change the World* (Old Tappan, NJ: Revell, 1970), 107.

Chapter 12 *Pleasantville*

1. Paula S. Fass, *The Damned and the Beautiful: American Youth in the 1920's* (New York: Oxford University Press, 1977), 13.

2. Irving Settel, *A Pictorial History of Radio* (New York: Grosset and Dunlop, 1967), 41, 47.

3. Access to network radio by evangelical Christians diminished drastically when networks turned to the liberal-leaning Federal Council of Churches to control what religious broadcasts aired. In response, evangelicals formed an association of independent Christian radio stations known as the National Religious Broadcasters in 1944. The movement that led to the formation of the NRB was a factor in the birth of the National Association of Evangelicals two years earlier.

4. Sterling North, "Literary Editorial," Chicago Daily News, May 8, 1940.

5. Greg Bjerg, "The Man Who Changed Comic Books Forever," http://www.damninteresting.com/?p=466.

6. Raymond J. Haberski Jr., http://www.encyclopedia.chicagohistory.org/pages/453.html.

7. John P. Sisk, "Exorcising Demons," a review of Frank Walsh, *Sin and Censorship: The Catholic Church and the Motion Picture Industry* (New Haven: Yale University Press, 1996), http://www.firstthings.com/article.php3?id_article=3622.

8. Stephen W. Paine, "Why I Do Not Attend Movies" (Houghton, NY: Houghton College Press, 1946).

9. Eugene Francis Clark, *A Son's Portrait of Dr. Francis E. Clark* (Boston: Williston, 1930), 169–71.

10. Jon Pahl, *Youth Ministry in Modern America: 1930 to the Present* (Peabody, MA: Hendrickson, 2000), 29.

11. Will H. Houghton, "Young People, This Is Your Page," *Moody Bible Institute Monthly*, September 1935, 21.

12. Based on statistics provided in Mendell Taylor, *Nazarene Youth in Conquest for Christ* (Kansas City, MO: Nazarene Publishing House, 1948), 16–18.

13. Ibid., 20.

14. Ibid., 21–22.

15. Ibid., 23.

16. Earle F. Wilde, "Our Young People's Work," *Herald of Holiness*, June 16, 1915. Also see Wilde, "Our Young People," *Herald of Holiness*, June 30, 1915, and "Our Young People: Choosing the Leader," *Herald of Holiness*, July 14, 1915.

17. Taylor, *Nazarene Youth*, 25–26.

18. Ibid., 48.

19. "A Short Review of the Activities of the Sw. Ev. Free Church of the United States of America, 1884–1924," 27, Evangelical Free Church of America Archives.

20. "Part One: History of the Minnesota Free Church Young People's and Sunday School Conference; Conference Grounds, Franson Memorial Park, Buffalo, Minnesota," June 1937, 2, Evangelical Free Church of America Archives.

21. *The Young People's Messenger* 3, no. 1 (September 15, 1923), Evangelical Free Church of America Archives.

22. Mel Larson, "F.C.Y.F. and Programs," *The Evangelical Beacon*, September 14, 1948, 16.

23. Jim Forstrom to Kurt Trucksess, October 20, 1998, Evangelical Free Church of America Archives.

24. The research contributing to this section comes from the insightful work of Richard Castleberry in preparation for his dissertation at Trinity Evangelical Divinity School.

25. Castleberry cites the minutes of the nineteenth annual assembly of the Churches of God.

26. Charles W. Conn, *Like a Mighty Army: A History of the Church of God* (Cleveland, TN: Pathway, 1996), 229.

27. Alda B. Harrison, "How to Organize and Conduct C. of G. Y. P. E.," (Cleveland, TN: Church of God, 1938), 1.

28. Richard Castleberry, e-mail message to author, August 8, 2008.

29. Ibid.

30. Mennonites should not be confused with the Amish who emerged from the Mennonite tradition at a later date and reacted more dramatically against the control of technology in modern life.

31. Much of the research regarding Mennonite youth ministry is based on the research of Bob Yoder and his students at Goshen College.

32. Bob Yoder, "A Historical Review of Mennonite Youth Ministry in the Past 120 Years," unpublished paper done in association with Steve Nolt, PhD, at Goshen College, May 11, 2005.

33. Elmer Ediger, *Youth Fellowship Manual for Local Youth Groups* (Newton, KS: Young People's Union, 1953).

34. Jonny Gerig Meyer, "A Program, an Organization, and a Movement: The Rise and Fall of Churchwide Mennonite Youth Fellowship, 1948–1968," unpublished paper, 24.

35. Paul Fleischmann, "25 Years of Networking: Then and Now," *Network Magazine* (Winter 2005): 4.

36. Paul Fleischmann, "The Miracle of God's Provision," *Network Magazine* (Winter 2006): 4.

37. *Network News* 6, no. 1 (Winter 1988), 2.

Chapter 13 *Friday Night Lights*

1. Orville Anderson, "Worland, Wyoming: God's Western Workshop," *Youth for Christ Magazine* 10 (January 1953): 12–16.

2. "Wanted: A Miracle of Good Weather and the 'Youth for Christ' Rally Got It," *Newsweek*, June 11, 1945, 84; "Youth for Christ Now Covers 1,450 Cities," *Minneapolis Star*, February 12, 1949, 8.

3. Mel Larson, *Youth for Christ: Twentieth Century Wonder* (Grand Rapids: Zondervan, 1947), 39.

4. "The History of Youth for Christ," *Christian Life and Times* (July 1946): 58–59; Oscar T. Gillian, "Youth for Christ," *Christian Life and Times* (September 1946): 4; Larson, *Youth for Christ*, 39–50.

5. Carl F. H. Henry, "Accent on Youth," *Sunday* (January 1945): 18–19.

6. Torrey Johnson and Robert Cook, *Reaching Youth for Christ* (Chicago: Moody, 1944), 46–49.

7. Jim Rayburn III, *Dance, Children, Dance* (Wheaton: Tyndale, 1984), 121–29.

8. William R. De Plata, *Tell It From Calvary* (New York: Calvary Baptist Church, 1972), 61–62; "Christian Youth Theatre Launched," *Evangelical United Action* 6 (December 1, 1947): 11.

9. "Youth Center Movement," *Moody Monthly*, July 1936, 556.

10. Eleanor Nazarenus, "An Analysis and Evaluation of Youth for Christ International," MA thesis, Northwestern University, 1946, 7; Charles T. Lampman, "Young Man with a Vision," *Christian Life Magazine* (June 1948): 65–69; Percy Crawford, "Television Pays Off," *Youth for Christ Magazine* (August 1951): 36–38.

11. Percy Crawford, "A Modern Revival," *Revelation* (August 1932): 325, 349–50.

12. Larson, *Youth for Christ*, 35.

13. Gilbert L. Dodds, "A Survey of Youth for Christ," MA thesis, Wheaton College, 1948, 8–22.

14. Two biographies of Jack Wyrtzen are Forest Forbes, *God Hath Chosen* (Grand Rapids: Zondervan, 1948); and Harry Bollback, *The House that Jack God Built* (Schroon Lake, NY: Word of Life Fellowship, 1972).

15. Marvin Goldberg, "Youth Alone and Liked," *Sunday* (April 1946): 54–55; Forbes, *God Hath Chosen*, 43–51.

16. Frank S. Mead, "Apostle to Youth," *Christian Herald* (September 1945): 16.

17. Forbes, *God Hath Chosen*, 116–24.

18. Though Jim Rayburn and the Young Life Campaign were never organizationally linked to Youth for Christ International, they shared a concern for reaching youth for Christ.

19. "Young Life Campaign 1943 Annual Report," Herbert J. Taylor Papers, Archives of the Billy Graham Center, Wheaton College, Folder 28, Box 69, Collection 20; Newspaper clippings from "[D]allas Morning," Archives of the Billy Graham Center, Wheaton College, Folder 7, Box 11, Collection 20.

20. Char Meredith, *It's a Sin to Bore a Kid* (Waco: Word, 1978), 38–45.

21. For an early biography see Mel Larson, *Young Man on Fire* (Chicago: Youth for Christ International, 1945).

22. Johnson and Cook, *Reaching Youth*.

23. "Truman Longs for Revival," *Christian Life Magazine* 12 (November 1949): 33.

24. Harold John Ockenga, "America's Revival Is Breaking," *Christian Life* 12 (March 1950): 20–22f; Harold John Ockenga, "Revival Is Here!" *Youth for Christ Magazine* (April 1950): 8–13f.

25. Lynne and Bill Hybels, *Rediscovering Church* (Grand Rapids: Zondervan, 1995), 23–42.

Part 5 Jazz Fusion

1. See Thomas L. Friedman, *The World Is Flat* (New York: Farrar, Straus and Giroux, 2005); and Friedman, *Hot, Flat, and Crowded* (New York: Farrar, Straus and Giroux, 2008).

Chapter 14 *Into the Woods*

1. Mark H. Senter III, *The Coming Revolution in Youth Ministry* (Wheaton: Victor, 1992).

2. *Digest of Educational Statistics* (2007), Chapter 2: Elementary and Secondary Education, table 52.

3. *Digest of Educational Statistics* (2007), Chapter 2: Elementary and Secondary Education, table 40.

4. *Digest of Educational Statistics* (2007), Chapter 2: Elementary and Secondary Education, table 105.

5. W. A. Henry III and N. S. Mehta, "Beyond the Melting Pot," *Time*, April 1990, 28–35.

6. *Digest of Educational Statistics* (2002), Chapter 2: Elementary and Secondary Education, table 42.

7. Ralph Keyes, *Is There Life after High School?* (New York: Little, Brown, 1976).

8. Donald Posterski and Reginald Bibby, *Canada's Youth: "Ready for Today"* (Ottawa: Canadian Youth Foundation, 1989), 55.

9. Mike Yaconelli, "Where's Your Passion? (Part I)," *Journal of Christian Camping* 22 (March–April): 6.

10. Stated in brief, they identified some core values: thriving as a healthy, trusting organization; abiding in a personal and corporate relationship with Jesus; developing people through spiritual nurture, emotional wholeness, and ministry effectiveness; cultivating unity and embracing diversity; excelling as a learning organization; practicing responsible evangelism for lost youth; multiplying spiritual leaders; pioneering and expanding locally and globally; partnering with and through the church; and giving away our passion, people, knowledge, and resources. Cited from "Future Search: A Case for Deep Change in YFC/ USA" (video produced by YFC/USA).

11. The additions called for maintaining financial stability in the movement through unified marketing and funding; knowing our distinctive contribution within the body of Christ; providing services to and collaboration with community leadership and agencies; and enjoying a national visibility through an active public relations strategy.

12. *Youth for Christ Board Member Handbook* (Denver: Youth for Christ/USA, 2003), 55.

13. *Inside Young Life* (June/July 1997).

14. *Inside Young Life* (January/February 1998).

15. *Inside Young Life* (February/March 1996).

16. *Inside Young Life* (December 1999/January 2000).

17. This number includes only summer campers in order to provide an accurate comparison with 2000.

18. 2007 Young Life Annual Report.

19. Dal Shealy and Pat Springle, *One Way 2 Play* (Nashville: Nelson, 1995).

20. Annual reports of Fellowship of Christian Athletes did not continue to report volunteer statistics.

Chapter 15 *Mr. Holland's Opus*

1. Mark Lamport et al., "The State of the Profession of Youth Ministry," *Christian Education Journal* (Autumn 1992): 85–107.

2. Mark W. Cannister, *"A Brief History of the Association of Youth Ministry Educators,"* http://www.aymeducators.org/?page=AYMEHistory.

3. Introductory texts were especially plentiful including (in alphabetical order by author/ editor): Warren S. Benson and Mark H. Senter III, *The Complete Book of Youth Ministry* (Chicago: Moody, 1987); Wesley Black, *An Introduction to Youth Ministry* (Nashville: Broadman, 1991); Kenda Creasy Dean, Chap Clark, and Dave Rahn, eds., *Starting Right: Thinking Theologically about Youth Ministry* (Grand Rapids: Zondervan, 2001); John M. Dettoni, *Introduction to Youth Ministry* (Grand Rapids: Zondervan, 1993); Richard R. Dunn and Mark. H. Senter III, *Reaching a Generation for Christ: A Comprehensive Guide to Youth Ministry* (Chicago: Moody, 1997); Roy G. Irving and Roy B. Zuck, eds., *Youth and the Church: An Approach to Christian Education of Youth* (Chicago: Moody, 1968); Lawrence O. Richards, *Youth Ministry: Its Renewal in the Local Church* (Grand Rapids: Zondervan, 1972); David Roadcup, *Ministering to Youth: A Strategy for the 80's* (Cincinnati: Standard, 1980); Duffy Robbins, *This Way to Youth Ministry: An Introduction to the Adventure* (Grand Rapids: Zondervan, 2004); Elmer L. Towns, *Successful Biblical Youth Work* (Nashville: Impact, 1966); D. Campbell Wyckoff and Don Richter, *Religious Education Ministry with Youth* (Birmingham, AL: Religious Education Press, 1982); Roy B. Zuck and Warren S. Benson, eds., *Youth Education in the Church* (Chicago: Moody, 1978).

4. Paul Fleischmann, "Using Your Connections: Networking with Your Peers," *Youthworker Journal* 3, no. 2 (Summer 1986): 43.

5. "Who is the National Network of Youth Ministries?" *Network Magazine* 27, no. 4 (Winter 2004): 22.

6. "Who is the National Network of Youth Ministries?" *Network Magazine* 23, no. 1 (Spring 2005): back cover.

7. Doug Clark, "Closing the Gap: Can It Be Done by 2000?" *National Network of Youth Ministries* (July 1997): 3.

8. In personal correspondence to the author, Paul Fleischmann reported, "We do have verified research that indicates, for example, that evangelism on campuses that employed Challenge 2000 commitments increased evangelism by 200%." What is not so clear is what the baseline was for measuring this growth in evangelism.

9. "The Challenge: Every Student, Every School, Every Community," *National Network of Youth Ministries* 19, no. 1 (March 2001): 9.

10. Doug Tegner, "The Need for Affinity," *National Network of Youth Ministries* 9, no. 2 (June 2001): 5.

11. "Affinity Network Report," *Network Magazine* 24, no. 3 (Fall 2006): 24.

12. Lynn Ziegenfuss, "Building Bridges with Your Community," *Network Magazine* (Spring 2005): 15–19; "Mobilizing New Mentors through Faith and Community Collaborations," *Network Magazine* 23, no. 2 (Winter 2006): 12–13.

13. "Sixteen Years in the 'Pole Position': Roots and Impact of See You at the Pole," *Network Magazine* 23, no. 4 (Winter 2005): 6.

14. Jeff Martin, "Taking Faith to the Field," *Network Magazine* 24, no. 3 (Fall 2006): 10–11.

15. Josh Weidmann, "I Have A Dream," *National Network of Youth Ministries* 18, no. 3 (August 2000): 11, 17, 21; "One School, Big Vision," *National Network of Youth Ministries* 16, no. 3 (September 1998): 9.

16. NNYM does an annual survey of members that may call this into question, but the survey is a self-selecting sample that nets results from about 20 percent of the membership. Such samples are not very reliable and may reflect primarily the responses of members more loyal to the networking ideal. In the 2007 survey, results reported that 49 percent of respondents were over the age of thirty-five and only 12 percent were under the age of twenty-five. One would question if this was an accurate reflection of youth workers in North America. *Network Magazine* 25, no. 4 (Winter 2007): 30–31.

17. The connection with Moody Bible Institute ended in 1990 when the ministry became an independent organization based first in Wheaton, Illinois, and later in Elburn, Illinois.

18. The eleven denominations include: The Evangelical Free Church of America, Fellowship Baptist of Canada, United Brethren in Christ, the Associated Gospel Churches of Canada, the Christian and Missionary Alliance of Canada, Fellowship of Atlantic Baptist in Canada, Grace Brethren, Evangelical Presbyterian, Conservative Baptist, Christian and Missionary Alliance of the United States, and the Free Methodist Church.

19. Mike King, *Presence Centered Youth Ministry* (Downers Grove, IL: InterVarsity, 2006); Chris Folmsbee, *A New Kind of Youth Ministry* (Grand Rapids: Zondervan/Youth Specialties, 2006).

20. The youth ministry led by Doug Fields at Saddleback Church, Lake Forest, California, is the other headliner youth ministry as the third millennium begins.

21. C. Peter Wagner, *Your Church Can Grow* (Glendale, CA: G/L Publications, 1976).

22. Comment by Doug Fields in response to the author, March 12, 2009.

23. Doug Fields, *Purpose Driven Youth Ministry* (Grand Rapids: Zondervan, 1998).

24. Rick Warren, *The Purpose Driven Church* (Grand Rapids: Zondervan, 1995).

25. Fields, *Purpose Driven Youth*, 46.

26. Ibid., 87.

27. Mark DeVries, *Sustainable Youth Ministry* (Downers Grove, IL: InterVarsity, 2008), 11.

28. Fields, *Purpose Driven Youth*, 160.

29. DeVries, *Sustainable Youth Ministry*, 19.

30. Mark DeVries, *Family Based Youth Ministry* (1994; repr., Downers Grove, IL: InterVarsity, 2004).

31. DeVries, *Sustainable Youth Ministry*, 53.

32. Fernando Arzola Jr., *Toward a Prophetic Youth Ministry* (Downers Grove, IL: InterVarsity, 2008).

33. Efrim Smith and Phil Jackson, *The Hip-Hop Church* (Downers Grove, IL: InterVarsity, 2005).

34. Sam George, *Understanding the Coconut Generation: Ministry to the Americanized Asian Indians* (Niles: Mall, 2006).

35. Francis E. Clark, *The Christian Endeavor Manual* (Boston: United Society of Christian Endeavor, 1925), 12.

36. Char Meredith, *It's a Sin to Bore a Kid* (Waco: Word, 1978).

37. Mark Yaconelli, *Contemplative Youth Ministry* (Grand Rapids: Zondervan, 2006), 45.

38. Steve Wright, *Rethink: Decide for Yourself, Is Student Ministry Working?* (Wake Forest, NC: Inquest, 2007), 54.

Epilogue

1. Jon Pahl, *Youth Ministry in Modern America: 1930 to the Present* (Peabody, MA: Hendrickson, 2000), 73–90.

2. William R. Myers, *Black and White Styles of Youth Ministry: Two Congregations in America* (New York: Pilgrim, 1991).

Select Bibliography

Adelson, Joseph, ed. *Handbook of Adolescent Psychology*. New York: Jon Wiley and Sons, 1980.

Alston, Wallace McPherson. "A History of Young People's Work in the Presbyterian Church in the United States (1831–1938)." ThD thesis, Presbyterian School of Theology, 1943.

"The American Christian Teen-ager Survey." *Youth for Christ Magazine*, April 1960.

Armitage, Thomas. *History of the Young People's Baptist Union of Brooklyn*. New York: T. R. Jones, 1890.

Arzola, Fernando, Jr. *Toward a Prophetic Youth Ministry*. Downers Grove, IL: InterVarsity, 2008.

Atcheson, Wayne. *Impact for Christ: How FCA Has Influenced the Sports World*. Grand Island, NE: Cross Training, 1994.

Balmer, Randall. *Mine Eyes Have Seen the Glory*. New York: Oxford University Press, 1989.

Bandura, Albert. *Social Foundations of Thought and Action: A Social Cognitive Theory*. Englewood Cliffs, NJ: Prentice-Hall, 1986.

Barclay, Wade Crawford. *The Methodist Episcopal Church, 1845–1939: Part Two*. New York: Board of Missions of the Methodist Church, 1957.

Barkun, Michael. "The Awakening Controversy." *Sociological Analysis* 46, no. 4 (1985): 425–43.

Barna, George. *Real Teens*. Ventura, CA: Regal, 2001.

Baucham, Voddie T., Jr. *Family Driven Faith*. Wheaton: Crossway, 2007.

Beasley, Steven Dewayne. "The Development of the Church Training Program of the Southern Baptist Convention: A Historical Review." EdD diss., Southern Baptist Theological Seminary, 1988.

Bennet, James E. "The Revival in Our Midst." *Sunday School Times* 86, March 25, 1944.

Bennett, Lerone, Jr. *Before the Mayflower: A History of Black America.* Chicago: Johnson, 2003.

Benson, Clarence H. *The Sunday School in Action.* Chicago: Moody, 1932.

Benson, Warren S., and Mark H. Senter III. *The Complete Book of Youth Ministry.* Chicago: Moody, 1987.

Berry, Joseph F. *Four Wonderful Years.* New York: Hunt and Eaton, 1893.

Bjerg, Greg. "The Man Who Changed Comic Books Forever." http://www.damninteresting.com/?p=466.

Black, Wesley. *An Introduction to Youth Ministry.* Nashville: Broadman, 1991.

———. "Youth Ministry Comes of Age." *Search* 23, no. 3 (Spring 1993): 8.

Bollback, Harry. *The House that ~~Jack~~ God Built.* Schroon Lake, NY: Word of Life Fellowship, 1972.

Boyd, Charles Arthur. *Young People at Work in Baptist Churches.* Philadelphia: Judson, 1928.

Boylan, Anne M. *Sunday School: The Formation of an American Institution, 1790–1880.* New Haven: Yale University Press, 1988.

Bremner, Robert H., ed. *Children and Youth in America: A Documentary History.* 2 vols. Cambridge, MA: Harvard University Press, 1970–71.

Briggs, Phillip H. "Patterns in Southern Baptist Youth Ministry." *Baptist History and Heritage* 26, no. 4 (October 1991): 4–12.

Bright, Bill. *Come Help Change the World.* Old Tappan, NJ: Revell, 1970.

Bronenbrenner, Urie. *The Ecology of Human Development: Experiments by Nature and Design.* Cambridge, MA: Harvard University Press, 1979.

Button, H. Warren, and Eugene F. Provenzo Jr. *History of Education and Culture in America.* Englewood Cliffs, NJ: Prentice-Hall, 1983.

"Cadets of Temperance." In *The Cyclopaedia of Temperance and Prohibition,* 60. New York: Funk and Wagnalls, 1891.

Cannister, Mark W. "A Brief History of the Association of Youth Ministry Educators." http://www.aymeducators.org/?page=AYMEHistory.

"The Challenge: Every Student, Every School, Every Community." *National Network of Youth Ministries* 19, no. 1 (March 2001): 5.

Chaplin, William Knight. *Francis E. Clark: Founder of the Christian Endeavour Society*. London: British Christian Endeavour Society Union, 1902.

Chaplin, W. Knight, and M. Jennie Street, eds. *Fifty Years of Christian Endeavour*. London: British Christian Endeavour Union, 1931.

Clark, Eugene Francis. *A Son's Portrait of Dr. Francis E. Clark*. Boston: Williston, 1930.

Clark, Francis E. *The Children and the Church, and the Young People's Society of Christian Endeavor, as a Means of Bringing Them Together*. Boston: Congregational Sunday School and Publishing Society, 1882.

———. *The Christian Endeavor Manual*. Boston: United Society of Christian Endeavor, 1925.

———. "A Familiar Letter from the President of the United Society." *The Golden Rule*, October 31, 1889, 74.

———. *Memories of Many Men in Many Lands: An Autobiography*. Boston: United Christian Endeavor Society, 1922.

———. *Ways and Means*. Boston: D. Lothrop, 1890.

Coble, Christopher Lee. "Where Have All the Children Gone? The Christian Endeavor Movement and the Training of Protestant Youth, 1881–1918." ThD thesis, Harvard Divinity School, 2001.

Coleman, James S., and Thomas Hoffer. *Public and Private High Schools: The Impact of Communities*. New York: Basic Books, 1987.

Coletta, Paolo E. *William Jennings Bryan: Political Puritan, 1915–1925*. Lincoln: University of Nebraska Press, 1969.

Collins, William J. "When the Tide Turned: Immigration and the Delay of the Great Black Migration." *Journal of Economic History* 57, no. 3 (September 1997): 607–32.

Conley, John Wesley. *History of the Baptist Young People's Union of America*. Philadelphia: Griffith and Rowland, 1913.

Conrad, Leslie, Jr. "Lutheran Youth Organizations." In *The Encyclopedia of the Lutheran Church*, vol. 3, edited by Julius Bodensieck, 2548–53. Minneapolis: Augsburg, 1965.

Courtoy, Charles Webb. "A Historical Analysis of the Three Eras of Mainline Protestant Youth Work in America as a Basis for Clues to

Future Youth Work." DMin project, Divinity School of Vanderbilt University, 1976.

Cremin, Lawrence A. *American Education: The Metropolitan Experience, 1876–1980*. New York: Harper and Row, 1988.

———. *The Transformation of the School*. New York: Vintage Books, 1964.

Cuyler, Theodore L. Archives. Princeton Theological Seminary, Special Collections.

Cuyler, Theodore Ledyard. *Recollections of a Long Life*. New York: American Tract Society, 1902.

Dean, Kenda Creasy. *Practicing Passion*. Grand Rapids: Eerdmans, 2005.

Dean, Kenda Creasy, Chap Clark, and Dave Rahn, eds. *Starting Right: Thinking Theologically about Youth Ministry*. Grand Rapids: Zondervan, 2001.

De Lacy, William H. "Juvenile Courts." In *The Catholic Encyclopedia*, 8:586–87. New York: Robert Appleton, 1910.

De Plata, William R. *Tell It from Calvary*. New York: Calvary Baptist Church, 1972.

Dettoni, John M. *Introduction to Youth Ministry*. Grand Rapids: Zondervan, 1993.

DeVries, Mark. *Sustainable Youth Ministry*. Downers Grove, IL: InterVarsity, 2008.

Dodds, Gilbert L. "A Survey of Youth for Christ." MA thesis, Wheaton College, 1948.

Donnelly, Harold I. "Christian Youth at Work." *International Journal of Religious Education* 12 (July 1936): 21–22.

Downing, Gary Willard. "Incarnational Witness: A Model of Ministry Linking Young Life to the Organized Church." DMin project, Luther-Northwestern Seminaries, 1978.

Dragastin, S. E., and Glen H. Elder Jr., eds. *Adolescence in the Life Cycle*. New York: Halsted Press, 1975.

Drucker, Peter F. *Innovation and Entrepreneurship: Practices and Principles*. New York: Harper and Row, 1985.

Dunn, Richard R., and Mark H. Senter III. *Reaching a Generation for Christ: A Comprehensive Guide to Youth Ministry*. Chicago: Moody, 1997.

Edgar, Walter. *South Carolina: A History*. Columbia: University of South Carolina Press, 1998.

Eisenstadt, S. N. *From Generation to Generation*. London: Free Press of Glencoe, 1956.

Elder, Glen H., Jr. "Adolescence in Historical Perspective." In *Handbook of Adolescent Psychology*, edited by Joseph Adelson, 3–46. New York: Jon Wiley and Sons, 1980.

Elkind, David. *All Grown Up and No Place to Go*. Reading, MA: Addison-Wesley, 1984.

The Endeavor Hymnal for Young People's Societies, Sunday Schools and Church Meetings. Boston: United Society of Christian Endeavor, 1901.

Erb, Frank Otis. *The Development of the Young People's Movement*. Chicago: University of Chicago Press, 1917.

Eshelman, Paul. *The Explo Story*. Glendale, CA: Regal Books, 1972.

Estep, W. R. "A Thousand Lives for China: Lottie Moon." In *More than Conquerors*, edited by John D. Woodbridge, 56–62. Chicago: Moody, 1992.

Evangelical Free Church of America Archives. "Part One: History of the Minnesota Free Church Young People's and Sunday School Conference; Conference Grounds, Franson Memorial Park, Buffalo, Minnesota," 2. June 1937.

———. "A Short Review of the Activities of the Sw. Ev. Free Church of the United States of America, 1884–1924," 27.

———. *The Young People's Messenger* 3, no. 1 (September 15, 1923).

Ewing, George W. *The Well-Tempered Lyre: Songs and Verse of the Temperance Movement*. Dallas: Southern Methodist University Press, 1977.

Fass, Paula S. *The Damned and the Beautiful: American Youth in the 1920's*. New York: Oxford University Press, 1977.

Fields, Doug. *Purpose Driven Youth Ministry*. Grand Rapids: Zondervan, 1998.

Fleischmann, Paul. "Results After Twenty Years." *National Network of Youth Ministries* 19, no. 1 (March 2001): 4.

———. "Using Your Connections: Networking with Your Peers." *Youthworker Journal* 3, no. 2 (Summer 1986): 42–45.

Flood, Charles Bracelen. *Lee: The Last Years*. Boston: Houghton Mifflin, 1981.

Folmsbee, Chris. *A New Kind of Youth Ministry*. Grand Rapids: Zondervan/Youth Specialties, 2006.

Forbes, Forest. *God Hath Chosen*. Grand Rapids: Zondervan, 1948.

Fowler, James W. *Stages of Faith*. New York: HarperCollins, 1981.

Gangel, Kenneth O., and James C. Wilhoit. *The Christian Educator's Handbook on Spiritual Formation*. Wheaton: Victor, 1994.

Gillespie, Franklin B. "Youth Programs of the United Presbyterian Church—An Historical Overview." *Journal of Presbyterian History* 59, no. 3 (Fall 1981): 309–82.

Gilligan, Carol. *In a Different Voice*. Cambridge, MA: Harvard University Press, 1982.

Gleason, Michael F. *When God Walked on Campus*. Dundas, ON: Joshua, 2002.

Gordon, Anna A. *The Temperance Songster*. Cincinnati: Fillmore Music House, 1904.

Graham, Philip. *The End of Adolescence*. Oxford: Oxford University Press, 2004.

Gutek, Gerald L. *Education and Schooling in America*. Englewood Cliffs, NJ: Prentice-Hall, 1983.

———. *A History of the Western Educational Experience*. New York: Random House, 1972.

Hall, G. Stanley. *Adolescence: Its Psychology and Its Relations to Physiology, Anthropology, Sociology, Sex, Crime, Religion, and Education*. London: Appleton and Company, 1904.

Hampel, Robert L. "Influence and Respectability: Temperance and Prohibition in Massachusetts, 1813–1852." PhD diss., Cornell University, 1980.

Handbook of the Methodist Youth Fellowship. Nashville: General Board of Education of the Methodist Church, 1953.

Hansot, Elizabeth, and David Tyack. *Managers of Virtue: Public School Leadership in America, 1820–1980*. New York: Basic Books, 1982.

Harner, Nevin C. "A Decade of Youth Work in the Churches." *Religious Education* 38, no. 1 (January–February 1943): 25–30.

Henry, W. A., III, and N. S. Mehto. "Beyond the Melting Pot." *Time*, April 9, 1990, 28–31.

Heywood, Colin. *A History of Childhood*. Cambridge: Polity, 2001.

Hine, Thomas. *The Rise and Fall of the American Teenager*. New York: Perennial, 2000.

Hoffman, Elisha A. *Songs of the New Crusade*. Chicago: Hope, 1876.

Hollingshead, August B. *Elmtown Youth*. New York: John Wiley and Sons, 1949.

Hopkins, C. Howard. *History of the Y.M.C.A. in North America*. New York: Association, 1951.

Hopper, Myron T. "Young People's Work in Protestant Churches in the United States." PhD diss., University of Chicago, 1938.

Horgan, T. "Christian Endeavor Society." In *New Catholic Encyclopedia*, 2:639. New York: McGraw-Hill, 1967.

Houghton, Will H. "Young People, This Is Your Page." *Moody Bible Institute Monthly*, September 1935, 21.

Howard, David M. *Student Power in World Evangelism*. Downers Grove, IL: InterVarsity, 1970.

Hull, Asa. *Hull's Temperance Glee Book*. Boston: O. Ditson, 1877.

Irving, Roy G., and Roy B. Zuck, eds. *Youth and the Church: An Approach to Christian Education of Youth*. Chicago: Moody, 1968.

Isaacson, Walter. *Benjamin Franklin: An American Life*. New York: Simon and Schuster, 2004.

Jenny, Gerald. *The Young People's Movement in the American Lutheran Church*. Minneapolis: Augsburg, 1928.

Johnson, Torrey, and Robert Cook. *Reaching Youth for Christ*. Chicago: Moody, 1944.

Junior Carols. Boston: United Society of Christian Endeavor, 1906.

Kazin, Michael. *A Godly Hero*. New York: Knopf, 2006.

Keillor, Garrison. *Lake Wobegon Days*. New York: Penguin Books, 1985.

Kett, Joseph F. *Rites of Passage: Adolescence in America 1790 to the Present*. New York: Basic Books, 1977.

Keyes, Ralph. *Is There Life after High School?* New York: Little, Brown, 1976.

King, Mike. *Presence Centered Youth Ministry*. Downers Grove, IL: InterVarsity, 2006.

Kirn, Walter. "Will Teenagers Disappear?" *Time*, February 21, 2000, 60–61.

Kohlberg, Lawrence. "The Development of Modes of Moral Thinking in the Years 10 to 16." PhD diss., University of Chicago, 1958.

Krug, Edward A. *The Shaping of the American High School: 1880–1920*. Milwaukee: University of Wisconsin Press, 1969.

Ladd, Tony, and James A. Mathisen. *Muscular Christianity: Evangelical Protestants and the Development of American Sport*. Grand Rapids: Baker Books, 1999.

Lamport, Mark, et al. "The State of the Profession of Youth Ministry." *Christian Education Journal* (Autumn 1992): 85–100.

Larson, Mel. "F.C.Y.F. and Programs." *The Evangelical Beacon*, September 14, 1948, 16.

———. *Young Man on Fire*. Chicago: Youth for Christ International, 1945.

Lerner, Richard M., and Lawrence Steinberg, eds. *Handbook of Adolescent Psychology*. 2nd ed. New York: John Wiley and Sons, 2004.

Levinson, Daniel J. *The Seasons of a Man's Life*. New York: Knopf, 1978.

Little, Sara. "Youth Ministry: Historical Reflections Near the End of the Twentieth Century," 1997. www.ptsem.edu/iym/research/lectures/downloads/1997/1997%20Little%20Youth%20Ministry.pdf.

Lleran-Muney, Adriana. "Were Compulsory Attendance and Child Labor Laws Effective? An Analysis from 1915 to 1939." *The Journal of Law and Economics* 45, no. 2 (2002): 401–35.

Lovelace, Richard F. *The American Pietism of Cotton Mather*. Grand Rapids: Christian University Press, 1979.

———. *Dynamics of Spiritual Life*. Downers Grove, IL: InterVarsity, 1979.

Lynd, Robert S., and Helen Merrell Lynd. *Middletown: A Study in American Culture*. New York: Harcourt, Brace and World, 1929.

———. *Middletown in Transition: A Study in Cultural Conflict*. New York: Harcourt, Brace, 1937.

Lynn, Robert W., and Elliott Wright. *The Big Little School: 200 Years of the Sunday School*. Birmingham, AL: Religious Education Press, 1980.

Marsden, George M. *Fundamentalism and American Culture*. New York: Oxford University Press, 1980.

———. *Jonathan Edwards: A Life*. New Haven: Yale University Press, 2003.

Marshall, Mary-Ruth. "Precedents and Accomplishments: An Analytical Study of the Presbyterian Youth Fellowship of the Presbyterian Church in the United States, 1943–1958." EdD diss., Presbyterian School of Christian Education, 1993.

Mather, Cotton. *Religious Societies: Proposals for the Revival of Dying Religion by Well-Ordered Societies for That Purpose*. Boston: 1724.

McCabe, James D., Jr. *Lights and Shadows of New York Life*. Philadelphia: National Publishing Company, 1872.

McClung, Charles Harvey. "The Development of the Denominational Youth Program in the Presbyterian Church in the U.S.A., 1881–1954." PhD diss., University of Pittsburgh, 1957.

McClusky, Evelyn M. "The Miracles Worked in 'Miracle Book Club.'" *Sunday School Times*. January 22, 1938, 61.

———. *Torch and Sword*. Oakland: Miracle Book Club, 1937.

Meredith, Char. *It's a Sin to Bore a Kid*. Waco: Word, 1978.

Miller, John. *Back to the Basics*. Colorado Springs: Young Life, 1991.

Moberg, David O. *The Church as a Social Institution*. 2nd ed. Grand Rapids: Baker Books, 1984.

Moody, William Revell. *Life of D. L. Moody*. New York: Macmillan, 1930.

Nazarenus, Eleanor. "An Analysis and Evaluation of Youth for Christ International." MA thesis, Northwestern University, 1946.

Niles, Katherine Evelyn. "A Survey and Critique of Young People's Societies." *Religious Education*, June 1929, 526–35.

Nyberg, John. "Youth for Christ Now Covers 1,450 Cities." Reprinted by permission from the *Minneapolis Star* of February 12, 1949, in *Youth for Christ Magazine*, May 1949, 52–53f.

Ockenga, Harold John. "America's Revival Is Breaking." *Christian Life* 12 (March 1950): 20–22f.

———. "Revival Is Here!" *Youth for Christ Magazine*, April 7, 1950, 8–13f.

"1 in 5 Blacks Drop Out." *Chicago Tribune*, November 11, 2003, sec. A.

Orr, J. Edwin. *The Second Evangelical Awakening in America*. London: Marshall, Morgan and Scott, 1952.

Pahl, Jon. *Hopes and Dreams of All*. Chicago: Wheat Ridge Ministries, 1993.

———. "What's History Got to Do with It? Understanding the Roots of Youth Ministry in America," 2004. http://www.youthspecialties .com/articles/topics/pastpresentfuture/history.php.

———. *Youth Ministry in Modern America: 1930 to the Present*. Peabody, MA: Hendrickson, 2000.

Peters, Clarence. "Developments of the Youth Programs of the Lutheran Churches in America." ThD thesis, Concordia Theological Seminary, 1951.

Piaget, Jean. *The Child's Conception of the World*. Paterson, NJ: Littlefield, Adams, 1960.

Posterski, Donald, and Reginald Bibby. *Canada's Youth: "Ready for Today."* Ottawa: Canadian Youth Foundation, 1989.

Powers, Bruce. *Growing Faith*. Nashville: Broadman, 1982.

Putney, Clifford. *Muscular Christianity: Manhood and Sports in Protestant America, 1880–1920*. Cambridge, MA: Harvard University Press, 2001.

Rayburn, Jim, III. *Dance, Children, Dance*. Wheaton: Tyndale, 1984.

Reed, James E., and Ronnie Prevost. *A History of Christian Education*. Nashville: Broadman and Holman, 1993.

Rice, Edwin Wilber. *The Sunday School Movement and the American Sunday School Union*. Philadelphia: Union, 1917.

Richards, Lawrence O. *Youth Ministry: Its Renewal in the Local Church*. Grand Rapids: Zondervan, 1972.

Rike, Phyllis I. "International Society of Christian Endeavor." In *The Encyclopedia of Modern Christian Missions*, edited by Burton L. Goddard, 341. Camden, NJ: Nelson, 1967.

Roadcup, David. *Ministering to Youth: A Strategy for the 80's*. Cincinnati: Standard, 1980.

Robbins, Duffy. *This Way to Youth Ministry: An Introduction to the Adventure*. Grand Rapids: Zondervan, 2004.

Ross, Dorothy. *G. Stanley Hall: The Psychologist as Prophet*. Chicago: University of Chicago Press, 1972.

Santrock, John W. *Adolescence*. 8th ed. New York: McGraw-Hill, 2001.

Schlesinger, Arthur M., Jr. *The Cycles of History*. New York: Houghton Mifflin, 1986.

Senter, Mark H., III. *The Coming Revolution in Youth Ministry*. Wheaton: Victor, 1992.

———. "The Youth for Christ Movement as an Educational Agency and Its Impact upon Protestant Churches: 1931–1979." PhD diss., Loyola University of Chicago, 1989.

Settel, Irving. *A Pictorial History of Radio*. New York: Grosset and Dunlop, 1967.

Seymour, Jack L. *From Sunday School to Church School*. Washington, DC: University Press of America, 1982.

Shanley, Walter J. "Temperance Movements." In *The Catholic Encyclopedia*, vol. 14, edited by Charles G. Hebermann, Wilhelm Liese, and Joseph Keating, 482–93. New York: Robert Appleton Company, 1912.

Shealy, Dal, and Pat Springle. *One Way 2 Play*. Nashville: Nelson, 1995.

Skinner, B. F. *About Behaviorism*. New York: Knopf, 1974.

Skinner, Betty Lee. *Daws*. Grand Rapids: Zondervan, 1974.

Smith, Christian, and Melinda Lindquist Denton. *Soul Searching*. New York: Oxford University Press, 2005.

Smith, Efrim, and Phil Jackson. *The Hip-Hop Church*. Downers Grove, IL: InterVarsity, 2005.

Smith, Frederic. *The Jubilee of the Band of Hope Movement*. London: United Kingdom Band of Hope Union, 1897.

Smith, J. Warren. "Youth Ministry in American Methodism's Mission." *Methodist History* 19, no. 4 (July 1981).

Smith, James Bryan. "Spiritual Formation of Adolescents." In *The Christian Educator's Handbook on Spiritual Formation*, edited by Kenneth O. Gangel and James C. Wilhoit, 247–57. Wheaton: Victor, 1994.

Snyder, Charles R. "Nothing But Water: The Rise of Temperance and the Emergence of the American Temperance Society." PhD diss., Southern Illinois University, 1990.

Steinsapir, Carol. "The Ante-Bellum Total Abstinence Movement at the Local Level: A Case Study of Schenectady, New York." PhD diss., Rutgers University, 1983.

Taylor, Herbert J. Papers. Wheaton College, Billy Graham Center Archives.

Taylor, Mendell. *Nazarene Youth in Conquest for Christ*. Kansas City, MO: Nazarene Publishing House, 1948.

Tegner, Doug. "Affinity Networks Plan, Pray." *National Network of Youth Ministries* 20, no. 1 (March 2002): 7.

Thompson, Earnest Trice. *Presbyterians in the South*. Vol. 3, *1890–1972*. Richmond: John Knox, 1973.

Toppin, Edgar A. *A Biographical History of Blacks in America Since 1528*. New York: David McKay, 1971.

Towns, Elmer L. *Successful Biblical Youth Work*. Nashville: Impact, 1966.

"Truman Longs for Revival." *Christian Life Magazine* 12 (November 1949): 33.

Trumbull, H. Clay. *The Sunday School: Its Origin, Mission, Methods, and Auxiliaries*. New York: Scribner's, 1911.

Tyack, David B. *Turning Points in American Educational History*. New York: John Wiley and Sons, 1967.

Tyrrell, Ian R. *Sobering Up: From Temperance to Prohibition in Antebellum America, 1800–1860*. Westport, CT: Greenwood, 1979.

Vieth, Paul H. *The Church and Christian Education*. St. Louis: Bethany, 1947.

Vygotsky, Lev S. *Thought and Language*. Cambridge, MA: MIT Press, 1962.

Wagner, C. Peter. *Your Church Can Grow*. Ventura, CA: Regal Books, 1984.

"Wanted: A Miracle of Good Weather and the 'Youth for Christ' Rally Got It." *Newsweek*, June 11, 1945, 84.

Warder, Graham. "Selling Sobriety: How Temperance Reshaped Culture in Antebellum America." PhD diss., University of Massachusetts Amherst, 2000.

Wells, Amos R. *Expert Endeavor*. Boston: United Society of Christian Endeavor, 1911.

———. "A New Religious Force." *The New England Magazine*, June 1892.

———. *The Officers' Handbook: A Guide for Officers in Young People's Societies, With Chapters on Parliamentary Law and Other Useful Themes*. Boston: United Society of Christian Endeavor, 1900.

———. *Prayer Meeting Methods*. Boston: United Society of Christian Endeavor, 1916.

Wells, David F. *No Place for Truth, or, Whatever Happened to Evangelical Theology?* Grand Rapids: Eerdmans, 1993.

West, Elliott, and Paula Petrik, eds. *Small Worlds: Children and Adolescents in America, 1850–1950*. Lawrence, KS: University Press of Kansas, 1992.

Westerhoff, John. *Will Our Children Have Faith?* New York: Seabury, 1976.

Wilcox, Mary. *Developmental Journey*. Nashville: Abingdon, 1979.

Wilde, Earle F. "Our Young People's Work." *Herald of Holiness*, June 16, 1915. Quoted in Mendell, *Nazarene Youth*, 23.

"William Jennings Bryan Recognition Project." http://www.agribusinesscouncil.org/bryan.htm.

Willke, J. C. "Christian Endeavor, International Society of." In *Encyclopedic Dictionary of Religion*, edited by Paul Kevin Meagher, Thomas C. Obrien, and Sister Consuelo Maria Aherne, 745–46. Washington, DC: Corpus, 1979.

Willson, Meredith. *The Music Man*. New York: G. P. Putnam's Sons, 1958.

Witt, Elmer N. "125 Youthful Years." In *Superservant: Resource for Youth Ministry* 4, no. 3 (Summer 1972): 11–18. St. Louis: Board for Youth Services, The Lutheran Church—Missouri Synod.

Wright, Elbert Joseph. *Virginia Baptist Training Union History*. Richmond: Baptist Training Union, 1947.

Wright, Steve. *Rethink: Decide for Yourself, Is Student Ministry Working?* Wake Forest, NC: Inquest, 2007.

Wyckoff, D. Campbell, and Don Richter. *Religious Education Ministry with Youth.* Birmingham, AL: Religious Education Press, 1982.

Yaconelli, Mark. *Contemplative Youth Ministry.* Grand Rapids: Zondervan, 2006.

———. *Growing Souls.* Grand Rapids: Zondervan, 2007.

Yaconelli, Michael. *Dangerous Wonder.* Colorado Springs: Navpress, 1998.

Yaconelli, Mike. "Obituary." *The Wittenburg Door,* October 1971, 10.

Youth for Christ Board Member Handbook. Denver: Youth for Christ/ USA, 2003.

Zuck, Roy B., and Warren S. Benson, eds. *Youth Education in the Church.* Chicago: Moody, 1978.

Index

12209